COMPLETE
CROCHET
HANDBOOK

STACKPOLE BOOKS

An imprint of Globe Pequot, the trade division of The Rowman & Littlefield Publishing Group, Inc.

4501 Forbes Blvd., Ste. 200

Lanham, MD 20706

www.rowman.com

Distributed by NATIONAL BOOK NETWORK

800-462-6420

The original German edition was published as Häkeln – Das Standardwerk.

Copyright © 2021 frechverlag GmbH, Stuttgart, Germany (www.topp-kreativ.de)

This edition is published by arrangement with Anja Endemann, ae Rights Agency, Calvinastr. 23, 10557 Berlin, Germany

PROJECT MANAGEMENT AND EDITING: Miriam Heil

EDITING: Helene Weinold-Leipold, Violau, Germany; Regina Sidabras, Berlin, Germany

PROOFREADING: Friederike Ahlborn, Sindelfingen, Germany

COPYWRITING: Eveline Hetty-Burkart (pages 98–135, 174–193, 212–224, 295–299, 314–316, 334–337), Beate Hilbig (pages 10–25, 28–56, 84–95, 160–173, 194–197, 236–247, 255–282, 300–305, 310–311, 322–328), Béatrice Simon (pages 57–81, 138–159, 225–235, 283–294, 306–309, 317–319, 329–333), Stephanie vat the Linden (pages 96–97, 312–313), Herbert Justen (pages 248–254), Bärbel Born (pages 200–206), Jennifer Stiller (pages 207–209), Tina Hees (pages 340–343)

ILLUSTRATIONS: Ursula Schwab, Handewitt, Germany

LAYOUT: Sandra Gramisci, Büro für Kommunikationsdesign, Munich, Germany

GRAPHIC DESIGN: Petra Theilfarth

TRANSLATION: Katharina Sokiran

PHOTOS: frechverlag GmbH, 70499 Stuttgart, Germany; lichtpunkt, Michael Ruder, Stuttgart, Germany

We have made every effort to ensure the accuracy and completeness of these instructions. We cannot, however, be responsible for human error, typographical mistakes, or variations in individual work.

British Library Cataloguing in Publication Information available

Library of Congress Cataloging-in-Publication Data

Names: Hetty-Burkart, Eveline, author. | Hilbig, Beate, author. | Simone, Beatrice, author.

Title: Complete crochet handbook / Eveline Hetty-Burkart, Beate Hilbig, and Beatrice Simone.

Other titles: Häkelmuster. English.

Description: First edition. | Lanham, MD : Stackpole Books, an imprint of Globe Pequot, the trade division of Rowman & Littlefield Publishing Group, 2023. | Includes index.

Identifiers: LCCN 2023005106 (print) | LCCN 2023005107 (ebook) | ISBN 9780811772013 (paper ; alk. paper) | ISBN 9780811772020 (epub)

Classification: LCC TT820 .B71813 2023 (print) | LCC TT820 (ebook) | DDC 746.43/4—dc23/eng/20230223

LC record available at https://lccn.loc.gov/2023005106

LC ebook record available at https://lccn.loc.gov/2023005107

Printed in China

First Edition

COMPLETE
CROCHET
HANDBOOK

Eveline Hetty-Burkart, Beate Hilbig, Béatrice Simon

STACKPOLE BOOKS

Essex, Connecticut

Blue Ridge Summit, Pennsylvania

Contents

HATS, SOCKS AND MITTENS

STITCH PATTERNS

CREATIVE CROCHET

RESOURCES

DEAR READER,

Crochet is more popular than ever before! It is so much more versatile than it might seem at first. With yarn and hook, everything from dense, sturdy potholders to light and airy lace shawls can be made in a wide array from utility stitches to delicate lace creations.

The variety of stitches, techniques, and pattern possibilities is almost innumerable even for old crochet hands. And once in a while you are bound to encounter unfamiliar terminology or methods that are not immediately apparent at first glance. Who wouldn't like to have a comprehensive reference book that helps in every situation? Here it is!

Basic techniques are explained step by step for those who have never held a crochet hook before, but even experienced crocheters will find new tips and tricks here. Fascinating special techniques, such as Tunisian crochet, Knooking, double-sided crochet, or hairpin lace, await to be (newly) discovered, and offer challenges for the experienced crocheter.

It also pays to venture outside one's own comfort zone, since the crochet community constantly turns more international and widely connected, especially thanks to the internet, where foreign-language patterns beckon and inspiration can be gained. Here, too, this book can help with international crochet terms and useful tips.

We wish for this book to gain a permanent place in your crochet library, and to always be your loyal companion!

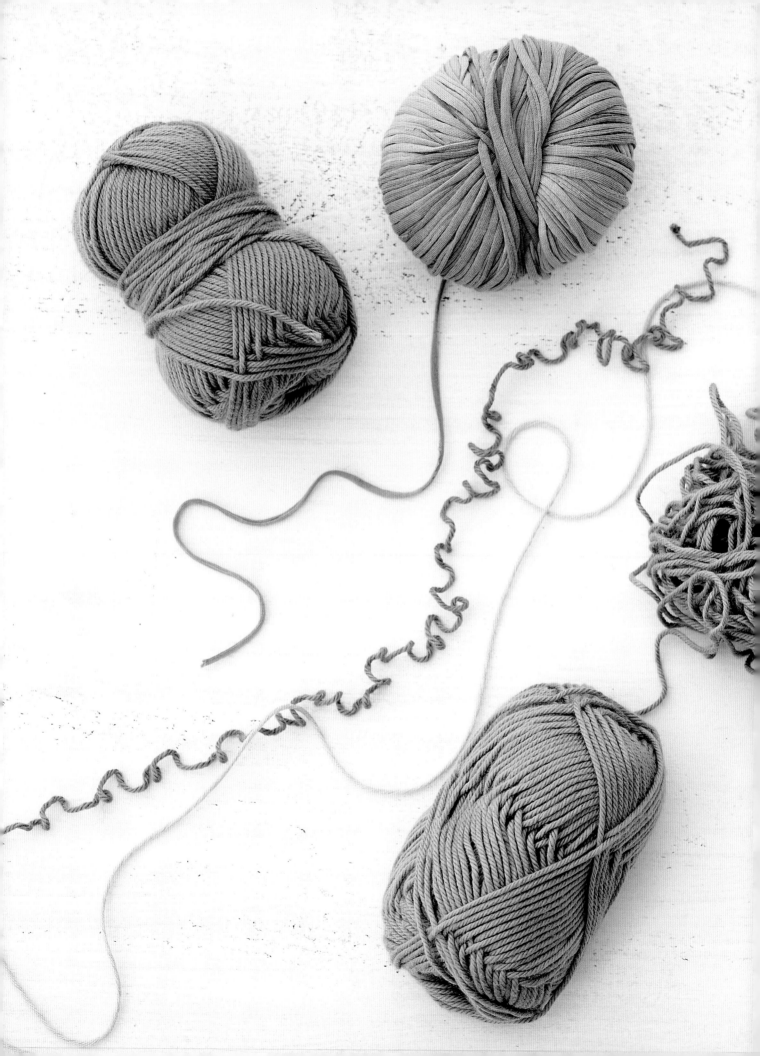

Yarn, Hooks, Notions

Before the first stitch comes choosing a yarn and hook. Besides these, there are many other pretty and useful tools that make crocheting even more enjoyable.

Yarn and Fiber

Not only are crochet yarns offered in a wide variety of colors and colorways, but the unique character of each yarn is also determined by different yarn types, fiber blends, yarn weights, and yarn construction. In the past, traditional cotton and linen yarns were considered typical crochet thread for filet crochet and lace work. Lately, other fiber types and materials have been increasingly gaining in popularity.

 Depending on fiber content, a yarn can be warming, cooling, or even temperature regulating. To choose the **RIGHT YARN** for a crochet project, it is important to know the **PROPERTIES** of the different fibers.

FIBERS AND THEIR PROPERTIES

Crochet yarns can be manufactured from natural or synthetic raw materials. Natural fibers are obtained from either plant cellulose fibers or animal protein fibers. Synthetic fibers can be produced from natural raw material sources as well as from man-made polymers.

NATURAL CELLULOSE FIBER

Cotton provides plant hair; flax, hemp, ramie, and jute provide soft fibers that can be blended with other fibers during manufacture. Different types of cellulose fiber have different properties.

COTTON

Cotton is harvested from the seed pods of the cotton bush. The cotton plant belongs to the Malvaceae (or mallow) family and grows in countries with tropical and subtropical climates. Its fine seed hairs consist mainly of cellulose. In the center of the fiber is the lumen, an air-filled cavity that works as a water reservoir and is surrounded by several partitions that serve as filters and give the fiber high stability and resistance but only a low elasticity. Its outer wall consists of a loose cellulose layer that is moisture absorbing. The fiber is further protected by a layer of fat, wax, cellulose, and pectins.

Owing to its low elasticity, cotton wrinkles easily. Wrinkling can be diminished through the addition of polyester. Since not much air can be encapsulated with this structure, cotton is only moderately warming.

Cotton can absorb about 20 percent of its own weight in vaporous moisture without feeling clammy. It only slowly releases already-absorbed moisture. Since it almost always contains some residual moisture, cotton hardly charges electrostatically. Thanks to its delicateness and softness, it is very skin friendly.

Cotton may be machine washed, spun dry, and steam ironed.

RAMIE AND HEMP

Ramie and hemp fibers are linen-like bast fibers harvested from the stems of the ramie plant (a type of nettle) and from the stems of the hemp plant, respectively. Both fibers are very tear resistant, durable, and not prone to pilling. For this reason, they are well suited as a natural alternative to blending with synthetics in manufacturing wool yarns, to increase abrasion resistance.

LINEN

Linen fiber is obtained from the stem of the flax plant, one of the oldest cultivated plants. It is similar in structure to cotton fiber and consists mainly of cellulose molecule chains. Because of the vegetable glue surrounding the fibers, linen is stiffer, with a smoother surface, and thus less pliable than cotton. Linen looks glossier than cotton, is more dirt repellent, and does not pill. This fiber is very durable and tear resistant but has little elasticity and is therefore very prone to wrinkling.

Yarns and fabrics made from linen hardly trap air and also cannot be roughened. In contrast, flax, being a cellulose fiber, is itself a good heat conductor. Therefore, garments made from linen do not warm but are always crisp and cool to the touch. Linen is very absorptive; it quickly absorbs moisture, releases it back into the environment equally quickly, and does not become electrostatically charged.

Linen is mostly used blended with other fibers. It increases the yarn stability and is ideal for summer yarns. Linen can be subjected to machine washing at high temperatures as well as the spin cycle. Before ironing, it always needs to be well moistened in order to smooth out wrinkles.

PROTEIN FIBER

Natural protein fiber is harvested by shearing or combing out animal fur and hair or by stripping and spooling up cocoon filaments.

WOOL

Sheep continue to be the most important raw material supplier for yarn production. Different countries of the world are home to various breeds of sheep, which have adapted to the respective climatic conditions and therefore provide wool with different properties.

Virgin wool, obtained exclusively from living animals, is the most valuable wool. Lambswool is the wool of a not-yet-a-year-old animal shorn for the first time and thus is especially soft. The finest of all sheep's wools originates with merino sheep.

Chemically, wool is a protein fiber and belongs to the group of keratins. Its outer layer consists of scales that are very dense in fine wool hairs and spread more apart in coarser wool hairs. Individual scale cells overlap each other as in the trunk of a palm tree. Prolonged friction causes the tiny scales to interlock with each other, forming lint and knots on the surface in the process. While these can be easily shaved with special tools, this process lets the fabric become thinner and weaker over time.

On top of the cuticle layer of the wool fiber is the epicuticle, a thin membrane that repels water and dirt but is permeable by water vapor. Wool fibers can slowly absorb up to 40 percent of their own weight in water vapor without feeling damp.

Under regular conditions, wool cannot be charged electrostatically.

The fiber owes its high elasticity to the spiral-shaped inner structure. For this reason, wool hardly tends to wrinkle and regains its original shape after having been subjected to tension and pressure, especially after hanging out in humid air.

Wool's resistance to tearing and abrasion is rather low. Especially when damp, stretch damage occurs easily. For this reason, hand-washed woolens should never be wrung out.

Wool keeps its wearer exceptionally warm. Thanks to the highly crimped fiber structure, it traps a lot of insulating air, and the protein substance itself has a thermo-insulating effect. These warming properties can be further enhanced by fulling and felting.

Wool is susceptible to moth damage. This issue can be prevented by storing small pieces of cedarwood (or other commercially available products) in the closet between the woolen items. While repelling moths, the scent of cedarwood is not overbearing when wearing woolen clothes and also dissipates very quickly in the air. When the cedarwood has dried out after a few years of use, it can be refreshed by sanding with sandpaper or by applying a few drops of cedarwood oil.

! When wool fibers submerged in suds are subjected to **STRONG FRICTION**, the fibers swell, and the scales become so interlocked that they can no longer be separated and form a **SOFT, DENSE, FELTED FABRIC**, which keeps out wind and moisture. This is used for deliberate felting of crocheted garments (> page 312).

> **!** Processing of luxury fiber in **PURE FORM** is rather laborious. For this reason, many of these fibers are blended with virgin sheep's wool. The warming and lightweight properties complement and harmonize well with each other.

> **!** Since pure silk yarns are quite **EXPENSIVE**, silk is often blended with other fibers. A blend of pure new wool and silk, for example, has the same warming and moisture-regulating properties as a pure new wool yarn while at the same time being much more delicate and softer than a pure virgin wool yarn.

Since wool fiber has naturally dirt-repellent properties, woolen clothes can be washed even at low temperatures in the gentle cycle or by hand. Washing temperatures higher than 86°F (30°C) and regular detergent should be avoided. Neutral or wool detergents keep the pH well above the critical alkaline range in which wool fiber felts. The wool washing programs of many washing machines prevent stretching damage by offering short spinning cycles with low rotational speed. Moist woolen garments should not be line dried but spread out flat to dry. Only woolen items made of specially manufactured yarns may be dried in the dryer. This will always be noted on the ball band. If possible, pure wool should be ironed or steamed at temperatures below 320°F (160°C), and only while covered with a damp cloth or using a steam iron. Dry ironing at too high temperatures can kill woolen items, causing the fiber to lose its memory.

ANIMAL HAIR

Especially fine and soft fibers with excellent thermal properties come from llama and alpaca. These animals are protected from severe cold in the Andean highlands of South America by their soft fur.

Equally luxurious is fine camel hair, which comes from the Bactrian camel or dromedary. Premium cashmere fibers are obtained from the combed-out undercoat of the cashmere goat, which is native to eastern India, China, and parts of the Himalayas.

Mohair fiber originates with the Angora goat; for the coveted kid mohair, only very young goats are sheared. Unlike sheep wool fiber, mohair fiber does not felt.

The interior of the hair of the pure white Angora fiber from the Angora rabbit traps air in its cells. This quality gives the hair an especially low weight and a particularly high heat retention capacity but also results in it becoming electrostatically charged and being very susceptible to moth damage.

SILK

Silk is the name given to the fibers obtained from the filaments of some insect species. The most important for textile processing come from the cocoons of mulberry silkworms, especially the mulberry silk moth, which has been reared in captivity for centuries in China and Japan.

A raw silk filament consists of the protein fibroin and the silk bast, sericin, which is also a protein. The silk bast that holds the two fibroin threads of the cocoon together is dissolved in boiling water, exposing the silk filaments to be fed into a spinning reel.

Seven to ten cocoon filaments from the center of the cocoon are plied to form a raw silk thread called reel silk. Leftovers of the cocoon that can no longer be reeled off are processed into spun silk (schappe silk). Bourette silk is made from short silk fibers that are left over from the manufacture of schappe silk and brushed out. Wild silk (tussah silk) comes from the tussah moth still living in the wild. Processing the pupated cocoons is considerably more difficult and costly than for those of the farmed mulberry silkworm. The silk fiber has a smooth outer structure and encloses hollow spaces in its interior. It can absorb about a third of its weight in moisture without feeling moist to the touch. Since it absorbs moisture quickly, it does not charge electrostatically.

The delicacy and softness of silk caress the skin. Silk is pliant and wrinkles little. Unlike sheep's wool, with its curly hairs, silk feels smooth against the skin and can even be a little clingy when slightly damp. Silk has a temperature regulating effect, cooling in summer and warming in winter. It has the highest tensile strength of all natural fibers. Since it is very smooth, it offers few opportunities for attack by fiber abrasion. However, silk is sensitive to light—it becomes brittle and fades.

Silk yarns should not be washed in water warmer than 86°F (30°C) and should be spun only very gently. Since silk, just as pure new wool, is sensitive to bases (alkaline), only neutral or mild detergents should be used. Washed silk garments should be laid flat until nearly dry (still slightly damp) and then ironed wrong side out. Water vapor from steam irons or steaming with a damp cloth can leave water stains on silk. Pure silk should never be folded, as it can break at the creases. For this reason, pure silk garments can only be stored rolled up or on hangers.

SYNTHETIC FIBERS FROM NATURAL POLYMERS

Cellulose is the main component of plant cell membranes. For its extraction, woods rich in cellulose are preferred, mainly spruce and beech wood, which are shredded into sawdust. By boiling the wood chips in either acidic or alkaline solutions, the cellulose they contain can be separated from its other components.

Depending on how the extracted cellulose is further processed, it can be used to produce viscose with wearing characteristics similar to cotton or acetate fibers with silk-like properties. Through variations in the manufacturing process, other types of synthetic fibers with different fiber properties can also be made.

In addition to cellulose, animal proteins such as milk proteins (casein) and vegetable proteins from corn, bamboo, or soybeans can be used for the production of polymeric regenerated fibers. Synthetically derived fibers of natural origin emerge on the market as alternative additives to increase the friction stability of wool yarns. It appears that the main focus for this seems to be the marketing impact when the usual synthetic additives can be replaced by a fiber of "natural origin," or when a yarn with a milk or soy content is advertised. Whether a synthetic fiber yarn made from natural raw materials should be considered a natural product continues to be the subject of much debate.

SYNTHETIC FIBERS

Polyamide, acrylic, and spandex are entirely man-made. They are an inexpensive alternative to more expensive natural fibers and can be used in blends to supplement them.

Since these synthetic fibers have no voids in the fiber structure, the moisture absorption of synthetic fibers is generally very low and can only be marginally improved by texturing the yarn or by producing hollow fibers. These fibers become highly electrostatically charged, as without moisture retention, they have no way of dissipating charges.

However, synthetic fibers are very elastic, wrinkle resistant, and have great resistance to tearing and abrasion. These qualities make them attractive as reinforcing blends to all delicate and less tear-resistant yarns. Synthetic additives can compensate for some of the natural weaknesses of fibers, provide more elasticity for cotton or linen yarns, improve care properties, and make yarns easier to dye. Likewise, many novelty yarns incorporating metallic, glitter, or fringe elements can only be made of synthetic fibers specially produced for the intended purpose.

THE RIGHT YARN

Besides personal preferences for one material or another, the intended use is also important for the selection of a yarn. When substituting for the yarn listed in a crochet pattern, if at all possible a yarn of the same fiber content and with comparable yardage should be chosen, to ensure the gauge matches that of the pattern, and the finished garment will have the same fit.

! A crocheted piece made in cooling cotton has a higher weight than the same piece worked in warming wool. This means that a piece of cotton yarn is shorter than a piece of wool yarn of the same weight. Therefore, the **TOTAL YARN WEIGHT NEEDED** will be accordingly higher.

14

! The **MORE THE STRANDS ARE TWISTED**, the higher the number of twists per 1 yard or meter, the more **TEAR RESISTANT** the yarn will turn out, the smaller its volume and higher its density, and the harder it will feel to the touch. In reverse, a yarn will drape **MORE SOFTLY**, be fluffier and more absorbent, but also more susceptible to breakage, **THE LESS TWIST** it gets during spinning.

X Yarn types with special properties can be manufactured using **DIFFERENT FIBER BLENDS**. For example, mixing in polyester improves wrinkle resistance in a linen yarn and gives a wool yarn greater durability, while adding in polyamide turns a wool yarn into one that is easier to care for, and blending with cotton makes a silk yarn more cost-effective.

X Strips cut from **FABRIC REMNANTS** have been on the market for some time in skeins or cones for retail sale.

SPINNING AND PLYING

In order to give structure to the collated fiber, it needs to be spun. The spinning direction can be either clockwise, resulting in an S-twist, or counterclockwise for a Z-twist. The number of wraps per 1 yard or meter of yarn indicates how tightly the yarn has been plied. A yarn indicated as "400S" has been plied with 400 wraps per 1 yard (or meter) with an S-twist in a clockwise direction. Individual strands can then be plied with each other. Depending on the desired effect for the yarn's construction, strands of either the same or a different twist direction are twisted together in one or more stages. Crochet yarns will often be plied as 2-, 3-, or 4-ply.

Special ways of spinning of the individual plies, combining different materials and colors, or subsequent dyeing, will result in different yarn effects. For bouclé yarns, for instance, smooth strands are combined with loopy strands; in thick-and-thin yarns, thicker sections alternate with thinner ones at different intervals. In fringe or eyelash yarns, long individual strands or yarn clusters are tightly twisted into a foundation strand. A heathered effect can be achieved by intensive blending of differently colored fibers before spinning.

OTHER MATERIALS

Very pretty and unusual effects can be achieved by crocheting with uncommon materials instead of the usual wool or cotton yarn.
Fine to medium wire can be used to create three-dimensional and malleable jewelry or bowls. Strips of cut plastic bags or fabric remnants make a very dense crocheted fabric, which is, for instance, well suited for home décor or sturdy bags (*Crocheting with non-traditional materials > page 314*).

RETAIL YARN

YARNS SOLD IN SKEINS, HANKS, CONES, OR SPOOLS

Crochet yarns are usually sold in bullet skeins, donut balls, cones, or hanks of 1.75 oz (50 g) each. Sock yarns are also offered as skeins or hanks of 3.5 oz (100 g) or 5.3 oz (150 g), each sufficient to make a pair of socks. Particularly luxurious yarns or those with a low yarn weight and high yardage are also sold in amounts of 0.9 oz (25 g).

Yarns offered as skeins or wound onto cones can be immediately used. Cones are worked off from the outside to the inside. Thanks to their own weight and large base, they are stable enough not to be toppled over as the yarn unwinds. The working yarn from a bullet skein should best be used from the inside out to prevent the skein from rolling around during work and getting tangled.

Hanks of yarn have to be first wound into a ball or cake before they can be used for crocheting. This can be done manually, the old-fashioned way, by hanging the opened hank over the back of a chair or around the outstretched arms of another person while winding it into a ball by hand. However, this can become tedious when several hanks need to be wound at once for a larger crochet project. Here, a

! Stay relaxed! When wool yarns are wound with **EXCESSIVE TENSION** and crocheted up this way, the yarn will revert to its original tension after the first wash, causing the garment or other finished item to significantly shrink.

X A good match! When shopping for yarn, make sure that all skeins come from the **SAME DYE LOT**, and purchase enough for your whole project. Only with luck will it be possible to buy more yarn of the same dye lot later on. It will be much easier to buy more initially and return leftover whole skeins afterward! Inquire about your store's time frame for returns at the time of purchase.

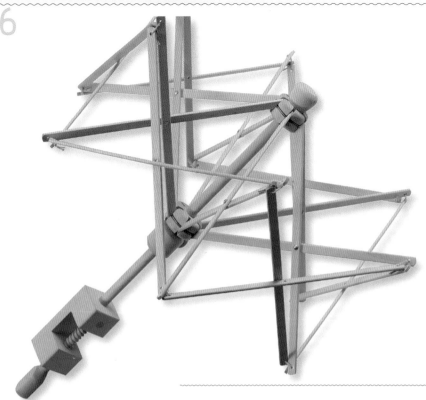

special yarn ball winder will come in handy. Most of them are powered by hand crank and wrap the yarn—fed through a yarn guide, around a center spool. When leaving the inner yarn end long enough, the finished yarn cake can be easily lifted from the center spool and used from the center out. If a second person to hold the hank of yarn is not available, the hank can be placed onto a yarn swift, which, just as the ball winder, can be securely attached to the tabletop by a clamp. The yarn swift can be adjusted to the diameter of the hank and is designed to rotate freely so that the yarn unwinds on its own due to the tension of the winder. While in use, the swift should be free of lint or yarn remnants and able to rotate unobstructed.

••• More information about the GAUGE SWATCH can be found on page 95.

YARN LABEL

Everything you need to know about the yarn you can learn at one glance from the ball band. Among the most important information is the fiber content of the yarn, as well as weight and yardage of the individual skein. The yardage always pertains to the weight of the individual skein.

The listed gauge will usually apply to a swatch knitted in stockinette stitch and therefore won't be very helpful for crochet. Here, always take note of the gauge stated in the pattern and, in any case, crochet your own gauge swatch!

The color number refers to a certain hue from a whole line of colors, whereas the dye lot number indicates the batch in which this particular skein has been dyed. Skeins with the same color number but different dye lots may seem to be the same color at first glance, but a significant difference may appear in the finished item after the yarn has been crocheted up.

••• Common CARE SYMBOLS are compiled on page 345.

Additionally, besides yarn line and brand name, details about the manufacturer will be given, including contact information for questions and complaints, as well as the country in which the yarn has been manufactured.

The care symbols printed on the yarn label are the same ones as used for clothing.

Always the Right Hook

A crochet hook and matching yarn are the basic equipment for every crochet project. Choosing the right tool is not an easy task: There are hooks from different materials, each with their specific properties, and, depending on crochet technique, even in different shapes. Different special techniques require their specific hook types as well.

[X] Crafters affected by nickel allergies and rheumatism should, if at all possible, **NOT USE STEEL CROCHET HOOKS,** but choose crochet hooks made of other materials.

[X] Those who want to enjoy their bamboo crochet hooks for a long time should opt for hooks made of sturdy **BAMBOO.**

[X] Crochet hooks made of **PRECIOUS WOODS** are expensive to purchase and therefore need diligent care. For maintenance, they should be rubbed with a small amount of **LINSEED OIL.** Rough spots, if any, can be smoothed with very fine grit sandpaper (at least 800 grade) or finest steel wool, and the hook reoiled after polishing. Some manufacturers of artisan wooden hooks do offer **REPAIR SERVICES.**

[!] In crochet hooks **WITHOUT GRIP,** the shaft transitions directly into the handle without any part in between. Very thin thread crochet hooks are often **SEPARABLE** between shaft and handle. For safe storage, the shaft of the crochet hook is inserted into the hollow handle, which serves as a sleeve.

MATERIALS

Crochet hooks of nickel-plated steel are very smooth and hard, and always feel cool to the touch. Loops glide easily over the hook with only minimal drag. Since steel is very weighty, crochet hooks made from this material are offered in tiny to very tiny hook sizes. Since they are so hard, the tip won't break under normal circumstances. Steel crochet hooks are offered as thread crochet hooks in a size range from sizes 0.6 mm (US steel hook #12) through 1.75 mm (US steel hook #4/0), and for yarn in sizes 2.0 mm (US steel hook size 4) and larger.

Crochet hooks made of powder-coated aluminum are a good alternative to steel crochet hooks. These metal crochet hooks are much lighter, however not quite as smooth as steel ones. While still providing a good degree of hardness, the smaller hook sizes are especially prone to accidental bending. Aluminum crochet hooks are sold in sizes 2.0 mm (US steel hook #4) and up. Owing to the sturdiness of the material, hairpin lace looms, as used for hairpin lace crochet, are very often made of aluminum as well.

Bamboo crochet hooks are lightweight and feel warm to the touch. They are softer than metal hooks and, especially in smaller hook sizes, can easily deform. Under normal circumstances, the tip won't break. Bamboo crochet hooks tempt the crocheter to work at a progressively looser

gauge. It is recommended to frequently recheck gauge during work, and compare the stitch appearance. This type of hook is sold in a size range from 2.0 mm (US steel hook # 4) through 8.0 mm (US L-11).

Crochet hooks of rosewood, ebony, kingwood, or other types of wood are truly caressing to hold. Often made from scrap wood from musical instrument production and being polished especially smooth, they feel pleasantly warm to the touch. This needle type, too, tempts the crafter to crochet more loosely. They are offered in a size range from 2.0 mm (US steel hook #4) through 8.0 mm (US L-11).

Crochet hooks of laminated birch wood are an alternative to hooks made from bamboo or precious woods. Due to the special technology in the manufacturing process, these crochet hooks are especially sturdy and polished to a smooth finish. They come in sizes from 2.0 mm (US steel hook #4) and larger.

Plastic hooks have been around for a long time. They are lightweight and sport a smooth surface. Since the manufacturing process allows for producing hollow hooks, even very large hook sizes can be manufactured, which, despite their diameter, still rest comfortably in the hand. Plastic crochet hooks in smaller sizes are often reinforced by a metal core.

THE "ANATOMY" OF A CROCHET HOOK

The typical form of a crochet hook is that of an elongated stick, which can either be of equal thickness throughout or feature a shaped grip that makes holding the crochet hook easier, with a small hook at the tip.

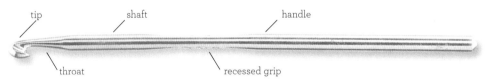

The **tip,** also called point, should be small so it will fit through the stitches easily, but not too small either, since this would make it harder to grasp the working yarn. Ideally, it should have a rounded shape, so the tip can smoothly slip through the stitches and loops without getting

caught. The **hook** serves for grasping the working yarn and pulling it through.

The **throat** is a crochet hook's narrowest spot. It constitutes the most important part, since here the working yarn is in constant movement. It should be as smoothly rounded as possible so that the yarn can be moved quickly and easily during crocheting. If the throat is too angular, the yarn can get caught on it, which disrupts the flow of crochet. Due to the strength of the material, the throats of metal crochet hooks are usually somewhat narrower and rounder than those of wooden hooks.

Directly after the throat follows the shaft. At the shaft, the hook size of the crochet hook is measured. The diameter of the shaft determines the size of the stitches. A thin shaft produces small and tight stitches, a thicker shaft larger and looser stitches accordingly. As a rule, thin yarns are worked with thinner hooks, thick yarns with thicker hooks.

The grip is a flattened spot that makes holding the crochet hook easier, so that one does not slide back and forth on the handle during crocheting. For beginners, this grip can prove very useful, as it provides a good way to practice holding the needle. Experienced crocheters, however, may find it not essential.

The handle as continuation of the shaft constitutes the remainder of the crochet hook. It will most often be about 5 inches (12.7 cm) long, including the grip, if the model has one. Crochet hooks can come with a variety of different handle designs. To make crochet hooks in smaller sizes easier to hold, the needle proper (most often made of steel) is often anchored within a thicker handle of sturdy plastic. More recent developments trend toward ergonomically shaped handles made of soft plastic material.

X Very SLICK CROCHET HOOKS without grip can be made easier to hold by placing a RUBBER SLEEVE or MASKING TAPE OVER THE HANDLE. Colorful MODELING CLAY is another means to make your own handles for crochet hooks.

! With the help of CONVERSION TABLES, it can be determined which US, UK, or JAPANESE hook sizes correspond to sizes in millimeters (> page 340). Conversion tables can also be found on the internet.

CROCHET HOOK TYPES

Depending on technique and intended use, different crochet hooks may be needed for different purposes.

THREAD CROCHET HOOKS

Thread crochet hooks are thin, fine crochet hooks with a delicate, sturdy steel tip. These are used when working with fine and finest cotton or silk yarns, particularly for lacework.

REGULAR CROCHET HOOKS

Regular crochet hooks (used for fine to jumbo yarns) are thicker crochet hooks, no matter what material they are made of. They can be used for crocheting with all commercially available yarns. For some time now, double-ended crochet hooks featuring points in different hook sizes at both ends have been available, too. Double-ended crochet hooks are the more economical alternative to two individual crochet hooks purchased separately.

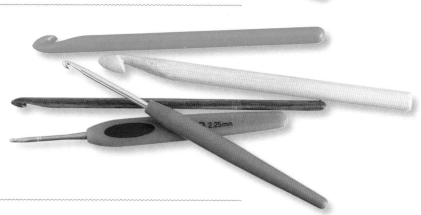

X Screw- or click-based interchangeable systems for Tunisian crochet hooks are often compatible with the corresponding **INTER-CHANGEABLE KNITTING NEEDLE SYSTEMS** by the same manufacturer.

! Occasionally, you can also find Tunisian crochet hooks with two tips pointing in **OPPOSITE DIREC-TIONS**. The orientation of the tip doesn't matter. It is important that both ends be the **SAME SIZE**.

! Hairpin lace looms can come as **ADJUSTABLE SYSTEMS**, too, with rods that can be inserted into a spacer as needed. Multiple openings in the spacer allow to **ADJUST** the **SPACING BETWEEN** the rods. Sometimes, the bottom part is also removable, allowing for finished loops to be released from the bottom of the loom to make longer pieces of lace.

TUNISIAN CROCHET HOOKS

Tunisian crochet hooks are used for the Tunisian crochet technique (> *page 225*). With a length of about 9.8–11.8 inches (25–30 cm), they are noticeably longer than regular crochet hooks, since this technique involves having multiple loops on the hook at the same time. They can consist of either a long, rigid needle or a short, straight needle without grip, extended at the non-hook end by an attached flexible cord. Both needle types feature a stopper at the end, which prevents open loops from slipping off the needle. Tunisian crochet hooks with points at both ends are used for crocheting in the round or for special stitch patterns. They are not to be confused with double-ended crochet hooks (> *page 19*). Both tips of a Tunisian crochet hook point in the same direction and are of the same size. Tunisian crochet hooks are also available as flexible screw- or click-based interchangeable systems, where needles and cords can be combined as needed.

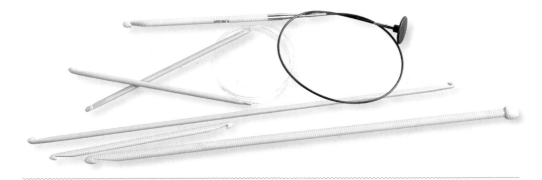

KNOOKING NEEDLES

Knooking needles are special needles for "Knooking" (> *page 255*), a technique using a crochet hook and a sturdy cord for holding stitches to create a knitted fabric. At the back end, they have an eye, through which the cord for holding stitches is threaded.

HAIRPIN LACE LOOMS

The hairpin lace loom, traditionally also called a fork, is the tool for creating hairpin lace crochet or fork work (> *page 283*). A hairpin lace loom consists of two parallel rods or prongs around which loops are crocheted.

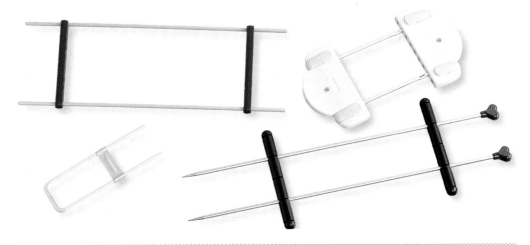

Useful
Notions

Craft stores and specialized retailers offer a wealth of different gadgets that make crocheting even easier and more comfortable. Some of them are indispensable; others are just so pretty that one simply wants to have them, although common household items such as a paper clip or regular rubber band would do as well.

MEASURING, SEWING, FINISHING

A needle/hook gauge or needle size guide helps to find the right size hook in a large assortment of differently sized hooks. Often, circular holes that correspond exactly to the diameter of the individual hook sizes are punched or drilled into a disc of particularly strong material. Since the size of a crochet hook is measured at the shank, the crochet hook has to be passed through the hole in the gauge in order to be measured. Sometimes the tip of a crochet hook is, however, a little thicker than its shank. For this type, a guide with widened openings/slots is useful.

With a swatch ruler, the gauge can be measured especially easily. For this, lay the crochet piece to be measured flat on an even surface, and place the frame on top, so that it is horizontally aligned with a row of stitches and vertically as parallel as possible to a column of stitches or a section of the stitch pattern. If necessary, nudge the crocheted fabric into place. Now the number of stitches and rows in 4 x 4 inches (10 x 10 cm) can be counted easily inside the cut-out opening. This way, you can check your individual gauge and, if desired, use this measurement to convert a pattern to a different yarn weight or measurements.

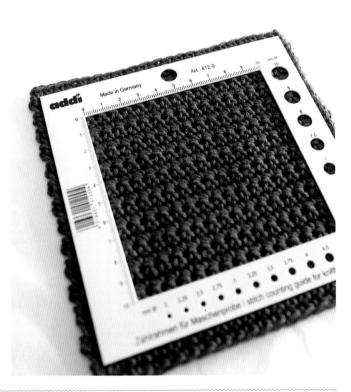

A MULTIFUNCTIONAL TOOL COMBINING a swatch ruler with a needle gauge guide for knitting needles and crochet hooks is nearly essential.

More information about the **GAUGE SWATCH** can be found on page 95.

For sewing together separate crocheted parts, you will need a thick, dull, tapestry needle that won't split the yarn. As basic equipment, one tapestry needle each is recommended in sizes 14 and 16.

To weave in yarn tails or embroider onto crocheted fabric, you should have needles in sizes 18 to 22, both with and without sharp tips (tapestry for dull tips, chenille for sharp). For crochet projects in thicker yarns, you may opt to additionally purchase even thicker needles. Eye size should be chosen with the goal in mind that the working yarn can be easily threaded through the eye, and the latter will create large enough gaps in the fabric for the working yarn to glide through when held double.

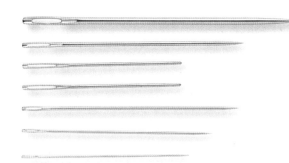

X You can also opt for checking off every row or round worked on a piece of NOTEPAPER.

X While a color is not in use, it can be secured by inserting it into the SLIT OF THE BOBBIN, thus preventing the working yarns from different bobbins from getting tangled.

Stitch markers are used in crochet to mark important spots. To prevent the marker from getting permanently embedded in the crocheted fabric, closed ring-type stitch markers, as known from knitting, cannot be used for crochet—only those that can be opened and closed like small safety pins are suitable. They can be attached to the crocheted fabric to mark individual stitches—for instance, to denote increase and decrease spots—or to keep track of the number of already-worked rows or rounds.

Yarn bobbins are helpful when working in the intarsia technique (> page 222), where multiple sections are worked in the same color and you don't want to use a separate whole skein of yarn for each color block.

A measuring tape should always be at hand to check the width and height of the crochet project. A retracting measuring tape is very practical and can be stowed away easily in your project bag.

Scissors are, of course, indispensable for making clean cuts when breaking the working yarn.

Yarn holders are offered in different types. Some consist of a board with several rods, each designed to hold one skein of yarn. When crocheting with multiple colors, every skein will stay in its place, and the yarns won't tangle. Special yarn bowls feature one or more slits at their sides for the yarn to be fed through, while the bowl itself keeps the ball of yarn contained. As an alternative, every ball can be placed into its own plain bowl or into a mason jar of sufficient dimensions.

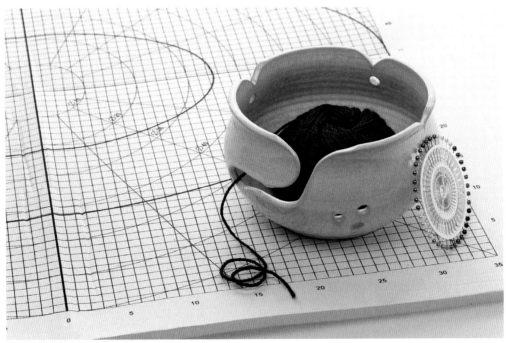

Blocking pins are larger tailor pins with a less sharp tip than their regular counterparts. As a rule, they are rustproof, but since, as compared to tailor pins, they are sold in relatively small quantities, they are significantly more expensive.

A blocking and steam-ironing mat with printed grid in inch or centimeter graduation simplifies the process of pinning crocheted pieces to the required measurements. A steam iron is a good alternative to steam blocking with moist cloths of linen or cotton fabric.

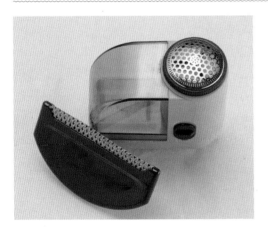

For the care of delicate wool or mohair garments, the following are recommended: a mohair brush (with which the mohair can be raised again after a wash), a wool comb to remove pilling tufts, and a fabric shaver and lint remover, which can battle even larger bumps and knots.

If a crocheted project is to be elaborately embroidered, a thimble is also worth its expense.

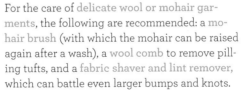

X Other yarn holders consist of just one SINGLE DOWEL ON A BASE onto which the skein of yarn is placed. This allows for easily winding off the yarn FROM THE OUTSIDE, too, without the need for pulling at the yarn. The tension resulting from the crochet movement will usually be sufficient to set the yarn in motion.

X There are some things needed for crocheting that you can't touch with your hands like hooks and yarn: GOOD LIGHTING, a comfortable place to sit, and a RELAXED POSTURE. All of the above can also be achieved in a companionable setting or with pleasant background music.

When space constraints are a problem during road trips, a **PATTERN KEEPER** comes in handy when working with charts. It helps to keep track of the already-worked rows.

USEFUL GADGETS FOR CRAFTING ON-THE-GO

A project bag, stocked with a second set of all important tools and ready to accommodate the current crochet project on the go, is a small luxury that should be indulged if you like to crochet while outside of your own abode. Such a bag should be large enough for your project and tools to fit comfortable and easy to carry. Ideally, it will have several interior compartments or pockets in which to stow various implements. A small tube of hand cream also comes in handy.

It may also be worthwhile to get two to three additional smaller closeable fabric pouches. One of the pouches will hold everything needed for securing and weaving in ends, such as a variety of embroidery and tapestry needles, a few safety pins, and a pair of scissors. The second bag will be for auxiliary tools, such as a tape measure or retractable tape measure, a small calculator, a pencil, a small notepad, and a few stitch markers. A third bag would have space for one or two spare skeins and the crochet pattern.

THE PROJECT BOOK

Whether you are among those who always first finish their current project before beginning another one, or if you tend to start multiple projects and, depending on your mood, continue to work sometimes on this one and sometimes on that one, bringing a little order into your crochet projects is worth the effort.

The most important tool for this is certainly your project book, in which you will log every started crochet project. Even more important than project name, date, or headline is the first yarn label pasted into it. It contains all of the important information about the yarn—from the fiber content to the care instructions; the gauge and color-number to the dye lot. If, in addition, you also paste the purchase receipt into the book, you can always look up where you bought the yarn.

The first entry should be the actual hook size used. If working from a pattern, you will also want to note the pattern name, the origin of the pattern (book title and page, or website URL) in order to be able to relocate it in case it should get misplaced, the size worked, and the available yarn amount.

If you don't have access to the pattern at all times, it is also helpful to copy the schematic or crochet charts and likewise paste them into the project book.

Very important are entries about all modifications to the original pattern. If, for instance, you crochet one sleeve shorter than stated in the pattern, the second sleeve should be of the same length, even if you are going to work on it a whole year later.

Organizing Yarn Stash and Crochet Projects

Who wouldn't be familiar with it: the yarn stash piling up at home without having a specific crochet project in mind yet and the hooks, which are actually always just where you are not looking for them? Just a few resources will go a long way for bringing a little order to your supplies!

Yarn supplies can be safely stored in cardboard storage boxes with lids. In these, they can be sorted by color, fiber content, yarn weight, or manufacturer. When boxes are accordingly marked, it will be very easy to find every yarn.

For wool yarns, it is also recommended to place skeins of the same dye lot together into a transparent plastic bag and close it, for instance, using a freezer bag clip. This way, they are kept mothproof but can still be easily viewed when searching for a yarn.

Alternative to cardboard storage boxes are stackable plastic boxes with lids. If storing wool yarns in open air, such as in a basket, a few pieces of cedarwood should definitely be put between the hanks or skeins for mothproofing.

Crochet hooks, a sizable collection of which can very easily accumulate over time, can be kept simply and decoratively in small vases or pen holders. Likewise, small, sturdy cardboard storage boxes or old wooden boxes are popular. Lovingly decorated in your very own design, they will turn into true treasure chests for your crochet hooks. To avoid injury while searching for hooks, the sharp tips of tiny steel crochet hooks should be protected by sticking them into a small piece of foam. Sewn crochet hook rolls provide a pretty and convenient storage solution for home and travel as well.

Tunisian crochet hooks can be likewise stored upright in a vessel, or those with attached flexible cords can be stored in transparent sheet protectors. Because of their size, hairpin lace looms can also be stored in sleeves of this kind.

For the storage of other crochet notions, a dedicated basket or a sewing box comes in handy to provide a permanent home for every tool to which it can be returned after having been used. Tapestry needles, stitch markers, scissors, tailor pins, and similar smaller items should be additionally placed into a small fabric pouch, to be stored together with the other tools.

! HEADS UP, MOTHS! Crochet projects from wool that have been paused for a longer time should by all means be stored in a mothproof way. Generally, it should be sufficient to store them **AIRTIGHT IN A PLASTIC BAG**, possibly together with a piece of cedarwood. For smaller projects, freezer bags with zip closure work very well.

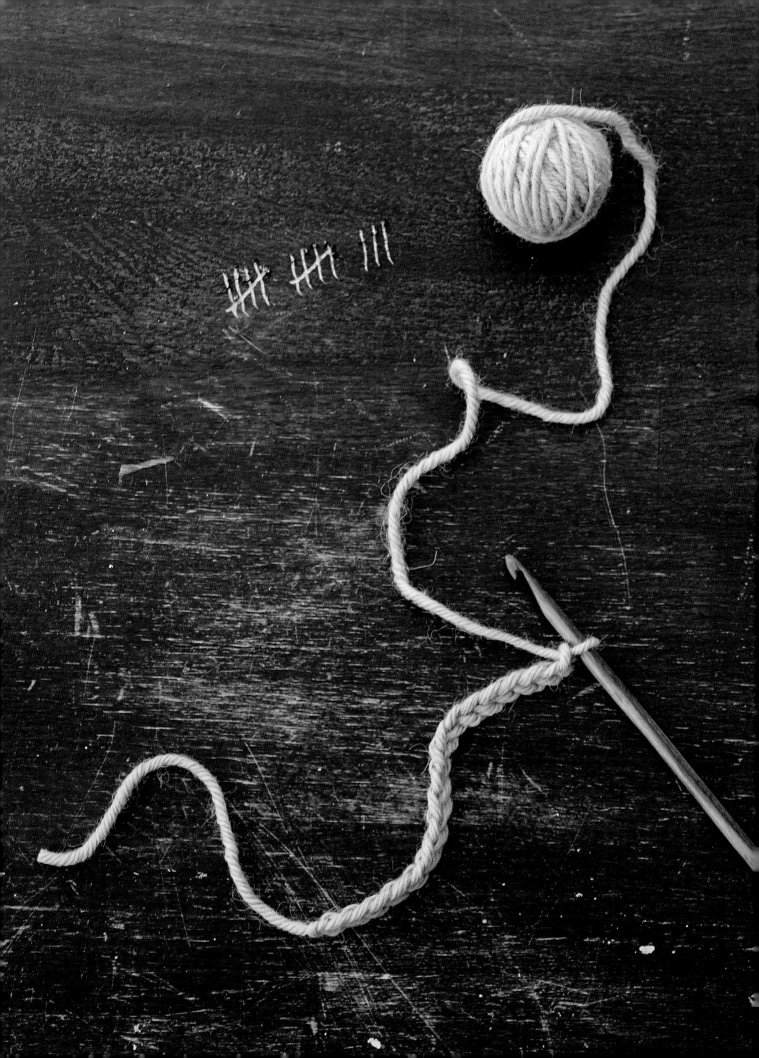

Crochet Stitches and Techniques

Stitches, stitches, and even more stitches: basic stitches, modified stitches, special stitches. Once you've learned the stitches, then you're ready for the techniques that turn your stitches into crocheted pieces: foundation chain, crocheting in rows and in the round, and finishing off . . . with new special tips for old crochet hands, too!

Before You Begin

Before crocheting the first stitches, you should familiarize yourself with a few crochet basics. What are the various parts of a crochet piece? How does the first loop get onto the hook and how should the hook, the yarn, and the crocheted piece be held?

WHAT IS WHAT?

To make a crochet piece, all you need is a ball of yarn and a crochet hook. In the beginning, you will place a slipknot onto the crochet hook. All further stitches will grow from this single loop, and you will always have at least one loop on your crochet hook. Depending on the type of stitch worked, there might be two or more loops at the same time on the hook during crocheting.

The working loop is the open loop of yarn that remains on the hook after having completed a stitch. The working yarn is the strand of yarn you are crocheting, which has not been crocheted yet, leading from the hook to the ball of yarn. The piece of extra yarn before the beginning slipknot is called the working yarn.

The foundation row is the bottom edge of the crocheted piece, which serves as a base for the crocheted fabric above it. It consists of either a crocheted chain, into which the stitches of the first row are worked, or stitches worked onto each other. The choice of foundation row depends on the intended use for the crocheted piece (crocheted chain > *page 57*, foundation crochet stitches > *page 59*).

Stitches represent a variety of basic and special stitches worked individually, each in its specific method. Basic stitches are all commonly used stitches of which the crocheted piece is composed, such as chain stitches, single crochets, or double crochets. To the category of special stitches belong all stitches created in a more complex way, such as crossed double or treble crochet, bullion stitch, or groups of stitches consisting of several individual stitches but counting as one stitch, such as popcorn stitches or cluster stitches.

Every stitch type creates a crocheted fabric with its typical stitch appearance. Small, compact stitches, such as single crochets, produce a tight and firm crocheted fabric, while large, longer stitches, such as treble crochets, create a more translucent and supple fabric.

Stitch patterns and effects are achieved by skillful combination of different stitch types. From just a number of basic stitches, manifold stitch patterns of different character can be designed, for instance, textured patterns, three-dimensional patterns, or lace patterns.

The top edge of the crocheted piece consists of the two loops of every crochet stitch. The front and back loop of the stitch appear as a horizontal V.

X When crocheting simple patterns, your work-in-progress can be set aside without any problems, since there is always **ONLY ONE LOOP** on the hook. To prevent the crocheted fabric from unraveling, just pull at the loop to make it larger. When working in more complicated stitch patterns, it is however recommended to always complete a row or a heightwise pattern repeat to avoid mistakes when resuming work on the piece later.

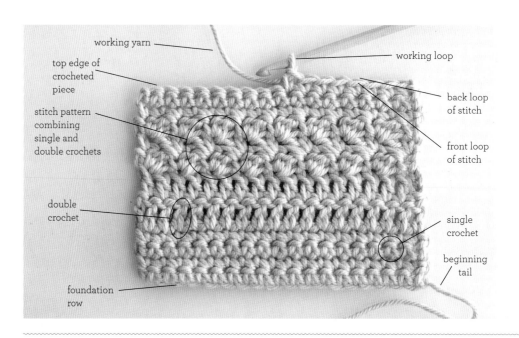

working yarn

working loop

top edge of crocheted piece

back loop of stitch

stitch pattern combining single and double crochets

front loop of stitch

double crochet

single crochet

beginning tail

foundation row

HOLDING HOOK AND YARN
Holding the crochet hook and feeding the yarn are the first important basic steps for crocheting.

HOLDING THE CROCHET HOOK
The crochet hook as a small, handy tool should lie in the hand comfortably. There are two basic methods for holding the hook.

One way is holding the crochet hook from below, like a pen, with the hook end located about 1.2 inches (3 cm) in front of the middle finger and pointing forward. If the crochet hook has a thumb rest, index finger and thumb will rest on this part

Another way is holding the crochet hook from above, like a knife, with the hook end about 1.2 inches (3 cm) in front of the index finger and pointing forward. If the crochet hook has a thumb rest, the thumb will rest on this part.

FEEDING PATH AND TENSION OF THE YARN
The feeding path is the way in which the yarn is led through the fingers while holding it at tension. The working yarn should be held with even tension to create an even stitch appearance. Just as with holding the crochet hook, there are multiple ways to feed the yarn. The tension on the yarn will be greater the more often the yarn is wrapped through or around the fingers.

Unwind some yarn from the ball. The working yarn hangs down behind the pinky finger of the left hand. Now lead the yarn around the fingers of the left hand using one of three possible ways:

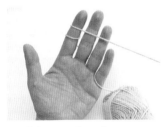

Lead the yarn from front to back between pinky finger and ring finger. Wrap the yarn around the index finger from back to front twice.

Or "weave" the yarn, starting at the pinky finger, over and under the fingers, and wrap it around the index finger twice.

Or just wind the yarn around the index finger two times.

HOLDING THE CROCHET HOOK AND THE WORK-IN-PROGRESS
The crochet hook is held in the right hand. It should rest in the hand loosely. Make sure that the hook faces forward, to the viewer. Lead the working yarn over the fingers of the left hand. At the same time, hold the crocheted piece with its top edge in a horizontal position so it will be easier to insert the hook into the stitches.

! Every crocheter needs to try out individually which position of the crochet hook feels best. Here, it is important to hold the hook LOOSELY and comfortably, without straining the hand in the process. With a little practice, you will soon develop your very own personal "style of crocheting." Knitters often prefer holding from above, as they are used to holding knitting needles this way.

! Leave a BEGINNING TAIL of about 8 inches (20 cm). This is sufficient to be woven in at the end of the project. For crocheted pieces requiring seaming, the beginning tail can be used later to sew the pieces together. In this case, leave an accordingly longer beginning tail.

✗ Before crocheting, make sure that hands and fingernails are smooth, to prevent the yarn from getting caught on any rough parts, which would disrupt the flow of crochet. A small tube of HAND CREAM kept in your crochet basket will be useful.

Stitches

A crocheted piece is made of stitches worked next to each other and atop each other. These can be either all stitches of the same type or different types of stitches combined into a clever stitch pattern.

BASIC STITCHES

Basic stitches are a few common stitches that are the basis of all crochet work and which can be combined into a wide array of stitch patterns.

THE BEGINNING SLIPKNOT

Every crocheted piece starts with a slipknot. This will be the first loop, also called the working loop, out of which the first stitch will emerge. The beginning slipknot can be adjusted in size.

BEGINNING SLIPKNOT AND SUPPLYING THE YARN OVER THE LEFT HAND

! With a little practice, you will be able to create the beginning slipknot, adjust the size of the beginning slipknot, and start working in an **UNINTERRUPTED** workflow.

1 Lead the yarn around the fingers of the left hand (feeding path > *page 29*) and wind it in a counterclockwise direction around the thumb once. Hold the yarn tail with the remaining three fingers of the left hand.

2 Now lead the crochet hook through the loop on the thumb from bottom to top, and, going over the crossed strands, grasp the strand coming from the index finger with the crochet hook, and pull it through.

3 At the same time, remove the thumb from the loop, making sure that the loop doesn't slip from the hook. Pull the beginning slipknot tight, but still sitting on the hook loosely. The size of the beginning slipknot can be adjusted by pulling at the working yarn.

4 Hold the beginning slipknot by the knot below the crochet hook. This way, you can start crocheting immediately, without further interruption.

BEGINNING SLIPKNOT OVER THE RIGHT HAND

 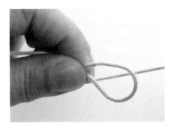 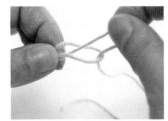

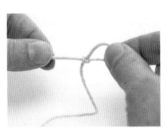

1 Place the yarn over the index finger of the right hand, and cross it, so that the working yarn is located in back. A loop has formed over the index finger.

2 Hold the crossed strands with the left thumb and index finger, take the loop off the index finger, and rotate it to the right, so that it is located above the yarn tail.

3 With your index finger, pull the yarn tail through the loop, and tighten the knot.

4 The size of the loop can be adjusted by pulling at the working yarn.

YARN OVER: THE LOOP ON THE HOOK

Making a yarn over or making a loop on the hook is the action of placing the working yarn onto the crochet hook to be able to grasp it with the crochet hook. You may make a yarn over either before inserting the hook into a stitch or after insertion to complete the stitch.

A yarn over can be used for creating stitches. Here, before inserting the hook, the working yarn is placed around the crochet hook one or more times.

Grasping the working yarn in order to finish an individual stitch is also called a yarn over. Depending on the type of stitch worked, the working yarn may be placed onto the hook one or more times and pulled through the insertion point or through the loops of the stitch.

X Supplying the working yarn always **FROM BELOW**, with a little practice, creates a pleasant **WORKFLOW**.

! Certain stitch types, such as double crochets, require yarn overs **BEFORE AND AFTER INSERTING THE HOOK.**

Before making a yarn over, the working yarn is always located behind the crochet hook.

When the yarn over is made to create a stitch, the yarn is placed on the hook before inserting the hook to work the stitch. For this, lead the crochet hook underneath the working yarn from front to back around the working yarn so that it rests on the hook. Then insert the hook into the appropriate stitch.

When making a yarn over to grasp the working yarn and pull it through, insert the hook first into the appropriate stitch and then pull the working yarn through the insertion point and the loops of the stitch as directed.

TWISTED STITCHES

The yarn over can, *after inserting the hook*, be placed on the hook the opposite way, grasping the working yarn from above.

After the stitch has been completed, this results in the stitch looking slightly twisted.

WRONG YARN OVER BEFORE INSERTING HOOK

If you place the yarn over of a double crochet the other way around before inserting it into the stitch, after inserting the hook into the stitch, you will find completing the stitch the regular way very awkward. Trying anyway to work the double crochet will result in a completely different-looking stitch.

Correct yarn over

Wrong yarn over

Three double crochets with wrong yarn over

THE CHAIN

A chain is a crocheted loop. It is used, for instance, in the foundation chain when chaining, for height adjustment at the beginning of a row or round, or one after the other in the form of a chain arc or bridge within a stitch pattern (Making a foundation chain > page 57).

crocheted chain from the front

crocheted chain from the back

1 Make a yarn over, grasp the working yarn . . .

2 . . . and pull it through the loop on the hook. The chain appears as a V-shaped loop below the hook. On the wrong side of work, this creates small perpendicular bumps between individual chains.

INSERTING THE HOOK INTO A STITCH

If not otherwise stated in the instructions or the stitch pattern, when crocheting into existing stitches, the hook is always inserted under both V-shaped top loops of the stitch.

SLIP STITCH

Slip stitches are the smallest stitches. They are very shallow and practically consist of only one single loop. Slip stitches are used to join in the round, to finish and reinforce edges and borders, to join crocheted motifs, to crochet parts together, or, as surface crochet, for embellishing crocheted fabric. Slip stitches can also be used to crochet whole pieces of fabric, but since the stitches are so tiny, this technique is seldom used to crochet a whole piece (*slip stitch crochet > page 261*).

Slip stitches worked in rows

1 To make a slip stitch, insert the hook, make a yarn over and grasp the working yarn, and pull it through the insertion point and . . .

2 . . . immediately through the working loop.

! Slip stitches tend to turn out too tight when making a whole fabric out of them. For this reason, always **CROCHET LOOSELY**, to be able to insert the hook into the stitch more easily.

X **SLIP STITCHES WORKED IN ROWS** create a sturdy, dense crocheted fabric that can be used, for instance, for belts or shoulder straps in bags (*slip stitch crochet > page 261*).

SINGLE CROCHET

The single crochet stitch is the easiest of the basic stitches and perhaps the most often used one. Single crochets are small and produce a fabric with a dense, compact stitch definition.

Single crochets worked in rows

1 To work a single crochet, insert the hook, make a yarn over, and pull the working yarn through the fabric. Pull the loop thus created larger until it reaches the height of the working loop. There are 2 loops on the hook now.

2 Make another yarn over, and pull the working yarn through both loops on the hook at once. The body of the single crochet stitch is small and V-shaped.

X Crocheted fabric made with only single crochets has a distinctive stitch appearance: two rows together create tiny "STARS" or "flowers" arranged next to each other and stacked on top of each other. This effect can be incorporated into stitch patterns to its advantage.

X To prevent a fabric worked in single crochet from turning out **TOO DENSE**, you can work using a crochet hook in a **LARGER HOOK SIZE** than recommended.

X The sturdy and compact stitch definition has the merit that pieces worked in single crochet will hold up better to **WEAR AND TEAR**. For this reason, this stitch can be used for bags, pillows, blankets, or small rugs and mats.

••• Single crochets can be modified in many ways. A few **VARIATIONS** can be found on pages 40 and 41.

EXTENDED SINGLE CROCHET

The extended single crochet is a variation of the single crochet. The stitch definition appears looser, which results in a fabric that feels suppler to the touch, and due to the slightly elongated shape the stitch pattern looks more airy. Since the stitch is more elastic than single crochet, it is often used for crocheting socks, for which reason it is called sock stitch in some languages.

Extended single crochets worked in rows

1 Insert the hook into the stitch, make a yarn over, and pull the working yarn through the fabric. There are 2 loops on the hook now.

2 Make another yarn over and pull the working yarn through the first loop on the hook. There are again 2 loops on the hook.

3 Make another yarn over and pull the working yarn through both loops on the hook at once. Extended single crochets resemble two single crochets stacked atop each other.

HALF DOUBLE CROCHET

A half double crochet is, after the single crochet stitch, the next basic stitch heightwise. It is likewise compact, the crocheted fabric appears similarly dense and sturdy, but has more elasticity.

Half double crochets worked in rows

 Half double crochets are often used in combination with other basic stitches **TO CREATE DISTINCTIVE PATTERNS.**

 Thanks to the additional yarn over, the stitch turns out thicker. For this reason, fabrics crocheted using half double crochet stitches **CONSUME MORE YARN** than those worked in single crochet.

1 Before inserting the hook, make a yarn over onto the hook.

2 Then insert the hook, make a yarn over and pull the working yarn through the fabric. There are 3 loops on the hook now.

3 Make another yarn over and pull the working yarn immediately through all 3 loops on the hook at once.

4 The half double crochet stitch is easily recognizable by its slightly elongated body with a short diagonally placed loop.

DOUBLE CROCHET

The double crochet stitch is one of the most often used basic stitches. Because of the yarn over and the additional step involved, the stitch turns out elongated and therefore taller than single crochets and half double crochets. Its stitch appearance is looser, and a distinctive linear texture is created.

Double crochet worked in rows

1 Before inserting the hook, make a yarn over onto the hook.

2 Then insert the hook, make a yarn over and pull the working yarn through the fabric. There are 3 loops on the hook now.

3 Make another yarn over and pull the working yarn through the first 2 loops on the hook at once.

4 Now make another yarn over and pull the working yarn through the remaining 2 loops on the hook at once.

5 The double crochet is recognizable by an elongated post (body of the stitch) with a diagonally placed loop in the center.

TREBLE CROCHET

Treble crochets are elongated, tall stitches. They produce a loose and sheer-looking fabric. Treble crochets are used, for instance, in combination with other basic stitches to create filigree-like patterns or as connective bars in lace crochet.

Treble crochets worked in rows

When treble crochets are worked, the **TOTAL YARN AMOUNT NEEDED** increases significantly in comparison to other stitch types. For one row of treble crochet, a length equal to approximately 21 times the width of the row should be calculated: To work a row of about 4 inches (10 cm), you will need a yardage of 84 inches (214 cm) of yarn.

1 Before inserting the hook, make 2 yarn overs onto the hook.

2 Then insert the hook and pull the working yarn through the fabric. There are 4 loops on the hook now.

3 Make yet another yarn over and pull the working yarn through the first 2 loops on the hook at once. There are 3 loops on the hook.

! When crocheting treble crochets and taller stitches, make sure that during all working steps the working yarn is held at an **EVEN TENSION**, so the slanted loops resulting from the yarn overs don't turn out too loose.

4 Make another yarn over and pull the working yarn through the first 2 loops on the hook. There are 2 loops on the hook.

5 Now make another yarn over and pull the working yarn through the remaining 2 loops on the hook at once.

6 The treble crochet stitch is recognizable by its long post (body of the stitch) with 2 slanted loops stacked atop each other.

EXTENDED DOUBLE CROCHET (EDC), EXTENDED TREBLE CROCHET, ETC.

Extended stitches are made by adding an extra step of "yarn over, pull a loop through" to a basic stitch. Half double crochets and double crochets involve different numbers of working steps. To work a half double crochet, in one working step, the working yarn is pulled through 3 loops on the hook together at once, for double crochet, the loops are worked off in two working steps, two together at a time. For in-between sizes with intermediate steps between double crochet and taller stitches, the number of yarn overs for the next taller stitch is placed onto the hook, and then the loops are, as done for double crochet, worked off together in pairs, until finally 3 loops remain on the hook. These 3 loops are worked together once after having made a new yarn over.

EXAMPLE: THE EXTENDED DOUBLE CROCHET (EDC)

1 The next taller stitch after the double crochet would be the treble crochet. Therefore, 2 yarn overs are placed onto the hook.

2 Then insert the hook, make a yarn over and pull the working yarn through the fabric. There are 4 loops on the hook now.

3 Make another yarn over and pull the working yarn through the first 2 loops on the hook at once. There are 3 loops on the hook.

4 Make another yarn over, grasp the working yarn and pull it through all 3 loops on the hook together at once.

5 Because of the additional yarn over at the beginning, the extended double crochet is taller than a regular double crochet but shallower than a treble crochet.

MODIFYING STITCHES BY INSERTING THE HOOK A DIFFERENT WAY

A stitch is composed of the body of the stitch (post) and the top of the stitch. The word "post" refers to the whole stitch, the phrase "top of the stitch" to the upper part of the stitch with front and back loops of the stitches, which lie horizontally, forming a V shape. In most cases, the top of the existing stitch is the spot where the hook is inserted for a new stitch. When inserting the hook, it is inserted through both loops of the stitch unless otherwise stated *(Inserting the hook into a stitch > page 32)*.
Even stitch patterns consisting of just a basic stitch type can be modified in a variety of ways by slightly changing the way of inserting the hook or by using completely different methods of inserting. Patterns and effects can also be achieved by including the post itself, or by inserting the hook not into the stich but in the space between stitches.

INSERTING THE HOOK THROUGH THE FRONT OR BACK LOOP ONLY

The loops of the top of the stitches can be used independently of each other as insertion points for the hook. Regardless of whether the right or wrong side of the fabric is facing up, the loop of the stitch closer to the viewer is called the front loop of the stitch, and the loop behind it the back loop of the stitch. When working a row, while only inserting the hook through one of the two loops, the unused loop will form a fine horizontal line. All basic stitches are suitable for being worked this way.

Slip stitches worked through the back loop of the stitch only.

Single crochet, worked in right-side rows through the back loop, in wrong-side rows through the front loop of the stitch only: This creates a fine horizontal line in every row.

Double crochet, worked in every row through the back loop of the stitch only: This creates a fine horizontal line in every other row.

INSERTING THE HOOK THROUGH THE FRONT LOOP ONLY

When inserting the hook, go under the front loop of the stitch only, making sure to not accidentally grasp the back loop of the stitch. Work the stitch as usual. The unused back loop of the stitch creates a fine horizontal line on the back side of the fabric.

INSERTING THE HOOK THROUGH THE BACK LOOP ONLY

When inserting the hook, go through the back loop of the stitch only, making sure to not accidentally grasp the front loop of the stitch. Work the stitch as usual. The unused front loop of the stitch creates a fine horizontal line on the front side of the fabric.

X Other pattern effects can be achieved by changing the way of inserting within the same row. This creates an interesting **BROKEN RIB** pattern.

HORIZONTAL RIDGES

Patterns with ridge effects can also be achieved by working stitches into the backs of previous stitches. The loops of the stitch will align themselves on the crocheted fabric into a cable-like horizontal ridge. How the pattern will look is determined by whether it is worked in rows or working in rounds: If working in rows, when crocheting a row, the back of the stitch from the previous row will be located on the front side of the work, which means the hook has to be inserted from the front of the work. The loops of the stitches lean to the back. If it is desired that the loops of the stitches are all on the same side of the fabric, in every other row, the hook needs to be inserted into the stitch from the back of the work.

To work a single crochet, insert the hook on the front of the work from bottom to top into the short, horizontal loop under the front loop of the stitch, make a yarn over, and grasp the working yarn; pull the yarn through the loop on the hook as usual to finish the stitch.

Single crochets worked in rows

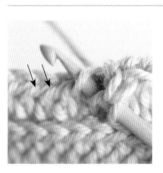

To work a half double crochet or double crochet, make a yarn over onto the hook, insert the hook on the front of the work from bottom to top into the horizontal loop under the front loop of the stitch, make a yarn over and grasp the working yarn; pull the yarn through the loops on the hook as usual to finish the stitch.

Half double crochets worked in rows

If working in rounds, however, the back of the stitch is always on the wrong side of the crocheted fabric. This means that the loops of the stitch will lean to the front in every round.

To work a single crochet on the wrong side of the fabric, insert the hook from top to bottom into the short horizontal loop under the back loop of the stitch, make a yarn over and grasp the working yarn; pull the yarn through the loop on the hook as usual to finish the stitch.

Single crochets in the round

To work a half double crochet or double crochet, make a yarn over onto the hook, on the wrong side of the fabric, insert the hook from top to bottom into the horizontal loop under the back loop of the stitch, make a yarn over and grasp the working yarn; pull the yarn through the loop(s) on the hook as usual to finish the stitch.

Half double crochets in the round

When crocheted in the round, the ridges of single crochet and half double crochets are very close to each other. This can be used to its advantage for items such as **NECKBANDS**, **BUTTON BANDS**, or **CUFFS**.

WORKING BETWEEN STITCHES

Suitable for this way of inserting are all taller stitches, meaning all stitches from double crochet up. Due to their height, gaps form between stitches, into which the hook can be inserted with ease.

Here, the hook had been inserted in the space between half double crochets.

Here, the hook had been inserted in the space between double crochets.

1 To work a stitch, make a yarn over onto the hook, and insert the hook into the space between 2 stitches of the previous row or round.

2 Pull the working yarn through, and work the stitch as usual. This aligns the stitches slightly staggered to the stitches of the previous row or round.

CENTER SINGLE CROCHET (CSC)

Center single crochet, or waistcoat stitch, is a very compact and dense stitch; the crocheted fabric appears flat and smooth. To work a center single crochet, insert the hook into the post of the stitch of the previous row. Due to having turned at the end of the row, the back of the single crochets of the previous row will be located on the right side of work in the current row. The back of a single crochet consists of the front loop of the stitch, the post of the stitch, a short loop located under the top of the stitch, and 2 other short loops resembling upside-down Vs.

To work a center single crochet, insert the hook between the two legs of the upside-down V, immediately below the short horizontal loop, and then work the stitch as usual.

Center single crochets worked in rows

! Always work center single crochet very **LOOSELY** in order to be able to easily insert the hook into the post of the stitch. Stitches will turn out loosely if the loop resulting from pulling the working yarn through is pulled slightly longer.

TWISTED STITCHES

When inserting the hook in the opposite direction (i.e., from back to front) into the stitches, the stitches will twist, creating a different stitch appearance.

Twisted single crochets worked in rows

Twisted half double crochets worked in rows

Twisted double crochets worked in rows

TWISTED SINGLE CROCHET

1 Insert the hook into the stitch through both loops of the stitch from back to front, with working yarn behind the hook.

2 Bring the working yarn to the front of work, making a loop onto the hook, and pull the working yarn through . . .

3 . . . and pull it even with the working loop above the crocheted piece.

4 Then finish the stitch the usual way.

TWISTED DOUBLE CROCHET

1 To work a twisted double crochet, make a yarn over onto the hook, and insert the hook from back to front as done for a twisted single crochet.

2 Bring the working yarn to the front of work, making a loop onto the hook, and pull the working yarn through . . .

3 . . . and pull it even with the working loop at the top edge of the crocheted piece. The newly created loop and the yarn over already appear twisted.

4 Now finish the double crochet the usual way.

POST STITCHES

For post stitches, the hook is not inserted through the loops of the stitch—the working yarn is led around the post of a stitch instead. This way of inserting the hook produces a three-dimensional effect. The posts bulge, while the unused loops of the stitches create horizontal ridges, located on either the right side or the wrong side of the crocheted fabric. Single crochets are the smallest stitches that can be worked this way, but it is especially effective for all stitches from double crochet up, since their elongated posts are easy to work around.

There are two different ways to work around the post. The hook can be inserted around the post either from the front or from the back, creating front or back post stitches.

FRONT OR BACK POST SINGLE CROCHETS

When single crochets are worked as post stitches, the result is a very dense, textured fabric that can be developed into appealing stitch patterns. The three-dimensional effect is not quite as pronounced as with front or back post double crochet.

Checkerboard pattern in front and back post single crochet, alternating 3 front post stitches and 3 back post stitches, and shifted after 3 rows

---

Front post single crochet

1 Insert the hook on the front side of the fabric from front to back to front around the post of the stitch of the previous row from right to left, causing the post of the stitch to bulge toward the front of the work.

2 Grasp the working yarn, pull it through behind the stitch . . .

3 . . . and pull it even with the working loop along the top edge of the crocheted piece. There are now 2 loops on the hook.

4 Finish as for a regular single crochet.

The loops of the single crochets of the previous row are located on the back side of the fabric. The post stitches appear prominently raised on the front side of the fabric.

Back post single crochet

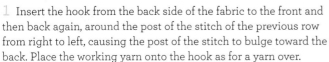

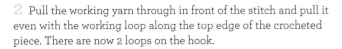

1 Insert the hook from the back side of the fabric to the front and then back again, around the post of the stitch of the previous row from right to left, causing the post of the stitch to bulge toward the back. Place the working yarn onto the hook as for a yarn over.

2 Pull the working yarn through in front of the stitch and pull it even with the working loop along the top edge of the crocheted piece. There are now 2 loops on the hook.

3 Finish as for a regular single crochet.

The loops of the single crochet stitches of the previous row are located on the front side of the fabric, and protrude prominently. The single crochets are located on the back side of the fabric.

X Raised stitches appear **DENSE AND VOLUMINOUS** in the crocheted fabric. For this reason, they are a very good choice for **POTHOLDERS.**

FRONT AND BACK POST DOUBLE CROCHET (RAISED STITCHES)

Whenever "raised stitches" are mentioned, this usually means raised double crochet. However, in the same way, all stitches taller than double crochet can be worked as raised stitches as well.

Ribbing pattern of raised stitches, alternating 2 front post double crochets and 2 back post double crochets

Regular front post double crochet

The top loops of the double crochet stitch of the previous row are located on the back side of the fabric. The double crochet prominently protrudes on the front side of the fabric..

1 Make a yarn over onto the hook. Insert the crochet hook from front to back to front (right to left) around the post of the indicated double crochet. The double crochet bulges toward the front of the fabric.

2 Grasp the working yarn and pull it through behind the double crochet. There are 3 loops on the hook.

3 Now finish the double crochet the usual way.

Regular back post double crochet

On the front side of the fabric, the top loops of the double crochet stitch of the previous row appear, protruding prominently. The double crochet is located on the back side of the fabric.

1 Make a yarn over onto the hook. Insert the crochet hook from back to front to back (right to left) around the post of the indicated double crochet. The post of the double crochet bulges toward the back of the fabric.

2 Grasp the working yarn and pull it through in front of the double crochet. There are 3 loops on the hook.

3 Now finish the double crochet the usual way.

X A profusion of three-dimensional textured patterns can be created using different **STITCH COMBINATIONS.** Also very appealing are **COLOR-WORK PATTERNS INVOLVING TWO OR MORE COLORS** in raised stitches.

WORKING IN THE CHAIN SPACE

In stitch patterns, individual stitches or groups of stitches are often separated from each other by chains, which can be called a chain space or chain arc. Chain arcs often skip a certain number of stitches. The chains either function and count as individual stitches or, in lace patterns, can be used to bridge gaps to create a mesh or web-like fabric. Unless otherwise stated, the hook is not inserted into individual chain stitches of the chain, but the new stitches are worked around the chain, which is called "working into the chain space."

Trellis pattern worked in the chain space

1 For each stitch, insert the hook below the chain arc from front to back, and then make a yarn over and pull the working yarn around the chain to the front and along the top of the chain.

2 Finish each stitch the regular way.

WORKING MULTIPLE STITCHES INTO ONE STITCH

Shell and fan patterns are created from double or treble crochets or taller stitches worked either into the same stitch or into the same chain space. This lets the stitches fan out into the desired shape. Since this increases the overall stitch count, stitches have to be either decreased or skipped in a different spot within the pattern repeat.

Fan pattern of 3 double crochets and chain arcs

Shell pattern of 7 double crochets and single crochets

To work a shell or a fan, respectively, always work the indicated number of stitches into the same insertion point. The stitches converge at the bottom.

! In **PATTERNS**, it can happen that even a **SINGLE CHAIN STITCH** is called a chain space or chain arc, although, strictly speaking, it is not an arc.

! If instructions state to insert the hook **INTO INDIVIDUAL CHAIN STITCHES OF THE CHAIN**, always insert so that **2 LOOPS** of the chain sit on the hook. Working either in the chain space or into individual chain stitches creates a different stitch appearance, especially in patterns using multiple colors.

··· The instructions for the **PEACOCK TAILS** can be found on page 328, for the Trellis pattern see page 325.

! When working stitches in rows below, always make sure that the working yarn is led **LOOSELY** up to the current row, since the crocheted piece might constrict otherwise

Two-color pattern of single crochets and single crochets worked in rows below.

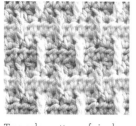

Two-color pattern of single crochets and treble crochets worked in rows below.

! Double and treble crochets worked in rows below require a little practice for stitches to turn out evenly and lie flat on top of the crocheted base fabric **NEITHER TOO TIGHTLY NOR TOO LOOSELY.**

X A treble crochet spans 3 rows of single crochets.

SPIKE STITCHES

Spike stitches are stitches for which the hook is not inserted into a stitch of the previous row but into the corresponding stitch located a few rows below. Depending on the pattern, this can be 2, 3, or even 4 rows below. Using different stitch types and ways of inserting the hook, interesting three-dimensional textures can be created. Through a well thought-out arrangement of multiple colors, appealing color gradients can be achieved.

SINGLE CROCHET SPIKE STITCH ON SOLID CROCHETED FABRIC

Spike stitches don't stand out much from the crocheted fabric if the working yarn is to be pulled through a solid crocheted base fabric. The working yarn goes around on the front and back of work.

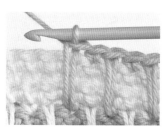

1 If instructions state to work, for instance, a single crochet 3 rows below, beginning at the next stitch of the previous row, count down 3 rows vertically. Insert the hook into that stitch . . .

2 . . . pull the working yarn through . . .

3 . . . and pull this loop longer until it reaches the height of the current row at the top of the crocheted piece.

4 Then finish the single crochet as usual.

DOUBLE CROCHET SPIKE STITCH IN TEXTURED PATTERNS

With double crochets or treble crochets, interesting three-dimensional textures can be achieved by working the stitches into stitches located several rows below that had been previously skipped. The height of the double crochet stitches "bridges" the distance to the height of the current row at the top of the crocheted piece. The spike stitch then sits in front of a crocheted base fabric of shallower stitches.

1 For treble crochets, first make 2 yarn overs onto the hook; next, insert the hook into the indicated stitch located below.

2 For this step, first insert the hook from front to back into the stitch, and then lead it through to the front again through the hole.

3 Place a yarn over onto the hook and pull the working yarn through.

4 Then finish the treble crochet as usual, taking care to keep the working yarn at an even tension so that after having worked off all loops of the treble crochet the top of the stitch ends up at the height of the current row, and the post of the stitch lies flat on top of the crocheted base fabric.

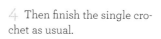
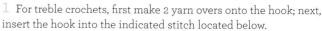
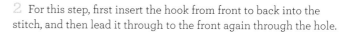
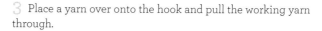

CROSSED STITCHES

Being narrow and tall, all stitches from double crochet up are especially well suited for creating various stitch patterns. With crossed stitches, versatile, slightly three-dimensional effects can be created. The easiest way to cross stitches is to work two double crochets one after another, but switching the insertion points (inserting into the second stitch first).

CROSSING DOUBLE CROCHETS TO THE RIGHT

1 To work the first double crochet, make a yarn over onto the hook, insert the hook into the stitch after the next one, and finish the double crochet the usual way.

2 To work the second double crochet, make a yarn over onto the hook, and insert the hook behind the first double crochet into the skipped stitch.

3 Pull the working yarn through the fabric. The first double crochet is located in front.

4 Then finish the double crochet the usual way. The double crochet located in front goes from bottom left to top right.

CROSSING TREBLE CROCHETS TO THE LEFT

1 To work the first treble crochet, make 2 yarn overs onto the hook, insert the hook into the stitch after the next one, and finish the treble crochet as usual.

2 To work the second treble crochet, make 2 yarn overs onto the hook, insert the hook into the skipped stitch in front of the first treble crochet . . .

3 . . . and bring the tip of the hook to the front of work again, in front of the first treble crochet.

4 Pull the working yarn through the fabric. The first treble crochet is located in the back.

5 Then finish the treble crochet as usual. The second treble crochet is located in front, pointing from bottom right to top left.

Double crochets crossed to the right with one row of single crochet in between

! DOUBLE CROCHETS are sometimes hard to **CROSS TO THE LEFT**, since it is fiddly to bring the tip of the hook to the front again when inserting for the second double crochet. **THE SAME LOOK** can also be achieved by allowing the hook to remain in the back after inserting for the second double crochet and pulling the working yarn through so that it will wrap itself around the post of the first double crochet, and then finishing the second double crochet the regular way. The crossed double crochets will then be joined together. This creates a slightly different stitch appearance from that of separately crocheted double crochets.

Treble crochets crossed to the left with one row of single crochet in between

CROCHETING CABLES

Cables are created by working double crochets as post stitches onto a background of shallower stitches such as single crochets or half double crochets *(Post stitches > page 41)*. When crocheting cables, the stitches of the cables are crossed in regular intervals. This is always done in right-side rows, and cable stitches are always worked as front post stitches. Between cables, the stitches of the background fabric are worked. In wrong-side rows, all stitches are always worked in the stitch used for the background fabric.

Cabled to the right with front post treble crochet

Cabled to the left with front post treble crochet

CABLE 2/2 (4 FRONT POST TREBLE CROCHETS WORKED ONTO A BACKGROUND OF HALF DOUBLE CROCHET)

Work the background fabric for this cable pattern as follows:

Rows 1 and 2: Work in half double crochet.

Row 3 (RS): Over the desired width of the cable, work front post treble crochet around the half double crochets of Row 1, and then work the remaining stitches in half double crochet.

All following WS rows: Work in half double crochet.

All following RS rows: Always work half double crochets into half double crochets and front post treble crochets around the front post treble crochets of the previous row.

CABLING TO THE RIGHT

1 For a cable of 4 front post treble crochets, work the first two stitches around the posts of following third and fourth post treble crochets.

2 Now, for the next front post treble crochet, make 2 yarn overs onto the hook, and then insert the hook behind the two already-worked treble crochets and around the first post stitch from left to right.

3 Yarn over and pull the working yarn toward the top of the fabric.

4 Finish the treble crochet the regular way.

5 Then work the fourth stitch around the second skipped stitch behind the already-worked stitches. The first two front post treble crochets are located in front and go from bottom left to top right.

Continue working in pattern, working half double crochet fabric and crossing front post treble crochets on top of each other in every right-side row.

CABLE CROSSING TO THE LEFT

1 For a cable of 4 front post treble crochets, work the first two stitches around the following third and fourth front post treble crochet.

2 Now, for the next front post treble crochet, make 2 yarn overs onto the hook, and insert the hook in front of the two already-crocheted stitches and behind the first skipped treble crochet (front to back to front).

3 Finish the front post treble crochet the regular way.

4 Then work the fourth stitch in the same way around the second skipped stitch. The two front post treble crochets worked last are located in front, going from bottom right to top left.

Continue working in pattern, working half double crochet fabric and crossing front post treble crochets on top of each other in every right-side row.

! THE TALLER the stitches, THE EASIER it is to cable them. The stitches, loosely arranged on the background fabric, create a pretty raised texture.

! Working cable crossings requires some practice, especially when the hook must be inserted behind already-worked stitches for CABLING front post stitches TO THE RIGHT.

SPECIAL STITCHES

"Special stitches" are those stitches worked a completely different way than basic stitches, for instance, bullion stitch or Solomon's knot. The phrase is also an umbrella term for groups of stitches consisting of several basic stitches combined but counting as one stitch, such as bobbles.

TREBLE CROCHET AND TALLER

Treble crochets and up are all stitches of the double crochet family that are taller than double crochet. Their only difference is the number of yarn overs placed onto the hook before inserting. For treble crochets, those are 2 yarn overs, for double treble crochets, 3 yarn overs, for triple treble crochets, 4 yarn overs, and so forth. With every additional yarn over, the process of working off the loops extends by one working step (treble crochets > page 35).

DOUBLE TREBLE CROCHET

Double treble crochet worked in rows

1 To work a double treble crochet, make 3 yarn overs onto the hook, insert the hook into the next stitch, make a yarn over and pull the working yarn through the fabric. There are 5 loops on the hook.

2 Now, one after another, yarn over and pull through two loops. First, only 4 loops will remain on the hook . . .

3 . . . then 3 loops . . .

4 . . . and finally, only 2 loops remain on the hook.

5 Crochet these 2 loops off together. The yarn overs create 3 slanted loops on the post of the stitch.

! Crocheted pieces made up completely of treble crochets or taller stitches are rather uncommon. The most well-known **APPLICATION** for treble crochets and taller stitches is in eyelet and lace patterns. They also serve as connecting bars between lace motifs.

! **THE TALLER** the stitch, **THE HIGHER THE NUMBER OF CHAINS** that need to be worked in turning for height-adjustment chains (turning or height adjustment chains > page 64).

OVERVIEW TREBLE CROCHETS AND TALLER

stitch type	yarn overs before inserting hook	steps for working off loops	slanted loops in the post	turning or height-adjustment chains
treble crochet	2	3	2	4
double treble crochet	3	4	3	5
triple treble crochet	4	5	4	6
quadruple treble crochet	5	6	5	7
quintuple treble crochet	6	7	6	8

X AND Y STITCHES

In X and Y stitches, double crochet and treble crochet are combined to produce a very tall and cleverly shaped stitch.

X STITCH

The X stitch is created in several working steps.

X stitch with a 1-stitch gap between the legs

1 First, make 2 yarn overs onto the hook, insert the hook into the stitch after the next one (skipping 1 stitch), and pull the working yarn through the fabric. There are 4 loops on the hook.

2 Grasp the working yarn and pull it through the first 2 loops on the hook at once. There are 3 loops on the hook.

3 Now place another yarn over onto the hook, insert the hook into the stitch after the next one (skipping 1 stitch), and, again, pull the working yarn through the fabric. There are 5 loops on the hook.

4 Grasp the working yarn and pull it through the first 2 loops on the hook at once. Only 4 loops remain on the hook now.

5 Grasp the working yarn again and pull it through the first 2 loops on the hook at once. Only 3 loops remain on the hook now.

6 Work off the last 3 loops on the hook in two working steps as done for a double crochet.

7 Now chain 1, and then make a yarn over onto the hook; next, insert the hook into the center of the crossed posts, grasping the 2 loops located in front with the hook.

8 Grasp the working yarn and pull it through the 2 loops of the crossed posts. There are again only 3 loops on the hook.

9 Work off the last 3 loops on the hook in two working steps as done for a double crochet. The crossed treble crochet has been completed. The chain creates a space of 1 stitch between the upper legs.

> ! X and Y stitches are **TALL STITCHES:** They have the same height as treble crochets. For stitch patterns with straight side edges, either work 1 treble crochet each at the beginning and the end of the row or replace the first treble crochet with 4 chains.

X stitches with a space of 1 stitch between the posts and the stitches

> ! X stitches are **NOT** to be **MIXED UP** with crossed stitches (*Crossed stitches > page 45*).

Y stitches and inverted Y stitches alternated, with a space of 1 stitch and 1 row of single crochet in between

Y STITCHES

Y stitches can be used to create stitch patterns, but are also applied as connecting bars between crocheted motifs.

Inverted Y stitches (Eiffel Tower stitches)

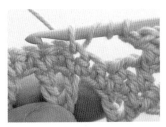  

1 First, make 2 yarn overs onto the hook, insert the hook into the stitch after the next one (skipping 1 stitch), and pull the working yarn through the fabric. There are 4 loops on the hook.

2 Grasp the working yarn and pull it through the first 2 loops on the hook at once. There are 3 loops on the hook.

3 Now place another yarn over onto the hook, insert the hook into the stitch after the next one (skipping 1 stitch), and, again, pull the working yarn through the fabric. There are 5 loops on the hook now.

4 Grasp the working yarn and pull it through the first 2 loops on the hook at once. Only 4 loops remain on the hook.

5 Grasp the working yarn again and pull it through the first 2 loops on the hook at once. Only 3 loops remain on the hook now.

6 Work off the last 3 loops on the hook in two working steps as done for a double crochet.

Y stitches

The **SPACING** between bottom or top legs can be adjusted by skipping 2 stitches for the bottom legs, and chaining 2 between the upper legs.

1 Make 2 yarn overs onto the hook, and insert the hook into the spot where the Y-stitch is supposed to be placed. Work off the loops on the hook as done for a treble crochet.

2 Then chain 1, make a yarn over onto the hook. Insert the hook in the center of the treble crochet, directly above the lower one of the slanted loops . . .

3 . . . and pull the working yarn through the fabric. There are 3 loops on the hook now.

4 Work off these remaining 3 loops on the hook in two working steps as done for a double crochet.

HERRINGBONE HALF DOUBLE CROCHET

Herringbone half double crochet is a pretty variation of half double and double crochet.

1 Make a yarn over onto the hook, insert the hook, make another yarn over, and grasp the working yarn.

2 Now pull the working yarn through the fabric and through the loop on the hook at once.

3 Then work off the remaining 2 loops on the hook at once.

Herringbone half double crochet worked in rows.

X Herringbone half double crochet stitches are **SHALLOWER** than double crochet. To reach the needed height, 2 turning or height adjustment chains will be sufficient (*turning or height adjustment chains > page 64*). If instructions state to turn with false half double crochet, work a false half double crochet (*> page 65*).

BOBBLES

Bobbles are groups of stitches composed of half double crochet or double crochet that are worked into the same stitch or space and crocheted together in the last step of the stitch. The stitches are positioned close together, creating small spherical shapes. There are flat bobbles, consisting of half double crochet, and "regular" bobbles, made of plain double crochet. Chain stitches, too, can be used to create bobble-like structures. Chain bobbles resemble picots protruding from the background fabric. Another bobble variation is slanted bobbles, which are worked around the post of a stitch from the previous row.

CHAIN BOBBLES

Chain bobbles are worked in right-side rows in conjunction with single crochets.

Chain bobbles on a background fabric of single crochet

1 Work single crochet up to the spot where the bobble is supposed to be placed. Then crochet a chain consisting of as many chains as indicated in the instructions.

2 Insert the hook from the front under the left leg of the single crochet worked last . . .

3 . . . make a yarn over, and pull the working yarn through the fabric. There are 2 loops on the hook now.

4 Then insert the hook into the next stitch, make a yarn over, and pull the working yarn through the fabric. There are 3 loops on the hook.

5 After having made a last yarn over, pull the working yarn through all 3 loops on the hook at once.

In the following wrong-side row, work in single crochet, and push the bobble to the back of the work so that it will later end up on the right side of the crocheted fabric, securing it in place.

! In the **WRONG-SIDE ROW**, make sure to work into the **ORIGINAL STITCHES** only, avoiding accidentally inserting the hook into the bobble base. Otherwise, an unwanted extra stitch will be created.

! The **SIZE** of the bobble is determined by the **NUMBER** of chains worked. It should be at least 4 chains, so that the bobble will have enough space to bulge.

Flat bobbles on a background of single crochets

X BOBBLES CROCHETED IN ROWS BELOW are worked in right-side rows. They are created when inserting the hook during a right-side row into the **BACK LOOP OF THE STITCH** only, and in the next right-side row working the bobble into the unused front loop of the stitch. This places the bobble on top of the background fabric. Since a bobble worked in a row below is supposed to count as 1 stitch, the stitch in the current row has to be skipped to compensate.

FLAT BOBBLES OF HALF DOUBLE CROCHET

As the name suggests, flat bobbles are less prominently protruding from the background fabric. To enhance their three-dimensional effect, they are often worked onto a background of shallower single crochets. Flat bobbles are worked in wrong-side rows, since they, owing to the shallower surrounding stitches, bulge toward the back of the work and will therefore be bulging on the right side of the fabric.

1 To work the first half double crochet, make a yarn over onto the hook, insert the hook, and pull the working yarn through the fabric.

2 Then, for each one of 3 more half double crochets, make a yarn over onto the hook, insert the hook into the same stitch, and pull the working yarn through the fabric. On the hook are now 2 loops each for every half double crochet, plus the working loop (9 total loops).

3 Yarn over and pull the working yarn through all loops on the hook at once, except for the working loop.

4 After having made a last yarn over, work the remaining 2 loops off together.

BOBBLES OF DOUBLE CROCHET

Bobbles of double crochet create an especially prominent bulge. Here, too, it is true that the effect is more pronounced the shallower the stitches of the background fabric are. Bobbles of double crochet need to be worked in wrong-side rows since the bobble stitches bulge toward the back on account of the shallower surrounding stitches. This later places the bobbles on the right side of the fabric. Between individual bobbles, any number of stitches can be worked.

Bobbles of double crochet on a background of half double crochet

1 For every double crochet, make a yarn over onto the hook, insert the hook in the same stitch, pull the working yarn through the fabric, and work off the first 2 loops. On the hook are now 1 loop each for every double crochet, plus the working loop.

2 Yarn over and pull through all loops on the hook at once.

3 Finally, pull the working yarn taut—the finished bobble bulges toward the back of the fabric.

SLANTED BOBBLES

Slanted bobbles are placed horizontally to the background and can be made of either half double crochet or double crochet. They are worked *in a right-side row* onto a background fabric of half double crochet or double crochet, since these stitches have an elongated post around which the hook can be inserted for the slanted bobble.

Example:
Slanted bobble of 5 double crochets on a background of half double crochet

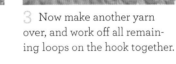

1 To work the first double crochet, make a yarn over onto the hook, as for a front post (double) crochet *(> page 42)* insert the hook behind the post of the half double crochet of the previous row located directly underneath, and pull the working yarn through the fabric. Work off the first 2 loops of the double crochet.

2 Work 4 more double crochets the same way around the post of the same half double crochet.

3 Now make another yarn over, and work off all remaining loops on the hook together.

Slanted bobbles on a background of half double crochet.

! Since the **SLANTED BOBBLE** counts **AS ONE STITCH**, the following stitch in the current row has to be skipped to compensate.

BULLION STITCH

The bullion stitch, sometimes called roll stitch, is based on the bullion stitch in embroidery, also known as coil stitch. It requires some practice to work the bullion stitch evenly, but the effort is well worth it since this stitch looks very impressive.

1 To work a bullion stitch, first wind the working yarn around the crochet hook several times as done for a yarn over. Depending on the desired length of the bullion stitch, this can be about 5 to 7 times.

2 Insert the hook into the next stitch, make a yarn over, and pull the working yarn through the fabric.

3 Then make another yarn over, and pull the working yarn through all loops on the hook at once.

4 Fasten the bullion stitch by chaining 1.

Bullion stitch on a background of half double crochet

X Bullion stitch can be worked especially well **IN BULKY YARNS**.

X Patterns involving bullion stitch are sometimes called **BULLION PATTERNS**.

X In the **FREEFORM CROCHET** technique, bullion stitches are very popular for their slightly **THREE-DIMENSIONAL LOOK**, which makes them perfect for use in intricate patterns.

! The WORD "cluster stitch" is NOT used CONSISTENTLY IN CROCHET PATTERNS. Often, it is also used for stitches that are worked into the same stitch but also crocheted together at the top, although these are not technically "cluster stitches." (Bobbles > pages 51–53, Popcorns see below).

CLUSTER STITCHES

In cluster stitches, several stitches originally worked in different insertion points are then crocheted together at the top (i.e., several stitches are turned into one stitch). Since this approach reduces the overall stitch count, either stitches have to be increased again in a different spot within the pattern repeat or chain arcs have to be added for compensation. Often, the cluster stitches of the following row are staggered in alternating chain spaces.

Cluster stitches in the chain space

1 To work a cluster stitch of double crochets, start with an unfinished double crochet, leaving the last 2 loops on the hook.

2 Work all other double crochets unfinished, too, likewise leaving the respective last loop on the hook. On the hook are now: 1 loop for every double crochet, plus the working loop.

3 Now make another yarn over, and pull the working yarn through all loops on the hook at once. The stitches converge at the top.

POPCORN STITCHES

Popcorn stitches are prominently protruding groups of stitches that can be used to great effect in patterns. They are worked into the same stitch, but, unlike in bobbles, here the stitches are not crocheted together at the top—instead, every stitch is worked separately and later all stitches are pulled together at the top. Compared to bobbles, popcorn stitches have a more elongated shape.

Popcorn stitch on a background of double crochet

1 To make a popcorn stitch, in a right-side row, work, for instance, 5 double crochets into the same stitch. Finish each double crochet separately.

2 Now remove the hook from the working loop, return to the first double crochet, and insert the hook from front to back into this double crochet.

3 Place the working loop onto the hook again, and pull it through the double crochet. The 5 double crochets will get pulled together at the upper edge.

4 The finished popcorn stitch will prominently bulge toward the front.

5 Secure the popcorn stitch with a tightly worked chain 1. In the following wrong-side row, crochet into the chain as into a regular stitch; the popcorn stitch will count as 1 stitch.

SOLOMON'S KNOT

Solomon's Knot, Hailstone, Love Knot, Crochet Love Knot, Lover's Knot, True Lover's Knot, and Knot Stitch—this stitch goes by many names.

All those different names refer to the same stitch: a chain pulled long, which at its tip is secured with a single crochet worked into the back bar of the chain. This creates a loose filigree-like stitch, which can be used either on its own or in combination with other stitches to produce a mesh-like fabric or lace patterns. When working patterns involving Solomon's knot, other stitches are always worked into the single crochet that anchors the knot.

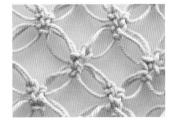

Mesh pattern in Solomon's knot

1 First, chain 1. Pull the working loop to a length of about 0.4–0.6 inches (10–15 mm) (or as stated in pattern instructions).

2 Make a yarn over, and pull the working yarn through the elongated loop, while holding the elongated loop so that the two strands of the loop are located to the right, and the working yarn to the left.

3 Now insert the hook between the doubled-up loop and the single strand of working yarn, make a yarn over, and pull the working yarn through the fabric.

4 Finish the single crochet the regular way. The Solomon's knot has been secured in place by the single crochet.

5 To create mesh fabric, work another Solomon's knot, and then insert the hook into a knot of the previous row that is still unused and has not yet been joined to other knots so far.

6 Work a single crochet.

Now crochet 2 more knots, and every time attach the second knot to the knot after the next one of the previous row.

! When working patterns in Solomon's knot, make sure that the loops are **ALWAYS** pulled to **THE SAME LENGTH.**

! Solomon's knot can be combined in various ways into mesh or **NET FABRIC.** The arrangement can be worked following the instructions for the respective stitch pattern or according to one's own imagination.

X Thanks to the net-like texture of the pattern, pieces crocheted in this pattern will adjust to many shapes. Lantern **COVERS** or **VASES** can be decorated especially nicely with crocheted filigree-like lace patterns this way.

Two-color braided loops on a background of half double crochet

[X] Whether tone-in-tone or in strong contrasts, multiple colors can be combined into pretty LONG COLOR REPEATS.

[X] If the loops are SPACED NOT TOO FAR APART, two columns of loops can be later crossed with each other LIKE CABLES.

[!] The CROCHETED CHAIN for a loop should always be slightly longer than TWICE THE HEIGHT of the finished loop to allow the loops to lay on the background fabric loosely. If the chain is too short, the whole crocheted piece will constrict.

[•••] How to work TWO-COLOR STRIPES is explained on page 213.

BRAIDED LOOPS

More than consolidated groups of stitches can be used to create stitch patterns. Simple crocheted chains can be arranged during crocheting in a way to achieve special pattern effects as well.

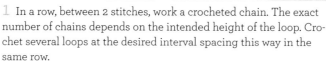

1 In a row, between 2 stitches, work a crocheted chain. The exact number of chains depends on the intended height of the loop. Crochet several loops at the desired interval spacing this way in the same row.

2 In the following wrong-side row, this produces a gap in the loop spot.

3 This gap will be closed when crocheting into the next stitch in that row.

4 Continue to work loops in every right-side row until the desired height has been reached, always placing new loops directly atop the loops of the preceding row. All finished loops stay on the right side of the fabric. Before working the last right-side row, beginning at the bottom, pull each loop directly above through the loop below it with a crochet hook (similar to a chain stitch).

5 Once all loops have reached the top edge, work this row in single crochet. When reaching a spot where a top row loop needs to be anchored, insert the hook first from front to back under the loop and then into the stitch behind it.

6 Work a single crochet to attach the loop.

Basic Techniques

No matter whether making a hat, bag, or garment, to combine individual stitches into a crocheted piece, a few basic techniques need to be mastered. How to start a crochet project, how to crochet in rows or rounds, how to join a new ball of yarn, and how to secure that last stitch—all this will be explained in the upcoming chapter.

BEGINNING CHAIN

To create crocheted pieces, individual stitches and stitch patterns are worked into a base of stitches, loops, or chains. The most common method is a beginning or foundation chain. While in the pattern instructions, the beginning chain is not counted as a row or round. The first row or round is worked into the beginning chain and therefore is worked differently than the following rows or rounds, which will be worked into previous stitches.

WORKING THE BEGINNING CHAIN

After the beginning slipknot, as many chains are worked as stated in the instructions and as needed for the required number of stitch pattern repeats. In the first row or round of the project, the hook is then inserted into these initial chains.

While the beginning chain should not be crocheted too tightly, so the hook can be easily inserted into these initial chains later, it should not be worked too loosely, either, so it won't twist around itself. The side of the chain where the V-shaped loops of the chain are visible is the right side or front of the work. All V-shaped loops have to be on this side of the work. The wrong side or back of the crocheted chain shows a row of small ridges or bumps.

The chains of the beginning chain lie practically perpendicular to the stitches of the future stitch pattern and, most of the time, this chain will be shorter than the width of the rows to be crocheted onto it. If working the beginning chain too tightly, a piece crocheted in turned rows will therefore form an inverted trapezoid shape. To create a proper rectangle, the beginning chain should be worked loosely: Either form taller chains or work the beginning chain using a crochet hook 0.5 to 1.0 mm (about 2 to 4 steps in US sizes) larger than the hook used for the project.

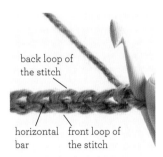

back loop of the stitch

horizontal bar

front loop of the stitch

COUNTING CHAINS

To check whether the correct stitch count for the piece or motif has been created or, for height-adjustment chains (> page 63), to crochet the first stitch into the correct chain, it is important to be able to properly count the chains: always begin counting at the chain worked last, immediately below the hook (do not count the loop on the hook), and count back toward the beginning slipknot.

5 4 3 2 1

X The NUMBER OF BEGINNING CHAINS has to match the required stitch count indicated FOR THE STITCH PATTERN. In projects with very long rows, it will be easier to keep track when marking every 10th or 20th chain with a STITCH MARKER or a piece of waste yarn in a contrasting color.

X It is recommended to work the BEGINNING CHAIN slightly LONGER than required for the stitch pattern. The first few extra chains not needed for the first row can later be removed by cutting off the beginning slipknot and then dissolving the chains up to the last stitch of Row 1.

How to crochet CHAINS is explained on page 32.

X To ensure that you are starting with the CORRECT STITCH COUNT, you can work WITH TWO SKEINS: Use one skein to crochet the beginning chain and another to work the first row or round. This way, you can easily add missing chains after the fact or dissolve extra ones. For this, begin the first row not at the side of the working loop, but at the other end of the chain, where the beginning slipknot is.

How to crochet into both sides of the beginning chain is explained on page 69.

Depending on yarn and hook used, it might happen that a larger **HOLE** forms underneath the back loop of the stitch when pulling the working yarn through. This can be remedied by pulling at both ends of the crocheted chain.

Crocheters with foresight leave **A LONG BEGINNING TAIL** hanging before making the beginning slipknot, to be used later to crochet any missing chains. If additional chains are not needed, the long beginning tail can be used to sew pieces together if needed.

To create a **NEAT EDGE**, it is important to always insert the hook **INTO THE SAME SPOT** of every chain, for instance, always through the back loop.

This **METHOD** of crocheting into the foundation chain is especially useful if the edge is to be **LATER CRO-CHETED INTO**, since both loops of the stitch stay unused now and can be crocheted into later.

CROCHETING INTO THE BEGINNING CHAIN

There are four different ways for inserting the hook into the beginning chain.

Through the back loop of the chain

When working the stitches of Row 1, insert the hook through the back loop of the chain only. If the crocheted chain is placed with V-shapes facing the viewer, this will be the top strand.

The bottom edge looks neatly twisted or braided.

Through the back loop of the chain and the horizontal ridge

Inserting the hook through the back loop of the stitch and the horizontal ridge of the chain creates a more compact edge than with inserting through the back loop of the stitch only, since the hook is inserted deeper. When viewing the crocheted chain from the top, these are the two top strands.

The bottom edge looks less twisted.

Through the front and back loop of the chain

Just like with all other basic stitches, the hook can also be inserted through both the front and the back loop of the chain. This method also produces a very sturdy edge, but it does need a little practice to look tidy.

Only the ridges are visible at the bottom edge.

Under the horizontal ridge (in the back bumps)

For this method, the crocheted chain is tilted toward the viewer, so that the back of the chain with the little back bumps is visible, and the V-shaped loops of the crocheted chain are in back, facing away from the viewer. The hook is inserted through the back bumps of the chain.

This creates an especially tidy edge.

BEGINNING WITH FOUNDATION STITCHES

This method has the big advantage in that it produces a much more elastic edge than using a beginning chain. Instead of working the entire chain first, before every stitch, a chain is worked and then the stitch is worked into that chain. Therefore, it is easy to make just the number of stitches needed to begin your piece. With this technique, the beginning chain and the first row are worked at once.

 Foundation stitches are also useful if within a crocheted piece **SEVERAL STITCHES** need to be **INCREASED** at the edge (> page 100).

FOUNDATION SLIP STITCH

1 Chain 2, insert the hook into the second chain from the hook, and pull the working yarn through the fabric.

2 Yarn over and pull through both loops on the hook at once.

3 Insert the hook under the leftmost outer loop, and pull the working yarn through the fabric. Grasp the working yarn again, and pull it through both loops on the hook at once.

Repeat Step 3 continuously until the required stitch count has been reached.

FOUNDATION SINGLE CROCHET

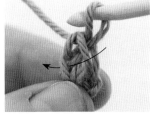

1 Chain 2, insert the hook into the second chain from the hook, and pull the working yarn through the fabric. You will have two loops on your hook

2 Yarn over and pull the yarn through the first loop on your hook. This is your chain stitch.

3 Yarn over and pull through both of the loops on your hook. The first foundation single crochet has been completed.

4 To work the base chain of the next single crochet, insert your hook into the space between the chain made in step 2 and the single crochet.

Repeat Steps 2 to 4 continuously until the required stitch count has been reached.

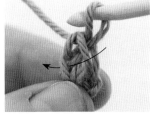 It may be helpful to **MARK** the **CHAIN** located below the hook with your thumb after Step 2. This makes it easier to see where to insert the hook in Step 4.

! Here, the **FIRST STITCH** has been replaced by **A CHAIN**. Don't forget to work into it when crocheting into the second row!

FOUNDATION HALF DOUBLE CROCHET

> Here, the **FIRST STITCH** has been replaced by **CHAINS**. Don't forget to work into them when crocheting into the second row!

> It may be helpful to **MARK** the **CHAIN** located below the hook with your thumb after Step 2. This makes it easier to see where to insert the hook in Steps 4 and 5.

1 Chain 3, make a yarn over onto the hook, insert the hook into the third chain from the hook, and pull the working yarn through the fabric.

2 Yarn over and pull through the first loop on the hook. This has created the chain at the base of the half double crochet.

3 Yarn over and pull through all 3 loops on the hook at once. The first half double crochet has been completed.

4 To work the next half double crochet, make a yarn over onto the hook, and then insert the hook between the chain created in step 2 and the half double crochet just created (i.e., to the right of the second loop from the left). Pull the working yarn through the fabric.

Repeat Steps 2 to 4 continuously until the required stitch count has been reached.

FOUNDATION DOUBLE CROCHET

> Depending on the **DESIRED STITCH PATTERN**, foundation stitches can likewise be used with treble crochet, double treble crochet, or other stitch types. Begin with the required number of **HEIGHT-ADJUSTMENT CHAINS** (> page 64), plus chain an additional 1.

1 Chain 4, make a yarn over onto the hook, insert the hook into the fourth chain from the hook, and pull the working yarn through the fabric.

2 Yarn over and pull through the first loop on the hook. This creates the chain at the base of the double crochet.

3 Yarn over and pull the working yarn through the first two loops on the hook at once.

4 Yarn over a third time and pull through the two loops on the hook at once. The first double crochet has been completed.

5 To work the next double crochet, make a yarn over onto the hook, and insert the hook under the two loops of the chain made in step 2. Pull the working yarn through the fabric.

Repeat Steps 2 to 5 continuously until the required stitch count has been reached.

BEGINNING PICOT EDGE

Picots are often used as decorative finishing for edges and decorative bands, but can also be used very well for the beginning edge. First, a chain is crocheted, consisting of chains and other stitches, which form the picots. In the first row or round of the crocheted piece, the hook will then be inserted into the stitches of the pattern thus created.

PICOTS FROM CHAINS WITH A SLIP STITCH

1 Chain 3 and insert the hook through the back loop only of the third chain from the hook.

2 Yarn over and pull the working yarn through the chain and through the loop on the hook at once, forming a slip stitch.

3 Repeat Steps 1 and 2 continuously until the picot edge has reached the desired length.

PICOTS FROM CHAINS WITH A SINGLE CROCHET

1 Chain 3 and insert the hook through the back loop only of the third chain from the hook.

2 Yarn over and pull the working yarn through the chain, and work a single crochet.

3 Repeat Steps 1 and 2 continuously until the picot edge has reached the desired length.

PICOTS FROM CHAINS WITH A DOUBLE CROCHET

1 Chain 3, make a yarn over onto the hook, and insert the hook through the back loop only of the third chain from the hook.

2 Complete the double crochet as usual.

3 Repeat Steps 1 and 2 continuously until the picot edge has reached the desired length.

! **OPTIONS** for the beginning picot edge technique are numerous. To achieve a different look from the examples shown here, for instance, the **INSERTION POINT** for the slip stitch or the single crochet can be varied, inserting the hook through both loops of the stitches instead of through the back loop only (> page 58).

X Afterward, the **PICOT EDGE** can be crocheted into in different ways (> page 62).

PICOTS FROM CHAINS AND 2 DOUBLE CROCHETS

1 Chain 3, make a yarn over onto the hook, and insert the hook through the back loop only of the third chain from the hook.

2 Complete the double crochet as usual.

3 Make a yarn over onto the hook, insert the hook into the same insertion point as the first double crochet, and work another double crochet.

4 Repeat Steps 1 through 3 continuously until the picot edge has reached the desired length.

PICOTS FROM CHAIN STITCHES, 1 DOUBLE CROCHET, AND 1 TREBLE CROCHET

1 Chain 3, make a yarn over onto the hook, and insert the hook through the back loop only of the third chain from the hook.

2 Complete the double crochet as usual.

3 Make 2 yarn overs onto the hook, and work a treble crochet into the same insertion point as the double crochet.

4 Repeat Steps 1 through 3 continuously until the picot edge has reached the desired length.

WORKING INTO A PICOT EDGE

For the stitches of the first row or round, after having worked the number of height-adjustment chains required by the stitch pattern, the hook is inserted either into the chains of the picot edge or below them.

Picot edge with slip stitches: 1 stitch each into the third chain and into the insertion point of the slip stitch

Picot edge with single crochets: 2 stitches each around the post of every single crochet

Picot edge with 1 double crochet: 3 stitches each around the post of every double crochet

Picot edge with 1 double crochet and 1 treble crochet: 3 stitches each around the post of every treble crochet, and 1 stitch into the insertion point of double crochet and treble crochet; the double crochet stays unused.

CROCHETING IN ROWS

To crochet in rows means to work up to a certain spot—in most cases, the end of the row—then to turn the work and continue on the other side of the fabric, crocheting back to the starting point. Right-handed crocheters always crochet from right to left into the stitches of the previous row (or the beginning chain), while left-handed crocheters work from left to right.

The beginning chain counts as "Row zero." Row 1 and all other odd-numbered rows are called right-side rows and form the public side of the fabric (the better-looking or right side of the crocheted piece), the second and all other even-numbered rows are called wrong-side rows and form the non-public side of the fabric (the wrong side). All stitches have a distinct front and back, with different stitch appearances.

X Sometimes, it can happen that a crocheted piece starts with a WRONG-SIDE ROW, when the actual reverse side of the stitch pattern looks better and it is therefore desired to show it ON THE PUBLIC SIDE of the fabric. The first and all other odd-numbered rows will then form the non-public side (back of work), the even-numbered ones the public side (front of work). If this happens, it will always be specially mentioned in the pattern instructions.

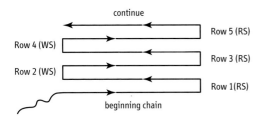

Single crochets worked in rows

Double crochets worked in rows

Turning can be done in either one of two directions—it is, however, important to always turn the same way to ensure that the first stitches of every row look the same throughout. Special attention should be paid to the beginning and end of every row since in these places something different is worked than in the middle part of the row and there is a risk of inadvertently increasing or decreasing stitches, resulting in a misshapen crocheted piece.

THE BEGINNING OF A ROW

WORKING HEIGHT-ADJUSTMENT CHAINS

Because crochet stitches have a certain height, crochet hook and working yarn have to be brought up to this height at the beginning of the row so that the row will have an even upper edge. After having worked the beginning chain, for this purpose, so-called height-adjustment chains have to be worked. (In subsequent rows, they are often called turning chains.)

The number of required chains is determined by the stitch type to be worked (table > page 64). These height-adjustment chains typically replace the first stitch of the first row, which cannot be worked the regular way. When pattern instructions mention height-adjustment or turning chains, it will often be noted that these chains "replace the first stitch" or "count as the first stitch."

! When the turning or height-adjustment chains at the beginning of a row do NOT COUNT AS A STITCH, they are not counted as insertion points at the end of the next row, NOT CROCHETED INTO, and just left unworked.

Example of a first row with 20 stitches
After having worked a beginning chain of 20, work is rotated by 90°, and an additional 3 chains are worked for height adjustment. The 20th chain of the beginning chain would be the basis for the first double crochet of the first row, which, however, is being replaced by the height-adjustment chains. To work the second double crochet of Row 1, the hook is then inserted into the 19th chain of the beginning chain (i.e., into the 5th chain as counted from the crochet hook).

••• Different ways for inserting the hook into the chains are explained on page 58.

The pattern writer could also have decided that these height-adjustment chains should be worked in addition to the stitch count listed for the row, which will be noted in the instructions either as "does not replace the first stitch" or as "does not count as a stitch." How to work the stitches will stay the same, only the way to count them will be different.

Example of a first row with 20 stitches

After having worked a beginning chain of 20, work is rotated by 90°, and an additional 3 chains are worked for height adjustment. Here, too, the 20th chain of the beginning chain is the basis for the first double crochet of the first row, which is now worked directly into this chain (i.e., into the 4th chain as counted from the crochet hook).

WORKING TURNING CHAINS

Since work is turned for the second and all following rows, from the second row onward the chains are no longer called height-adjustment but turning chains.

These turning chains can be worked at the end of the previous row, before turning, or one can first work the last stitch of the previous row, turn work, and then work the required number of turning chains. In this case, too, the turning chain can either count as a stitch or not.

When the turning chain counts as a stitch, the hook is inserted for the second stitch of the row into the next-to-last stitch of the previous row. This spot is located slightly to the left of the post of the next-to-last stitch of the previous row. If not otherwise stated in the instructions, the hook is inserted through both loops of the respective stitch.

If the first stitch is not replaced by a turning chain, the first stitch is to be worked directly in the last stitch of the previous row.

X When height-adjustment or turning chains COUNT AS A STITCH, the crocheted piece will have STRAIGHT EDGES. If height-adjustment or turning chains do NOT COUNT AS A STITCH, the EDGES will be slightly WAVY, which can be used for decorative purposes. This decorative feature is, however, asymmetrical, since the height-adjustment or turning chains appear staggered for even- and odd-numbered rows. With shallow stitches, such as single crochet, a nice decorative effect with a picot-like look at the edges of the crocheted piece can be achieved this way.

! For the FIRST STITCH AT THE BEGINNING OF THE ROW, it is especially important to insert the hook exactly at the CORRECT SPOT. It is very tempting to insert the hook into the next available spot, which, however, is the base of the first stitch of the row. In this case, a stitch is inadvertently increased. It is best to slightly stretch the work widthwise, and to watch carefully which of the stitches are the next-to-last and the last stitch of the previous row. One or more turning chain(s) which replace the first stitch of a row should end up EXACTLY ATOP THE LAST STITCH of the previous row. To work the second stitch of the new row, the hook is inserted slightly to the side of the next-to-last stitch of the previous row.

Number of height-adjustment or turning chains required

stitch type in rows or rounds	number of height-adjustment or turning chains
slip stitch	0
single crochet	1
half double crochet foundation half double crochet	2
double crochet foundation double crochet	3
treble crochet foundation treble crochet	4
double treble crochet foundation double treble crochet	5

The listed numbers for height-adjustment or turning chains are recommendations. Very tight crocheters may have to work 4 chains as a stand-in for the first double crochet; for looser crocheters, 2 chains might be sufficient.

When chains replace the first stitch of every row, the second stitch of the row is always worked into the next-to-last stitch of the previous row. The last stitch of every row is worked into the top chain of the height-adjustment chain.

If the chains are next to the edge and don't replace a stitch, the first stitch of every row is worked directly into the last stitch of the previous row. The last stitch of the row is worked into the first actual stitch of the previous row; the chains are not crocheted into.

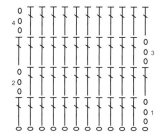

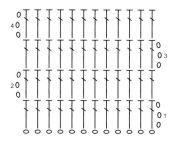

TURNING WITH A FALSE DOUBLE CROCHET

To bring crochet hook and working yarn up to the required height before beginning a row worked in double crochet, there is an option to work a so-called "false" double crochet, which also counts as the first stitch. To work the second double crochet of the new row, the hook is then inserted into the next-to-last stitch of the previous row.

Two advantages of this beginning stitch are: 1) it does not create a hole between itself and the following stitch, as is the case when starting a row with a turning chain, and 2) the first stitch more closely resembles the other stitches of the row.

1 Turn work before beginning a new row. Pull the working loop upward to the height of a double crochet.

2 Press the loop with your finger against the crochet hook to hold it in place, and then move the crochet hook in a counter-clockwise direction around the loop.

3 The top of the loop secured with your finger at the far right is the working loop; the double-stranded loop serves as yarn over on the crochet hook.

4 Now yarn over and pull the working yarn through in back of the double-stranded yarn over on the hook, pulling it through to the front.

5 There are now 2 loops on the hook.

6 Yarn over and pull through both loops on the hook at once. A false double crochet has been completed.

7 Continue working double crochet, working the first actual double crochet of the row into the next-to-last stitch of the previous row.

! When pulling the WORKING LOOP up to the height of the current row, it should be NEITHER TOO LONG NOR TOO SHORT. With time and practice, you will get a feeling for the correct length of the loop.

X Beginning a row with a false double crochet is best suited for ONE-COLORED CROCHETED PIECES, but less so for crocheted pieces involving color changes, for which STANDING STITCHES (> page 77) are the better choice. If false double crochets shall be nevertheless used for striped colorwork patterns, the color needs to be changed during the last stitch of the previous row (> page 78).

! What applies to a false double crochet can also be applied to OTHER STITCHES: For a false half double crochet, pull up the loop a little shorter and, when pulling the working yarn through for the first time, pull it through underneath the yarn over and through the working loop. For a false treble crochet, pull up the loop a little higher accordingly, and place the double-stranded loop onto the hook (instead of 2 yarn overs). For treble crochets and taller, it is especially important to press the working loop securely against the hook with your finger.

> ❗ For the last stitch, the hook should **NOT** be inserted into the **GAP** between the next-to-last stitch and the height-adjustment or turning chain, to avoid making the existing hole even larger.

> ✖ In order to avoid overlooking the **LAST INSERTION POINT**, it is helpful to mark the last height-adjustment or turning chain of the previous row with a **STITCH MARKER**.

> ❗ If the previous row had been started with a **FALSE DOUBLE CROCHET**, the hook is inserted for the last stitch of the current row as usual under **BOTH TOP LOOPS** of this false stitch.

> ❗ Since the working yarn is **BEING CUT** at the end of every row, it likewise has to be woven in every time, unless the yarn tails are to be used as **DECORATIVE FRINGE**.

THE END OF THE ROW

For the first row after the beginning chain, the end of the row does not present any particular difficulty. To work the last stitch of the first row, the hook is inserted into the first stitch of the beginning chain, directly adjacent to the beginning slipknot. From the second row on, it is important to watch out whether the first stitch of every row is being replaced by a turning chain or whether the latter does not count as a stitch and is located outside of the edge. In order to avoid accidental decreases at the edges, the first stitch of the previous row should not be overlooked.

If the turning chains are located next to the first stitch, outside of the edge, and don't count as a stitch, then the last stitch is crocheted into the first actual stitch of the previous row, without crocheting into the chains.

If, however, the chains replace the first stitch, then the last stitch of the next row is worked into the topmost one of the height-adjustment or turning chains. Usually the easiest way to do this is to insert the hook through one loop of the stitch only. However, the height-adjustment or turning chain may stretch, creating a larger, unsightly hole. Therefore, it is better to insert the hook through both loops of the top chain of the height-adjustment or turning chain, either through the back loop of the stitch and the back bump (third loop) or—which is not always easy but looks much better—under the front and the back loop that create the V in the chain.

Chains do not replace the first stitch

Inserting the hook through the back loop of the stitch

Inserting the hook through the back loop of the stitch and the back bump (third loop)

Inserting the hook through both loops of the stitch

WORKING RIGHT-SIDE ROWS ONLY

For flat pieces crocheted in rows, it is also possible to work all rows on the right side only. This makes for a very smooth, homogeneous stitch appearance, since only the front of all stitches is visible.

At the end of every row, the working yarn has to be cut, work is not turned, and every new row starts again at the first stitch of the previous row. The working yarn has to be joined anew in this spot every time and brought up to the required height with either height-adjustment chains or standing stitches (> page 77).

This produces a stitch definition just like that of pieces crocheted in the round (> page 67), in which the crocheted piece is likewise not turned and the right side of work always faces the viewer. Since the hook is always inserted just slightly to the right of the stitch of the previous row, the crocheted piece will turn out slanted if the hook is always inserted into the first stitch of the previous row. This can be avoided by shifting the beginning of the row alternately to the left and to the right. For this, at the beginning of the row, alternate inserting the hook once into the first stitch and working the row as usual and the next time into the second stitch of the row, working two stitches into the same stitch and leaving the first stitch unworked. The stitch count worked per row stays unchanged.

Single crochet worked in right- and wrong-side rows

Single crochet worked on the right side only

CROCHETING IN ROUNDS

When crocheting in rounds, the work is not turned; instead, the last stitch of a row is connected to the first stitch of the same row, thus joining the row into a round. Unlike working in turned rows, it is always crocheted on the right side only, so that only the front of all stitches is visible. For most stitch types, this has a considerable effect on the stitch appearance.

THE BEGINNING OF THE ROUND

There are various methods to start a crocheted piece worked in the round. Just like for crocheting in rows, in most cases a base is needed, into or around which the hook can be inserted.

BEGINNING FROM A SINGLE CHAIN

After the beginning slipknot, first 1 chain is worked, and then as many height-adjustment chains are worked as needed for the stitches of the first round: 1 height-adjustment chain for single crochet, 2 for half double crochet, 3 for double crochet, and so forth (> page 64). For all stitches of the first round, the hook is then inserted into the first chain after the beginning slipknot.

With just one single chain as base for the first round, only a small hole is created in the center of the crocheted piece; however, the inherent size of this chain is fixed, so there is not much leeway for the total number of stitches for the first round. The first round should have between 6 and 8 stitches. If rounds with more or fewer stitches are needed, an adjustable opening like an adjustable magic ring or magic circle (> page 68) is the better choice.

BEGINNING WITH A RING OF CHAINS

A piece crocheted in the round can also be started with a crocheted chain, which is joined into a ring shape with a slip stitch.

1 Best practice is to form the crocheted chain into a ring shape, and then insert the hook into the first stitch of the crocheted chain and work a slip stitch. This way, the beginning tail is moved to the side and won't be in the way during further work. The knot of the beginning slipknot before the first chain disappears within the stitches.

2 After the ring has been closed, the appropriate number of height-adjustment chains for the desired stitch type must be worked. The stitches of the first round are now worked not into individual chains, but around the crocheted chain. For the first loop of every stitch, the hook is inserted under the crocheted chain, in the center of the ring.

With this method of starting, the size of the opening in the center can be varied by casting on a different number of chains. Additionally, higher stitch counts can be worked in the first round than would be possible with beginning from a single chain.

X You can work THREE-DIMENSIONAL ROUND SHAPES such as spheres or tubes (> page 122), as well as many other FLAT SHAPES, in the round, starting in the center and then working around it (> page 116).

! After the beginning chain has been formed into a ring shape, the hook is inserted for the slip stitch either THROUGH THE BACK LOOP OF THE STITCH or THROUGH BOTH LOOPS OF THE STITCH forming the V of the first chain after the beginning slipknot. Then HEIGHT-ADJUSTMENT CHAINS are worked AS A REPLACEMENT FOR THE FIRST STITCH OF THE ROUND. Only for single crochet does the height-adjustment chain not count as a stitch—knowing this will be important later when joining to the beginning of the round.

X When making a TUBE-SHAPED PIECE, start by crocheting a chain as long as the planned circumference of the tube and join into the round with a slip stitch (> page 70). In the first round, crochet not around the chain but INTO INDIVIDUAL CHAINS, working 1 stitch into every chain.

! When a TUBE SHAPE is NOT desired, the number of chains in the beginning chain always has to be MUCH SMALLER than the number of stitches in the first round. In this case, the stitches of the first round will be evenly distributed around the ring. The hook needs to be easily inserted into the ring, so the number of chains cannot be too small. For a first round containing at least 10 to 12 stitches, a ring of 4 or 5 chains will typically be worked.

⊠ Even though the magic circle could be made larger anytime by loosening it, it is much more practical to leave the ring **LARGER IN THE BEGINNING**, pulling it smaller later.

⊠ Since the **OPENING** of a magic ring is rather **LOOSE** and, especially with very **SMOOTH, SLIPPERY YARNS** such as silk or rayon, comes undone easily, it is recommended to **SECURELY WEAVE IN** the beginning tail as soon as possible before continuing work.

❗ Because closing the double-stranded ring involves pulling at the yarn tail with force, this method is suited especially for **STURDIER YARNS** such as cotton or heavily plied yarns, which are less prone to breaking when pulled at.

BEGINNING WITH A MAGIC CIRCLE

The single-strand magic circle is sometimes also called an adjustable loop. It starts with forming the working yarn into a single-stranded loop.

1 The yarn tail is placed in the right hand. Using your left hand, lead the working yarn from the front over the beginning tail, crossing the strands.

2 Now pull the working yarn through the loop with your fingers.

3 This has created a loop above the magic circle, into which the crochet hook can be inserted. The ring itself stays large (but can be made smaller by pulling at the yarn tail if desired), and the loop created this way is made somewhat smaller by tightening the working yarn, so that it sits closer to the magic circle.

4 Now you can start working the number of height-adjustment chains required for the stitch type of the first round. The stitches of the first round will be crocheted around the single-stranded loop of the magic circle.

5 When the required stitch count for the first round has been worked, the magic ring is cinched smaller by pulling at the beginning tail, which adjusts the size of the center opening. This method has the big advantage that the size of the opening can be adapted as needed. When the ring is pulled smaller, the stitches of the first round evenly distribute themselves around the opening.

BEGINNING WITH AN ADJUSTABLE MAGIC RING

The adjustable magic ring is a variation of the magic circle. It can be cinched even tighter than a simple magic circle, so that the opening is completely and permanently closed.

Option 1

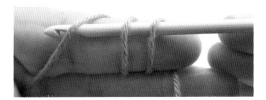

1 To make an adjustable magic ring, wind the beginning tail from front to back around the left index finger 2 times, with the beginning tail at the right, and the working yarn connected to the skein at the left. Then insert the crochet hook from the right under the 3 strands on the finger, and pull the working yarn through from the far left under the two other stands.

2 Remove the finger from the double-stranded magic ring and cinch the loop on the crochet hook smaller by pulling at the working yarn, and then pull the loop closer to the ring.

3 The first round begins with working the number of height-adjustment chains required for the stitch type of this round. The stitches of the first round will be crocheted around the double-stranded loop of the magic ring.

4 When the required stitch count for the first round has been worked, the ring is pulled smaller in two working steps. First, pull at the yarn tail. The ring constricts, with a small loop remaining.

5 Pull at the yarn tail once more. You will notice a slight resistance. Join with a slip stitch and close the ring.

Option 2

1 Lead the yarn over the index finger, and wind it in a counterclockwise direction around the thumb once. Hold the yarn tail in place with your middle finger, ring finger, and pinky finger.

2 Insert the hook under the thumb strand, and pull the strand from the index finger through. This has created a small loop.

3 Again pull the same strand from the index finger through the loop on hook. Around the thumb you now have a double strand at the front and a single strand at the back. Remove the thumb from the loop.

4 The first round begins, as for a single-strand magic circle, with working the number of height-adjustment chains required for the stitch type of this round. The stitches of the first round will be crocheted around the double-stranded loop of the magic ring.

5 When the required stitch count for the first round has been worked, the ring can be closed in one movement by pulling at the yarn tail.

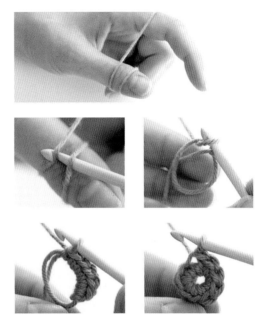

X The two **VARIATIONS** for adjustable magic rings are very similar. Option 2 is somewhat easier to work, while Option 1 is better protected against accidental unraveling of the initial ring.

CROCHETING ALL AROUND A BEGINNING CHAIN

Oval or rectangular flat crocheted pieces worked from the inside out are started by crocheting all around a crocheted chain.

Just as done for working in rows, after having crocheted a beginning chain, the first row is worked with the appropriate number of height-adjustment chains (which count as a stitch) required for the stitch type. Having reached the end of the row, when working in double crochet, 7 stitches are worked into the last stitch (i.e., the first chain of the beginning chain), which automatically rotates work by 180° (instead of turning as done for working in rows). Depending on where the hook had been inserted into the crocheted chain for working the first side, the following insertion points for crocheting into the unused loops on the opposite side of the chain are now available:

· insertion point at first side ➜ insertion point at other side
· back loop of stitch ➜ front loop of stitch and third loop in back
· both V-shaped loops of the stitch ➜ third loop in back
· third loop in back ➜ both V-shaped loops of the stitch

Once the end of the bottom side of the beginning chain has been reached (the spot where the height-adjustment chain emerges), 6 stitches are worked into the last stitch (which, at the same time, is also the last stitch of the beginning chain); then work is rotated again 180° at the end of the round. In this spot, only 6 stitches are necessary (instead of the 7 stitches needed at the other end of the beginning chain) because the first height-adjustment chain does count as a first stitch. The first round has now been completed, and at its end, just needs to be joined with a slip stitch (> page 70) in preparation for beginning the second round.

Depending on where and how increases take place in subsequent rounds, the same beginning chain crocheted into all-around can be the base for either an oval or a rectangle.

X If you crochet **FEWER STITCHES** into both ends of the beginning chain during the first round, the **SHAPE OF THE FINISHED PIECE** changes. It will turn into a tube closed at one end since its beginning is not a flat oval. This is how flat bags can be worked, for example.

X Sometimes at the end of the round, it is rather hard to spot the first single crochet or the topmost height-adjustment chain into which the hook has to be inserted **FOR THE SLIP STITCH** to join into the round. If the respective stitch is marked with a **STITCH MARKER** immediately after it has been worked, it can later be spotted much easier.

X It is not recommended to insert the hook **THROUGH ONE LOOP OF THE first STITCH** of the previous round **ONLY**, since this bears a risk of the stitch opening, creating a **HOLE**.

! For **FABRICS CROCHETED IN SINGLE CROCHET**, it is helpful to work **A HEIGHT-ADJUSTMENT CHAIN** at the beginning of the round, which **DOES NOT COUNT AS A STITCH** and will be ignored later when joining into the round. In this case, the first single crochet of the new round is worked atop the first single crochet of the previous round, inserting the hook into the same spot from which the working loop on the crochet hook emerges.

X If instructions state for the next round to be worked in **DOUBLE CROCHET OR TALLER STITCHES**, the round can also be begun with a "false double crochet." Without turning work, pull the loop of the slip stitch used for joining to the appropriate height, and work a "false double crochet" (> page 65).

JOINING IN ROUNDS

The most common method to join in rounds consists of working a slip stitch into the first stitch of the round.

For rounds in single crochet, the first stitch of the round will be the first single crochet; the height-adjustment chain at the beginning does not count as a stitch. If not otherwise stated in the instructions, the hook is inserted under both top loops of the stitch.

For taller stitches, the slip stitch is worked into the topmost chain of the height-adjustment chain. It is easiest to insert the hook through the back loop of the stitch and the third loop in the rear, so that the front of the chain stays visible.

Another way is to insert the hook under the two loops of the stitch creating the V, to achieve a similar look as for the other stitches.

In all cases, the crochet hook with the working yarn has now ended up in the correct spot to start the next round: at the base of the first stitch for the next round and atop the first stitch of the previous round.

For some pieces working in rounds in lace patterns, it is useful to begin and end the next round not exactly above the first stitch of the previous round but staggered slightly to the right. For this, the previous round is not joined with a slip stitch, but with a single crochet or a half or double crochet, depending on the distance required to the first stitch of the previous round according to the stitch pattern worked.

To insert the hook, the same rules as for joining in rounds with a slip stitch apply here, too.

BEGINNING SUBSEQUENT ROUNDS

The first round has been joined, working yarn and crochet hook are located above the first stitch of the previous round, and have now to be brought up to the required height in order to work the following stitches.

1 First, work height-adjustment chains, which count as a stitch: for instance, 2 for a half double crochet, 3 for a double crochet (> page 64).

2 Now crochet the second stitch of the second round into the next stitch of the previous round. Heads up! Do not mix up this insertion point with the spot where the height-adjustment chain emerges if, according to the pattern, every stitch is supposed to be worked into the corresponding stitch of the previous row.

Only if the pattern states to work 2 double crochets into the first stitch of the previous round—for instance, for flat, round crocheted pieces with increases in every round—is the hook inserted into the spot where the height-adjustment chain emerges.

TURNED ROUNDS

Working in turned rounds makes sense when you want to create a certain stitch appearance or pattern. Since here, at the end of the round, after having joined into the round, working direction changes and the crocheted piece is turned as for crocheting in rows, the same stitch appearance as for crocheting in turned rows is produced, too: Front and back of all stitches are visible. You start with a normal round in which the fronts of the stitches appear on the right side of the fabric; then, in Round 2 and all other even-numbered rounds, the back of the stitches will be visible on the right side of work.

Wanting to insert the hook for the **FIRST STITCH AFTER TURNING** through both loops of the V of the nearest stitch is very tempting. This V, however, belongs to the first stitch of the previous round (either height-adjustment chain counting as a stitch or false stitch). When instructions state to work every stitch into the corresponding stitch of the previous round, **THE HOOK SHOULD NOT BE INSERTED IN THIS SPOT.** If, by contrast, stitches are to be increased by working 2 stitches into the same stitch, then do insert the hook in this spot to work 2 stitches into the first stitch.

Oval crocheted in joined rounds. Only the front of the stitches is visible.

Oval crocheted in turned rounds. Front and back of the stitches are visible.

The first round is joined as usual with either a slip stitch or other stitches; then work is turned and the next round begins with the appropriate number of height-adjustment chains above the first stitch of the previous round. To work the second stitch of the second round, the hook is then inserted (on the wrong side of work, since work had been turned) into the last actual stitch of the previous round (not into the spot where the height-adjustment chain emerges).

Work and join all further rounds this way, and always make sure to insert the hook into the correct spot.

SPIRAL ROUNDS

Just as with working in regular joined rounds, the crocheted piece is not turned at the end of the round. Therefore, always only the front of the stitches is visible. However, rounds are not joined here: The first stitch of the new round is just worked above the first stitch of the previous round, resulting in spiral-shaped rounds.

SPIRAL ROUNDS IN SINGLE CROCHET

Beginning with a ring
Work starts with either a magic circle or an adjustable magic ring (> page 68); then 1 chain is worked for height adjustment, which does not count as a stitch. Into the ring, 6 single crochets are worked. The first stitch is marked with a stitch marker.
Without joining in rounds, the first single crochet of the second round is now worked directly into the first single crochet of the first round.

Beginning with a single chain

If a spiral round begins with a single chain (> page 67), this creates a height-adjustment chain. This should not be crocheted into at the transition to the second spiral round but needs to be skipped. The first stitch of the second round is worked directly into the first single crochet of the first round.

To be able to easily and accurately **COUNT** the rounds, it is helpful to mark the first stitch of every new round with a **STITCH MARKER,** since the transition from one round to the next is barely distinguishable from the remainder of the round. A piece of waste yarn used as a **COUNTING THREAD,** which is always alternatingly moved to the back and front between the last and first stitch, comes in handy as well.

When working in spiral rounds, the **SNAIL SHAPE** will be emphasized even more when inserting the hook **THROUGH THE BACK LOOP OF THE STITCH ONLY** for every stitch from the second round on. The unused front loops of the stitches then form a slightly elevated spiral line.

This method can also be used for **SHORTER OR TALLER BASIC STITCHES**. The "transitional stitches" for this must be made longer or shorter (i.e., crocheted over more or fewer stitches), working the different basic stitches in order of their height. For treble crochet, for instance, double crochet and extended double crochet should be additionally used; for half double crochet, single crochet is sufficient.

SPIRAL ROUNDS IN DOUBLE CROCHET

With progressive beginning

Spiral rounds in double crochet, or taller stitches, are generally crocheted the same way as spiral rounds in single crochet. However, the different height of the stitches between first and second round results in a significantly larger height gap than for single crochet, so that the first double crochet of the second round cannot simply be worked into the first double crochet of the first round.

This can be resolved by gradually replacing the first few double crochets of the first round with single crochets and half double crochets; these transitional stitches create a kind of approach ramp for the first few double crochets of the second round, which allows for a neat, gentle transition between the first two rounds of the crocheted piece. Here, too, it is recommended to mark the first stitch of the round with a stitch marker that will be carried up in subsequent rounds.

1 Begin by making a magic circle or adjustable magic ring (> page 68). Work 1 height-adjustment chain (does not count as a stitch), and then work 2 single crochets (placing a stitch marker in the first single crochet), 2 half double crochets, and 8 double crochets into the ring.

2 The first round of 12 stitches has been completed, and the ring can be pulled closed. Now work the first double crochet of the second round directly into the first single crochet of the first round.

To produce a flat piece, in the second round, work an increase in every stitch (2 double crochets into every stitch); in the following rounds, work an increase in every 2nd, every 3rd, every 4th stitch, and so forth. In all other rounds, no more adjustments for transition are needed.

Beginning with the actual stitches

This method is somewhat easier to work, but the center opening does not look as neat as with the first method.

Work 6 chains, plus 3 height-adjustment chains replacing the first double crochet. Form the crocheted chain into a ring shape, but do not join with a slip stitch. Now work the first double crochet directly into the first chain of the round (i.e., the 9th chain from the hook).

To create a flat shape, continue as described for progressive beginning.

ENDING SPIRAL-SHAPED CROCHETED PIECES

Ending with a step

If you are not bothered by a small step at the end of the last round, you can just fasten off after the last stitch (single crochet or double crochet) (> *page 80*).

Single crochet spiral with stepped end

Double crochet spiral with stepped end

Smooth finish

To finish the crocheted piece with a jogless and smooth edge, for a piece worked in single crochet, after the last stitch work 1 slip stitch each into the next 3 stitches.

For a piece worked in double crochet, after the last double crochet of the last round, work an additional 3 half double crochets, 3 single crochets, and 3 slip stitches (one each) into the next 9 double crochets.

! There are various methods for joining new working yarn. Important for all of them is that old and new yarn tails should be securely **ANCHORED** in the crocheted fabric at the join.

JOINING NEW WORKING YARN

When you notice the end of a skein approaching, you can opt for joining new working yarn either at the end of a row, to be able to hide the ends in the edge and seam later, or in the middle of the row. The denser or fuller a stitch pattern looks, the easier it will be to weave in any yarn tails and hide them in the crocheted fabric.

NEW WORKING YARN IN THE SAME COLOR

The following methods are only suitable for joining new working yarn in the same color, for instance, when joining a new skein, as they do not produce a clearly defined transition. Which method to use in each individual case depends on the yarn weight, construction, and fiber content of the yarn.

RUSSIAN JOIN

This method is better suited for thinner yarns. The result is a single strand, which has been doubled over a couple inches, and is slightly thicker than usual but with which you can continue to work the regular way.

1 When from the old yarn about 6 inches (15 cm) are left, thread the yarn tail into a tapestry needle and weave the last few inches of the yarn tail back into the strand, creating a loop.

2 Then thread the new yarn into the tapestry needle, lead it with the tapestry needle through the previously created loop of the old tail, and likewise weave the beginning tail of the new yarn over a couple inches back into the strand of new working yarn.

FELTING TOGETHER

This method is only suitable for feltable yarns; it will not work with yarns marked "superwash." Yarns can be of sheep's wool or other animal fiber, or yarn blends with high wool content. For plant-based yarns, a different method should be used, since these won't felt.

1 Place the end of the old yarn onto the beginning tail of the new yarn, overlapping over a couple inches, and slightly twist them around each other.

2 Using your palms and a small amount of water, rub the strands together until they felt onto each other.

THINNING OUT THE ENDS

Method 1—For Yarns of Felting Fibers

This method is rather meant for thicker yarns consisting of at least two strands plied with each other.

1 Thin out the tails of the old and the new yarn over approximately the same length: first, manually unply the strands, twisting opposite the plying direction, and, on both yarns, cut off half the number of individual strands of which the yarn is composed. (For single-ply yarns, such as roving, cut out half of the fiber.)

2 The remaining partial strands of both yarn tails can now be felted together. Over the length that had been cut, a new strand of regular thickness has been created, which can be handled like a normal strand.

Method 2—For Yarns of Non-felting Fibers

If the yarn used is not feltable, the above-mentioned method of thinning out can be slightly modified: thin out the strands as described for Method 1 over a length of about 8 inches (20 cm) each, but don't cut them. Let one half of the current working yarn hang in back of work, loop the other half together with half of the new strand. When continuing to crochet, hold each loop together with the respective yarn tail so they won't come undone, working with two strands held together. Later, thread all ends through to the wrong side, and hide them there.

NEW WORKING YARN IN THE SAME OR A DIFFERENT COLOR

In the following methods, the working yarn is changed between two stitches in a clearly defined spot, making it suitable for joining a new skein in the same or a different color.

WITH A BEGINNING SLIPKNOT

Joining a new skein with a beginning slipknot works best at the beginning of a new row or round.

In rows

1 Turn work, and thread the cut end in the old color through the last working loop to secure (= the previous row has been completed, > page 80), make a beginning slipknot (> page 30) with the new yarn, and place it onto the crochet hook. Insert the hook into the last stitch of the previous row . . .

2 . . . and pull the working yarn through the fabric and through the working loop at once, forming a slip stitch.

3 Now, after having worked either the required number of height-adjustment chains or a "false double crochet" (> page 65), continue in stitch pattern.

In rounds

For a crocheted piece worked in the round, join the old round with a slip stitch and thread the cut end in the old color through the last working loop to secure. Then make a beginning slipknot with the new color (> page 30) and join it by inserting the crochet hook into the topmost height-adjustment chain replacing the first stitch of the previous round, and pull the working yarn though the fabric, through this stitch, and through the beginning slipknot. After that, begin the new row or round, as usual, with the required number of height-adjustment chains.

Other stitch types

This method of joining new working yarn also works the same way for stitches taller than double crochet, as well as for single crochets.

If taller stitches shall be worked without height-adjustment chains since their stitch appearance is different from that of the actual stitches of the stitch pattern, you can, after having threaded the cut end in the old color through the working loop to secure the last stitch of the previous row, and made a beginning slipknot, immediately start working the stitches of the stitch pattern.

1 The beginning slipknot in the new color is on the crochet hook. Now place as many yarn overs onto the hook as needed for the first stitch to be worked and insert the hook into the last stitch of the previous row.

For stitches taller than double crochet, as well as for single crochets, new working yarn can be joined this way.

2 Finish the stitch as usual.

This method can also be applied when working in rounds and in turned rounds. In those cases, it won't be necessary to stagger the beginning of every new round, since the beginning stitch looks just like all other stitches, creating a uniform stitch definition throughout.

Weaving in ends

At the conclusion of the work, always carefully undo the knot of the beginning slipknot using a dull tapestry needle, cross the yarn tails, and weave them in within the stitches of the crocheted fabric (> page 154).

STANDING BEGINNING STITCHES

If you want to save yourself the trouble of untying the knots, instead of a beginning slipknot, you can just place the new working yarn from back to front over the crochet hook once and work the first stitch the regular way. This is referred to as "standing stitch" or "beginning stitch."

Taller basic stitches

1 Place the working yarn over the hook once like a yarn over (= replaces working loop). Press this yarn over firmly to the hook with your finger. Then place the number of yarn overs required for the respective stitch type (here: double crochet) onto the hook, insert the hook into the last stitch of the previous row, and pull the working yarn through the fabric.

2 Finish the stitch as usual until only the last loop of the stitch and the yarn over as provisional working loop remain. Continue to firmly hold the latter.

3 Pull the working yarn through the last loop of the stitch and underneath the yarn over on the hook. The standing stitch has been completed.

! Generally, yarn tails should be woven in on the wrong side of work within stitches of the SAME COLOR.

! The FIRST STITCH can be worked better if pressing with a finger onto the first loose yarn over, this way SECURING it against the crochet hook.

! Standing stitches will ALWAYS have ONE YARN OVER MORE on the hook than needed for the actual stitch because the first yarn over replaces the working loop.

! This technique can also be used for **WORKING IN THE ROUND** and in turned rounds.

Single crochets

This method works the same way for single crochet, too.

1 Place the working yarn over the hook once like a yarn over (= replaces working loop) and hold it in place. Then insert the hook into the last stitch of the previous row.

2 Pull the working yarn through the fabric. Then yarn over and pull through the first loop on the hook and underneath the yarn over/working loop.

3 The standing single crochet has been completed.

WITH PROVISIONAL KNOT

This is not a traditional—but a very easy—method to join in new working yarn.

When only 4 inches (10 cm) remain from the current working yarn, knot the new working yarn directly to the last stitch (leaving a beginning tail of 4 inches [10 cm] hanging) around the old strand, push the knot through to the wrong side of the fabric (i.e., during a right-side row or in a round, to the back, during a wrong-side row, to the front), and continue working height-adjustment chains or false double crochets at the beginning of the row or round with the new yarn.

When work on the piece has been finished, carefully undo the knot using a dull tapestry needle, cross the yarn tails, and weave them in on the wrong side of the fabric. When changing colors, make sure that the woven-in end does not show through to the right side of the fabric.

WHILE WORKING LOOPS OFF THE HOOK

A new piece of working yarn can also be joined very inconspicuously at the transition from one stitch to the next. This can happen either when changing colors or skeins within the row or at the end of the last row before the change.

X The **FIRST STITCH OF THE NEW ROW** can be worked either with height-adjustment chains or with false double crochet after the working yarn has been changed during completion of the last stitch of the previous row.

X The working yarn in the new color can be pulled through with the crochet hook and the yarn tail **LEFT HANGING** on the wrong side of work until **WOVEN IN**. The new working yarn can also be loosely **KNOTTED** with the old color, moving the knot close to the adjacent stitch.

At the end of the row

1 Using the old working yarn, complete the stitch until 2 loops remain on the crochet hook. Pull the working yarn in the new color through.

2 Crochet the last 2 loops together using the new yarn.

3 Turn work, and work the first stitch of the new row with the new color.

For single crochet, crochet the loop off the hook using the new color immediately after having pulled the first loop through.

Within a row

To change a skein or color within the row, complete the last stitch before the color change join, except for the last 2 loops, finishing the last step of the stitch in the new color.

After that, continue with the new yarn, keeping both yarn tails on the wrong side of the work.

For single crochet, crochet the loop off the hook using the new color immediately after having pulled the first loop through.

! Changing colors while crocheting loops off the hook does not work with SLIP STITCHES since, in this case, there are no "last 2 loops" which could be crocheted together in the new color. With this technique, a yarn in a new color can only be added AT THE END OF A ROW if the color change is to remain unnoticeable.

Within or at the end of a round

When crocheting in rounds, a new working yarn in a different color is joined within the round the same way as for crocheting in rows (see above). To join the new color at the end of the round, there are two options:

OPTION 1

1 Complete the last stitch of the round except for the last 2 loops. Now, to join into the round, insert the hook into the topmost height-adjust-ment chain or under the two V-shaped loops of the stitches of the first stitch of the round, and pull the new working yarn through.

2 Without making another yarn over, pull the new loop through the last 2 loops of the last stitch of the round. Now you can immediately start the new round.

! In this method, the beginning of the round SHIFTS with every round by 1 STITCH TO THE RIGHT, since the height-adjustment chains are located above the last double crochet of the round and not above the height-adjustment chains of the previous round.

X The COLOR CHANGE can also be worked MORE CONVE-NIENTLY for both methods if the ends of the old and the new color are temporarily KNOTTED TOGETHER in the back of the work. After having completed the piece, the knots are dissolved and the yarn tails crossed and then carefully woven in.

! When joining into the round, the LAST STITCH OF THE PREVIOUS ROUND should NOT BE OVERLOOKED since with this method the height-ad-justment chains also emerge from this last stitch and not from the height-adjustment chains of the previous round.

! These two methods can also be used FOR TURNED ROUNDS. The only difference to joined rounds or spiral rounds is that the work is turned at the end of every round.

OPTION 2

1 Complete all steps of the last stitch of the round, but don't join into the round yet. To join into the round, insert the hook into the topmost height-adjustment chain or under the two V-shaped loops of the first stitch of the round, and pull the new working yarn through and at the same time through the last loop of the round.

2 Now you can continue with the first stitch of the new round (height-adjustment chain or "false stitch").

FINISHING OFF

When work on the piece has been completed, break the working yarn at least 4 inches (10 cm) after the last stitch and secure the end to prevent the crocheted piece from unraveling. There are several options to do this.

SECURING THE TAIL AT THE END OF THE ROW

When a crocheted piece worked in rows has been completed, the working yarn is usually located at the end of the last row.

SECURING WITHIN THE LAST STITCH

 Since this option for ending is not very sturdy, the **YARN TAIL** should be **RATHER LONG** so it won't escape from out of the stitches.

After having completed the last stitch, break the working yarn and pull the working loop longer so that the end of the yarn slips out of the stitch and can be woven in. The end of the crocheted piece is at the same height as the last stitch and is barely noticeable.

SECURING WITHIN THE WORKING LOOP

This option for ending is **VERY STURDY** and not prone to coming undone on its own.

After the last stitch has been completed and the working yarn has been cut, pull the yarn tail completely through the working loop. This produces a sturdy ending that is slightly higher than the row. The height difference can be evened out while weaving in the tail.

SECURING WITH A SINGLE CHAIN

Owing to the **ADDITIONAL CHAIN**, a little "STUD" forms at the end of the work. While this is aesthetically not very pleasing, it can be hidden later in a seam or an edging.

If you want to make absolutely sure that the tail cannot become undone later, you can work an additional single chain after the last stitch and then break the working yarn and pull the tail all the way through the working loop.

Then tighten the yarn end pulled through to secure the closure.

SECURING THE TAIL WHEN WORKING IN ROUNDS

SECURING WITHIN THE JOINING STITCH OF A ROUND

For pieces crocheted in rounds, the last round is usually joined, most often with a slip stitch, but other stitch types can be used, too.

To finish work, after having joined the round, break the working yarn leaving an end of at least 4 inches (10 cm) after the last stitch and pull the yarn tail completely through the last working loop.

! If **THE LAST ROUND IS NOT JOINED**, or if work ends in the middle of the round, resulting in a small jog, the yarn tail is secured the same way as at the end of a row (> page 80).

The top edge of the crocheted piece shows clean V shapes, but the yarn tail dangles rather loosely and thus will have to be properly secured while being woven in later.

The yarn tail can be much better secured if, before pulling the cut end through to finish, you first make an additional yarn over onto the crochet hook and pull it through the working loop. Nevertheless, the yarn tail still needs to be woven in later.

This ending looks slightly elevated but is well secured.

... How to weave in yarn tails is explained on page 154.

SECURING WITH A FALSE STITCH (SEWN BIND-OFF)

With the help of a tapestry needle and the yarn tail, you can also imitate a V-shaped stitch so that the final round of the work appears completely closed and the end of the round is less noticeable. During the same working step, the yarn tail can also be woven in.

1 Finish the last round completely, but do not join. Break the working yarn, leaving an end of at least 4 inches (10 cm) after the last stitch. Now pull the working loop longer so that the tail slips through the last two loops.

2 Thread the yarn tail into a tapestry needle and lead it from front to back under either the two top loops of the topmost height-adjustment chain or the top of the first stitch at the beginning of the round.

3 Bring the tapestry needle back to the last stitch, insert it from top to bottom into the center of the V . . .

4 . . . and bring it to the back through the two top loops of the last stitch. Now weave in the yarn tail.

5 The top edge of the crocheted piece now looks even and joined. The sewn-off stitch does not stand out from the remaining stitches.

Shaped to Perfection

Crocheting only straight pieces can become boring—get on with real shapes! Checklist to get you started: understanding crochet instructions, shaping crocheted pieces with increases and decreases, and incorporating details such as buttonholes and zippers.

Understanding
Crochet Patterns

A crochet pattern contains all the information pertaining to a crocheted piece, independent of elements of style and design. Anyone who understands the general concept and meanings of the terms can, based on this information, adapt any pattern to other desired measurements or to yarns with a different gauge.

LAYOUT AND CONTENTS OF A PATTERN

The crochet pattern describing a garment is divided into different sections, each of which contains important information for the successful outcome of your crochet project.

SIZE

The listed size gives a general idea of the dimensions of the finished garment. For articles of clothing, the indicated **clothing size** provides a first idea of whether the garment will have the correct fit. For accessories such as bags and scarves, measurements are given for the height and width; for items of a circular shape, most often diameter or circumference are noted. Finished sizes for three-dimensional items, such as stuffed toys, are usually based on circumference and height.

If the pattern for a garment contains **numbers for multiple sizes**, these are usually listed in ascending order, beginning with the smallest size. All numbers are then listed in the pattern next to each other either divided by slashes or dashes or partially enclosed in parenthesis or brackets. If the pattern contains only one number, it applies to all sizes.

GARMENT PATTERN/SCHEMATIC

In the garment pattern or schematic, all parts of the crocheted piece are individually shown, labeled with all measurements. This way, you will know in advance, and can check during work, which shape and size each individual part should have.

"ONE SIZE FITS ALL": Catchall sizes should be relied on for scarves or stoles at most. Since clothing sizes are not internationally standardized, for all other garments, the numbers in the schematic should be **COMPARED** to the measurements of a well-fitting garment **OF A SIMILAR SHAPE** and, on the basis of this, the appropriate size chosen or the pattern instructions adapted to one's own measurements.

Garment schematics can be true to scale, but they are not always. If you want to work from a **GARMENT SCHEMATIC AS A PATTERN IN FINISHED SIZE**, you should therefore not enlarge the garment schematics with a photocopier but, based on their measurements, create your own personal garment pattern.

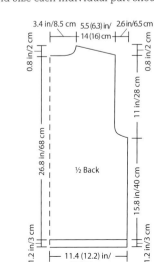

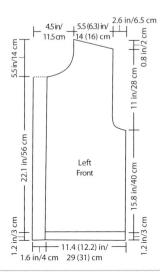

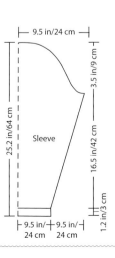

MATERIALS

All materials needed to create the item are usually listed, including yarn, hook size, and, if necessary, any notions such as stitch markers, tapestry needle to weave in ends, or accessories, such as buttons, zippers, or beads.

Yarn information usually contains the yarn name, manufacturer, color or colorway (name and/or number), and the required amount, often also the fiber content of the yarn and its yardage. Also important is information about the **gauge swatch**, which can be found in every pattern. Equipped with this information, you can quickly **find alternatives** if a certain yarn should not be available or you want to use a different yarn than the pattern calls for.

The **recommended hook size** should always be checked against what works for your own gauge swatch *(> page 95)*. Make sure to check the pattern instructions for the stitch pattern used for the gauge swatch so you can properly compare your own swatch against the sample!

STITCH PATTERNS

Stitch patterns used in a pattern are provided as either a crochet chart *(> page 91)* or written-out row-by-row instructions *(> page 90)*. In a crochet chart, every stitch is represented by a symbol. In some patterns, symbols are explained right next to the crochet chart; in books or in magazines containing multiple patterns, symbol explanations are usually either listed in one spot or consolidated in a table.

Stitch patterns provided in written form are described in detail row by row or round by round. To save space, they will often contain numerous abbreviations *(> page 344)*.

GAUGE SWATCH

The gauge is one of the most important facets of the whole pattern. All numbers in a pattern, such as stitch count, row count, number and placement of increases or decreases, are calculated based on the gauge. Only if **your own gauge matches the one stated in the pattern**, will your crocheted item have the **listed measurements and/or the appropriate fit**. Especially if using a different yarn than listed in the pattern, a gauge swatch is essential. If you want to work a pattern in a yarn with a different gauge than the yarn for which the pattern was calculated, retain the garment schematic, and calculate all measurements based on the new gauge. Additional information about gauge can be found on page 95.

CROCHET PATTERN

The actual crochet pattern describes **all working steps** from beginning to finishing the crocheted piece. It is grouped into **detailed descriptions of all individual parts** for the item, usually beginning with the largest piece. To be able to compare whether all working steps have been rendered correctly so far, often stitch counts, after a certain working step, are listed, too. If a part is to be worked more than once, it also states how many of each piece are to be worked.

In the "finishing" section (sometimes also called "making up"), besides the order of work for sewing the pieces together, all other finishing work such as working crocheted edgings, sewing on buttons, or attaching decorative elements, is also explained.

X It is recommended to purchase the **WHOLE YARN AMOUNT** for the project, and preferably one extra skein, at once since all skeins used in the same project should be from the same dye lot and have the same **DYE LOT NUMBER**. In specialized yarn stores, you can ask to have additional skeins laid away for some time. Many local yarn stores will also accept returns on leftover unused skeins in original packaging within a certain period.

X Before starting, you should **COMPLETELY READ THROUGH** the **WHOLE PATTERN ONE TIME**, including all abbreviations, stitch patterns, and crochet charts or colorwork charts. This way, you get a quick overview of the design and the order of work. It will also quickly become apparent whether any questions or clarifications need to be addressed in advance.

BASIC TERMS AND PHRASES IN CROCHET PATTERNS

* (ASTERISKS)/FROM * TO */FROM * (ON)...
* asterisks can be found in patterns in phrases such as "repeat from * to * " or "repeat from * ." They indicate that the instructions listed between asterisks, or after a single asterisk, are to be repeated either continuously or as often as stated. Instructions between or after asterisks can, for instance, describe a pattern repeat, or a repeating increase or decrease of stitches.

In patterns, it can happen that within a repeat listed between asterisks, further repeats must be inserted. Every one of the inserted repeats is marked with an additional asterisk. The next would therefore be marked with **, yet another one with ***, and so forth. If there are several instructions between asterisks, you will have to pay close attention to always repeating the appropriate section. It will help a lot to mark these different repeats in different colors.

AT BOTH ENDS OF THE ROW/AT BOTH ENDS/ON BOTH SIDES To achieve a symmetrical shape, the same instructions are being worked at the same height of the crocheted piece, at the same time, at both ends of the row. When stitches must be increased or decreased "at both ends of the row," the increases or decreases are to be worked at the beginning and at the end of a row (> pages 100 and 105).

BEGINNING CHAIN The beginning chain (> page 57) is the foundation, or the beginning, on which the crocheted piece is built up and onto which the first row or round is being crocheted. The pattern instructions will list the exact number of chains needed for the beginning chain. Often, additional chains are mentioned that are to replace the first stitch of the first row. If chains replace the first stitch, instructions will state into which chain from the hook to insert the hook when beginning the first row. After having worked Row 1, the stitch count should be checked to avoid mistakes in the number of stitches.

BEGINNING TAIL/ENDING TAIL Beginning and ending tails are extra pieces of yarn hanging out from the crocheted fabric either at the beginning or end of a crocheted piece or at the beginning or end of a skein or a color. They must be woven in after having completed the crocheted piece (> page 154).

BEGINNING WITH A WRONG-SIDE ROW If the more presentable side of a stitch pattern is created on what is actually the wrong side of the crocheted fabric, the counting method changes. Right- and wrong- side rows are switched. In stitch patterns and colorwork charts, it can be easily spotted if work starts with a wrong-side row, since the odd row numbers for right-side rows are shown not as usual to the right of the chart but to the left of it.

BRACKETS/PARENTHESES Angular Brackets [ ] indicate that all stitches listed within these brackets have to be read as a group of stitches, and often also have to be worked into the same insertion point. Example: "[2 single crochets, 1 double crochet] into the same stitch," whereby the addendum is not always specially mentioned.

Parentheses ( ) often contain more detailed explanations than brackets. Example: "1 double crochet into the next double crochet (the middle one of 5 double crochets of the previous round)" explains the specific insertion point—namely, center stitch from a group of five stitches of the previous round.

Both brackets and parentheses can also be used to consolidate groups of stitches that, in their entirety, are to be worked multiple times consecutively. "(2 dc, 1 sc) 3 times" means that here, you will crochet into a total of 9 stitches.

Additionally, brackets and parentheses can separate different numbers for different sizes from each other.

COLOR CHANGE When working with multiple colors, the color has to be changed within the crocheted piece (> page 76). The working yarn in one color will be left hanging and a new strand in a different color will be used as the new working yarn. The transition from one color to another can happen either within a row/round or at the beginning of a new row. The unused working yarn can be left hanging or hidden within the following stitches.

CONTINUOUSLY "Continuously" is often mentioned in pattern instructions in conjunction with color sequences, stitch pattern sequences, or pattern repeats. It means that these parts of the instructions are to be repeated or performed consecutively as often as possible until either the end of a row/round has been reached or there are not enough stitches left any more to work a full repeat.

CROCHETING OFF TOGETHER To crochet loops off the hook together (> page 102) means that stitches are crocheted together. For this, the working yarn is first pulled through the indicated stitches or loops on the hook until one loop for every stitch worked, plus the working loop, remain on the hook. Then a new yarn over is

X For garments, **MARKING THE MOST IMPORTANT STEPS, STITCHES, AND NUMBER OF ROWS** gives a good overview of how the item is constructed and what techniques are required.

made onto the hook, and the working yarn is pulled through all loops at the same time. Depending on how many stitches are worked off together, the stitch count decreases.

DECREASING/DECREASE When decreasing, the number of stitches in a crocheted piece is being reduced. Decreases (> page 102) serve the purpose of either shaping the crocheted piece or creating a stitch pattern. During decreases, always make sure that the number of stitches matches the stitch count listed in the pattern instructions or required for the pattern repeat of the stitch pattern.

EDGES All outer edges of a crocheted piece are considered "edges of the crocheted piece," which can later be seamed or finished with an added border or edging. The edges of a crocheted piece are categorized as:

a) bottom edge of the crocheted piece = the beginning edge,

b) top edge of the crocheted piece = the row worked last, and

c) side edges of the crocheted piece = the edges at the right and left side of the piece.

EVEN- AND ODD-NUMBERED ROWS The rows in a pattern are numbered continuously. The first, and thus odd-numbered row, is the row after the beginning chain or foundation row. If not otherwise stated, odd-numbered rows form the front of work, even-numbered rows the back of work of a crocheted piece. In crochet charts, row numbers for odd-numbered rows are located to the right, those for even-numbered rows to the left of the charts (i.e., always at the side where the rows starts).

FROM THE HOOK/FROM HOOK When counting along a beginning chain, chains are not counted from the beginning tail to the crochet hook, but the other way around from the crochet hook back toward the beginning tail.

FRONT OR BACK LOOP OF THE STITCH Every completed stitch presents at the top of the current row as horizontally positioned loops in the shape of the letter V. The two legs of the V are called "loops of the stitch." The part of the stitch that makes up the front leg is called the "front loop of the stitch"; the one that makes up the back leg is the "back loop of the stitch." This term is always related to which side of the work is presently facing the viewer—the same loop of the stitch can therefore be considered "front

loop" when being worked into and "back loop" when the work is turned.

These two loops of the stitch are also called top loops of the stitch. For certain stitch patterns, it might be necessary to insert the hook only through the front or back loop of the stitch (> page 37). When this is the case, it will always be specially mentioned in the pattern instructions.

HEIGHT-ADJUSTMENT CHAINS/TURNING CHAINS "Height-adjustment chains" is the name for chains that are worked to reach the height of the first stitch when crocheting in the round. Height-adjustment chains can be worked additionally, and do not count as a stitch when they are located between two stitches. In most cases, they replace the first stitch. When joining into the round, the slip stitch is always worked into the topmost chain of the crocheted chain that replaces the first stitch. The chains additionally worked at the beginning of the very first row are likewise called height-adjustment chains.

"Turning chains" is the name for chains that are worked to reach the height of the first stitch of the following row from the second row when crocheting in turned rows. They prevent the crocheted piece from constricting at the sides. Turning chains can be worked additionally, and do not count as a stitch. They can be seen as small arcs at the side edges of the crocheted piece. They can, however, also replace the first stitch of the row. In this case, the last stitch at the end of a row must be crocheted into the topmost chain of the crocheted chain that replaces the first stitch.

The exact number of height-adjustment or turning chains needing to be worked depends on the height of the stitches (> page 64).

INCREASING/DECREASING EVENLY DISTRIBUTED To avoid unsightly bulges when decreasing several stitches in a row or round, they are decreased not all at once, but spaced out in evenly distributed spots.

Example for a decrease: For a stitch count of 40 stitches, 8 stitches are to be decreased evenly distributed. This means that in this row or round, every 4th and 5th stitch must be crocheted together.

Example for an increase: For a stitch count of 40 stitches, 8 stitches are to be increased evenly distributed. This means that in this row or round, 2 stitches must be worked into every 5th stitch.

X When photocopying the pattern for personal use, you can mark all important facts with a highlighter. If the printed crochet charts are rather small, they can also be conveniently enlarged to the desired dimensions with the photocopier.

Even if using just one skein, you can work **WITH TWO STRANDS OF YARN HELD TOGETHER.** For this, pull one strand as usual from the middle of a center-pull skein and take the second strand from the outside of the skein.

Small **NUMBERED TAGS,** which are attached to the stitch markers, make **ORIENTATION** easier.

INCREASING/INCREASE When increasing, the number of stitches in a crocheted piece rises. Increases (> page 98) serve the purpose of either shaping the crocheted piece or creating a stitch pattern. When working increases, special effort should be made that the number of stitches in the crocheted piece matches the stitch count listed in the pattern instructions or required for the pattern repeat of the stitch pattern.

IN FRONT OF WORK/IN BACK OF WORK This specification always refers to the side of the work currently facing the crocheter, whether that is the actual right or wrong side of the crocheted fabric.

INSERTING THE HOOK IN A ROW BELOW When crocheting stitches worked "in a row below," the hook for the new stitch is inserted not under the loops of the stitch of the previous row or round but into a stitch one or several rows or rounds below into which, in most cases, another stitch has already been crocheted earlier. This way of inserting the hook is mostly used for creating stitch patterns. At the top edge of the crocheted piece, the following stitch into which the hook would have "normally" been inserted is now being skipped in the current row. In some stitch patterns, the hook will be inserted into stitches below that had been previously skipped. These stitches worked in rows below are finished in front of the base fabric, which makes them appear raised.

INSERTION POINT The insertion point is the spot into which the hook is inserted for a new stitch, before pulling the working yarn through the fabric. If not otherwise stated, this will be at the top edge of the crocheted piece, under both loops of the stitch for the following stitch (> page 32). It is, however, also possible that instructions call for working only through the back or the front loop of the stitch. The insertion point can also be in an entirely different spot, for instance, one or several rows below, between two existing stitches, or approaching the stitch from the wrong side of the fabric. If the insertion point is different from what is normally expected when working a stitch pattern, this point will be mentioned.

JOINING A ROUND WITH A SLIP STITCH When crocheting in the round, usually the end of the round has to be joined to its beginning before the next round can be started (> page 70). This means that the first and the last stitch must be joined. This is usually done with a slip stitch, which, after the last regular stitch of the round has been completed, is worked into the first stitch of the same round.

JOINING NEW YARN When crocheting with multiple colors or when a new row/round has to be continued in a different spot, such as when working motifs, the working yarn has to be joined anew. This is usually done by attaching the new working yarn with the help of a slip stitch (> page 33).

LEAVING STITCHES UNWORKED To decrease several stitches at the end of a row, the last stitches are not crocheted into, but just left unworked. The crocheted piece is turned a few stitches before the end of the row has been reached. The edge of the crocheted piece is therefore moved inward by the number of stitches decreased/left unworked.

MAIN PATTERN The main pattern is the stitch pattern in which an item is mainly worked. If several stitch patterns are to be worked in approximately equal proportions, they are usually consecutively numbered and named Stitch Pattern 1, Stitch Pattern 2, and so forth. When crocheting, make sure to always work the appropriate current stitch pattern.

MARKING/STITCH MARKERS It is very helpful to mark certain rows, rounds, or individual stitches: for instance, the beginning of the round when working in the round, increase and decrease rows or rounds, pattern repeats, and so forth. This can be done in different ways. A marking thread is a piece of yarn in a contrasting color that is placed between two stitches within a row or round or at the beginning of a round. The ends should hang down about the same length in front and back of the work. Marking threads are useful only as short-term markers, as they can easily slip out. For row- or round-counting purposes, a longer counting thread can also be moved from front to back after a certain number of rows, and later back again. Stitch markers are small safety-pin-type rings or clips made of metal or plastic that are used to mark individual stitches, rows, or rounds. They are sturdy and, owing to the way they are anchored in the fabric, safe from falling out.

MIRROR-INVERTED "Mirror-inverted" is another word for "in reverse." For symmetrically crocheted pieces, the right half has to be worked mirror-inverted or in reverse to the left half; for garments, for instance, Right and Left Front or Right and Left Sleeve will be worked mirror-inverted to each other.

Example for a symmetrically crocheted piece: If in one row, the second and third stitch are to be crocheted together, then, at the end of the row, the third-to-last stitch likewise is to be crocheted together with the next-to-last stitch.

Example for the Right and Left Front: If at the Right Front, neckline shaping decreases are worked at the right edge of the piece, then, on the Left Front, neckline shaping decreases are to be worked at the left edge of the piece.

PATTERN REPEAT The repeat or pattern repeat is a self-contained unit of a stitch pattern, consisting of a certain number of stitches and rows or rounds, and being repeated multiple times widthwise and heightwise. Crochet charts or written instructions for the stitch pattern often show or describe the pattern repeat only once and specify how often it is to be worked. Always pay attention to whether it has been stated how often the pattern repeat must be worked in total or how often it is to be repeated after having been worked for the first time.

PREVIOUS ROW/PREVIOUS ROUND The previous row/previous round is always the row or round that had been worked immediately before the row or round that is currently in the process of being worked.

RIGHT AND LEFT EDGE OF THE CROCHETED PIECE The indication of the location of the edge always refers to the position as viewed from the crocheter onto the crocheted piece when the front of work is facing up.

RIGHT SIDE OF WORK The right side of work is always the "better-looking" side of a crocheted piece, which will later be worn or displayed on the outside or public side of the piece.

RIGHT-SIDE ROW The right-side row is the row that is worked while the front of work of the crocheted piece is facing up. If not otherwise stated, all odd-numbered rows are right-side rows. In crochet charts, row numbers for right-side rows are located to the right of the chart.

RIGHT SIDES FACING EACH OTHER Two crocheted pieces are placed together with the front of work (= outsides) facing each other—they are now "right sides facing each other" and thus "wrong sides out." This technique is done mostly during finishing, when sewing or crocheting pieces together. After individual parts have been joined, the crocheted piece is turned so that in the finished object, the right sides of the fabric are located on the outside and seams on the inside.

SKIPPING/LEAVING OUT/PASSING OVER To skip a stitch or stitches means to insert the hook not in the immediate-following stitch, but to leave the following stitch (or a certain number of stitches) unworked, not crocheting into them, and insert the hook into a stitch (or certain number of stitches) further to the left. This is used for creating stitch patterns. Often, chain arcs are used to bridge skipped stitches.

SPIRAL ROUNDS These are rounds that are crocheted continuously in spirals without joining round at the end of the round before starting the next one. Spiral rounds are often worked in shallow stitches only, such as a single crochet.

TURNING WORK At the end of a row, the crocheted piece is turned to the other side so that the beginning of the new row is again located at the right, and therefore in working direction. Front and back of the crocheted piece trade places. For left-handed crocheters, it is exactly the other way around since they work their rows or rounds in the direction from left to right.

WEAVING IN/SEWING IN/HIDING ENDS To weave or sew in ends, or to hide them, means to thread and anchor yarn tails on the wrong side of the fabric or the back of a crocheted piece. Hiding ends should, if possible, be done in the most invisible way. In addition to that, the working yarn should be woven in securely so that it cannot escape from the crocheted fabric (> page 154).

WITH TWO STRANDS OF YARN HELD TOGETHER/DOUBLE-STRANDED To work with two strands of yarn held together means that two strands of the working yarn from the same or different skeins are held together and crocheted with as one working yarn.

WORKING IN ROWS When working in rows, the work has to be turned at the end of every row since the working direction goes always from right to left (for left-handed crocheters, from left to right). After having turned, alternatingly the front or the back of the crocheted piece will face up.

WORKING IN THE CHAIN SPACE/AROUND A CHAIN Chain arcs are often employed to create stitch patterns, and are crocheted into or around in later rows or rounds. When working the stitches, the hook is not inserted into any individual chains of the chain arc, but into the space under the chain (> page 43). The bases of

X If you need QUICK HELP WITH QUESTIONS, you can get it from various sources. Often, manufacturers and publishers have established hotlines that you can consult. The Internet also offers a variety of craft and crochet forums, where you can gather useful tips.

! Depending on the stitch pattern, it might be necessary to crochet INTO INDIVIDUAL CHAINS OF A CHAIN ARC. If this is needed, it will be specially mentioned in the instructions.

the stitches worked will then go around the chain.

WORKING IN THE ROUND When working in rounds without turning, the working direction is always the same. In most cases, the front of the work will face outward. A distinction is made between rounds that are joined with a slip stitch and spiral rounds (> *page 71*), which are worked without a clearly defined transition between rounds. In special situations, "turned rounds" (> *page 71*) can also be worked. In this case, the crocheted piece is turned at the end of each round and even-numbered rounds are worked on the wrong side of the fabric.

WORKING INTO THE SAME INSERTION POINT To crochet into the same insertion point means to work two or more stitches one after another into a single spot of the previous row or round. This procedure is used either to increase stitches or to create stitch patterns. In shell patterns, for instance, up to 9 stitches can be worked into the same stitch (> *page 43*).

WORKING LOOP After having completed a stitch and before beginning a new stitch, a single loop always remains on the hook. This loop is called the working loop.

WORKING YARN Working yarn is the name for the strand of yarn leading from the working loop to the ball of yarn and being used to crochet with.

WRONG SIDE OF WORK The wrong side of the work is in most cases the less presentable side of a crocheted piece, which will be later in the finished piece either on the inside or on the back. This is the side where all ends should be woven in.

WRONG-SIDE ROW The "wrong-side row" is the row that is worked while the back of the work is facing up. Usually, all even-numbered rows are wrong-side rows. In crochet charts, row numbers for wrong-side rows are shown to the left of the chart.

WRONG SIDES FACING EACH OTHER Two crocheted pieces are placed together with the back of work (= wrong sides) facing each other—they are now "wrong sides in." This is done mostly during finishing, when sewing or crocheting pieces together.

PRESENTATION OF CROCHET PATTERNS

Crochet patterns and stitch patterns can be presented in different ways: either in written form, as instructions written out row by row in words, or as a crochet chart shown in symbols. Often, a crochet pattern can also contain other useful content, such as a chart for a colorwork pattern or a schematic for finishing.

WRITTEN OUT ROW-BY-ROW INSTRUCTIONS

Stitch patterns given in text form describe in detail row by row or round by round how the stitch pattern should be worked. For this, the stitch pattern is always explained in working direction (i.e., every stitch or every action is listed in order from right to left). For simple patterns consisting of one or just a few stitch types, instructions of this kind are still relatively short and easy to understand; for more complicated patterns, this way of notation can make the pattern very long. To save space, abbreviations are used for the most common terms (> *page 344*).

Main stitch patterns are mostly presented in form of written-out row-by-row instructions since the pattern repeat on which the stitch pattern is based is in most cases only a few stitches in width and a few rows or rounds in height. Listed are first the stitch count of the pattern repeat and, if needed, extra stitches. If, for instance, the instructions for a stitch pattern state "stitch count a multiple of 6 + 2 (additional stitches)," for the foundation chain, a multiple of 6 stitches and 2 additional stitches have to be worked (i.e., 14 stitches, 20 stitches, 26 stitches, etc.). In some stitch patterns, numbers for the required stitch count also list the number of height-adjustment or turning chains if any are required (> *page 64*). After the details about the exact stitch count, all subsequent rows or rounds needed for a heightwise pattern repeat are described in detail. Lastly, it will be explained which rows or rounds are to be repeated for a complete heightwise pattern repeat.

Some books contain photographs of **STITCH PATTERN SWATCHES** for commonly known stitch patterns. This gives you a good idea of the construction and texture, such as the openness or density of the crocheted fabric or the effects of color and color repeats.

CROCHET CHART

A crochet chart is the graphic depiction of a stitch pattern (i.e., drawn instructions containing all relevant information about a stitch pattern or motif). Ever since crochet charts have been invented, even complicated stitch patterns can be presented in an easily understandable format, no matter whether they are worked in rows or in the round.

In crochet charts, every stitch has been assigned a certain character or symbol. Since the use of these characters or symbol is not standardized, every crochet chart should always be accompanied by a symbol legend or explanation of symbols from which the meaning of individual symbols can be gained. This symbol explanation can either be placed next to the chart or, in books or magazines, be found in a central location in the form of a consolidated table or list (> page 340).

Using these symbols, a graphical representation of the crochet work can be created that exactly shows which stitch types have to be worked in which order. Where to insert the hook for every stitch is evident from the spot where the symbol for the stitch is placed in relation to the stitch(es) of the previous row or round. Crocheted pieces are worked either in rows or in rounds, and charts are set up in different ways to show the working order.

CROCHETING IN ROWS

Pieces crocheted in rows begin with a chain, or foundation row, above which the first row will be located. This row is worked from right to left. For a better overview, rows are consecutively numbered, with the row number shown at the side of the chart from which the row begins. Right-side rows are to be read from right to left, wrong-side rows from left to right. This way, you can keep track and easily reorient yourself anytime if you forget whether you are currently working a right- or wrong-side row.

If a certain number of stitches must be repeated within a row, these are either enclosed in brackets or noticeably separated from the rest of the pattern by vertical lines. These stitches are called the pattern repeat (= patt rep) or just repeat. If the stitches of the pattern repeat are located in the center of a row, where before it and after it additional stitches are worked, first the stitches shown before the pattern repeat are to be worked once, then the stitches of the pattern repeat are worked as often as indicated, and finally the row is finished by working the stitches after the pattern repeat once. How often the pattern repeat needs to be worked will be stated in the accompanying text. Pattern repeats can also be differentiated from the remainder of the chart by color. Pattern repeats of multiple rows or rounds that need to be repeated heightwise can also be marked in one or the other way.

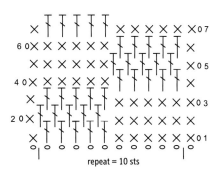

repeat = 10 sts

o = 1 chain (ch)

X = 1 single crochet (sc)

╪ = 1 double crochet (dc)

CROCHETING IN ROUND

Pieces crocheted in round often start from a ring of chains or a magic circle (> pages 67 and 68) in the center. The first round is then worked into this ring, working the stitches in the chain space around the ring. As an alternative, the first round can also be worked into a single chain (> page 67).

All subsequent rounds are then worked around the center point outward, increasing the stitch count in each round so that the size of the piece increases. The crochet chart shows exactly in which spots stitches will be increased. Rounds are always to be read and crocheted from right to left (i.e., in a counterclockwise direction). Individual rounds are consecutively numbered; numbers are always noted to the right of the beginning of the round. Rounds are usually joined, meaning they are closed with a slip stitch before a new round begins (> page 70).

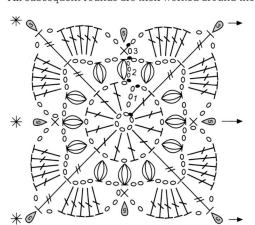

! LEFT-HANDED CROCHETERS start every row or round always in their own working direction (i.e., will work right- and wrong-side rows in the OPPOSITE DIRECTION), beginning at the end of the chart without a row number. When crocheting in the round, left-handed crocheters work IN A CLOCKWISE DIRECTION.

! Often, symbols used in crochet charts look similar to their crocheted counterparts so that a crochet chart gives a first IMPRESSION OF THE STITCH PATTERN.

! For working in the round using shallow stitches, SPIRAL ROUNDS can also be worked. When working in spiral rounds, rounds are continuously crocheted atop each other without transition (spiral rounds > page 71).

JOINING MOTIFS

Individual motifs can be joined into a larger patchwork of crocheted elements. This can be done either at the end by crocheting the motifs together or during crocheting by joining as you go. Spots in which motifs need to be joined are specially marked in the crochet chart, often with arrows, stars, or crosses *(crochet chart > page 91 bottom)*.

INDIVIDUAL STITCHES

Individual stitches are shown as **non-joined symbols** next to each other. Every basic stitch is marked with a symbol reserved for it and can thus easily be distinguished from all other stitches.

Examples:

- o = 1 chain (ch)
- ● = 1 slip stitch (sl-st)
- ✕ = 1 single crochet (sc)
- ⊤ = 1 half double crochet (hdc)
- = 1 double crochet (dc)
- = 1 treble crochet (tr)

! A detailed **TABLE OF CROCHET SYMBOLS** can be found on pages 340–343.

GROUPS OF STITCHES

Groups of stitches are **individual stitches joined to each other** that are shown in the chart as fan shapes. If symbols converge at the bottom, they are all worked into the same stitch; if symbols converge at the top, they are crocheted (worked off) together.

Examples:

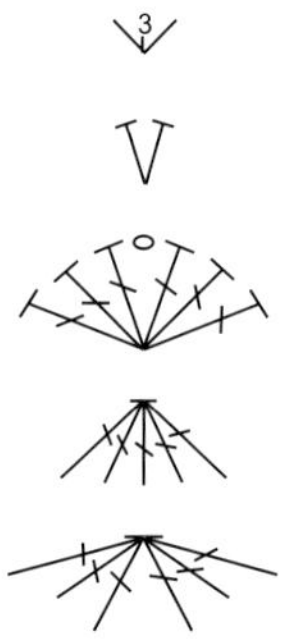

- = 3 single crochets into the same stitch
- = 2 half double crochets into the same stitch
- = 3 double crochets, 1 chain, 3 double crochets into the same stitch
- = 5 double crochets crocheted together
- = 6 double crochets crocheted together

SPECIAL STITCHES

Special stitches can be worked in a **completely different way** than regular stitches or may consist of a **variety of basic stitches** for which either the hook is inserted in a special way or that are combined into a group of stitches with its own typical look.

Examples:

- = 1 single crochet worked below
- = 1 front post double crochet
- = 2 crossed double crochets
- = 1 X-stitch in double crochet
- = 1 cluster stitch of 4 half double crochets crocheted together
- = 1 cluster stitch of 5 double crochets crocheted together
- = 1 popcorn of 5 double crochets
- = 1 Solomon's knot

SCHEMATICS

Besides stitch pattern and colorwork charts, additional working steps or facts, such as about the **placement of individual elements**, are visualized in the form of schematics.

Individual motifs of crocheted patchwork compositions are crocheted or sewn together in a certain order into a larger unit of crochet work. Schematics show the exact arrangement of the motifs and can, in addition to colors and names or numbers of motifs, also contain the working direction for each individual motif.

For crocheted pieces consisting of individual motifs that are joined during the work, the arrangement is usually visualized in the schematic to make it easier to keep track where motifs currently worked are to be attached. Especially with motifs crocheted onto existing parts, a schematic is essential and very helpful since placement mistakes are difficult to correct.

If you want to create your **OWN MOTIF-BASED DESIGNS**, it is strongly advisable to **DRAW** a few motifs true to scale **ON PAPER,** cut them out, and place them together in a large arrangement. This way, you can determine how the motifs can be meaningfully combined into a large unit. Additionally, you can mark the **JOINING STITCHES** on the motifs and then draw up a schematic.

Grid-style charts are used particularly often when larger areas are worked IN ONLY ONE STITCH TYPE, but in TWO OR MORE COLORS, such as potholders or intarsia work for bags, pillows, or blankets.

GRID CHARTS

In the filet crochet technique (> page 236), in Tunisian crochet (> page 225), and for colorwork patterns (> page 212), instead of a regular crochet chart, grid charts are often used. In a grid chart, every box contains a piece of information.

TUNISIAN CROCHET CHARTS

In charts for Tunisian crochet, every box contains one stitch. The boxes are of rectangular shape and contain two small symbols arranged one on top of the other that indicate how the stitch is to be worked in right-side rows or wrong-side rows. Often, the different directions of the work are additionally represented by arrows at the edge of the counting chart (Tunisian crochet > page 225).

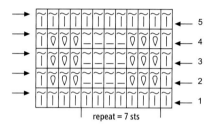

⊓ = 1 Tunisian simple stitch

⊔ = 1 Tunisian purl stitch

⍉ = 1 Tunisian knit stitch

→ = direction of work

FILET CROCHET CHARTS

In filet crochet, a mesh background is crocheted using only chains and double crochets, into which patterns can be incorporated by "filling in" boxes to create ornaments or shapes. Every box in the mesh background corresponds to a box in the chart. Filled boxes in the chart signify that the respective box in the mesh background is to be filled in with double crochets. As in a regular crochet chart, rows are consecutively numbered, and here, too, row numbers for right-side rows are odd numbers on the right and those for wrong-side rows are even numbers to the left of the chart (Filet crochet > page 236).

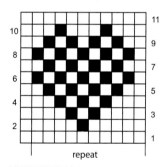

☐ = 1 empty box = 1 double crochet, 2 chains

■ = filled box = 3 double crochets

COLORWORK PATTERN CHARTS

For colorwork patterns, the crocheted fabric can be shown in the form of a colored chart. Every box in it corresponds to a stitch, which is to be worked in the indicated color.

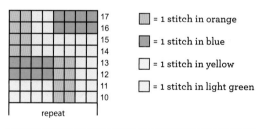

☐ = 1 stitch in orange

☐ = 1 stitch in blue

☐ = 1 stitch in yellow

☐ = 1 stitch in light green

THE GAUGE

Based on the projected measurements for your crocheted piece, the exact number of stitches widthwise and of rows or rounds heightwise has to be calculated before starting work. Basic stitches differ in height and width so that for every stitch pattern individual measurements have to be determined. Exact measurements can be found out with the help of a gauge swatch.

Gauge depends in particular on the yarn weight. The thicker the yarn, the larger the stitches turn out, and the fewer the number of stitches needed to cover a certain width. The stitch pattern itself also affects the gauge. Crossed stitches, such as in cables or post stitches, constrict the crocheted fabric so that more stitches will be needed. Stitch patterns with many holes, such as mesh patterns, are rather loose and run wider, so that you get by with fewer stitches.

Hook size, individual crochet style, and the fiber content of the yarn have an impact on the gauge as well. Before every crochet project, you should therefore take the time to diligently make a gauge swatch, to make sure that the measurements given in the pattern or the measurements calculated by you will be matched.

CROCHETING A GAUGE SWATCH

To determine gauge, always refer to the numbers stated in the pattern instructions. For numbers gained from yarn labels, if no separate crochet gauge is listed, the numbers on the ball band cannot be used for crochet projects since they refer to knitted swatches worked in Stockinette stitch.

Chain one-and-a-half times as many stitches as are stated for 4 inches (10 cm). Work in the indicated stitch pattern to a height of 6 inches (15 cm). Use the hook size recommended in the pattern instructions. Then pin the swatch to a suitable surface with tailor pins, lightly steam, and let it dry. Using a measuring tape, measure a section of 4 inches (10 cm) each widthwise and heightwise and mark the boundaries with tailor pins. Now count the number of stitches in width and the number of rows in height per 4 inches (10 cm). Write down these numbers as well as the hook size used. This is the specific gauge for the particular yarn used for a specific hook size in a select stitch pattern.

ADJUSTING GAUGE

If the gauge of your crocheted swatch matches the required numbers, you can immediately proceed with working your project.

If you have counted more stitches and rows in 4 inches (10 cm) than stated in the pattern, you have worked too tightly. You need to repeat your swatch using a larger hook size. If you have counted fewer stitches and rows in 4 inches (10 cm), you have worked too loosely and need to repeat your swatch using a smaller hook size.

If, using a different hook size, the required gauge can be matched but either the crocheted fabric turns out significantly too dense or too loose or the stitch definition is not to your liking, you should make your own calculations based on a gauge swatch to your liking and convert the information from the pattern to these values.

The same it is true if you want to use a completely different yarn. In this case, try first the hook size recommended on the yarn label to work a gauge swatch.

If your gauge noticeably differs from the one listed in the pattern, REPEAT your swatch using a DIFFERENT HOOK SIZE to ensure that measurements are correct. If you start work on the project with a hook size that had been only guessed at, not actually tried, you are setting yourself up for disappointment.

QUICK CHECK! When about 1.2 inches (3 cm) have been crocheted, you can already preliminarily count the stitches. This gives you a rough idea of whether the hook size is approximately right. If you notice that your work is considerably looser or tighter than it should be, unravel these few rows, and change to a different hook size right away.

A SWATCH RULER (> page 21) is a very handy tool for counting your gauge swatch.

Body Measurements and Crochet Patterns

Taking accurate measurements is crucial for a well-fitting garment. For this reason, body measurements needed for the garment are taken at anatomically important spots of the body following defined rules.

BODY MEASUREMENTS

To take individual body measurements, the **measuring tape** should be held **close to the body** but not constricting. Measurements are taken **standing erect**, in a naturally relaxed pose. It is recommended to wear a tight-fitting t-shirt so that starting and ending points can be marked with tailor pins if necessary. To find the correct spot for the waistline, it can be marked with a narrow ribbon or piece of yarn. As a general rule, the closer a garment is supposed to fit to the body, the more detailed the measurements taken and the more closely the garment pattern matched to them.

MEASUREMENTS FOR TOPS

CHEST CIRCUMFERENCE Measure the largest circumference, horizontally over the **fullest point of the bust,** passing through under the arms, and slightly above the lower base of the shoulder blades.

WAIST CIRCUMFERENCE Measure at the **slimmest part,** and close the measuring tape in the front. This measurement is needed for fitted tops.

HIP CIRCUMFERENCE Measure horizontally around the **widest part of the hips.** Let the measuring tape slowly slide horizontally over the posterior, adjusting the length until the largest spot has been reached.

SHOULDER WIDTH The shoulder width is measured from the side of the neck to the top of **the upper arm.**

UPPER ARM CIRCUMFERENCE With relaxed arm, measure the **circumference of the arm under the armpit.** You will notice that the circumference of the dominant arm is often about an inch larger. This difference should usually be compensated for by the elasticity of the crocheted fabric. Only for sleeves with a very tight fit and if the difference between the arms is substantial it might be necessary to record circumferences for both arms separately and take this into account when crocheting the sleeves.

ARM LENGTH Measure the outer arm length **from the top of the shoulder point** over the tip of the bent elbow **to the outer wrist bone.** Your closed fist should rest at the waist, so that the elbow is angled by about 90 degrees.

ARMHOLE DEPTH Have the person being measured put a sheet of paper under their armpit so that the top edge is horizontal over their spine. Then measure from the seventh cervical vertebra along the spine down to the top edge of the paper strip.

X A measurement that does not originate with conventional tailoring but is useful for developing patterns for crocheted garments is the **ARMHOLE DEPTH.** To find it, place a measuring tape around the upper arm directly under the armpit. Starting from this tape, place a second measuring tape over the shoulder joint up to where the arm emerges, and measure.

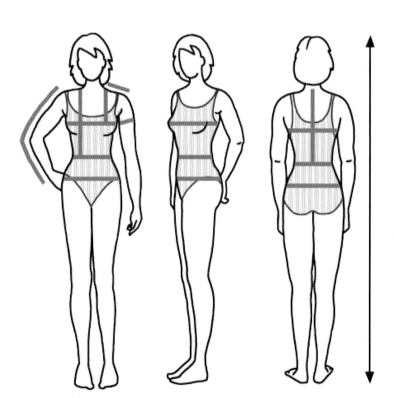

FRONT LENGTH Measure from the seventh cervical vertebra in the back along the neck toward the front beyond the bust point to the marked waist. Here, too, measure both halves of the body, write down the numbers and, if needed, continue working with a mean value. This measurement is needed for tops that emphasize the waist, such as with a peplum.

BACK LENGTH Lead the measuring tape from the seventh cervical vertebra along the spinal column to the marked waist.

BACK WIDTH With arms hanging down, measure from one side to the other side at the highest point of the bust at the transition from the shoulder blades to the armpit. At the end points of this line, the sleeve seams should be located.

MEASUREMENTS FOR HATS
HEAD CIRCUMFERENCE The measuring tape encircles the largest horizontal circumference of the head above the ears.

MEASUREMENTS FOR MITTENS
HAND CIRCUMFERENCE Measure the widest spot over the knuckles of the extended hand without encompassing the thumb. Fingers should be held close to each other.

MEASUREMENTS FOR SOCKS
FOOT LENGTH To be measured barefoot and with the body weight evenly distributed on both feet. The foot length corresponds to the distance between two horizontal lines, one touching the end of the longest toe, the other the heel.

FOOT CIRCUMFERENCE Place the measuring tape around the widest part of the forefoot. Measure barefoot and with the body weight evenly distributed on both feet.

INSTEP CIRCUMFERENCE/GIRTH With the foot outstretched and upright, measure over the heel and the top of the foot. This measurement determines the height of the gusset.

ANKLE CIRCUMFERENCE Measure the widest spot at the ankle.

CALF CIRCUMFERENCE Place the measuring tape around the widest part of the calf.

LOWER KNEE CIRCUMFERENCE Measure at the narrowest spot below the knee. This measurement determines the cuff width for knee-highs.

! Head circumference and neckline: The **HEADS OF BABIES AND TODDLERS** are in relation to the remaining body proportions noticeably larger than in adults. For this reason, it is recommended to also consider the head circumference measurement when crocheting sweaters that are pulled on over the head.

MEASUREMENTS IN SIZING TABLES AND CLOTHING SIZES
Unlike individual body measurements, measurements in sizing tables have been averaged from a series of measurements and matched with a size from the table. Measurements in sizing tables often differ significantly from industry to industry and from company to company. Many countries inevitably have their own sizing standards since body types differ regionally.

CLOTHING SIZES FOR ADULTS
Standard sizes for women refer to a body height from 65 to 68 inches (165 to 172 cm). For shorter woman below a body height of 65 inches (165 cm), there are petite sizes, for taller women with a height over 68 inches (172 cm) tall sizes.

CLOTHING SIZES FOR CHILDREN
Clothing sizes for children's garments are based on body height and are spaced in intervals of 2.4 inches (6 cm). Girls' sizes have a narrower waist than the sizes for boys, but a larger hip circumference. Proportions become slimmer with increasing size. For children whose figure deviates from the national average, there are slim and husky sizes.

! Not all sizes are the same. If you want to crochet a garment following a ready-to-use pattern, don't rely solely on the garment sizes listed in the instructions. In European **CLOTHING SIZES** alone, there are very big differences between nominally the same sizes: Italian clothing sizes for ladies are larger by three units than German clothing sizes, the French ones by one unit. US sizes also have different standards, which can vary among brands and manufacturers. It should also be noted that the proportions can differ significantly.

Increases and Decreases

Increasing and decreasing stitches—resulting in a higher or lower overall stitch count—is what shapes a crocheted piece. This allows you to produce garments with slanted sides or a sloping neckline, or to create rounded necklines, armholes, or sleeve caps, as well as to shape flat motifs such as granny squares, and to produce three-dimensional shapes.

INCREASING STITCHES

When working increases, the total stitch count rises either on account of additional individual stitches within the row or round or through multiple stitches added over a new section.

INCREASING INDIVIDUAL STITCHES

Whether at the edges or within a row or round, the principle of increasing individual stitches is the same: 2 stitches are crocheted into the same insertion point, thus "doubling" the stitch.

! Increases in HALF DOUBLE CROCHETS, DOUBLE CROCHETS, AS WELL AS TREBLE CROCHETS AND TALLER are made using this method of doubling stitches, too.

INCREASING INDIVIDUAL STITCHES WITHIN A ROW
Into the same insertion point as the stitch worked last (here: single crochet), crochet 1 stitch more. The stitch has been doubled; the stitch count increased by 1 stitch.

X Working MULTIPLE STITCHES INTO THE SAME STITCH creates effects, such as fans or shells (> page 43), or raised elements, such as bobbles (> page 51). These groups of stitches can be considered building blocks for stitch patterns.

X When increases are worked at GREATER INTERVALS, it is recommended to mark the LAST INCREASE with a stitch marker.

! If turning chains do NOT REPLACE THE FIRST STITCH (> page 64) when working in double crochet, work 2 double crochets each into the first and last actual stitch of the previous row.

INCREASING INDIVIDUAL STITCHES AT THE EDGES

For increases of single crochets at the side edges, work 2 stitches each into the first and into the last stitch of a row.

For taller stitches, such as double crochet, at the beginning of the row, after the turning chains, work the first double crochet directly into the last stitch of the previous row (the first stitch of the current row after having turned).

At the end of the row, work 2 double crochets into the topmost chain of the 3 turning chains.

INCREASING INDIVIDUAL STITCHES WITH CHAINS

An individual stitch can also be increased by a single chain worked between 2 stitches. This type of increase is relatively inconspicuous for single crochet—a short stitch—and blends well into the surrounding stitches.

In the following row or round, insert the hook at the increase spot either under the chain (in the chain space) or into the chain itself. The finished increases are barely noticeable in the surrounding single crochets.

1 In the appropriate spot, chain 1.

2 Work the next single crochet not into the same but into the following regular stitch.

In double crochet, when an individual stitch is increased by working a single chain, a small hole forms. If further increases are worked in regular intervals in the same spot, these holes can be deliberately used to accentuate the increase line.

X Increasing by way of a single chain is well suited for working in single crochet and WITH THICKER YARNS

THE POSITION OF THE INCREASED STITCHES

If individual increases are placed directly at the edges, stitches in this area appear to have step-like small jogs, which don't affect the overall shape. This increase type is common and is often used in filet crochet patterns.

To achieve a straight edge without steps, the individual increases are worked 1 stitch in from the edge. If a crocheted edging will be added later, this is the best setup for a straight-edge line. For this, at the beginning of the row, work 2 stitches into the second single crochet or the first double crochet after the turning chains, respectively. At the end of the row, work 2 stitches into the next-to-last stitch.

  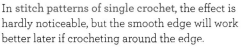  

In stitch patterns of single crochet, the effect is hardly noticeable, but the smooth edge will work better later if crocheting around the edge.

For double crochet, this method works the same way and yields a more noticeable visual difference: At left, increases have been worked directly at the edge; at right, 1 stitch in from the edge.

100

! If there is a special stitch pattern above the increased stitches with pattern repeats that repeat multiple times, when crocheting over the crocheted chain of the extension, the stitch pattern has to be **CONTINUED** matching the main part.

! If MULTIPLE STITCHES need to be increased WITHIN A ROW, this cannot be done in one spot, but the increases have to be worked as individual increases, evenly distributed within the row. Spacing the increases will result in a nice, even curve in the crocheted piece (> page 122).

! For taller basic stitches, add the appropriate number of TURNING CHAINS at the BEGINNING OF THE ROW (> page 64).

••• How to crochet into chains is explained on page 58.

INCREASING MULTIPLE STITCHES AT THE EDGES

If instructions state to "extend a crocheted piece at the same height at both ends of the row" by multiple stitches, additional stitches are to be added for the new sections (for example, when in a T-shaped pullover, the sleeves will be worked in one piece with the Front or Back). To ensure that the first row above the increases will be at the same height, the extensions are worked differently on the right and left edges. The method is shown here for single crochet, but the principle can also be used for other stitch types.

INCREASING MULTIPLE STITCHES AT THE BEGINNING OF THE ROW

The basis for an increase at the right edge of the crocheted piece (i.e., at the beginning of the row), must be prepared before turning at the end of the previous row.

1 Before turning, crochet a chain of the required stitch count plus any turning chains.

2 After having turned, work single crochet along the chain, working the first single crochet in the second chain as counted from the hook.

3 Continue the stitch pattern into the existing crocheted piece to the end of the row. The end of the row is at the same time the beginning of the increases at the left edge.

✗ The foundation stitch increase can be used for all stitch types. For double crochet and taller stitches, before inserting the hook for the base loop, place the number of yarn overs appropriate for the height of the stitch onto the hook (*beginning foundation stitches > page 59*).

INCREASING MULTIPLE STITCHES AT THE END OF THE ROW

Increases at the left edge are crocheted onto the end of the row one stitch after another with a so-called "base chain," which allows for the new stitches to be at the same height as the current row. Every base chain replaces a single beginning chain.

1 For the first stitch to be increased, insert the hook into the insertion point of the last single crochet and pull the working yarn through the fabric. There are 2 loops on the hook now.

2 Make a yarn over, and pull the working yarn through the first loop on the hook—the first base chain has been created. There are 2 loops on the hook now.

3 Place another yarn over onto the hook and pull the working yarn through both loops on the hook at once. The first single crochet has been increased.

4 For the second stitch to be increased, insert the hook into the base chain of the stitch worked before and pull the working yarn through. Grasp the working yarn again and first pull it through the base chain and then complete the single crochet as usual.

Repeat Step 4 continuously until the required number of stitches has been increased. From the next row on, continue the crocheted piece over the whole width.

INCREASING BY ADDING ON A FOUNDATION CHAIN

When increasing multiple stitches at the end of a row, there is a simple alternative to foundation stitches: A new beginning chain is crocheted onto the piece. This method is suggested if increases are needed for a long stretch, such as for the whole length of a sleeve, or are followed by a delicate lace pattern since, in this case, the beginning rows of the added sections at both ends of the row will look identical.

1 Work to the last 2 stitches of the previous row, remove the hook from the working loop, and place a stitch marker into the working loop. Leave the working yarn hanging. Now insert the hook into the last single crochet of the previous row, and join new working yarn here. Crochet a beginning chain for the required stitch-count. (Remember, do not count the turning chain!) Pull the yarn tail through the last loop.

How to crochet into chains is explained on page 58.

2 Place the marked working loop onto the hook again, and work to the end of the single crochets of the previous row.

Then work the stitch pattern above the new foundation chain. From the next row on, continue working over the full new width of the crocheted piece.

 Through crocheting multiple stitches together, a variety of **STITCH PATTERNS** can be created.

 When **MORE THAN 2 STITCHES** are worked off together, an inverted **FAN SHAPE** or a **BOBBLE** is created (> *page 52/53*). For this, first leave the last loop of every stitch on the hook, and finally pull the working yarn through all loops on the hook together at once.

DECREASING STITCHES

Decreasing stitches, too, is needed in the shaping of crocheted pieces, such as for armholes and necklines in garments. Through decreases, the stitch count is being reduced, either by a single stitch or by multiple stitches over a longer section.

DECREASING INDIVIDUAL STITCHES

Whether at the edges or within a row or round, the principle of decreasing individual stitches is the same: 2 stitches are crocheted together. Two stitches merge into one another so that only one stitch (2 loops of a V) remains to be worked into on the next round. This action is called "crocheting (off) together."

CROCHETING 2 SINGLE CROCHETS TOGETHER

1 When 2 single crochets are to be crocheted together, insert the hook for the first single crochet and pull the working yarn through. To work the second single crochet, insert the hook into the next stitch and pull the working yarn through. There are 3 loops on the hook now.

2 Pull the working yarn through once more, pulling it through all 3 loops on the hook at once. The stitches have been crocheted together, the stitch count has been reduced by 1, and 1 shared final loop has been created.

CROCHETING 2 HALF DOUBLE CROCHETS TOGETHER

1 When 2 half double crochets are to be crocheted together, for the first half double crochet, make a yarn over onto the hook, insert the hook, and pull the working yarn through the fabric—there are 3 loops on the hook now. To work the second half double crochet, place a yarn over onto the hook, insert the hook into the next stitch, and pull the working yarn through the fabric. There are 5 loops on the hook altogether.

2 Pull the working yarn through once more, pulling it through all 5 loops on the hook at once. The stitches have been crocheted together, the stitch count has been reduced by 1, and 1 shared final loop has been created.

CROCHETING 2 DOUBLE CROCHETS TOGETHER

1 When 2 double crochets are to be crocheted together, first work the first double crochet, except for the last 2 loops: make a yarn over onto the hook, insert the hook, pull the working yarn through, and then yarn over and pull it through the first 2 loops on the hook at once.

2 Repeat these steps for the second double crochet, inserting the hook into the next stitch. There are 3 loops on the hook now (= the respective last loops of both double crochets, plus the working loop).

3 Pull the working yarn through once more, pulling it through all 3 loops on the hook at once. Two double crochets have been crocheted together, the stitch count has been reduced by 1 stitch.

! When crocheting double crochets, TREBLE CROCHETS, AND TALLER STITCHES together, first complete every stitch individually UP TO THE LAST LOOP (i.e., crochet the loops off the hook in pairs with a yarn over in between). Finally, pull the working yarn through once more, pulling it through all loops on the hook at once.

SINGLE DECREASE BY SKIPPING ONE STITCH

A single stitch can also be decreased by skipping 1 stitch of the previous row or round. For single crochet, a shallow and compact basic stitch type, this way of decreasing is relatively inconspicuous and blends well into the surrounding stitches.

1 Before the decrease spot, work 1 single crochet as usual. To work the next single crochet, insert the hook into the stitch after the next one.

2 Work the single crochet as usual. 1 stitch stays unused; the stitch count has been reduced by 1.

For sloped sides, in evenly spaced rows, the first stitch and the next-to-last stitch of a row are skipped, which works especially well for crocheting with thicker yarns. For this, at the beginning of the row, after the turning chain, work the first single crochet into the second stitch of the previous row, and at the end of the row, skip the next-to-last stitch, and work 1 single crochet into the last stitch. When, however, this type of decrease is used with double crochet, a small gap forms, which disrupts the flow of the fabric. If further decreases are worked in regular intervals in the same spot, these holes can be used purposefully to accentuate the decrease edge. In the pictured example, the decreases are set in from the edge by 3 double crochets (*decrease stitches > page 104*).

! If a crocheted piece WITH SLANTED SIDE EDGES is being worked, the turning chains should not be located outside the edge of the crocheted piece, but always REPLACE the FIRST STITCH OF THE ROW. Otherwise, the edge won't have a nice-looking slant.

! In HALF DOUBLE CROCHET, TREBLE CROCHET, AND TALLER STITCHES, for an individual decrease directly at the beginning of the row, reduce the otherwise usual NUMBER OF TURNING CHAINS by 1 chain.

DECREASE AT THE EDGES

For decreases at the side edges, the two first and the two last stitches of a row are crocheted together.

For decreases in single crochet, crochet the first two single crochets at the beginning of the row together and at the end of the row crochet the next-to-last and the last single crochet together.

For taller stitches, such as double crochet, to decrease at the beginning of the row, work only 2 turning chains (i.e., 1 chain fewer than the usual 3 turning chains that would normally replace the first double crochet). Then work the first double crochet into the second stitch of the previous row. The row located above will later end in this stitch.

Continue the row, and for the decrease at the end of the row, crochet the last 2 double crochets together.

LOCATION OF DECREASE STITCHES

Placing individual decreases directly at the edges results in a compact stitch appearance with step-like, small offsets, which won't affect the overall shape much. This decrease type is very common and is often used in lace patterns.

For a smooth, jogless edge shape, individual decreases should be worked 1 stitch in from the edge. If instructions state to work an edging around the crocheted piece later, this is the best basis for a straight edge.

How to work decorative edgings around OUTSIDE EDGES is explained on pages 155–159. How to incorporate a border frame is described on pages 165–172.

Decrease at the edge in single crochet

Offset decrease in single crochet

Decrease at the edge in double crochet

Offset decrease in double crochet

At the beginning of the row, crochet the second and third stitch together. At the end of the row, work to the last 3 stitches, and then crochet the following 2 stitches together and finally work the last stitch. For comparison, both versions of the decrease are shown. When an edging is added, the result will be even more noticeable.

DECREASING MULTIPLE STITCHES

If a crocheted piece must be narrowed at the same height by multiple stitches at both ends of the row, decreases have likewise to be worked **differently at the right and left edge**. This can, for instance, be necessary to create angular armholes in garments. Round edges can also begin with decreasing multiple stitches (> page 109).

DECREASING MULTIPLE STITCHES AT THE BEGINNING OF A ROW

To decrease multiple stitches **at the right edge** of a piece, the stitches to be decreased at the beginning of the row have to be bridged. For this, **crochet along** these stitches of the previous row **with slip stitches**, which, being shallow, do not add much height. This will get you to the spot set in from the edge for the new beginning of the row and eliminates having to break the working yarn and joining it anew.

Before the row can be continued in the appropriate stitch pattern, height-adjustment chains must be worked to reach the required height, for instance, in the case of single crochet, 1 chain. This chain replaces the turning chain that would be normally worked at the beginning of the row and is usually crocheted before turning. In this case, the new row begins set in from the edge because of the decreases.

DECREASING MULTIPLE STITCHES AT THE END OF A ROW

To decrease multiple stitches **at the left edge** of a piece, the row ends by as many stitches earlier as need to be decreased. At the end of the row, the last stitches before the edge are not crocheted into. In pattern instructions, this process is often called "leaving stitches unworked."
The new edge of the crocheted piece shifts inward by the number of stitches to be decreased. This is followed by the turning chain, after which the crocheted piece is continued over a reduced width.

> **!** The principle of decreasing multiple stitches can also be **APPLIED TO OTHER BASIC** stitches. Be sure to consider the appropriate **NUMBER OF HEIGHT-ADJUSTMENT CHAINS** to be worked at the beginning of the row.

> **!** If **MULTIPLE STITCHES** are to be **DECREASED** within a row, this cannot be done all in one spot. Decreases have to be worked as individual decreases and **EVENLY DISTRIBUTED** within the row. This results in a curve in the crocheted piece (> page 122).

Shaping
Garments

Every garment is based on schematics for its individual pieces, which show the shape of each piece at one glance. Additionally, this graphic representation contains each part's measurements for length and width, and in most cases also references to the direction of work as well as the boundaries of stitch patterns. To shape the pieces of a garment according to the schematic, strategically placed increases and decreases are necessary.

HOW MANY STITCHES to increase for the desired width is calculated on the basis of the **GAUGE SWATCH** (> page 95).

SHAPING AT THE EDGES

If a crocheted piece is shaped at the edges only, the shape itself stays flat and the parts are later joined together by seams. To work a nicely shaped edge, two numbers are relevant: first, the total number of rows, in most cases heightwise, over which the respective shaping shall take place, as well as the stitch count that needs to be increased or decreased in total. Further important are frequency and distribution, which in turn depend on the desired shape—sloped, curved, or angular.

SHAPING AT INCREASE EDGES

Depending on the type and cut of a garment, it might be necessary to create horizontal, slanted, or curved edges. For this, either multiple stitches can be increased at once or a number of individual stitches can be gradually increased—or a combination of both increasing methods can be used.

HORIZONTAL INCREASE EDGE

If instructions state to "extend a crocheted piece at the same height at both ends of the row" by multiple stitches, all additional stitches are increased at once, as explained on page 100. The transition will turn out more rounded if already in the row worked before, 1 single stitch each is increased at both edges. Horizontal increase edges are often used in garments in which the sleeves are worked in one piece with the body in a T-shaped cut.

SLANTED INCREASE EDGE

To evenly widen a crocheted piece, 1 stitch each is increased in evenly spaced rows at both side edges. For this, divide the number of rows needed for the desired height by the total number of stitches to be increased for each side.

The resulting number shows in which row the increases must be repeated. If for instance, 5 stitches each shall be increased on both sides over 40 rows heightwise, in every 8th row, 1 increase each must be worked at the beginning and the end of the row. Slanted increase edges are often used for side sloping on Fronts and Backs as well as for sleeve tapering in sweaters and jackets.

CURVED INCREASE EDGE

To work a curved shaping at the edge, in most cases—but also depending on the stitch pattern—single and multiple stitch increases must be combined.

At the start of the curve, individual stitches must be increased in regular intervals, followed by increases in increments of multiple stitches per row. Curved increase edges can be found in overcast shoulders and batwing sleeves worked onto the body.

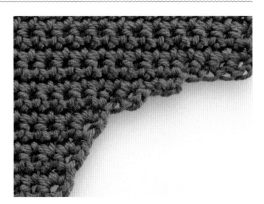

! If an **ARMHOLE** is worked above a sloped side edge, the last increase for the slope should be worked **SEVERAL ROWS BEFORE THE START** of the armhole decreases.

SHAPING AT DECREASE EDGES

Horizontal, slanted, or curved edges can be formed by decreasing in different ways. For this, sections are either skipped or "bridged," or individual or multiple stitches are decreased regularly and/or gradually.

HORIZONTAL DECREASE EDGE

If instructions state to "narrow a crocheted piece at the same height at both ends of the row" by multiple stitches, these sections either stay not crocheted into or are bridged with slip stitches. The crocheted piece is then continued over a reduced width.

This applies, for instance, to angularly shaped armholes in garments.

For a square neckline in the middle of the row, leave the number of stitches unworked that corresponds to the width of the neckline. Then complete both sides separately and with a new inside edge that goes to the inner point of the shoulder seam.

●●● How to decrease multiple stitches at the edges is explained **IN DETAIL** on page 105.

! To decrease 1 stitch, 2 stitches are **WORKED OFF TOGETHER** (> page 102).

✗ Placing decreases 1 stitch in from the edge creates a **STRAIGHT EDGE** into which an edging can be crocheted later (> page 104).

✗ When decreases for a sloped edge are worked in a **LACY STITCH PATTERN**, the section up to the outer insertion point has in most cases to be bridged with a **TALLER BASIC STITCH** than those in the actual stitch pattern.

SLANTED DECREASE EDGE

If instructions state to "evenly narrow a crocheted piece" at both side edges, 1 stitch each is decreased in evenly spaced rows. For this, divide the number of rows needed for the desired height by the total number of stitches to be decreased for each side. The resulting number shows in which row the decreases are to be repeated. If for instance, 6 stitches each shall be decreased on both sides over 36 rows, the first decrease is worked right at the beginning of the first row. Then 1 stitch each is decreased in every 6th row, 5 times more. After the last decrease, 5 rows are worked to the required height of 36 rows. Slanted decrease edges are used for raglan shaping and V-shaped necklines.

A **V-shaped neckline** consists of two slanted decrease edges. First, the crocheted piece is divided in the middle. Then both halves are continued separately, creating two new inside edges in the middle of the piece, which go up to the inner point of the shoulder seam.

When decreases are worked several stitches set in from the edge, the stitches at the edge run parallel to the slant and emphasize the decrease line. If the decrease spots are visibly separated by a change in stitch pattern, such as with a narrow border, the shape can also be specially highlighted.

MULTIPLE DECREASES FOR A SHALLOW SLOPE

Crochet stitches are of different heights. Between slip stitches, single crochet, and treble crochet and taller stitches, there is a significant height difference. For this reason, a wedge shape can be achieved using different basic stitches, beginning with slip stitch, continued with single crochet, half double crochet, double crochet, and treble crochet, and ending with double treble crochet. This difference can be used to develop a step-less sloping line within a row.

Smaller height differences are also created if in double crochet and taller stitches, the first loop is pulled longer. This can be factored in, too, during finer grading.

CURVED DECREASE EDGE

A pleasingly shaped curve for an armhole or neckline is produced if decreases of individual and multiple stitches are combined. At the start of the curve, first skip several stitches, leaving them unworked, and then gradually decrease fewer and fewer stitches in every row, so that the curve ascends shallowly. Then proceed to working individual decreases in evenly spaced rows. For an armhole, the curve transitions into a straight course of the edge. Similarly for the neckline—here, too, during the last rows, no stitches are decreased.

For taller basic stitches, shown in the example of double crochet in the photo at right, at the beginning of the row after the first multiple-stitch-decrease bridged with slip stitches, work 1 single crochet and 1 half double crochet one after another to create a jogless transition to the row height of double crochet. If decreasing evenly on both edges, end the row mirror-inverted (i.e., before the new end of the row, work 1 half double crochet, 1 single crochet, and 1 slip stitch).

Sleeve Cap

A sleeve cap can be divided into three segments for shaping:
- a curve, starting shallow and then rising,
- a slant in the middle part,
- a rounded peak, which first rises quickly and then proceeds gradually to the finished height.

The decreases for a sleeve cap begin, as described before for the armhole, with a shallow curve, which transitions into a slant by decreasing individual stitches in regular intervals. Subsequently, for the cap, more and more stitches at once are incrementally decreased, in opposite order to the curve at the beginning, until finally the remaining stitches in the middle of the sleeve—for a narrow sleeve over a width of about 2.4 inches (6 cm)—are left unworked, and the sleeve is completed.

X **TALL CROCHET STITCHES,** such as double crochet, produce a **STEPPED EDGE** if decreasing multiple stitches several times in a row by leaving them unworked (i.e., not crocheting into them and not bypassing them with slip stitches). "Steps" of this kind can be **AVOIDED** by using the different stitch heights to create a linear transition. In the example, 3 stitches per row have been decreased.

X To work a sleeve cap, a **PAPER CUTOUT IN ORIGINAL SIZE** is helpful so the shape can always be rechecked during crocheting.

SHAPING WITHIN THE CROCHETED PIECE

Increases and decreases within a crocheted piece can be cleverly incorporated into the stitch pattern so that they are barely noticeable or can be used deliberately as design elements. They are useful for changing width and creating shapes. Within the crocheted piece, increases and decreases can also be worked to minimize the number of seams. For example, in a raglan top crocheted from the neckline down in which Front, Back, and Sleeve(s) are worked in one piece, increases can be placed exactly in the raglan line spots.

GATHERING WIDTH AND RUCHING

Working evenly distributed decreases within a row or round reduces the stitch count and therefore the width of a crocheted piece. If a large number of stitches is decreased in the same row or round, a ruffle effect is created, which will be even more pronounced with an increasing number of decreases and makes for a great design element. In every decrease spot, 2 or 3 stitches should be crocheted together.

The opposite effect can be achieved with evenly distributed increases within a row or round. As more stitches are increased, the width becomes all the more abundant. This flaring width creates a ruffle or billowing effect.

SHAPING DARTS THROUGH INCREASES AND DECREASES

When garments are not crocheted in individual pieces but worked all in one piece, they don't have side seams in which shaping elements such as increases and decreases could be hidden. This is, for example, the case with pullovers crocheted in the round or when Fronts and Back for a jacket are worked in one piece. If a close-fitting design is desired nonetheless, so-called shaping darts can be included in spots at which seams would be otherwise located.

The word "darts" originates in tailoring, where fabric width is stitched down to obtain close-fitting shapes. In crocheting, the term is somewhat misleading because here shaping darts are not retroactively added but are included during crocheting by working increases or decreases. The increases or decreases are always placed in the same spot and at regular height intervals. The more rows or rounds located in between, the better a shaping dart will blend into the surrounding stitches. Additionally, it allows for a "softened" transition in the shaping, without causing unsightly bulges.

! To decrease 1 stitch, 2 stitches are crocheted together (> page 102). A double decrease is created when 3 stitches are crocheted together.

X Calculations for shaping darts should always be based on a SCHEMATIC WITH INDICATED MEASUREMENTS of the desired crochet project.

REDUCING WIDTH

To reduce width, decreases are worked atop each other at regular height intervals. For even distribution, determine from the gauge swatch how many stitches should be decreased for the desired width reduction and over what height this will have to happen. It should be noted that the first decrease needs to be placed with enough distance from the beginning edge. If, for instance, 8 stitches are to be decreased over 17 rows, calculate 17 ÷ 8 = 2 + 1 remainder row. The first decrease is worked immediately at the beginning of Row 1; then, in every other row, 1 stitch each is decreased, 7 times more. After the last decrease, 2 more rows are worked even to the required height of 17 rows.

  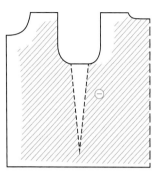

To work the actual decrease, mark the decrease spot (= spot in which otherwise a seam would be located) between 2 stitches with a piece of contrasting color yarn. Then, in the previously calculated distribution, alternating between before and after the marking, crochet 2 stitches each together. In the photo, the total width to be reduced has been marked, too.

This way, for a top worked bottom-up, for instance, the width from the hip in the direction of the chest can be reduced, as shown in the schematic.

ADDING IN ADDITIONAL WIDTH

To add in additional width, increases are worked atop each other at regular height intervals. For even distribution, determine from the gauge swatch how many stitches must be increased for the desired additional width and over what height this will have to happen. If, for instance, 8 stitches are to be increased over 17 rows, calculate 17 ÷ 8 = 2 + 1 remainder row. The first increase is worked immediately at the beginning of Row 1; then, in every other row, 1 stitch each is increased, 7 times more. After the last increase, 2 more rows are worked to the required height of 17 rows.

  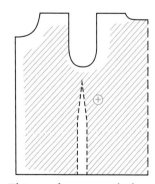

To work the actual increase, mark the increase spot (= spot in which otherwise a seam would be located) between 2 stitches with a piece of contrasting color yarn. Then, in the previously calculated distribution, alternating between before and after the marking, work 2 stitches each into the same insertion point. In the photo, the total width to be added has been marked, too.

This way, for a top worked top-down, additional width can be added from the waist down, as shown in the schematic.

SLEEVE TAPERING can also be worked with decreases within the crocheted piece for a sleeve crocheted top-down in the round.

More information about gauge can be found on page 95.

SLEEVE TAPERING can also be worked with increases at regular intervals within the crocheted piece for a sleeve crocheted bottom-up in the round.

Working a garment in one piece **ENTIRELY SEAMLESS** sounds tempting, considering how much seaming can be eliminated. However, it is important to keep in mind that seams stabilize the shape of a large crocheted piece and are especially useful for heavy yarns.

> **!** **A SINGLE DECREASE** can be worked by skipping a stitch *(> page 103)*. To work a **SINGLE INCREASE,** a single chain can be added between two stitches *(> page 99).*

WAIST-SHAPING INCREASES AND DECREASES

For tops crocheted seamlessly in one piece, waist-shaping increases and decreases are placed at the sides where the side seams between Front and Back would normally be found. For garments worked bottom-up, they are created by first reducing width from the hip to the waist, as described on page 111, and then subsequently, adding in width again from the waist to the armhole. The decrease or increase spot, which had been marked with a piece of contrasting color yarn, hereby falls on the imagined side seam.

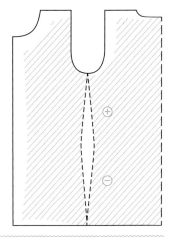

ACCENTUATED WAIST

When the waist is to be additionally emphasized, first the imagined side seam is marked as center line, and 1 increase or decrease each is placed before and after this center line—overall at a distance of 2 to 3 stitches. Make sure to increase or decrease 2 stitches instead of 1 for each increase or decrease row in this case. In the photo, to the right and the left of the marked center line, increases and decreases have been worked with a distance of 1 stitch each in between. Additionally, the reduced or added width has been marked in the photo.

ADDITIONAL WAIST-SHAPING DARTS

If the pattern calls for a very close fit for a top, additional waist-shaping darts can be included. These are to be placed vertically on the Back and Front. The distance to the center of Back and Front depends on garment size, the shape of the pattern, and on the desired final result you want to achieve.

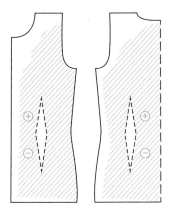

FURTHER SHAPING OPTIONS

There are a few more options for shaping a crocheted piece while it is being worked. These either use the height differences between different stitch types or work increases or decreases inconspicuously into the stitch pattern.

SHORT ROWS

Short rows make it possible to work more rows over part of the stitches than over the remainder of the initial row. They are a method for incorporating rounded edges or inserts. A row is "short" because all of the stitches in the row are not crocheted into; the work on the row is terminated before the actual end of the row. At the same time, the height differences of the stitches are used for "advancing and receding" in a jogless transition, making short rows better suited for pieces crocheted in taller stitch types. A short row can bevel the edge either at both ends of the row or just at one side. A nice curve can be created when shortening several rows atop each other by multiple stitches each.

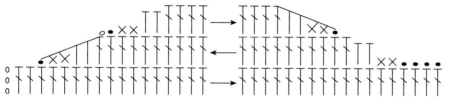

●●● CROCHET
SYMBOLS are explained on pages 340–343.

In garments, horizontal bust darts, a shallow neckline, or shoulder sloping can be shaped with short rows. A generous hem width can also be added this way to crocheted garments worked sideways.

WORKING SHORT ROWS

Let's look at an example: When working a crocheted piece in double crochet, the first short row starts with 1 slip stitch, 2 single crochets, and 2 half double crochets to achieve a jogless transition to the row height of double crochet.

The end of the row is worked in the opposite order. To do this, the stitches are crocheted off the hook along the slanted edge one after another a special way: In the first working step of each stitch, 1 loop remains on the hook—for 1 double crochet, make a yarn over, insert the hook and pull a loop through, crochet the first 2 loops off the hook together, and then make another yarn over onto the hook and crochet it off; for each one of 2 half double crochets, make 1 yarn over onto the hook, insert the hook, and pull the working yarn through the fabric, and then crochet 2 loops off the hook together; for each one of 2 single crochets, insert the hook, and pull the working yarn through the fabric, and then crochet 1 loop off the hook; for 1 slip stitch, insert the hook, and pull the working yarn through the fabric—there are a total of 7 loops on the hook now.

! The NEW END of the short row is located before the first shallower stitch that had been worked to shorten the row. For every subsequent short row, the wedge has to be started sufficiently ahead of this previous end of the row.

Short rows are a great option to add **WAVE-SHAPED BORDERS** to garments and blankets.

In the second working step, going back, first crochet the first loop off the hook by itself, and then, one after another, crochet 2 loops together; finally, crochet the last 3 loops together. Chain 1 and turn. Work the next short row the same way.

CROCHETING INTO SHORT ROWS
After the last short row has been worked, continue working over all stitches again, regardless of the different stitch heights: The crocheted piece has been shaped without having worked any seam at all.

The stitches at the beginning of the rows can be crocheted into as usual. Into the stitches that had been crocheted off the hook the special way at the end of the rows, for every stitch insert the hook under the vertical loop of the stitch.

USING THE DIFFERENCES IN STITCH HEIGHT
Crochet stitches are of different heights (> *page* 64), which can be used for shaping crocheted pieces.

In the first example, in every other row, stitches of different heights have been combined, which creates narrow wedges. In the second example, wedge-shaped rows are worked directly one after another, which results in a greater curvature.

CHANGING HOOK SIZE

A shape can also be changed by regularly changing hook sizes. For this, begin with a crochet hook 0.5 mm (about 2 US size steps) smaller than the smallest one recommended on the yarn label. After having worked a few rows, go up in hook size in increments of 0.5 mm. End with a hook size about 0.5 mm (about 2 US size steps) larger than the largest hook size recommended for the yarn. In the same way, the width, too, can be reduced.

! Keep in mind that different hook sizes also influence STITCH DEFINITION AND DRAPE of the crocheted fabric: dense and compact with smaller hook size versus airy and open with a larger crochet hook.

SHAPING BY PATTERN VARIATION

Increases and decreases can be so cleverly integrated into the stitch pattern that they are barely noticeable and appear to be used **on purpose** as part of the stitch pattern's design.

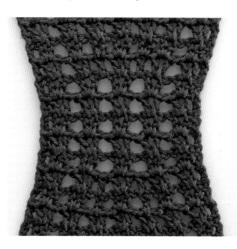

Using chains is an especially simple method for changing shape. The number of chains is gradually increased or decreased.

If width is to be added or reduced in a **more complex stitch pattern**, any existing pattern repeat must be faded out or newly introduced step by step over several rows or rounds. For this, increases or decreases should be placed in **suitable spots in the stitch pattern**—for instance where later in the stitch pattern 2 stitches will be worked into the same stitch anyway or will be crocheted together.

In this example, the increases are part of the emerging stitch pattern—the expansion appears as if it were created all on its own.

Flat Motifs

Round and rectangular motifs, ornamental flowers, and granny squares are started from the center, crocheted outward in the round, and constantly increased in diameter. Strategically placed increases are necessary for achieving the desired shape. Further increases must be usually worked in every round to keep the shape flat.

 How to work the popular GRANNY SQUARE can be found on page 317.

! The phrase "CROCHETING IN THE ROUND" is also used for angular flat shapes to express the difference to crocheting in turned rows.

 There are MULTIPLE WAYS to start a shape in the middle, which are explained in detail beginning on page 67.

X A circular shape can also be worked in SPIRAL ROUNDS, for which it is helpful to mark the beginning of the round (> page 71).

CIRCULAR SHAPE

To work a flat, round shape, within each round, stitches must be increased—evenly distributed. Increase spots are staggered in subsequent rounds; otherwise a polygon with pronounced increase lines would be created instead of a circle.

CIRCLE IN SINGLE CROCHET
Instructions
Begin the circle with 1 chain in the center (> page 67). Then work sc in rounds, beginning every round with ch1, and ending with 1 sl-st into the first sc to join.

Round 1: Work sc6.
Round 2: Double every st around—that is, work sc2 each into every st (= 12 sts).
Round 3: Double every other st around, work sc1 into all other sts (= 18 sts).
Round 4: Double every 3rd st around, work sc1 into all other sts (= 24 sts).
Round 5: Shift increase spots to place increases staggered between previous increases.

For this, first double the 2nd st, and then [double every 4th st] 5 times, work sc1 into all other sts (= 30 sts).
Round 6: Double every 5th st around, again shifting increase spots, work sc1 into all other sts (= 36 sts).
Following the established pattern, work the circle to the desired size, staggering the increases in every round.

CIRCLE IN DOUBLE CROCHET
Instructions
Begin with a magic circle (> page 68) in the center. Then work dc in the round, beginning every rnd with 3 height-adjustment chains (= replaces the 1st st of the rnd), and closing the round with 1 sl-st into the topmost one of the 3 chains.

 ABBREVIATIONS can be found on page 344.

 To learn how to work 2 stitches into the first stitch of the second round, see page 70, "Beginning subsequent rounds."

Round 1: Work dc15.
Round 2: Double every st around—that is, work dc2 each into every st (= 30 sts).
Round 3: Double every other st around, work dc1 into all other sts (= 45 sts).
Round 4: Double every 3rd st around, work dc1 into all other sts (= 60 sts).

Following the established pattern, work the circle to the desired size. For a circle worked in double crochet, too, increase spots must be staggered in every round worked.

CIRCLES IN DIFFERENT STITCH TYPES

Circular shapes can also be crocheted in different stitch types. The number of stitches required for the first round varies with stitch type.

stitch type	stitches in first round
single crochet	6
half double crochet	10
double crochet	15
treble crochet	18

In every new round, as many stitches are increased as are worked in the first round. This means that with every new round, there will be 1 stitch more between increase spots.

For double crochet and taller stitches, height-adjustment chains replace the first stitch of the round. From Round 4 or 5 on, increases must be placed staggered to the previous round to achieve a circular shape.

The fiber content of the yarn and the gauge of the crocheted fabric also have an impact on the above-mentioned benchmark numbers. With increasing diameter, it should be periodically checked whether the motif does still lie flat. If the outside edge curls upward, more stitches need to be increased; if the outside edge becomes wavy, the stitch count must be reduced.

How to **CROCHET IN THE ROUND** is explained in detail beginning on page 67.

SQUARE

A rectangle with sides of equal length can also be crocheted in different ways. Here, four variations for shaping a square are shown. The plain patterns in single crochet or double crochet direct attention to the way the corners are formed.

SQUARE IN SINGLE CROCHET

For a square in single crochet, increases are worked 4 times in every round at equal intervals. At every corner, 1 chain is worked.

Instructions

Begin the square with 1 chain in the center (> *page 67*). Then crochet in rounds, beginning every round with ch1, and ending with 1 sl-st into the first sc to join. From Round 2 on, insert the hook through the back loop of the stitches only (> *page 37*).

Round 1: * Sc1, ch1 (= corner), repeat from * 3 times more.
All following rounds: Into every sc of the previous rnd, work sc1, in the chain space (= corner), work [sc1, ch1, sc1].

Stitch sequences within **ANGULAR BRACKETS** [ ] are worked into the same insertion point.

The **INCREASES** at the **CORNERS** can also be worked with **DOUBLE CROCHETS** instead of **CHAINS** from Round 2 on. For this, before and after the treble crochet at the corners, work [2 double crochets each in the same insertion point] to achieve a flat shape.

ABBREVIATIONS can be found on page 344.

SQUARE IN DOUBLE CROCHET

For a square in double crochet, increases are worked 4 times in every round at equal intervals. The increases needed at the corners are supplemented by chains along the diagonals; there is also 1 treble crochet each.

Instructions

Begin the square with ch6 joined into a ring in the center (> *page 67*). Then work dc in the round, beginning every rnd with 3 height-adjustment chains (= replaces the 1st st of the rnd), and closing the round with 1 sl-st into the topmost one of the 3 chains.
Round 1: Work [3 height-adjustment chains, dc2] into the ring, ch3 at the first corner, * dc3, ch3 at the corner, rep from * 2 times more.
Round 2: Dc1 into every dc; at the corners, work [dc2, ch1, tr1, ch1, dc2] in the ch3-sp.
All following rounds: Dc1 into every dc; at the corners, work [dc2 in ch-sp of previous rnd, ch1, tr1 in tr, ch1, dc2 in ch-sp].

FROM CIRCLE TO SQUARE

A square can also be started with a circle-shaped center.

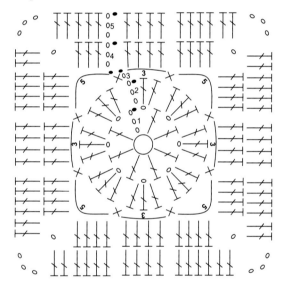

Instructions

Begin the square with a magic circle in the center (> *page 68*), and work Rounds 1 and 2 as for the circle in dc (> *page 116*). The stitch count in Round 2 must be a multiple of 4.
Round 3: Work according to the chart in sc, bridging sts with chains to create 4 corners.

Round 4: Work according to the chart, dc in ch-sp of the previous rnd, and ch1 at each corner.

Round 5 and all following rounds: Work according to chart, dc1 in every dc, and shape the corners.

SQUARE STARTED IN A CORNER

A square shape can also be worked in turned rows with a single increase spot, with diagonal increase lines from one corner to the opposite corner. Traditional potholders often are worked this way.

Instructions

For the textured ridge effect, work sc in back loop only in every row (> *page 37*).
Begin with ch2.
Row 1: Sc3 in the 2nd chain from the hook. The middle stitch of these 3 is the corner stitch.
All following rows: Sc1 into every sc, and sc3 into the middle stitch.

TRIANGLE

For a triangle worked in double crochet, increases are worked 3 times in every round at equal intervals. Corners are shaped by chains.

Instructions

Begin the triangle with a magic circle in the center (> page 68). Then work dc in the round, beginning every rnd with 3 height-adjustment chains (= replaces the 1st st of the rnd), and closing the round with 1 sl-st into the topmost one of the 3 chains.
Round 1: Work [3 height-adjustment chains, dc2] into the magic ring, ch4 for the first corner, * dc3, ch4 for the corner, repeat from * once more.
All following rounds: Dc1 into every dc, and for corner shaping [dc3, ch4, dc3] in ch4-sp of previous rnd.

HEXAGON

A hexagon consists of six corners and six sides of equal length. If increase spots are accented by chains worked in this spot, corners and angle lines will be emphasized. This classic shape can also be combined into a continuous and gapless field of motifs.
To work a hexagon in double crochet, increases are worked 6 times in every round at equal intervals. When dividing for the corners, the stitch count of the first round muat be a multiple of 6.

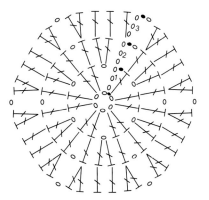

●●● An overview over the **CROCHET CHART SYMBOLS** can be found on pages 340–344.

Instructions

Begin the hexagon with ch6 joined into a ring in the center (> page 67).
Rounds 1–3: Work from crochet chart. Begin every rnd with 3 height-adjustment chains replacing the first dc and closing the round with 1 sl-st into the topmost one of the 3 chains.

If an even larger motif is desired, rep Round 3 continuously; the number of stitches between the corners will increase by 2 sts per round with every round worked.

OCTAGON

An octagon consists of eight corners and eight sides of equal length. The circular-shaped center must be large enough to provide room for corner shaping. For this, begin with a large ring of chains, leaving an opening in the center of the motif. The pictured motif has a circle worked in single crochet in the center, which keeps the center opening small. To work an octagon in double crochet, increases are worked 8 times in every round at equal intervals. To make the corner divisions even, the stitch count of Round 2 must be a multiple of 8.

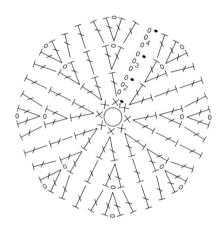

Instructions

Begin the octagon with a magic circle in the center *(> page 68).*
Round 1: Work sc8, join the round with 1 sl-st into the first sc.
Rounds 2–4: Work from crochet chart, beginning every rnd with 3 height-adjustment chains replacing the 1st dc, and closing the round with 1 sl-st into the topmost one of the 3 chains.

If an even larger motif is desired, work as for Round 4 continuously; the number of stitches between the corners will increase by 2 sts per round with every round worked.

OVAL SHAPE

An oval is composed of three shape elements: two half circles with a straight center part in between. In all rounds, over the curved sections, stitches must be increased at evenly distributed intervals to shape the round parts, as described earlier for the circular shape. The center part stays without increases.

To work an oval shape, a beginning chain is crocheted into all around from both sides (> page 69). To calculate the proper length of the foundation chain in the center, the following rule applies: desired length of the finished oval, minus the desired width. Based on gauge, the required stitch count can be calculated.

Instructions

Work into both sides of the beginning chain all around, beginning every round with ch1 and ending with 1 sl-st into the first sc to join. Shape the round parts at both ends as described earlier for the circular shape; between round parts, work the middle part in sc even without increases.

RECTANGLE

A rectangle starts like an oval from a foundation chain in the middle crocheted into on both sides all around (> page 69), but with increases at the ends, always worked in the same corner spots. The length of the foundation chain is calculated as described for the oval.

Instructions

Round 1: Work sc1 into every ch of the beginning chain. At the end of the chain, work [ch1, sc1, ch1, sc1] all into the same insertion point as the last sc. Continue the round, working sc into the unused loops on the opposite side of the beginning chain. At the end, work [ch1, sc1] into the same insertion point as the last sc, ch1, and join the round with 1 sl-st into the first sc.

All following rounds: Work sc1 into every sc; at each corner, in the ch-sp, work [sc1, ch1, sc1]. Begin every round with ch1, and end with 1 sl-st into the first sc to join.

RHOMBUS

In an equilateral rhombus, the angles of the corners are of different sizes, with identical angles at opposite corners. This difference must be taken into account when working the increases at the corners.

Instructions

Begin the rhombus with a foundation chain worked into from both sides (> page 69) as follows:
Round 1: Ch4, sc1 in the 2nd chain from the hook, [sc1, ch1, sc1] twice into the next 2 chains. Continue into the unused loops on the opposite side of the foundation chain, working [sc1, ch1, sc1] into the next chain, sc1 in the same insertion point as the first sc at the beginning of the round, ch1, and then join the round with 1 sl-st.

Rounds 2–5: Work from chart, inserting the hook for sc through the back loop of the stitches only (> page 37). Begin every round with ch1, and end with 1 sl-st into the first sc to join.

If an even larger rhombus shape is desired, further rep Rounds 4 and 5; the stitch count between the corners will increase by 1 st each per side with every round worked.

To **CREATE SHARPLY DEFINED CORNERS**, it is important to always place increases directly atop increase spots of the previous round.

An overview over the **CROCHET CHART SYMBOLS** can be found on pages 340–344.

Three-Dimensional Shapes

Three-dimensional shapes can be worked in the round practically "seamlessly." Increases as well as decreases, distributed evenly throughout the round, account for creating the three-dimensional shape. From basic spheres, rolls, or other curved figures, most often worked in single crochet, items such as animal or doll bodies can be created.

HALF-SPHERE AND SPHERE

To create a smooth curvature for a sphere, stitches must be increased and again decreased evenly distributed over the whole round. When more and more rounds are worked, increases are spaced farther apart, and it is also necessary to shift the increase or decrease spots from round to round. When the shape has reached its widest point, rounds are worked even (without increases or decreases) until a half-sphere has been created. To turn a half-sphere into a full sphere, after the straight section, decreases are worked in reverse, decreasing stitches at the same pace as the former increases.

HALF-SPHERE

Instructions

Begin the half-sphere with 1 chain in the center (> page 67), and then work sc in the round. Either work spiral rounds (> page 71) or begin every round with ch1 and end with 1 sl-st into the first sc to join.

Round 1: Work sc6.

Round 2: Double every st around—that is, work sc2 each into every st (= 12 sts).

Round 3: Double every 3rd st around, work sc1 in all other sts (= 16 sts).

Round 4: Double every 4th st around, work sc1 in all other sts (= 20 sts).

Round 5: Double every 5th st around, work sc1 in all other sts (= 24 sts).

Rounds 6 and 7: Work sc24 even without increases.

SPHERE

Instructions

Rounds 1–7: Work as described for the half-sphere.

Rounds 8 and 9: Work sc1 in each st (= 24 sts).

Round 10: Crochet every 5th and 6th st together, work sc1 in all other sts (= 20 sts).

Round 11: Crochet every 4th and 5th st together, work sc1 in all other sts (= 16 sts).

Round 12: Crochet every 3rd and 4th st together, work sc1 in all other sts (= 12 sts).

Round 13: Crochet all sts together in pairs throughout (= 6 sts).

Round 14: Work sc1 in each st (= 6 sts).

··· How **TO CROCHET IN THE ROUND** is explained beginning on page 67.

! When working a **SINGLE DECREASE**, 2 stitches are crocheted off the hook together (> page 102).

X In **SPIRAL ROUNDS**, there are no defined and therefore conspicuous transitions between rounds (> page 71), which is an advantage for three-dimensional shapes in single crochet. During work, however, it is easier to keep track if the beginning of the round is marked with a marking thread.

··· **ABBREVIATIONS** can be found on page 344.

! When the sphere is supposed to be **STUFFED** with fiberfill or other stuffing material, the latter has to be inserted before crocheting has been completed.

For crocheting a sphere there are no universal rules, just a few helpful key points. The material used, individual crochet style, and especially the size, all affect the finished piece. Based on the gauge swatch *(> page 95)*, the stitch count for the desired circumference is calculated, and the number of rows equal to one-quarter of the circumference determined—this yields the necessary height for half of the sphere.

Work starts as for a circular shape *(> page 116)*. The larger the sphere is supposed to become, the longer the circle stays flat and curves only a little with increasing circle diameter. If, for a flat circle, one would work 2 single crochets into every other stitch of the previous round, for a sphere shape, increases would be worked into every 3rd stitch—fewer stitches are increased, so the shape begins to curve.

In the following rounds, the intervals between increase spots are increased, and increases should also be staggered so that an even shape is formed. With an increasing number of rounds, more middle even rounds without increases have to be included, which causes the piece to curve faster. The last 2 or 3 rounds up to half-sphere size are always worked even without increases. The second half of the sphere will be decreased at the same intervals as the first half was increased.

The sphere is one of the basic shapes when crocheting small figures, often called **AMIGURUMI** *(> page 125)*. It can form the head or body of a figure.

ROLL OR TUBE

When a half-sphere shape is continued with further middle even rounds (without increases or decreases) than would form a sphere, a tubular shape (or roll) is formed, which can either be closed at the other end or stay open. This shape is often used for crocheted dolls or animals; it can be turned into a body, arm, or leg.

LARGE ROLL

Instructions

Rounds 1–4: Work as described for the half-sphere.

Work sc even without increases over all 20 sts around until the roll has reached the desired length. If the roll is supposed to be closed, now decrease sts as follows:

Round 1: Crochet every 4th and 5th st together, work sc1 in all other sts (= 16 sts).

Round 2: Crochet the 2nd and 3rd st together, and then [crochet every 3rd and 4th st together] 3 times, to shift the decrease spots, work sc1 in all other sts (= 12 sts).

Round 3: Crochet all sts together in pairs throughout (= 6 sts).

Break the working yarn leaving a long tail, thread the end into a tapestry needle, and thread it through the front loops of the sts of the last round. Pull taut to close the remaining opening in the center.

SMALL ROLL

Instructions

Begin the small roll with 1 chain in the center *(> page 67)*, and then work sc in the round. Either work spiral rounds *(> page 71)* or begin every round with ch1 and end with 1 sl-st into the first sc to join.

Round 1: Work sc6.

Round 2: Double every other st around—that is, work sc2 into every other st, sc1 into all other sts (= 9 sts).

Round 3: Double every 3rd st around, work sc1 into all other sts (= 12 sts).

Work sc even without increases over all 12 sts around until the roll has reached the desired length. To close the roll, decrease sts as follows:

Round 1: Crochet every 3rd and 4th st together, work sc1 into all other sts (= 9 sts).

Round 2: Crochet every 2nd and 3rd st together, work sc1 into all other sts (= 6 sts).

Break the working yarn, leaving a long tail, thread the end into a tapestry needle, and thread it through the front loops of the sts of the last round. Pull taut to close the remaining opening in the center.

Cylinders are the ideal base shape for **STORAGE BASKETS** of any size.

CYLINDER

If after a flat circular shape *(> page 116)* a tubular shape is added without increasing stitches, a cylindrical shape is formed.

As soon as no more stitches are increased, the edge folds up, creating the transition between circular shape and tube. The edge of the circular shape can also be accentuated, if desired.

If the first round without increases is worked, not as usual, into the top loops of the previous round, but the hook is inserted below the top loop of the stitch as for a back post single crochet *(> page 41)*, a prominent line is formed. For this, for every single crochet, insert the hook from back to front below the top loop and exit again after the post of the stitch, pull the working yarn through the fabric, and then finish up the single crochet. Owing to this way of inserting the hook, the top loops of the previously worked round are not located on top. The edge is emphasized all around, and the two shapes are clearly separated.

... ABBREVIATIONS can be found on page 344.

CONE

A cone is shaped by alternating rounds with and without increases. This shape evolves into the tip of a cone from the beginning. Just as with every three-dimensional shape, here, too, the number of increases and the number of intermittent rounds without increases impact the shaping. The more increases and the fewer intermittent rounds, the shallower the cone turns out.

Instructions

Begin the cone with 1 chain in the center *(> page 67)* and work sc in spiral rounds *(> page 71)*.
Round 1: Work sc5.
Round 2: Double every st around—that is, work sc2 each into every st (= 10 sts).
Round 3: Work 10 sc, without increases.

Round 4: Double every other st around, work sc1 in all other sts (= 15 sts).
Round 5: Work 15 sc, without increases.
Round 6: Double every 3rd st around, work sc1 in all other sts (= 20 sts).
Round 7: Work 20 sc, without increases.

Round 8: Double every 4th st around, work sc 1 in all other sts (= 25 sts).
Round 9: Work 25 sc, without increases.

If an even larger cone is desired, continue working in the established pattern, alternating rounds with and without increases.

OTHER THREE-DIMENSIONAL SHAPES

Especially when crocheting parts for doll or animal bodies, increases or decreases are strategically placed to shape small bulges—for instance, to form a nose or ears, or to reduce or enlarge the circumference of a part in an asymmetrical way, such as for a prominent belly.

The pictured shape begins as described for the large roll (> page 123). After the first 4 increase rounds, 3 more rounds are worked over all 20 stitches around. Then individual stitches are decreased over one half of the shape only, over the course of 2 rounds, until the width has been reduced to 14 stitches. The resulting shape could be a foot onto which a leg will be crocheted later. Careful stuffing with fiberfill additionally supports the shaping.

STUFFING a shape with fiberfill should not be underestimated. This step is crucial for the perfect appearance of the item. The shape gets its FINISHING TOUCHES, and even irregularities can still be adjusted in the process.

AMIGURUMI

Translated from Japanese, amigurumi means "knitted bundle." Typical amigurumi are very small, cute characters or small animals with an oversized, ball-shaped head with embroidered facial features. Individual parts of the body are worked in single crochet, most often separately and sewn together. Other objects in miniature format are sometimes called amigurumi as well.

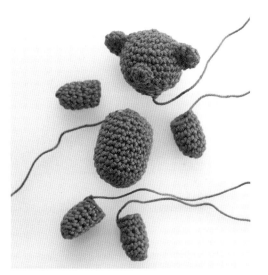

To crochet a character such as a mini teddy bear, a sphere is worked for the head, a closed roll for the body, open tubes as arms and legs, and tiny half-spheres for ears. A muzzle could be made of a single round of single crochet. It is important to crochet very densely, if necessary with a smaller crochet hook than listed for the yarn weight on the ball band. These individual shapes are stuffed with fiberfill, sometimes with weighted stuffing such as plastic pellets or dried lentils added. When sewing these shapes together, every stitch of the round or edge should be carefully incorporated.

Closures and Pockets

Appropriate closure options, such as buttonholes or zippers, as well as professionally incorporated pockets, are sophisticated details that give a crocheted item—no matter whether garment, handbag, or home accessory—the final touch.

BUTTONHOLES

Buttonholes can be incorporated different ways but should preferably be used in **dense fabrics in sturdy stitch patterns**, such as single crochet. They can be positioned horizontally or vertically. Placement, size, and number of buttonholes should be determined before beginning work on the crocheted piece and **marked in the schematic.** This is especially important if buttonholes are to be worked directly into the fabric, such as for a garment Front. It is best to first crochet the counterpart without buttonholes, since this allows for checking the placement of the buttonholes before they are worked. Another option for a button closure are **button loops on a chain arc base,** which are crocheted onto an existing edge. As a general rule, the buttonhole should always be just large enough to let the button pass through with ease. Its size depends on the diameter and thickness of the button.

HORIZONTAL BUTTONHOLES

A horizontal buttonhole is worked **within one row.** When buttonholes are placed near the edge of a garment Front, the buttonhole should be offset from the edge by half of the button's diameter plus 1 or 2 stitches. Additionally, it is to be considered whether the Front will later be finished with a crocheted edging, which would require the buttonhole to be placed within the edging rather than the actual garment Front. In **buttonhole bands worked sideways,** the positions of horizontal buttonholes should be distributed evenly spaced and between 0.6 and 1 inch (1.5 and 2.5 cm) in from the hemline or neckline—depending on the width of the button band and the size of the button.

Crochet the row up to the point where the buttonhole is to begin. If instructions state to work, for instance, a buttonhole over 5 stitches, work a corresponding number of chains at the same time skipping the same number of stitches in the current row. Then continue the row in pattern.

In the next row, work 1 single crochet into every chain. If the main pattern is a different one, continue it over the new chains.

! When **CROCHETING OVER** the buttonhole, crocheting into individual chains of the chain (> page 58) should be preferred over working into the chain space. Crocheting into the chain space (> page 43) would make the buttonhole not sturdy enough.

X To **REINFORCE** horizontal buttonholes, they can be embroidered around in buttonhole (blanket) stitch. For this, separate the plies of the project yarn and use only half. Stitch from left to right. Insert the needle from back through front through the fabric at the end of the buttonhole and move the thread to the right. Insert the needle below the top loop and move the tip of the needle over the thread. Pull the thread through—the first stitch has been completed. Stitch evenly around the edges of the slit, working 2 or 3 buttonhole stitches into each stitch of the crocheted fabric.

VERTICAL BUTTONHOLES

A buttonhole placed vertically is worked as a slit over several rows. Since it is less noticeable than a horizontal buttonhole, it is well suited for being directly incorporated into the body of the garment. This type of buttonhole is also recommended for narrow buttonhole bands worked separately.

Crochet the row up to the point where the buttonhole is supposed to begin, and then divide work and continue both halves separately until the specified height for the buttonhole has been reached. First, proceed working to the right of the buttonhole. To work the part to the left of the buttonhole, join the working yarn anew in the last stitch to the right of the buttonhole, and then finish the remainder of the row and turn to work more rows, making sure both sides end at the same height.

In the following row, work again over all the stitches—the end of the buttonhole slit has been closed.

For stitch patterns in tall crochet stitches, such as double crochet, small buttons can be passed through the gaps between the stitches, eliminating the need for buttonholes. To mark the buttonhole spot in the fabric, sew two adjacent stitches together on either side of the buttonhole.

Vertical buttonholes **KEEP THEIR SHAPE** when the buttonhole edges are reinforced with buttonhole stitch (> page 192).

BUTTONHOLE PLACEMENT should be considered during the **PLANNING** stage of a project. Will buttonholes be worked directly into the body of the garment or are they part of a button band crocheted onto the garment later (> page 165)? Will a decorative edging be added to the main part (> page 155)? Generally, the distance to the edge is another key point that needs to be taken into account.

CROCHETING INDIVIDUAL BUTTON LOOPS ONTO AN EDGE

Button loops are directly crocheted onto the edge of the Front after the crocheted pieces have been completed. First, the placement for the buttons is determined and marked with tailor pins.

Attach the yarn at the end point of the button loop, to the left of the marked button location. Crochet a chain the length of the planned button loop. Move the crocheted chain to the right and attach it with a slip stitch (> page 33) at the beginning point of the button loop, to the right of the marked button location.

Crochet around the chain arc from right to left in single crochet (> page 43) and finish with a slip stitch into the starting point (= the spot where the yarn had been attached). Break the working yarn and pull the working loop long until the tail has been pulled through. Thread the tail through to the wrong side and weave it in.

A button loop worked in **VERY THIN YARN** is delicate and inconspicuous. To crochet it, the project yarn can be separated into half the strands.

Individual button loops crocheted onto the edge can be worked in a **CONTRASTING COLOR** or all in different colors, turning them into a decorative embellishment.

For **LADIES GARMENTS**, buttonholes are worked on the Right Front, for men's, on the Left Front.

BUTTONS can also be **CROCHETED** to match the garment (> page 185).

SAME-ROW BUTTON LOOPS

Button loops can also be added during the last row of a button band or while adding a crocheted edging. The buttonhole row must be worked in single crochet.

1 At the beginning of the row, work 5 single crochets. For the first button loop, chain 5 chains (adjust the number of chains as needed for the button size). Move the crocheted chain to the right.

2 Remove the crochet hook from the working loop, and then insert the hook into the fifth single crochet from the left—this corresponds to the first single crochet at the beginning of the row. Now place the working loop on the hook again, and pull it through.

3 Working from right to left, crochet 8 single crochets in the chain space of the chain arc (> page 43), so that it arches slightly. Finish with 1 slip stitch (> page 33) into the last single crochet of the row, inserting the crochet hook through the front loop of the stitch and a vertical strand of the post.

4 Now continue either working the buttonhole band or crocheting along the edge. Work 6 single crochets (counted from the end of the button loop), and then work the chain for the next button loop, and move it to the right. The loops in the example are placed 1 stitch apart from each other. To adjust the spacing, if needed, move along the edge with more single crochets.

TWO-ROW BUTTON LOOPS

With this method, multiple button loops are created at the same time over the course of 2 rows. The loop itself will be less pronounced compared to crocheting in the chain space, creating a just slightly arched outer edge. Intervals between button loops depend on button position.

When 2 stitches are **CROCHETED TOGETHER**, 1 single stitch is decreased (> page 102).

Example: At the beginning of a right-side row, work 3 single crochets. To work the first loop, * chain 5, skip 3 stitches of the previous row, and then work 5 single crochets. Repeat from * all the time and, after the last loop, work only 3 single crochets more. Work 1 wrong-side row in single crochet, working 1 single crochet each into every single crochet and every chain of the previous row and at the same time crocheting together the single crochet before the chain with the first chain of the chain arc, as well as the last chain of

the chain arc and the single crochet after it. Finally, finish the top edge with slip stitches worked through the back loop.

INSERTING ZIPPERS

Inserting a zipper requires great accuracy as well as dexterity of the hands. **Crocheted fabric is flexible and stretchy**—even compact stitch patterns such as single crochet are not a rigid structure. To ensure that the zipper fits correctly, without either constricting or stretching the edges of the crocheted piece, it should **first only be basted or pinned** to the garment. Then the garment is tried on to check the fit.

A **separable zipper** is a good choice for casual garments. Inserting it into a jacket or zip neck sweater should always be done in such a way that **the back of work looks neat**, too, when the zipper is opened and the edge folds over. For this reason, the most presentable and sturdy method is to enclose the zipper on both sides by a crocheted band.

ONE-LAYER FACING ON THE OUTSIDE

For a one-layer band on the outside, a narrow edge of the crocheted piece itself is used to **cover the back of the zipper**. Into a **slip-stitch line of surface crochet**, a facing is then crocheted. The distance of the line of slip stitch to the edge equals the planned width of the facing. This is a good way to conceal not-quite-perfect edges as well.

On the right side of work, crochet a **line of slip stitch** between the 3rd and 4th stitch in from the edge (> page 193). For fabrics worked in single crochet, every slip stitch spans 1 row of the base fabric. The facing will be crocheted into the loops of the slip-stitch line of surface crochet. In the pictured example, the slip stitches, with their closed, streamlined stitch appearance, are used as embellishment for the facing. In Row 1 (= right side), the new slip stitches are worked **through the back loop** (> page 37) of the existing line of slip stitch.

Work another **5 rows of slip stitch** (> page 33), always inserting the hook **through the front loop of the stitch only**. The facing ends with a wrong-side row, its width must be exactly **identical** to that of the edge of the crocheted piece underneath it. At the other edge, work another band the same way.

Pin the closed zipper with tailor pins between the two bands beginning and end should not protrude over the edge of the Front, and the **chain** in the middle of the zipper should stay **uncovered**. Additionally, make sure that the crochet rows to both sides of the zipper are exactly opposite of each other. For sewing, use the project yarn or—if it is too thick—buttonhole thread in a matching color. Open the zipper and work back stitch (> page 189) to sew it on along the edges of the facing.

Sew on the edges of the facings on the wrong side in whipstitch (> page 192) with buttonhole thread. At both ends of the bands sew the narrow sides together using the yarn tails so that the **zipper tape** is fully **enclosed**.

The **DISTANCE** of the line of slip stitches **FROM THE EDGE** should equal the width of the zipper tape.

If the stitches for the zipper facing are **PICKED UP** from a slip-stitch line of surface crochet (> page 193), a clear border line is created.

A **SPECIAL ZIPPER** with loosely woven groove along the row of teeth **MAKES SEWING IN EASIER,** even with fabrics in thicker yarns.

X The zipper can also be simply placed **WITHOUT ADDITIONAL FACINGS** behind the open edges of the crocheted piece or behind bands crocheted onto the main part (> page 165) then sewn on. It will then, however, be **VISIBLE ON THE WRONG SIDE OF THE FABRIC**, including the zipper tape and the seam, and, if used on garments, can also irritate the skin. This method should therefore be reserved for non-clothing items such as pillowcases or bags.

X All facing solutions shown here can also be used for **OTHER STITCH PATTERNS** (> page 168). With shallow slip stitches, it is however easier to match the exact height of the zipper tape in crochet than with any of the taller stitches.

X When crocheting the facing to the line of slip stitch on the wrong side of the fabric, use a **SMALLER CROCHET HOOK**, which is easier to insert under the loops of the stitches.

! With both types of **ONE-LAYER BANDS**, the width of the crocheted piece itself stays the same; the width of the **TWO-LAYER BAND** will add to the width of the piece.

ONE-LAYER FACING ON THE INSIDE

If the edge of the crocheted piece is supposed to stay visible, it is also possible to **directly crochet** a one-layer band **onto the zipper tape** on the wrong side. A special zipper with loosely woven groove comes in handy for this purpose.

First, crochet a **line of slip stitches** (> page 33) along the loosely woven groove on the **wrong side** of the zipper, inserting the needle in **evenly spaced intervals into the groove**. For zippers without a special groove, the crocheted slip stitches can be replaced by chain stitch (> page 190) embroidered with a sharp needle. For the facing, work 1 right-side row in single crochet, and 3 rows of slip stitch through the front loop of the stitch only (> page 37). Crochet a facing onto the second zipper tape the same way.

Pin the zipper between the edges of the crocheted piece and the facing; the **zipper chain** should stay **uncovered**. Make sure the crochet rows to both sides of the zipper match. Open the zipper. Sew on the edges of the crocheted pieces with short stitches in whip or back stitch (> pages 192 and 189) and buttonhole thread in a matching color. **Sew on the edges of the facings on the wrong side of work.**

TWO-LAYER FACING

The two-layer band is an alternative to the facing described on page 129. With this method, facings are crocheted onto the main piece **on the outside as well as on the inside**.

For this, loosely crochet slip stitches close to the front edges of the crocheted pieces. **On the right side of the fabric**, work the stitches for the facing **into the slip stitches** and **on the wrong side of the fabric, into the visible single strand** of the surface crochet line. Make sure that both facings have the same number of rows. Place the closed zipper between the two layers of the facing and pin it in place, keeping the zipper chain in the middle uncovered. Open the zipper. Using back stitch (> page 189), first

sew on the outside facing and then the inside facing.

POCKETS

A pocket for a garment or accessory can be **crocheted separately** and sewn on afterward on the outside or be directly **incorporated into the crocheted piece** through a slit worked within the fabric with a pocket lining on the inside. A pocket is generally useful to have, but can also be a decorative embellishment, and is a great canvas for creativity.

PATCH POCKET

Rectangular, rounded, circular, or heart-shaped—a patch pocket can be crocheted **in any shape.** This pocket type also lends itself to a variety of options for sewing on and finishing for decoratively created pockets. It can be open at the top or be fastened with a button and buttonhole (> pages 126 and 185), or closed with a zipper. Patch pockets have the advantage of not needing to be planned right from the start of the crocheted piece. Their placement can be determined **after the item has been completed.**

RECTANGULAR POCKET

This **simple shape** is easy to work and embellish for added interest. The seam used for sewing on can also be a decorative element and accentuate the pocket's shape.

First, determine the **size of the pocket.** Measurements of 5.1 inches (13 cm) width and 5.5 inches (14 cm) height yield an average pocket size, but can be adjusted depending on the purpose of the pocket. Based on your **gauge swatch,** calculate the stitch and row count. End the pocket heightwise with a right-side row; as **finishing edging,** work a **wrong-side row of slip stitches through the front loop of the stitch only** (> page 37). This accentuates the edge in a subtle manner while at the same time **reinforcing** it.

Now decide on pocket placement and pin the pocket in place with tailor pins. **If both the base fabric and the pocket have the same stitch pattern,** make sure that the rows of **crochet are aligned** exactly atop each other. Using running stitch (> page 189), sew on the pocket with each sewing stitch spanning 1 crochet stitch or 1 crochet row and placing the stitches 1 crochet stitch or 1 crochet row in from the edge. At the corners, also stitch down over the edge of the pocket. Use contrasting color yarn in the same yarn weight as the project yarn and a dull embroidery needle.

More information about **GAUGE** can be found on page 95.

Using **RUNNING STITCH** (> page 189), a dashed line can be embroidered, which, when worked in a contrasting color yarn, creates an additional **COLORFUL ACCENT.**

POCKET WITH ROUNDED CORNERS

A pocket with rounded corners is the **traditional shape for jackets.** Adding crocheted edgings can change the style. Here the spectrum ranges from minimalist, in single crochets or crab stitch, up to playful narrow edgings with picots and other embellishments (Decorative edgings > page 155).

Just as for the rectangular pocket, first determine the size. Begin the pocket at the bottom edge with **increases at both ends for the curve**—each over an area of about 0.8 inch x 0.8 inch (2 cm x 2 cm). This still leaves some leeway for the final height of the pocket. End the pocket heightwise with a right-side row and, immediately after, continue the row at the side edge, adding a **single crochet edging** along the **edges of the pocket** (> page 156).

How to **INCREASE STITCHES AT THE EDGES** is explained in detail beginning on page 98.

Determine the pocket placement and pin on the pocket using tailor pins. **If both the base fabric and the pocket have the same stitch pattern,** make sure that the rows of **crochet are aligned** atop each other. Sew on the pocket with **invisible seam under the crocheted edging** using buttonhole thread in a matching color and working short back-and-forth stitches.

KANGAROO POCKET

A sewn-on double-sided scoop pocket, also called kangaroo pocket, is located on the Front and has two pocket openings starting at the side edges and following a diagonal line, similar to the shape of a trapezoid. The bottom edge can be either flush with the hemline of the garment or a facing or at a distance from it.

Shape and size of the kangaroo pocket are depicted in the schematic as a starting point for your own projects. To create the **short slope** up to the beginning of the pocket opening, **increase** 2 or 3 stitches **in regular intervals.** Work the **edges of the pocket openings** at both sides of the pocket **less steep** in the beginning (i.e., first decrease 1 stitch each in every other row, about 3 times, then in every other row, and, finally, in every 4th row). This shape is optically more pleasing if a facing or trim is to be added later. In the example shown, the finishing edging is worked in a right-side row, the top loops of which visually match the finishing of the other surrounding edges.

After that, crochet along the **side edges and the pocket openings.** For this, add slip stitches close to the edge (> page 193), and then, in a right-side row, work slip stitches through the back loop (> page 37). The shape will be **reinforced** by this. As an alternative, add any crocheted edging (> page 166) along the pocket opening. Determine the pocket placement and pin it on. If **having the same stitch pattern,** make sure that the rows of **pocket and garment Front align.** Additionally, in the center of the Front, mark the widthwise section of stitches corresponding to the top and bottom width of the pocket, to ensure that the pocket is placed in the middle.

To **sew on the pocket** along its straight upper edge, weave stitch by stitch the crocheted fabric under the top loops, alternating with catching 1 stitch within a row on the Front. Sew on the straight bottom pocket edge using back stitch (> page 189) over the width of 1 crocheted stitch each between Rows 1 and 2. Finally, stitch down both side edges located below the pocket opening.

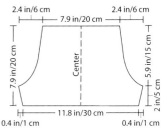

Shape and size of the kangaroo pocket

●●● How to **DECREASE** individual stitches at edges is explained in detail on page 104.

●●● Examples for **CROCHETED-ON EDGINGS** and instructions on how to work them can be found beginning on page 165.

X **VARIATION** of the kangaroo pocket: crochet two separate pocket halves mirror-inverted, place both pockets directly adjacent to the side seam, and sew on all around, except for the pocket opening.

SET-IN POCKETS

In set-in pockets, the **pocket lining** is **hidden on the inside** of the crocheted piece. Pocket placement, shape, and size must be determined before beginning work. Only in the last working step, a facing is added or the pocket slit finished with a plain edging to reinforce it and to prevent the edge from stretching with use.

HORIZONTAL POCKET

The pocket slit is located horizontally in the crocheted piece. Its placement must be carefully planned in advance. A **separately worked pocket bag** is joined to the main piece while it is being crocheted up. The edge of the pocket slit can be finished with either an added facing (> page 165) or a decorative edging (> page 155).

First, separately crochet a rectangular **pocket lining** of about 5.1 inches x 5.1 inches (13 cm x 13 cm). It must have 2 stitches more widthwise than the planned pocket slit. Now work the main part of the garment up to the height of the intended pocket opening, ending with a wrong-side row. Mark the width of the pocket opening. In the following right-side row, work up to the beginning of the pocket slit, leave the **stitches of the pocket slit unworked**, and instead, continue the row **immediately after**, working **over the edge of the pocket lining**, beginning in the 2nd stitch. Leave the last stitch of the pocket lining unworked, and continue the row after the second marking again over the main part of the garment. Now the pocket lining has been incorporated, and the main part of the garment is continued over the whole width, including the new stitches.

Crochet a **facing** (shown in a two-color stripe pattern in the pictured example) **along the pocket slit**: Attach new working yarn (> page 76) at the end of the slit, located at right, and work single crochet through the back loop only (> page 37). Work a total of 4 right-side rows (i.e., work every row with new working yarn from right to left), alternating colors 1 and 2. After the 4th row, work crab stitch edging (> page 156) in Color 2. Stitch down the narrow ends of the facing using the yarn tails.

On the wrong side of work, **sew on the pocket lining** in whipstitch (> page 193). Don't pull the **yarn too taut**, to prevent the pocket lining from showing through on the right side.

X While patch pockets are fine as interior pockets for purses and tote bags, the most **ATTRACTIVE SOLUTION** for garments is in most cases set-in pockets.

X If the project yarn is very thick, the pocket lining should preferably be worked in a **THINNER YARN** of the same color and fibers to keep the pocket flat and prevent unwanted bulk.

ZIPPERED POCKET

A set-in pocket can also be closed with a zipper. **For a horizontal pocket slit,** an opening as wide as the zipper's length and 1 or 2 rows in height is left in the main part of the garment.

Crochet the main part up to the height of the intended pocket opening, ending with a right-side row, but don't break the working yarn. Now mark the **length of the pocket slit** according to the length of the zipper. Work the following wrong-side row up to the end of the slit, break the working yarn, and pull it through the working loop (> page 80). After the second marking, attach new working yarn and continue the row to the end.

Now work a right-side row in which the width of the **left-out pocket slit** will be **bridged:** work up to the slit, and then crochet a chain for the second slit edge—the number of chains corresponds to the unused stitches of the first slit edge. After the end of the slit, continue the right-side row to the outside edge.

Now continue working the piece over the whole width again and, when **crocheting over the chain,** work the single crochets **into the back loop (third loop) of the chain** (> page 58) so that the two V-shaped loops of the stitch create a clean edge.

Sew in the zipper **underneath the edges of the slit using back stitch** (> page 189) and buttonhole thread in a matching color.

Separately crochet a rectangular pocket lining. It must be 0.8 inch (2 cm) wider than the width of the pocket slit, the height about 5.1 inches (13 cm) total plus 0.8 to 1.2 inches (2 to 3 cm) as the inside facing on the back of the zipper. Pin the pocket lining to the inside so that the **zipper is completely covered** and the top edge can be sewn on above the zipper tape (i.e., both ends should extend by the same amount). Sew on the pocket lining in whipstitch (> page 192).

The **pocket slit** for a zippered pocket can also be **worked at a slant.** For this, **divide work** at the beginning point of the pocket opening and continue working the **sections separately** with slanted edges and 2 stitches apart from each other. For the first one of the two slit edges, **decrease individual stitches in evenly spaced rows** (> page 102). To ensure that the second slit edge runs parallel to the first, a corresponding **number of stitches** must be increased here (> page 98). At the end point of the pocket opening, again crochet over both parts combined, bridging the skipped stitches with 2 chains.

SIDE-SEAM POCKET

This pocket version is functional and does not show. The **pocket slit** runs in the side seam of the garment.

Crochet a round-shaped **pocket lining**. To help, a **pocket template** is included on this page; size it as needed on a photocopier. The **straight edge of the template is where the lining will be later**

attached, which is also where the beginning chain should be located, making this edge relatively sturdy and perfect for attaching. Shape the pocket lining with increases and decreases (> *pages 98 and 102*) to match the shape of the template.

Along the side edges of Front and Back, mark the **pocket slit** locations. **Sew the straight beginning edge of the pocket lining onto the marked part of the side edge** of the Back in whipstitch (> *page 192*), starting between the first and second stitch from the edge and picking up every stitch on the pocket lining, creating an even seam.

Close the **side seam** of Back and Front above and below the attached pocket lining. **Add a crocheted edging** (> *page 155*) along the **pocket slit** on the Front to reinforce the edge and/or to accentuate it. On the wrong side of the Front, sew on the pocket lining in whipstitch.

⊠ Either work **A SINGLE-LAYER POCKET LINING,** which will be sewn to the wrong side of the main part, or make a **POCKET LINING IN TWO PARTS:** First, place the parts along the pocket slit, and then sew them together. The bag created this way will hang loosely on the inside of the garment. All set-in inner pockets can be worked in two layers using this method: This can be useful especially for pieces worked in lacy stitch patterns, for which it would not be feasible to sew the pocket lining to the main part, or where the pocket is not supposed to show on the outside. It is recommended to use a **THINNER YARN** for this purpose that matches the project yarn in color and fiber content and won't add too much bulk to the pocket bag.

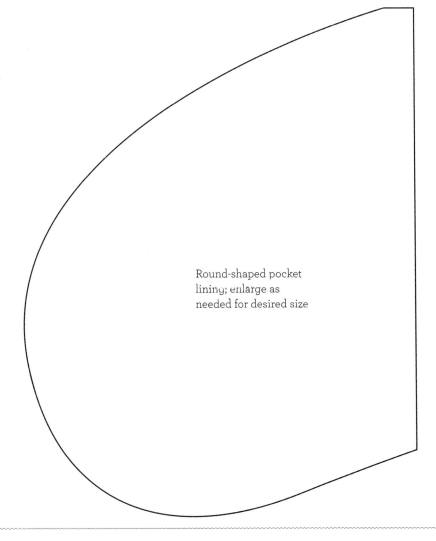

Round-shaped pocket lining; enlarge as needed for desired size

Finishing
Touches

For the perfect finish for your crocheted piece, individual parts are blocked and joined, and decorative details, such as borders and decorative bands, or embellishments, such as fringe and buttons, are attached.

Joining
Crocheted Pieces

Except for simple scarves or blankets worked in one piece, crocheted items often consist of several parts that have to be joined together eventually. For this process, there are two options: crocheting together using a crochet hook or sewing together with a tapestry needle or an embroidery needle with a blunt point. Both techniques have their advantages and disadvantages.

X Crocheted pieces should be SEWN OR CROCHETED TOGETHER LOOSELY so the seam matches the drape and stitch appearance of the crocheted fabric and the piece doesn't constrict. To achieve the desired result, you can try out DIFFERENT HOOK SIZES for crocheting together. When sewing together, make sure that the yarn is not pulled too taut for all stitches throughout.

X Before crocheting together, the parts should be attached, preferably WITH TAILOR PINS made of metal or wood, or basted together with a long RUNNING STITCH (> page 189). Take care to not accidentally catch the basting thread in the actual seam, so it can later be cleanly removed.

CROCHETING TOGETHER

Crocheting together is often used for pieces such as granny squares or other individual motifs featuring edges of the same length and matching stitches and row counts. Crocheting together is fast, and mistakes can be easily corrected by just pulling at the working yarn. However, with this technique, in addition to the edges of the crocheted pieces, a welt-like line of crochet stitches is created, which does add bulk. A crocheted seam can, however, also be used smartly as a design element.

Pieces to be crocheted together are in most cases placed together with wrong sides facing each other, so that the seam later shows on the right side of the fabric. In a similar way, the pieces can also be seamed on the wrong side—in this case, they are placed together with right sides facing each other. However, a crocheted join worked in single crochet or slip stitch often contributes bulk. If the parts to be joined don't have all top edges/stitches only (as do motifs crocheted in the round), top and bottom edges and side edges must be crocheted together in different ways.

CROCHETING TOGETHER WITH SLIP STITCHES

Since slip stitches are the shallowest basic stitches, seams in this technique turn out relatively flat.

A slip stitch join will place itself as a wide, flat seam onto one side of the edge. On the wrong side of work, short perpendicular stitches appear. This difference is not of much concern if the seam is worked in the same color as the pieces to be joined.

When the join is worked right sides facing each other, it will appear as short vertical lines after turning to the right side.

TOP AND BOTTOM EDGE

1 When the piece has been crocheted and the ends are woven in, place both crocheted pieces together, wrong sides facing each other.

2 Now first insert the hook into the first stitch of the row of the piece in front and then into the opposite stitch of the piece in back (which is the last stitch of the last row). Grasp the working yarn and pull it through both stitches at once. Chain 1.

3 Insert the hook again into the two first stitches and work 1 slip stitch.

4 Finally, insert the hook into the second stitch of the piece in front and into the corresponding opposite stitch of the piece in back, pull the working yarn through the fabric, pulling it through both stitches and through the loop on the hook at once. Continue in this manner to the end of the joining row.

CORNER

When the end of this edge has been reached, rotate work by 90° in a clockwise direction, and join the adjoining side edges at left. Since it is not possible to work more than one slip stitch into the same insertion point, continue working the first slip stitch at the new edge.

SIDE EDGES

The number of slip stitches needed **per row** for crocheting together along the side edges depends on the **height of the stitch** in which the crocheted piece has been worked and that appears at the edges. For pieces worked **in single crochet**, after the corner, the hook is inserted into the next pair of edge stitches from both pieces to be joined: crochet the edge stitch at the beginning/end of the row in the piece in front together with the edge stitch at the beginning/end of the row in the piece in back. Usually, 1 slip stitch is worked into every edge stitch (i.e., **1 slip stitch per row**).

For joining side edges of crocheted pieces **in taller stitches**, there are no fixed rules, just **guidelines**. If it has not been mentioned in the pattern instructions how many slip stitches to work in how many rows, it is recommended to test a few times over 3 or 4 rows to determine the correct number of slip stitches so the seam will neither bunch up nor pucker. The following methods as a rule of thumb give a few clues.

❗ **FOR TALLER STITCH TYPES**, the first stitch in **RIGHT-SIDE ROWS** is the height-adjustment chain: Here, the hook should be preferably inserted under the two top loops of the chain. In a **WRONG-SIDE ROW**, the hook is inserted as usual under the two V-shaped top loops.

❗ Just as when crocheting together two top edges in single crochet, the top or bottom edges of pieces crocheted **IN OTHER STITCH TYPES** are joined the same way. It is only important that both edges have the same number of stitches.

❗ For the crocheted join **AT THE SIDE EDGES** to look similar to that at the top edge, the hook should preferably be inserted **UNDER 2 STRANDS** of the pieces to be joined. If the hook is inserted only under 1 strand of the edge stitches, the "seam" will appear too skinny, while inserting under 3 strands (i.e., under the whole stitch), would add too much bulk.

Should the **NUMBER** of slip stitches gained from the number of height-adjustment chains at the beginning of the row prove to be **TOO HIGH**, the seam can be worked with a **SMALLER CROCHET HOOK** than the actual crocheted piece. This should provide enough room in the edge stitches to place the slip stitches.

In crocheted seams for all types of edge stitches, it is recommended to insert the hook **UNDER 2 STRANDS** to create a sturdy but not too thick join.

Method 1: As many slip stitches as height-adjustment or turning chains

As many slip stitches for each row are worked into the edge stitches as there are **height-adjustment or turning chains** at the beginning of the row, according to the **height of the respective stitch type**. With this method, for instance, for a crocheted piece worked in double crochet, 1 slip stitch is worked into the top, and 2 slip stitches into the post of the edge stitches of both pieces. For turning chains, the slip stitches can be worked directly into individual chains.

stitch type	number of slip stitches for joining
single crochet	1
half double crochet	2
double crochet	3
treble crochet	4
double treble crochet	5

Method 2: Number of height-adjustment or turning chains minus 1

Depending on the yarn used and how tightly or loosely the pieces had been crocheted, fewer slip stitches per edge stitch and row might be sufficient for a side seam: In this case, calculate **1 slip stitch fewer** than height-adjustment or turning chains needed for the respective stitch type. Work the first stitch of the seam into the top of the stitch, the remaining stitches into the post.

To compensate for the smaller number of slip stitches, the slip stitches are in this case worked more **loosely**. You can also adjust the **tension of the yarn** accordingly or use a **larger crochet hook** for crocheting the pieces together.

The total number of slip stitches is not as important as **JOINING** both pieces **AT AN EVEN PACE**.

Method 3: Alternating numbers of slip stitches

This method is a combination of the two techniques described earlier. When, for example, two pieces worked in double crochet are joined and 3 slip stitches (Method 1) prove too much (fabric ripples) but 2 slip stitches (Method 2) too little (fabric constricts), **alternatingly once 2 and once 3 slip stitches** can be worked per double crochet edge stitch.

CROCHETING TOGETHER IN SINGLE CROCHET

The pieces to be joined can also be placed **RIGHT SIDES FACING EACH OTHER** and be crocheted together on the wrong side in single crochet. Since single crochets are slightly taller than slip stitches, this type of seam often appears **QUITE BULKY**.

Unlike crocheting together with slip stitches, a seam in single crochet appears not only on one side of the two joined crocheted pieces but also sits clearly visible **directly on both edges** with the characteristic "V" of the crochet stitch around the edges of the crocheted pieces. For this reason, the front and back of work look almost identical.

When the join is worked **right sides facing each other**, it will appear as short vertical lines on the right side of work after turning.

TOP AND BOTTOM EDGES

In essence, crocheting together top and bottom edges in single crochet works the same as **for slip stitches** (> *page 139*). Place the crocheted pieces to be joined together with **wrong sides facing each other**, insert the crochet hook into the first stitch of the top row on the piece in front, and into the corresponding stitch on the piece in back. Grasp the working yarn and pull it through both stitches at once. Chain 1 for height adjustment and work the first stitch of the seam. Then insert the hook into the next 2 corresponding stitches of both pieces as usual (i.e., under the two top loops of the stitches) and work 1 single crochet. Continue working this way to the end of the top edge.

CORNERS

When the end of the top edge has been reached, work the last single crochet into the last pair of edge stitches of the pieces to be joined, rotate work 90° **in a clockwise direction**, and, into the same stitch, work another 2 single crochets—one for turning the corner, and one as first single crochet of the side seam. This means that the last stitch of the top edge in every crocheted piece is a corner stitch, into which 3 single crochets for transitioning to the side edge are to be worked.

For some yarns and designs, 3 single crochets in the corner stitch will appear **TOO BULKY**. If this is the case, the middle stitch can be **REPLACED BY A SINGLE CHAIN**.

SIDE EDGES

Just as in crocheting together **with slip stitches**, both crocheted pieces are joined with additional single crochets along the side edge.

To work the single crochets, the hook can be inserted under one strand of the edge stitches, under two strands, or under the whole edge stitch. The only important point is to insert the hook always **into the same spot** throughout to ensure a uniform stitch appearance at the edge. The more strands are enclosed within the single crochet of the seam, the sturdier, but also bulkier the edge will appear. Usually it is recommended to insert the hook under 2 strands of the edge stitches so that the side seam matches those at the top and bottom edge.

For the number of single crochets when crocheting together **SIDE EDGES, ALL THREE METHODS** described for slip stitches (> *page 140*) can be used. Since single crochets are wider than slip stitches, **METHODS 2 AND 3** are, however, the best choice.

For the actual **number of stitches required for each row**, similar rules apply as for joining **with slip stitches** (> *page 140*). However, the most visually appealing results are achieved with fabrics in shallow stitches, for which the hook needs to be inserted just once or at most twice. The taller the stitches are, the larger the variety of possible insertion points in the edge stitches: It can be height-adjustment or turning chains, tops or posts of stitches, or from the front or the back of these stitches. All these differences, as well as yarn used, can affect the appearance of the finished seam. Wool yarn's springiness can compensate for some irregularities, while smooth cotton often looks uneven.

It's worth the effort to crochet the side edges together **OVER A FEW ROWS PROVISIONALLY**, including trying out crochet hooks **OF DIFFERENT SIZES**, to achieve the optimal result.

When the **side edges** of crocheted pieces **in taller stitches** are worked into single crochet, a neat effect can be achieved by working multiple stitches around the post of the edge stitch.

To **BREAK UP** a seam or create a different effect, you can play around with different options and **COMBINE** them. You could, for instance, alternatingly work "1 single crochet, 1 slip stitch" into the edge stitches, or between 2 single crochets, skip 1 edge stitch, bridging it with 1 chain.

X A seam can also be accentuated as a design element by using a YARN IN A CONTRASTING COLOR.

! Even though weaving in yarn tails is tedious, the working yarn for seaming should NOT be TOO LONG, because being too frequently pulled through the stitches of the crocheted fabric puts a strain on it. Furthermore, it is easier to sew with strands APPROXIMATELY 20 inches (50 cm) long.

X A pretty VARIATION of the whipstitch seam for sewing motifs together is to only pick up the TWO LOOPS NEAR THE MIDDLE while seaming. On the right side of the fabric, the loops of the stitch not included in the seam are later visible.

SEWING TOGETHER

Sewing together with a tapestry needle appears more laborious at first, but produces **less noticeable seams** since only one strand connects the stitches, whereas when crocheting together the yarn for the seam stitches is always double-stranded. However, mistakes can only be corrected by cutting the seam, which always also harbors the danger of accidentally cutting into the crochet stitches.

When sewing, it is much easier than when crocheting together to join very **different pieces** to each other: sleeves to Fronts and Backs, or joining differently patterned and shaped pieces with non-matching stitch and row counts. This is, for instance, the case when a sleeve cap has to be sewn into an armhole.

Pieces to be sewn together are usually placed with **right sides facing each other** since the seam should not be visible from the right side. For sewing, the project yarn and a blunt tapestry needle with a large eye should be used.

WHIPSTITCH

Whipstitch can be used for **all kinds of seams**, and produces a flexible seam. It looks especially pretty for joining motifs in a contrasting color.

Work the whipstich in corresponding stitches over the edges of the pieces. If the seam is worked with wrong sides facing each other, the right side will show straight stitches while the stitches appear slanted on the wrong side of work.

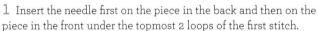

1 Insert the needle first on the piece in the back and then on the piece in the front under the topmost 2 loops of the first stitch.

2 Pull the working yarn through, lead the needle to the back again, and in the same way insert it through the appropriate next stitch of both pieces. The working yarn will place itself over the edges when the yarn is pulled through.

3 Continue in this manner, until the pieces are joined over the entire length.

When sewing, pick up **2 loops for each stitch** so the seam will be sturdy: For the top edge, these are the two V-shaped loops of the stitch; at the side edges, these are 2 strands each of the edge stitches (= chain or head and/or body of the stitches).

It is also possible to insert the needle only under one strand of the stitches, which will produce a flatter but less sturdy seam. Along the **top and bottom edge**, as a rule, 1 stitch is worked into every stitch, and at the **side edges**, as many stitches as correspond to the number of height-adjustment or turning chains of the respective stitch type (> page 64).

BACKSTITCH

While this seam uses up more yarn than other seams since the strands of the stitches are practically wrapped by the working yarn, it is very sturdy. Work from right to left.

On the right side of the fabric, the seam appears in the form of uniform stitches; on the wrong side of the fabric, it is twisted in a cord-like fashion. When opened and flattened out, two parallel stitches appear at a time.

1 Insert the needle from back to front through the respective second stitches of both edges, going under both top loops of the stitches.

2 Insert the needle from front to back through the first stitches of both edges, located to the right, and pull the working yarn through.

3 Insert the needle again 2 stitches further left through both layers, from back to front.

4 Insert the needle again at the end of the previous stitch, from front to back.

Repeat Steps 3 and 4 until you have reached the desired length. Having reached the last possible insertion point at the end of the edge, insert the needle from front to back, rotate work 90 degrees in a clockwise direction and sew the side edges together in the same way.
Orienting oneself for the number of stitches per row at the side edges at the number of height-adjustment or turning chains for the respective stitch type will in most cases yield too many stitches. For this reason, it is suggested to instead apply the formula "height-adjustment or turning chains minus 1" (> page 140, Method 2) as for crocheting together. For fabrics crocheted in single crochet or half double crochet, 1 or 2 backstitches per edge stitch or row should be worked.

! It is especially important to always lead the sewing thread on the wrong side of the fabric either OVER OR UNDER the strand of the previous stitch. DON'T CHANGE during seaming; otherwise the seam will turn out uneven.

! For all seams, individual stitches should be carefully TIGHTENED with the needle AFTER A FEW STITCHES to produce an even and not too loose seam.

MATTRESS STITCH

This seam is hardly noticeable from the outside and is often worked at the **side edges** of crocheted pieces. For the top and bottom edge of the crocheted piece, where the needle can be inserted immediately below the top loops, a slightly modified version of the mattress stitch can be used.

The seam looks identical from the front and back and, once opened and flattened, small V-shaped stitches show.

X It is best to pull the working yarn through **AFTER EVERY STITCH**.

! For pieces crocheted **IN TALLER STITCHES, MULTIPLE STITCHES PER EDGE STITCH OR ROW** should be sewn. For instance, 2 stitches for 1 double crochet, insert the needle directly **INTO THE EDGE STITCHES**, since the needle can be inserted "1 stitch in from the edge" only at the transition from one row to the next.

SIDE EDGES

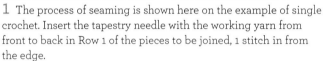

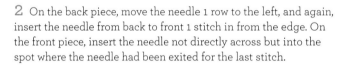

1 The process of seaming is shown here on the example of single crochet. Insert the tapestry needle with the working yarn from front to back in Row 1 of the pieces to be joined, 1 stitch in from the edge.

2 On the back piece, move the needle 1 row to the left, and again, insert the needle from back to front 1 stitch in from the edge. On the front piece, insert the needle not directly across but into the spot where the needle had been exited for the last stitch.

3 On the front piece, move forward one row, and insert the needle from front to back, on the back piece not directly across but into the spot where the needle had been exited for the last stitch.

4 This way, insert the needle in a zigzag path alternatingly into the edges of both pieces, and pull the working yarn through gently and not too tightly.

TOP AND BOTTOM EDGE

At the top and bottom edges of the crocheted pieces, where the needle can be inserted **directly under the two loops of the stitches**, mattress stitch is worked similarly to the side edges. When the seam has been completed and the working yarn pulled through at every stitch, this join is **barely noticeable**. Only the characteristic V-shapes of the stitches will be visible.

LADDER STITCH SEAM

This seam is **stretchy and relatively flat.** The tapestry needle is led in an angularly meandering path through the stitches at the top and bottom edge or through the rows at the side edges.

This seam looks identical from the front and back once opened; nearly parallel stitches in evenly spaced intervals are visible.

1 The process of joining is shown here on the example of the single crochet. First, insert the tapestry needle with the working yarn from front to back in Row 1 of the pieces to be joined. Then move the needle 1 row to the left and insert it parallel to the first stitch from back to front through both layers.

2 Again move 1 row to the left and again insert the needle from front to back through both layers parallel to the previous stitch. Continue in this manner until the end of the edge has been reached.

Just as at the side edges, this seam can also be worked at top and bottom edges, where it is possible to insert the needle directly under the two top loops of the stitches.

! For pieces crocheted **IN TALLER STITCHES, MULTIPLE STITCHES PER EDGE STITCH OR ROW** should be sewn (for instance, 2 stitches for 1 double crochet), inserting the needle directly **INTO THE EDGE STITCHES,** since the needle can be inserted "1 stitch in from the edge" only at the transition from one row to the next.

JOINING MISMATCHED EDGES

Individual parts of garments rarely have only straight edges, which would be necessary for joining row to row or stitch to stitch. Moreover, here also sometimes **stitches** have to be joined **to rows** or **round edges to straight ones.** Crocheted seams, if at all, can only be worked at the shoulders and/or the side edges. All other parts must be joined by sewing in the respective preferred technique. To make seaming easier, it is recommended to place the parts together edge to edge, and with right sides facing each other (or wrong sides facing each other, if a visible seam is desired as design element), temporarily attach them together **with tailor pins or running stitch** (> page 189). To correctly align the parts, pin them together **step-by-step:** Begin with the outer ends of the edges, and then pin the middle; proceed with the middle of the left half, and with the middle of the right half, and so forth. This approach makes it possible to evenly distribute the amount of the crocheted fabric at both edges before sewing together.

X If you want to be extra careful, you can **WASH, BLOCK, AND LET DRY** individual parts before seaming.

X As a general rule: **WORK A TRIAL RUN** and be flexible. If necessary, stitches of the same seam type might need to be of **DIFFERENT WIDTHS** in different spots.

Example: Sewing a sleeve cap into an armhole

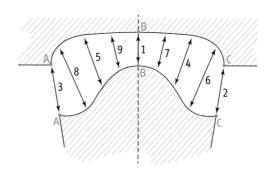

JOINING MOTIFS

Motifs are flat crocheted pieces in geometric shapes, worked in the round from the center out and often joined into larger items patchwork-style. They have only top edges all around, and often have the same stitch count at all edges—or at least such a regular shape that they can be easily joined, such as rectangles for which short edges are joined to short edges and long edges to long edges.

JOINING FINISHED MOTIFS

To join individual crocheted motifs, all methods of crocheting together or sewing together explained in this book (> pages 138-145) can be used. Individual motifs are placed together with edges flush. When motifs are joined with additional crochet work, small, decorative ornamental bands are created between the individual motifs.

SEWING AND CROCHETING TOGETHER

Depending on whether the joining seam will later be out of sight on the wrong side of the fabric or will be visible on the right side of the fabric as decorative element, motifs are placed together with either right sides facing each other or wrong sides facing each other, edge abutting edge and stitch abutting stitch.

! ROUND OR OVAL MOTIFS are in most cases only connected at their tangents, where a few stitches meet each other in a nearly straight line and can be joined. Since these seams are worked separately and always only over a few stitches, there are more ends to weave in.

Now the motifs can be crocheted together (> page 140), for instance, in single crochet. A single crochet seam stands out raised and can be emphasized even more by using contrasting color yarn. It can, however, also be worked on the wrong side of the fabric if it otherwise would add too much bulk.

Motifs can also be crocheted together with slip stitches. The seam in this case produces a broad, flat line on the right side of the fabric.

When sewing together motifs, you can experiment with the insertion point.

If motifs placed together with wrong sides facing each other are sewn together only through the two loops near the middle, the seam will be less noticeable, and the loops of the stitch not included in the seam form decorative lines.

If motifs placed together with wrong sides facing each other are sewn together only through the two outer loops, a seam of tiny slanted dashes is formed.

For motifs placed together right sides facing each other, the exact opposite effects are created.

JOINING WITH ADDITIONAL CROCHET WORK

Since joins with additional crochet work are supposed to show on the right side of the fabric, for joining, motifs are placed together with **wrong sides facing each other**. Then the hook is inserted alternatingly into the motifs—first into the stitches of the first motif, then additional stitches are worked, and then the hook is inserted into the stitches of the other motif.

With Basic Stitches

A pretty but subtle join is created if single crochet is worked between the edges of the two motifs.
A single crochet **seam** does not add too much volume and has a slight zigzag shape.

1 Place the motifs together with wrong sizes facing down. Work 1 single crochet into the first stitch of the motif in front. Then work 1 single crochet into the corresponding stitch of the motif in back.

2 Continue in this way, working 1 single crochet each, first into the next stitch of the motif in front and then into the opposite stitch of the motif in back.

Motifs can also be joined by crocheting with **taller stitches**. This will space the individual motifs farther apart. The taller the crochet stitch, the more pronounced the ladder-like texture created by the seam will turn out.

Joining with half double crochet

Joining with double crochet

WITH CROCHETED CHAINS

Small crocheted chains can also be employed for joining motifs in a very handsome way. The result is a filigree-like seam with a zigzag effect. With this method, 1 stitch **each** is skipped, which staggers the joining spots at both edges.

1 Place the motifs together with their wrong sides facing down. Work 1 single crochet into the first stitch of the motif in front, and then chain 3. Now work 1 single crochet into the second stitch of the motif in back and again chain 3.

2 Work 1 single crochet into the third stitch of the motif in front, chain 3, and then work 1 single crochet in the fourth stitch of the motif in back. This way, alternate working "1 single crochet each into the motif in front, chain 3, 1 single crochet into the motif in back, chain 3," while skipping 1 stitch of each edge.

X You may find crocheting motifs together easier if holding both motifs **IN YOUR HAND** using a finger as **SPACER** as shown for sewing together (> pages 142 and 143).

X What is true for motifs can also be applied to **OTHER CROCHETED PIECES**, such as for a **DECORATIVE, VISIBLE JOIN** at the sides or at the shoulders of a garment. It is important that the stitch count at both edges to be joined is identical. This allows for adding in afterthought width if the parts themselves are too small.

! Unlike crocheting together with single crochet (> page 140), in this method you **NEVER** crochet **THROUGH BOTH LAYERS** at once, but always alternatingly into the individual motifs to be joined

X A DIAGRAM is helpful for arranging the crochet motifs and planning the placement of the joins; for rectangular motifs, graph paper is recommended.

X Joins don't always have to be entirely uninterrupted. It is also possible to **JOIN** the motifs to each other just **AT THE CORNERS**. However, these finished objects are in most cases not as hard-wearing. Hexagonal motifs are particularly suitable for such types of filigree-like work.

ARRANGING MOTIFS

When finished motifs are joined to each other after having been completed, it is convenient to work in **longer joining stretches**. This way, at the end, fewer ends need to be woven in. To do this, it is necessary to plan the **layout** of the motifs and the **lines of joining** before starting the first join.

This is most easily done with **rectangular motifs**, which are joined in **straight lines** with a **narrow join** (for instance, with sewn seams, slip stitches, or single crochets), since here, no special provisions for the joins at the corners have to be made.

First, two motifs are joined together along one edge of each. Then this same join is continued without interruption over two more squares. Thus two sets of two motifs are joined together sharing a long side, while in the center they are only connected to each other at the join. Continue this way until the desired width has been reached. Now add one other motif at a time the same way onto each group of two, always onto one side edge of the strip. Work this way in strips until the finished length of the strip has been reached. Then join the still open edges of the motifs, sewing a long seam over the whole width or length. At the crossing points, just crochet or sew over the previously worked join.

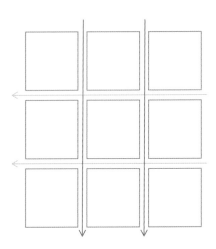

If rectangular motifs are to be joined through **additional crochet work**, joining is somewhat more complicated since the **corner formation** between the individual motifs is not as simple. For this reason, every crochet pattern should contain detailed directions on this topic. Here, this type of join will be explained by the example of joining four squares. Each motif is first completed individually. Then they are joined through additional crochet work in the form of groups of 3 double crochets forming a completely continuous join. How to work the join and shape the corners is explained on pages 150 and 151.

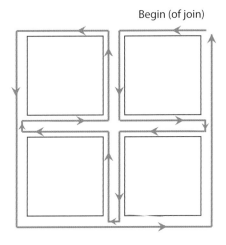

Begin (of join)

For motifs in **other shapes,** the path of the joining lines must be customized to their shape. Here, it can happen that not all edges can always be joined as part of a longer line. A few edges will remain, which have to be joined on an individual basis.

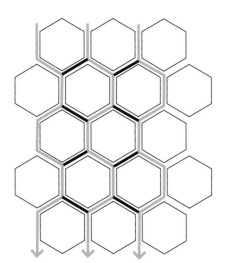

The motifs are now joined at the edges one stitch after another. At the corners, just continue **across the corner** to the next two edges to be joined, which should not present a problem since the join itself is narrow.

✗ If **ENDS NEED TO BE WOVEN IN** on small edges to be joined separately, this should preferably be done within the already-worked joining seams.

❗ To compose a rectangular larger item of motifs that are themselves not square-shaped or rectangular, under certain circumstances **HALF MOTIFS** or **SMALL IN-BETWEEN MOTIFS** in other shapes have to be crocheted to fill in gaps. An area made up of octagons will, for instance, need small squares to fill the spaces generated between motifs.

! In view of the diversity of crocheted motifs, the methods presented here for joining during crocheting can ONLY point out A FEW OPTIONS. Most crochet patterns provide DETAILED DIRECTIONS on how to join individual parts.

JOINING WHILE CROCHETING: "JOIN AS YOU GO"

With this type of joining, **only the very first motif** is **crocheted in its entirety.** All following motifs are **crocheted separately, except for the last round,** and joined with the other motifs during the last round. This has the clear advantage that at the end, only very few ends need to be woven in.

Using the following techniques, any number of motifs in a variety of shapes can be joined to each other. It is important to think about **which combined shape** the joined motifs will later have before starting the joining and whether, for instance, an **even distribution of colors** has to be considered. It is best to prepare a **diagram** that shows all motifs used in the appropriate layout and, if at all possible, including particulars for each one (> page 93). This will allow for crossing off already-worked motifs during crocheting, keeping you on track over which edges the currently worked motif will be joined with other completed motifs.

Depending on progress of work, motifs need to be joined along one, two, or three (or, for polygons, along multiple) edge(s). The remaining edges are just **crocheted** as usual **without joining.** Into these edges, other motifs might be crocheted later. When **solid larger items** are composed of individual motifs, it might be necessary to join all edges of a motif during crocheting.

JOINING IN THE SAME STITCH PATTERN

When the join is worked during the last round in the same stitch pattern as the remainder of the motif, a very inconspicuous join is formed. This is shown here on the example of a classic granny square (> page 317) made up of clusters of 3 double crochets and chain arcs of 2 chains.

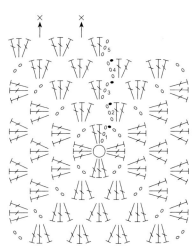

1 The first motif, consisting of 5 rounds, has been completed. Now the second motif is worked up to and including the fourth round. Still work the first double-crochet cluster of the fifth round as usual. Place the motif currently being worked centered onto the completed motif, wrong sides facing each other, making sure that the stitch patterns accurately match one another.

2 Now work 1 single crochet into the chain space between the double-crochet clusters of the completed motif, which is located in the back.

3 Continue the second motif with the next double-crochet cluster. In this manner, proceed working over the entire first edge.

∷ CROCHET SYMBOLS are explained on pages 340–343.

Corners have to be handled differently, depending on how many corners abut during the course of the work:

When only **two corners** abut, instead of 2 chains, 1 single crochet is worked in the chain space of the completed motif, plus 1 additional chain.

If **three corners** abut, the motif currently being worked is joined only to the corner of the immediately adjoining completed motif, as described for two corners.

If **two or three corners** abut, and if the currently worked corner is the last corner of the motif that is being joined, first the chain is worked and then the single crochet.

If **four corners** abut, 2 single crochets are worked into the corners of the motifs immediately adjoining to the right and to the left and are crocheted together. The corner of the motif located diagonally opposite is left out.

JOINING SOLID LAST ROWS

When the outer edge of a motif consists of a solid round of stitches, it, too, can be joined to another motif at every stitch during crocheting. Here, the process is shown on the example of double crochet. This creates a small zigzag-shaped elevation.

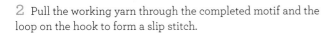

1 Finish the first motif completely, and complete the second motif except for the last round; then place both edges opposite of each other with right sides of work facing up. Begin the last round of the second motif. Work 3 chains (to replace the first double crochet) into the edge of the motif being currently worked. Now insert the hook from top to bottom into the opposite double crochet of the already-completed motif.

2 Pull the working yarn through the completed motif and the loop on the hook to form a slip stitch.

3 Work the next double crochet of the not-yet-completed motif; then insert the hook again into the opposite double crochet, and pull the working yarn through the fabric and through the loop on the hook. Work the whole edge in this manner.

For motifs like these, **at the corners**, often 2 stitches are worked into the same stitch with a short chain in between. If corners are joined to corners, first work the first double crochet into the corner stitch, then work 1 slip stitch in the chain space of the completed motif, and then work the second double crochet into the same insertion point as the first double crochet.

X It does not matter in which **ORDER** individual motifs for a larger whole item are crocheted and joined, as long as you **MAINTAIN** the **OVERVIEW**, and know which color has to be worked next, and where the current motif has to be crocheted onto the existing piece.

! If the motif has a **LONGER CHAIN SPACE** at the corners, it might be necessary to work a few chains, here, too, before and after the slip stitch, if needed. However, it should be **SIGNIFICANTLY FEWER CHAINS** in all than a regular chain arc in this spot would contain, so no larger holes are created.

WITH CHAIN ARCS

When joining with a chain arc, too, the first motif is **worked completely to the end**, and all other motifs are joined **during the last round** to one or more completed motifs. The example shown here is for a 4-round motif in the classic granny square stitch pattern (> page 317), consisting of clusters of 3 double crochets with chain arcs of 2 chains at the corners. The fifth round consists of chain-5 arcs.

 **CROCHET SYMBOLS** are explained on pages 340–343.

 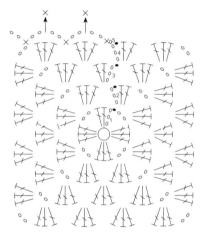

1 First, work all rounds of the first motif (including the chain-5-arcs) as well as Rounds 1–4 of the second motif. Place both motifs together centered, wrong sides facing each other, with stitch patterns correctly aligned. Now work the fifth round of the second motif, consisting of chain-5 arcs. For this, first, chain 2.

2 Work 1 single crochet in the appropriate chain space of the completed motif. Then work 2 additional chains and 1 single crochet into the chain space after the double-crochet cluster of the second motif. Continue, joining the edges in this manner to the end.

 If you want, you can join in the chain arcs **EVEN LESS CONSPICUOUSLY.** For this, in the joining spot, after having worked the 2 chains, remove the **HOOK FROM THE WORKING LOOP,** insert the hook from above in the chain space of the completed motif, pull the working loop through, and attach with 1 slip stitch in the chain space. Then proceed with 2 chains as described.

The **corners** have to be handled differently, depending on how many corners abut during the course of the work:

When only **two corners** meet, just as for the rest of the motif, 2 chains are worked, 1 single crochet in the chain space of the completed motif, and 1 single crochet into the corner of the motif currently being worked.

If **three corners** meet, the motif currently being worked is only joined to the corner of the immediately adjoining completed motif, as described for two corners.

If **four corners** meet, proceed as follows: chain 2, in the chain space of the corners adjoining immediately to the right and left, work 1 single crochet in each chain space, crocheting all single crochets together with a joined top, and then chain 2. Skip the diagonally opposite corner.

WITH PICOTS

Round motifs can, owing to their shape, only be joined **at individual points**. This can also be accomplished in an especially beautiful and smart way with picots (*> page 158*). In the example, a round motif with different stitch types is shown, the last round of which has been worked in picots of 3 chains and 1 slip stitch.

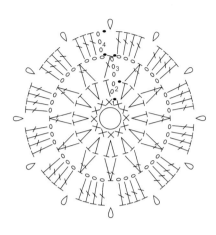

If **ROUND MOTIFS** are to be combined into a likewise round larger unit, start with a **CENTRAL MOTIF** and attach motifs in rounds around it. Just as well, round motifs can also be joined in strips into other shapes. Here, too, it is important to draw up a **DIAGRAM** in advance, showing the needed motifs and their arrangement. **COMPLETED MOTIFS** should be **MARKED** to make sure none of the joining spots will be overlooked.

1 First, finish the first motif completely, including the last round with picots. Work the next motif, except for the last round, and then work the beginning of the last round up to the first picot. Work the first chain of the picot. Then insert the hook from the back into the appropriate picot of the completed motif.

2 Work 1 single crochet.

3 To finish the picot being worked, chain 1 more, and work 1 slip stitch. Continue working the motif, joining the picots in this manner in all required spots with the picots of already-completed motifs.

If **the hook is inserted** into the picot **a different way**, the joining spot can be made to look even less conspicuous. For this, first remove the hook from the working loop, insert the hook from the top and from front to back through the picot, place the working loop on the hook again, and pull it through the picot. Now make a yarn over onto the hook, and pull the working yarn through the loop; then finish the picot. The joining spot appears inconspicuous and flat.

SECURING THE ENDS OF THE WORKING YARN

Except in the rare cases in which the yarn tails are used as decorative elements (for instance, as fringe in a scarf worked lengthwise), they must be either crocheted in during work or woven in neatly and carefully on the wrong side of the crocheted piece at the end.

CROCHETING IN YARN TAILS

Crocheting in yarn tails can be used for attaching a new skein of working yarn in the same color as well as for color changes (*Joining new working yarn > page 74*). This way, almost no ends need to be woven in upon completion of work.

Before the first stitch with the new yarn is worked, place the remaining approximately 4 inches (10 cm) of the old working yarn and the first 4 inches (10 cm) of the new working yarn, in working direction onto the stitches of the previous row or round, and work the following stitches as usual. Both strands are crocheted around over a width of 5 to 10 stitches this way, hiding the tails within the stitches. This works especially well with short stitches, which securely enclose the strands within.

In lace patterns, the color change should preferably be planned in a spot where the stitch pattern is rather solid and has enough stitches to enclose the ends within. Otherwise, it is also possible in lace patterns for the end of the old working yarn to be woven in within a chain arc. However, this method is only suitable for joining a new skein in the same color, not for a color change.

1 Before beginning the first chain, lead both tails over the working yarn to the back. Chain 1.

2 Then lead both tails over the working yarn to the front, and chain 1.

Repeat Steps 1 and 2 until the yarn tails have been securely crocheted in.

WEAVING IN YARN TAILS WITH A TAPESTRY NEEDLE

Loose yarn tails are woven in with a blunt tapestry needle after work on the piece has been completed. Thread a yarn tail of approximately 4 inches (10 cm) into the large eye of the needle, and lead the needle through the stitches on the wrong side of the fabric to hide the tail within the crocheted stitches. To prevent the yarn tail from becoming undone over time, it needs to be woven in first in one and then in the opposite direction.

X For especially **SLIPPERY YARNS**, which easily become undone, the yarn tail can be **UNTWISTED** and separated. Each end is then **WOVEN IN SEPARATELY**— here, too, with a change of direction.

! When weaving in yarn tails, make especially sure that **NO** yarn tails emerge **ON THE RIGHT SIDE OF THE FABRIC**.

Within a seam, yarn tails can be woven in especially well and inconspicuously. Thread the yarn tail into a tapestry needle and weave it in between the stitches of the two pieces in the joining spot. For this, stitch back and forth at least once.

Decorative Edgings

There are various reasons to finish the edges of a crocheted item with a crocheted edging: to improve the appearance of the edges, to reinforce them, or to additionally embellish them. Possible options include edgings in slip stitch, single crochet, or crab stitch, as well as ornate lace edgings. Often, a plain border with a simple combination of stitches is sufficient to spice up a finished item.

When a finished item consists of several parts, as with a blanket or garment, these parts are first sewn or crocheted **together**. After this, the edge is crocheted all around in plain crochet stitches (slip stitches, single crochet) or with simple stitch combinations (chains and single crochets, or double crochets and single crochets).

When crocheting into the edges at the **top and bottom edges** of the crocheted piece, the hook is inserted as usual into the stitches, as would be done for working another row or round. At the **side edges**, the hook is inserted into the edge stitches, and the new stitches evenly distributed as described for crocheting together side edges (> page 140).

An edge can also be decorated with a **SEPARATELY CROCHETED BORDER**. For this, a border of the desired width is first worked separately and then sewn to the edge of the main piece. This method is especially practical when the border is to be worked in a **DIFFERENT YARN** than the main part and with **A DIFFERENT CROCHET HOOK SIZE**. Furthermore, separately worked edgings can be designed more elaborately and freer of constraints—for instance, in regard to the direction of work—than with crocheting directly onto the main part (> page 160).

SLIP STITCH EDGING

Surface crochet in slip stitch creates a **very narrow edging** on the right side of the crocheted piece. This is often applied to reinforce the edge. In a contrasting color, it can also create a decorative accent.

At the top edge, insert the hook for the slip stitches (> page 33) into the **two top loops of the stitch**. At the corners, rotate work clockwise by 90° and continue crocheting into the side edge as described for crocheting together (> page 140).

It also looks very neat if the row of slip stitches is worked slightly set in from the edge (*Surface crochet in slip stitch > page 193*).

SINGLE CROCHET EDGING

An edging in single crochet is an especially simple and inconspicuous method for finishing the edges of a crocheted piece in a decorative way and, at the same time, to straighten them. If you want to accentuate it, work the single crochets in a contrasting color to the remainder of the crocheted piece.

When it is worked in the same yarn as the main part, a crocheted edging in single crochet has the same elasticity as the remainder of the crocheted piece. Crocheting around edges in single crochet works just as **crocheting together in single crochet** (> page 141), with the difference of **only** working **through one layer.**

A crocheted edging in single crochet can also very well serve **as the base** for other decorative edgings or bands (> page 160). It helps to straighten the edge of the crocheted piece in a neat way and can be used to adjust the **stitch count for the pattern repeat** of a border or edging if needed.

CRAB STITCH EDGING

Crab stitch is nothing other than single crochets going diagonally, which are worked **from left to right**—opposite to the usual direction of work. It creates a sturdy, cord-like finish. The hook is **at top and bottom edge** inserted in every stitch, **at the side edges,** as described for crocheting together (> page 140).

1 At the end of the last row or round, do not turn work. With the working loop still on the crochet hook, insert the hook into the last stitch and work 1 single crochet and 1 chain the regular way.

2 Then move the crochet hook to the right and insert the hook under the two top loops of the next-to-last stitch of the row. For this, hold the working loop with the right index finger and insert the hook through the fabric below it. Grasp the working yarn, without first placing a yarn over on the hook, just clasping the hook end from the top onto the working yarn.

3 Pull the working yarn through. The new loop is located to the left of the working loop.

4 Finish the single crochet as usual.

Repeat **Steps 2–4** until you reach the desired length, inserting the hook into the next stitch to the right of the previous one.

It can happen that **1 CRAB STITCH PER EDGE STITCH** is too much for the edging, causing the edging to **BUNCH**. When you have previously made sure that the stitch count at the edge **IS AN ODD ONE,** you can in this case alternate working 1 crab stitch and, skipping the next stitch, **CHAIN 1,** ending with 1 crab stitch.

SPIKE STITCH EDGING

At an edge with multiple solid rows or rounds in single crochet, a single crochet edging can be worked for which the hook is inserted not immediately into the stitches at the very edge but into stitches **one or more rows or rounds below.** These stitches worked below (> page 44) create motifs that look very decorative, especially in contrasting colors, and can be designed as desired. An especially attractive effect can be achieved by combining working single crochets below and crocheting them off together.

Instructions
Stitch count a multiple of 8.
* Work 5 sc into the edge. Crochet the following 3 sc together, inserting the hook as follows into one stitch after another: next st 1 row below, next st 2 rows below, next st 1 row below. Repeat from * continuously.

The edge patterns pictured here are just **EXAMPLES**. The **SIZE OF THE PATTERN REPEAT** can be easily customized by adjusting the number of stitches worked in-between or rows worked below.

Instructions
Stitch count a multiple of 6.
* Work 3 sc into the edge. Crochet the following 3 sc one after another, inserting the hook in rows below as follows: 1 row, 2 rows, and 3 rows below. Repeat from * continuously.

ABBREVIATIONS can be found on page 344.

Instructions
Stitch count a multiple of 7.
* Work 2 sc into the edge. Crochet the following 5 sc one after another, inserting the hook in rows below as follows: 1 row below, 2 rows below, 3 rows below, 2 rows below, 1 row below. Repeat from * continuously.

RUFFLE EDGING

Ruffles are created in a simple way: by crocheting more stitches than there are insertion points at the edge—so to speak, too many stitches for the available space. As a result, the ruffle edging ripples. To work a solid ruffle, into every edge stitch, for instance, 3 double crochets are worked, which are finally arranged into a narrow but deep edging.

Density and width of the ruffle can be modified by varying the number of rows or rounds and the number of stitches to be worked into the same insertion point. Onto the base of a first row with 2 double crochets per edge stitch, a second row with 1 double crochet and 1 chain is worked into every double crochet of the previous row. The resulting ruffle is wider but also more airy than the basic one. Since it consists of 2 rows, it needs to **begin with a wrong-side row**, so that the stitches of the second row later appear on the right side of the fabric.

Ruffles can be **VARIED IN MANY WAYS**—up to elaborate lace patterns, for instance, for a scarf in a romantic style.

X Picots can be modified through the **NUMBER OF CHAIN STITCHES**, the use of **SLIP STITCHES OR SINGLE CROCHETS** for anchoring, and through their **INSERTION POINTS**. Additionally, the **SPACING** between individual picots can be increased or decreased. Experimentation pays off!

••• **ABBREVIATIONS** can be found on page 344.

PICOT EDGING

Picots are tiny curves or peaks of a small number of stitches. They are applied in delicate lace patterns (*> page 301*) and when joining motifs (*> page 153*), but can also be used for decorating the edges of crocheted pieces in a simple way. Most often, picots consist only of chain stitches, slip stitches, and/or single crochets, but there are also numerous variations.

PICOT EDGING OPTION 1
This picot edging option stands out vividly from the top edge.

Instructions
* Work the desired number of single crochets up to the spot for the 1st picot. Then chain 3 and work 1 sl-st into the first of these 3 chains, inserting the hook under the outermost 2 loops of the chain. Repeat from * continuously.

PICOT EDGING OPTION 2
These picots sit closer to the top edge since the hook is inserted deeper for the anchoring stitch.

Instructions
* Work the desired number of single crochets up to the spot for the 1st picot, chain 3. Then work 1 sl-st, inserting the hook into the post of the last sc, between the two V-shaped legs. Repeat from * continuously.

PICOT EDGING OPTION 3
This picot variation is rather round and sits very shallow on the edge.

Instructions
* Work the desired number of single crochets up to the spot for the 1st picot, chain 3. Then sc1 into the same insertion point as the last sc.
Repeat from * continuously.

X The bobbles can be shaped **FLATTER WITH FEWER DOUBLE CROCHETS** and **EVEN ROUNDER WITH MORE DOUBLE CROCHETS CROCHETED TOGETHER**. The **STITCH COUNT** between the bobbles can be modified as desired.

••• How a **CLUSTER STITCH** is worked is explained on page 54.

POM-POM OR BOBBLE EDGING

This very decorative edging uses up more yarn than the previous ones but gives the edge of a crocheted piece a particularly sculptural effect. The rounded shape of the bobbles can be emphasized even more by nudging them into shape from back to front.

Instructions
Stitch count a multiple of 4.
* Work 3 sc, [sc1, ch2, 1 bobble of dc5tog, ch2, sc1] into the next st. Repeat from * continuously.

SHELL EDGING

Shell or fan patterns are very decorative. Since they are a combination of stitches worked over multiple stitches of the edge, it needs to be made sure before starting work that the stitch count of the edge matches that of the stitch pattern repeat. Shell patterns are usually worked over an odd number of stitches. This is also useful if later, when joining motifs (> page 146), the hook has to be inserted into the middle of the shell.

Instructions
Stitch count a multiple of 6 + 1 st extra.
* Work 1 sc, skip 2 sts, dc7 into the next st, skip 2 sts. Repeat from * continuously, ending with sc1 into the last st.

When having reached the corner of the top edge, work 3 single crochets into the corner stitch and continue the shells along the side edges, but here inserting the hook into the edge stitches. Patterns will usually contain all information needed for evenly inserting the hook at the edge. If these details should be missing, the required number of shells and thus even spacing of the insertion points can be calculated on the basis of the width of the shell.
The shells can also be worked in double crochet. For this, the stitch count should be a multiple of 8 + 1 st extra, 9 double crochets per shell will be crocheted, and 3 stitches skipped.

JAGGED EDGE

Spikes at the edge of a crocheted piece can be worked in different stitch patterns. The depicted edging is a simple modification of the shell pattern.

Instructions
Stitch count a multiple of 6 + 1 st extra.
* Work 1 sc, skip 2 sts, [dc3, ch1, dc3] into the next st, skip 2 sts. Repeat from * continuously, ending with sc1 into the last st.

The prettiest stitch appearance can be achieved if the finished crocheted piece, especially the edging, is blocked, pinning down individual chains at the corners of the peaks. Moisten the blocked finished crocheted piece and let it dry (> page 196).

X When **WORKING IN** the round, the additional stitch is not needed.

X A shell edging is easier to work after **FIRST** crocheting **ALL AROUND** the crocheted piece **IN SINGLE CROCHET** (> page 156).

X The shells of an edging don't have to be immediately followed by another, they can be separated by other stitches (such as single crochets) or other stitch patterns (such as picots). In this case, it should, however, be ensured before starting the edging that the **STITCH COUNT** of the edge is a **MULTIPLE OF THAT OF THE FULL PATTERN REPEAT.**

Borders, Edgings, and Bands

Borders, edgings, and decorative bands, whether crocheted with the main piece or attached afterward, lend a professional look to crocheted items, especially garments. Unlike plain one-row edgings, these edges are made up of multiple rows or rounds in a selected stitch pattern, which can be crocheted together with the main piece, crocheted onto the main piece afterward, or sewn onto it.

LACE TRIM

The word "trim" usually stands for crocheted lace and decorative bands, which are either directly **crocheted onto** an edge **or worked separately** and then joined to a base of crocheted or woven fabric. They are versatile and can be used as decorative finishing for completed garments, accessories, or furnishings. Lace trim looks especially delicate in very fine cotton thread at the edges of handkerchiefs.

CROCHETING BORDERS

Every border consists of a **pattern repeat** *(> page 88),* which is repeated continuously. Crocheted borders can be worked either lengthwise or widthwise.

BORDERS CROCHETED LENGTHWISE

Border with straight edge

Border with irregularly shaped edge

Lengthwise crocheted borders are worked in turned rows over the **whole width** of the border. The heightwise pattern repeat of the border therefore consists of **several rows,** which are repeated continuously. The border can be crocheted without interruption to the desired length.

Edgings with a **STRAIGHT SIDE EDGE** can later be easily joined to the **EDGE OF CROCHETED OR WOVEN FABRIC.**

When both edges are **DECORATIVELY SHAPED,** such as with arcs or spikes, the border cannot be directly crocheted onto the piece, but only **SEWN ONTO IT AFTERWARD.**

BORDERS CROCHETED WIDTHWISE

These borders are usually worked in turned rows onto a foundation chain over the **whole length** of the border (i.e., the widthwise pattern repeat consists of a **specific number of stitches** and is repeated continuously over the whole width).

When this border is to be sewn onto a main piece afterward, its length will have to be exactly calculated and crocheted to match since a **later extension is not possible.**

! Even for borders, a small **GAUGE SWATCH** should be rendered. This gives you a general idea about the border in progress, and you can evaluate whether it will match the woven or crocheted fabric in **LOOK AND WIDTH.**

CROCHETING BORDERS ONTO A CROCHETED EDGE

Borders as edge finishing for crocheted pieces are usually **wider and constructed more elaborately** than regular edge finishing such as single crochet or slip stitches edges, which are often limited to one row or round *(Decorative edgings > page 155)*. When crocheting a border **onto the edge of a crocheted piece**, at the **top and bottom edge**, the hook can be inserted directly into the stitches. At the side edges of the crocheted piece, it is recommended to first add a row of **single crochet** *(> page 156)*. Afterward, the border is crocheted onto this base, following the pattern instructions.

For borders worked **in the same yarn** as the main part of the crocheted piece, one stitch of the border corresponds to one stitch of the crocheted piece. It can also happen that the border is to be worked in a contrasting yarn, in most cases in a somewhat **thinner yarn weight**. If this is the case, a gauge swatch for the border should be worked.

1 Place the gauge swatch next to the edge of the main piece and mark a pattern repeat. Then count on the edge of the main piece how many stitches of the main piece correspond to one pattern repeat of the border. In the example shown, there are 7 stitches of the border pattern repeat to 6 stitches of the crocheted piece.

2 After calculating, crochet the border onto the main piece, if necessary increasing stitches within the pattern repeat to reach the stitch count needed for the border.

JOINING BORDERS TO WOVEN FABRIC EDGES

Lace borders are often added as decorative elements to items of woven fabric, such as handkerchiefs or tablecloths. When these edgings are directly crocheted onto the fabric, the necessity of sewing them on later is eliminated, and the transition looks very neat. For this, the fabric edges must be specially prepared. Especially well suited for this purpose are linen needlework fabrics, such as evenweave fabric, or denser woven linen fabrics as used for embroidery. Their countable fabric threads allow for accurate work.

X LINEN NEEDLE-WORK FABRICS are available in many different types. Their descriptions are based on the **THREAD COUNT** per square inch.

PREPARING FABRIC EDGES

There are different ways to prepare the edges of woven fabrics for attaching borders: hemming and crocheting around in single crochet, hemming and embroidering in chain stitch, or hemming and embroidering in buttonhole stitch.

! For coarsely woven fabrics (such as 8-thread count), it will often be sufficient to pull out **1 FABRIC THREAD**. For finer woven fabrics (such as 12- to 14-thread count), however, **2 OR 3 FABRIC THREADS** should be pulled out, so that the hook can later be inserted easily through the fabric edge. When multiple fabric threads are pulled, crocheting into the fabric edge produces a fine **HEMSTITCH-LIKE TEXTURE**, which creates an additional decorative effect.

X If you want to skip preparing the fabric edges, you can directly sew on the **CROCHETED BORDER BY HAND OR WITH YOUR SEWING MACHINE.** For this, hem the fabric, place the crocheted border overlapping approximately 0.2–0.4 inches (0.5–1 cm) over the hem, and sew on in back stitch/straight stitch.

! When crocheting into the edge later, insert the hook for the crochet stitches **BETWEEN THE KNOTS** of the buttonhole stitches.

Hemming and Single Crochet

Linen needlework fabric, 8-thread count

Linen needlework fabric, 14-thread count

1 Cut the fabric on the grain to the desired size + 0.3 inches (0.75 cm) and hem to presser foot width with the zigzag stitch of the sewing machine. Then carefully pull out one or more fabric threads 0.6 inches (1.5 cm) in from the fabric edge. How many fabric threads should be pulled out will depend on the fabric and the yarn weight of the crochet thread used.

2 Fold the edge of the fabric 0.3 inches (0.75 cm) to the back, and baste with sewing thread in short running stitches (> page 189). For this, a thinner thread in a matching color should be used.

3 Now crochet along the fabric edge in single crochet, making sure that the loops of the crochet stitches are always pulled to the very top of the edge so the fabric edge won't constrict. Depending on the thickness of the crochet yarn used, space the insertion points one or more fabric threads apart so the top edge of the line of crochet will be straight.

Hemming and Embroidering in Chain Stitch

1 Cut the fabric on the grain to the desired size + 0.4 inch (1 cm) seam allowance and hem with the zigzag stitch of the sewing machine to presser foot width. Fold the edge of the fabric 0.4 inch (1 cm) to the back and baste in running stitch (> page 189). Then approximately 0.2 inches (5 mm) in from the top edge, embroider a line of chain stitches (> page 190). Work the embroidered chain stitches evenly long, so that the hook can later be inserted easily into the loops of the stitches.

2 Then work single crochet into the embroidered chain stitches, inserting the hook through the top loop of the embroidered chain stitch only. Work the single crochets loosely at an even tension.

Hemming and Embroidering in Buttonhole Stitch

Cut the fabric on the grain to the desired size + 0.4 inch (1 cm) seam allowance and hem with the zigzag stitch of the sewing machine to presser foot width. Then fold the edge of the fabric 0.4 inch (1 cm) to the back and baste in a running stitch. Embroider around the edge of the fabric in buttonhole stitch, approximately 0.2 inch (5 mm) deep. Space the stitches evenly and make sure they are all of the same length.

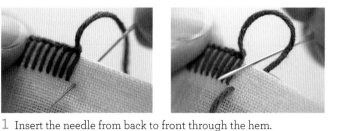
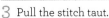

1 Insert the needle from back to front through the hem.

2 Bring needle and working yarn to the back over the edge of the fabric, and lead the needle from back to front through the loop of working yarn.

3 Pull the stitch taut.

Repeat Steps 1–3 continuously.

CROCHETING BORDERS ONTO PREPARED EDGES OF WOVEN FABRICS

After the fabric edges have been prepared, the loops of the single crochets or individual loops of the buttonhole stitches are now located at the outside edges. There are two main ways to get the border onto the edge: crocheting into a fabric edge to make a border and crocheting already-finished borders onto a fabric edge.

Crocheting into a Fabric Edge to Make a Vorder

In borders worked sideways, for the first row or round the hook is inserted directly into the top loops of the single crochets or between the knots of the buttonhole stitches, respectively, spacing insertion points one or more stitches or knots apart, depending on the type of the border. Then the border is worked in rows or rounds as instructed.

Crocheting Separately Crocheted Borders onto Edges

Borders already crocheted up separately can be attached to the prepared fabric edge in different ways.

Crocheting on with Chains

This technique of joining crocheted borders and woven fabric is suitable for all lace trimmings with a straight side edge, and especially for lengthwise crocheted edgings (> page 160).

1 Crochet the border in the required length and work one row of single crochet into the straight edge. Then block the border (> page 196).

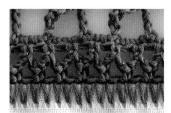 

2 Place the border along the edge of the fabric so the single crochets are located opposite each other. Attach the working yarn at the edge of the fabric, work 1 single crochet into the first single crochet, chain 2, 1 single crochet into the second single crochet at the edge of the border located at the bottom, * chain 2, 1 single crochet into the single crochet at the edge of the fabric after the next one, chain 2, 1 single crochet into the next but one single crochet at the edge of the border. Repeat from * continuously.

Working the Edging and Attaching the Border at the Same Time

When the fabric edge is crocheted around and the border crocheted onto it at the same time, one working step can be eliminated.

1 Crochet the border in the required length, work one row of single crochet into the straight edge, and block. Place the border against the edge of the fabric and with extended single crochet (> page 34), crochet onto it as follows: attach the working yarn at the edge of the fabric, * insert the hook through the fabric edge, pull the working yarn through the fabric, and pull the loop up to the top edge of the fabric. Yarn over and pull the working yarn through the first loop (there are 2 loops on the hook).

2 Insert the hook from back to front into the stitch at the bottom edge of the border, and pull the working yarn through, pulling it through the stitch at the border and the two loops on the hook at once. Repeat from * continuously.

When a ROW OF SINGLE CROCHET has been previously worked into the STRAIGHT EDGE of the border, even spacing between insertion points is much easier to manage.

Ready-to-use blanks are offered in many **DIFFERENT SHAPES** and colors. They can be crocheted around individually and used for items such as doilies. Often, you can also find shape templates for **CROCHETED PATCH-WORK**. Several templates are crocheted around and at the same time joined to produce a larger item.

Specialized yarn stores also carry **HANDKER-CHIEFS** with already-prepared perforated edges, to which you just need to add a **BASE ROUND OF SINGLE CROCHET** before the lace edging can be started.

If the holes are spaced too far apart for **VERY FINE CROCHET THREAD**, the gaps can be bridged with **CHAINS** between the single crochets in the base round.

Experienced crocheters can develop their own **CORNER SOLUTIONS** from the **EXISTING PATTERN REPEAT**. For this, two pattern repeats are placed at a **RIGHT ANGLE** to each other and a suitable stitch arrangement is worked out for the corner beginning with the first round. For chain arcs, it is important to estimate the correct number of chains needed at the corner.

READY-TO-USE WOVEN FABRIC BLANKS WITH PREPARED EDGES

Ready-to-use blanks have the advantage that the edges of the woven fabric are already-prepared with a **perforated edge**. Edgings on ready-to-use blanks are worked **in the round**. During the first round, single crochets are worked into the prepared holes.

Angular Shapes

1 First, work a base round of single crochet. For this, work 1 single crochet each into every hole. At the corners, always work 3 single crochets into the same hole.

2 Then crochet the edging onto this single crochet base round. Edgings for angular ready-to-use blanks must be tailored to the number of holes per side: The stitch count calculated from the pattern repeats for one side and corner have to correspond exactly to the number of holes along one side.

Round Shapes

1 First, work a base round of 1 single crochet into every hole.

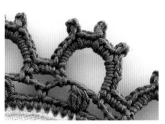

2 Then crochet the edging onto this single crochet base round. Edgings for round ready-to-use blanks must be tailored to the number of holes in the round: The stitch count calculated from the pattern repeat has to correspond exactly to the number of holes around the template.

SHAPING CORNERS IN EDGINGS

Crocheted edgings as trim for doilies are very popular. While borders crocheted in a straight line can be nicely folded into a corner shape, which is then attached to the fabric, this turns out rather bulky and often also looks unmatched.

To achieve attractive corner solutions, the pattern repeat for the edging is adapted to fit the corner, which is shown in a separate crochet chart. With this modification, work can proceed without interruption from one fabric edge to the next.

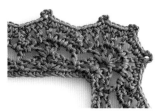

BANDS

Bands are worked at all edges of the crocheted piece that require a **reinforced edge.** They are also useful for **closures,** since buttonholes can be worked into the bands at the side edges, or a zipper can be sewn in *(buttonholes > page 126, zipper > page 129)*. Nice decorative effects can be achieved if the main pattern of the crocheted piece and the stitch pattern of the band are matched to each other. For example, stitches from the main part can be continued into the band or the stitch pattern of the band can be in a strong contrast to that of the main pattern. Bands along the side edges of crocheted pieces can be either **crocheted at the same time** or **added later.**

BANDS CROCHETED AT THE SAME TIME

Predominantly with blankets or pillows, bottom, top, and side bands adjoin each other. These bands look especially nice if they blend into each other **without interruption.** It should be noted that the stitches of the main pattern and the stitches of the band pattern must have **the same height.** When the stitches of the main pattern are shallower than those of the band pattern, the band will bunch. If, however, the stitches of the main pattern are taller than those of the band pattern, the band will constrict.

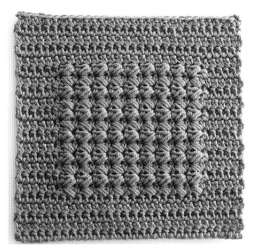

For bands crocheted at the same time as the main part, the **stitch count for the beginning chain** is calculated on the base of the stitch count for the main pattern + the number of stitches for the bands on both sides. First, work the bottom band in the stitch patterns for bands over all stitches widthwise to the desired height of the bottom band. Then, at both ends of the row, continue the stitch pattern of the band over the appropriate stitch count at the side edges, and work over the remaining stitches in the main pattern for the crocheted piece in between. At the desired height for the top band, work again over all stitches in the stitch patterns for bands.

BANDS CROCHETED ONTO THE MAIN PIECE

For bands crocheted on afterward, the stitches of the band are worked onto the crocheted edges of the completed crocheted piece, **right side of fabric facing up.**

At the **top edge** of the **crocheted piece,** the stitches for the band are worked into the **top loops of the stitches of the last row.** The stitches of the band run vertically upward in the **same direction** as the stitches of the main part.

X For bands crocheted directly onto side edges, it is recommended to make a **GAUGE SWATCH FOR THE BAND.** This way, it can be easily determined how many stitches of the band correspond to how many heightwise rows of the main stitch pattern. In the pictured sample, 8 rows of the stitch pattern correspond to 10 stitches of the band. After calculating, mark the edge of the crocheted piece with tailor pins or waste yarn in the appropriate intervals and then crochet onto it.

If a band is to be crocheted onto the **bottom edge of a crocheted piece**, it is recommended to work the stitches of Row 1 immediately after the foundation chain into the **third loop in the back of the chain** (> page 58). This way, the loops of the chains arrange themselves as top loops onto the bottom edge and can later be easily crocheted into. The stitches of the band point down vertically, **opposite to the direction of the stitch pattern.**

At the side edges, it is recommended to first work a row of single crochet (> page 156) into the edge. This way, the edge is being reinforced, and irregularities caused by the stitch pattern are smoothed out. The band lies nice and straight at the side edge.
Then work the band in the desired stitch pattern into the base row of single crochet. Viewing the crocheted piece in its later orientation, at the right-side edge Row 1 is worked from bottom to top; at the left side edge the other way around from top to bottom. The stitches of the band are rotated by 90° crosswise to the direction of the stitch pattern.

BANDS AROUND CURVED SECTIONS

For bands at **inner curves**, the band must be shortened with increasing height to prevent it from bunching. This is done by reducing the stitch count (i.e., stitches must be decreased in evenly spaced intervals around the bend). How many stitches to decrease depends on the shape of the inner curve: For heavily rounded edges, more stitches must be decreased than for less pronounced ones. Decreases are worked by crocheting 2 stitches together (> page 102).

For bands at **outer curves**, the band must be lengthened with increasing height to prevent it from constricting the crocheted piece. For this, the stitch count is increased (i.e., stitches must be increased in evenly spaced intervals along the curve). How many stitches to decrease depends on the shape of the outer curve: For heavily rounded edges, more stitches need to be increased than for less pronounced ones. Increases are always worked by crocheting 2 stitches into the same stitch (> page 98).

BANDS AT CORNERS

For bands at **inside corners**, with increasing height the band has to be shortened and likewise a corner shaped (i.e., the stitch count is being reduced). To work an inside corner, stitches must be decreased in every row or round always over the same spot. The number of stitches that must be decreased is determined by the shape of the corner: For heavily shaped inside corners, more stitches have to be decreased than for shallower corners.

For corners with an **inside angle of 90°**, from the first row/round on, in the center of the corner 3 stitches each are crocheted together (> page 102). In the first row/round, work to 1 stitch before the corner and then crochet together the last stitch before the corner, one stitch directly at the corner, and the first stitch after the corner. This decrease stitch will be the corner stitch for the following rows or rounds and is always crocheted together with the stitch before it and the stitch after it.

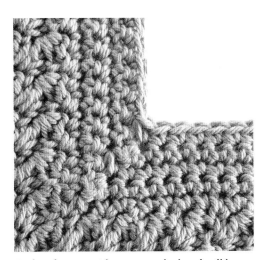 

For bands at **outside corners**, the band will become longer with increasing height (i.e., the stitch count must be increased). To work an outside corner, stitches need to be increased in every row or round, always in the same spot. The number of increases is determined by the shape of the corner: For heavily shaped outside corners, more stitches need to be increased than for less pronounced corners. For corners with an **outside angle of 90°**, during the first row or round, work up to the corner stitch and crochet 3 stitches into this same stitch (> page 98). The center stitch of this increase will be the corner stitch for the following rows or rounds, into which again 3 stitches will be worked.

✗ A VARIATION for corners with right inside angles: In every row or round, SKIP THE CORNER STITCH and crochet the stitch before it together with the stitch after it.

! Bands can be crocheted into OBTUSE ANGLE CORNERS if stitches are increased or decreased not in the corner stitch, but in the stitch before and after it.

Obtuse angle inside corner

Obtuse angle outside corner

Corners with very acute angles are created when multiple stitches are crocheted together at the corner, for instance 2 stitches each before and after the corner stitch.

Crocheted bands are also suitable for **KNITTED PIECES** since the crocheted fabric is **VERY DENSE**, and the bands are **NOT PRONE TO CURLING**.

STITCH PATTERNS FOR BANDS

There are numerous options for designing bands in decorative ways, creating eye-catching details for your crocheted pieces. Choosing the right stitch pattern plays an important role in this.

ALL-OVER STITCH PATTERNS FOR BANDS

For bands, those stitch patterns are especially well suited that have a closed all-over (and therefore dense and compact) texture. These stitch patterns reinforce the edge and have an additional decorative effect thanks to their specific stitch definition.

Since all crochet stitches have a distinctive front and back of the stitch, the **stitch appearance is different** depending on whether the band is crocheted **in rows or rounds**. This is of importance when, for instance, a neckband is worked in the round while the side edge will be crocheted into in rows.

In rows

In rounds

Single Crochets (> page 33) worked in rows yield a typical "little stars" stitch pattern. When crocheted in the round, the V-shaped bodies of the stitches are stacked atop each other. This stitch appearance looks more even.

In rows

In rounds

Extended single crochet (> page 34) worked in rows creates a stripe-like stitch pattern. Worked in the round, the stitch appearance looks more compact and even.

In rows

In rounds

Half double crochet (> page 34) in rows produces a fabric with narrow stripes that are noticeably distinguishable from each other. When crocheted in the round, the stitch appearance looks even more homogeneous.

X WIDE BANDS can be nicely decorated with a cord or tie (> page 180).

Herringbone half double crochet (> page 51) worked in rows appears as stripes. When crocheted in the round, this stitch type looks braided.

In rows

In rounds

Center single crochets (> page 39) produce a very dense, solid stitch pattern. Working in rows, the stitches stand slightly staggered to each other; in the round the stitches are exactly atop each other.

In rows

In rounds

Single crochet worked **into the back** of the **single crochets** of the previous row (> page 38), when crocheted in rows, creates individual horizontal ridges. When crocheted in the round, the ridges are packed closer to each other and appear like a band with a closed surface.

In rows

In rounds

In **stitch patterns** worked in turned rows, right- and wrong-side rows usually look very different. Since opposite rows stand out or recede, the crocheted fabric has a slightly sculptural effect. When crocheted in the round, the stitch patterns appear more uniform and two-dimensional.

In rows

In rounds

STITCH PATTERNS FOR BANDS WITH RIDGE TEXTURE

Patterns with ridge effects can be produced with stitches that prominently protrude from the background fabric. Best suited are post stitches (> *page 41*), especially raised stitches. If, for instance, 2 front post stitches and 2 back post stitches are alternated, vertical ridges are created. A band like this can be easily crocheted together with the main piece.

Most ridge-like stitch patterns, however, create horizontally positioned ridges. When these ridges are crocheted onto a side edge, the stitches will later be positioned 90 ° rotated, with ridges running from bottom to top.

ABBREVIATIONS
can be found on page 344.

Closely spaced wide ridges are created from half double crochets. Every ridge is worked over the course of 2 rows: Begin with a wrong-side row.

Row 1 (WS): Chain 2 extra, hdc through the back loop only the desired number of stitches (> *page 37*), chain 1, and turn.

Row 2 (RS): Hdc, working every hdc through the back loop of the hdc of the previous row and additionally into the unused loop 2 rows below.

Repeat Rows 1 and 2 continuously. Finish the band by turning the last wrong-side row without an additional turning chain and instead of hdc, work slip stitch.

Especially prominently protruding ridges are created from half double crochets for which in every row the hook is inserted into the back of the stitch of the previous row (> *page 38*). Finish the band by working a last right-side row in slip stitch.

A narrow zigzag texture is created from single crochets for which in every row the hook is always inserted into the back of the stitch only. Finish the band by working a last right-side row in slip stitch.

BANDS WORKED SIDEWAYS IN A RIDGE PATTERN

If a band is to be crocheted onto a top and bottom edge so that the ridge runs vertically to the top, it is separately crocheted in rows with only a few stitches, and at the same time in every other row attached to the main piece. At the bottom edge of the piece, it is best to work from left to right, so that the left edge of the band is joined to the edge of the main piece.

Band in Single Crochet Worked through the Back Loop of the Stitch Only

1 Attach the working yarn at the desired beginning of the band in the current row, looping on and work a beginning chain the intended width of the band. * Chain 1 extra, turn work, and work a right-side row in single crochet through the back loop of the stitch only (> page 37) into the crocheted chain, except for the last stitch.

2 Insert the hook into the last stitch and pull the working yarn through the fabric. There are 2 loops on the hook now.

3 Insert the hook front to back through the front loop of the next stitch at the edge of the main piece.

4 Yarn over and pull the working yarn through all 3 loops on the hook at once.

5 Then work 1 slip stitch through the front loop of the next stitch at the edge.

6 Now turn without an additional turning chain and work 1 wrong-side row in single crochet through the back loop only.

Repeat Steps 1–6 from * all the time, until the entire top or bottom edge has been crocheted into. Then continue the band without further transition directly along the side edge in rows, and crochet it to the desired width.

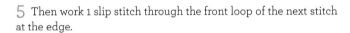
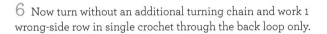
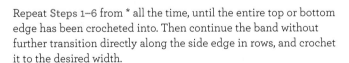

> When crocheting onto a side edge, a possibly **DIFFERENT STITCH HEIGHT** of the main pattern and the pattern of the band has to be considered, too. It is best to make a **GAUGE SWATCH** for the band, place it next to the side edge, and count how many rows of band and side edge correspond to each other. For bands in **HALF DOUBLE CROCHET** or double crochet, it might be necessary to **SKIP 1 STITCH AT THE EDGE**, to prevent the band from bunching.

If you want to rotate the ridges of the side edge by 90° to the band of the bottom edge, first work the band at the bottom edge. Then work the band at the side edge from bottom to top and first join it to the band at the bottom edge, and then crochet it onto the side edge as described.

X **KNOOKING** produces a **PLIABLE** and stretchy fabric that resembles knitting.

STRETCHY RIBBING

Stretchy ribbing can be worked in the "knooking" technique, which allows for producing elastic "knit-look" ribbing, which can be either crocheted over or knooked onto another crocheted piece *(knooking › page 255)*.

1/1 ribbing: Knook alternatingly "1 knit knook stitch, 1 purl knook stitch."

1/1 ribbing with twisted purls: Knook alternatingly "1 knit knook stitch, 1 purl knook stitch through the back loop."

2/2 ribbing: Knook alternatingly "2 knit knook stitches, 2 purl knook stitches."

CROCHETING OVER KNOOKED RIBBING

First, knook the ribbing in the desired width and height, and then bind off the stitches. Now crochet over the ribbing in the required stitch pattern, inserting the hook under the top loops of the stitches of the bind-off row at the top.

KNOOKING OVER THE EDGE OF A CROCHETED PIECE

To finish the top edge of a crocheted piece with ribbing, after having completed the last crocheted row, pick up 1 loop each from every crochet stitch, place it on the knooking hook, and knook the desired ribbing.

KNOOKING RIBBING ONTO A SIDE EDGE

Work one row of single crochet into the side edge of the piece *(› page 156)*. Then insert the knooking hook into every stitch and place 1 loop each onto the hook. Knook the ribbing in the desired stitch pattern.

NECKBANDS

Crocheted neckbands are **less stretchy** than knitted ones. A neckband therefore must be exactly fitted to the crocheted piece to prevent it from bunching or constricting, so it will lie **nicely flat**. For the design of neckbands, there are a multitude of options. Suitable stitches for neckbands are **shallow stitches**, such as slip stitches, single crochet, or half double crochet. Delicate lines can be achieved by changing the way of inserting the hook (> *page 37*). Strong contrasts, however, are created by post stitches (> *page 41*), surface crochet (> *page 193*), or sculptural elements, such as fringe (> *page 174*).

Neckbands with **angular shapes** are made if 1 or 2 stitches are always decreased in the same spot. The number of stitches required depends on the angle of the corner.

Simple Neckband in Single Crochet

Work decreases at the corners according to the angle of the corner, always in the same spot.

Row 1: Work slip stitches into the edge.

Row 2: Work single crochet into the edge of the piece, at the same time also grasping the back loop of the slip stitch.

Rows 3 and 4: Work sc.

Row 5: Work crab stitch.

For the inward curve on **round neckbands**, stitches must be decreased at even intervals.

Neckband with Loopy Fringe

Work the decreases to match the curve.

Row 1: Sc1, * ch7, sc1, repeat from * continuously.

Row 2: Sc1 into every sc of the previous row.

Row 3: Sc1 blo into every stitch of the previous row.

Row 4: Sl-st 1 flo into every stitch of the previous row.

Row 5: Sl-st 1 blo into every stitch of the previous row.

A **V-shaped neckline** has an acute angle. Depending on the angle of the corner, for the point multiple stitches must be crocheted together at the same time.

V-shaped Neckband with Surface Crochet in Slip Stitch

Decrease in every round as required for the angle.

Row 1: Work sc, inserting the hook about 0.4 inches (1 cm) in from the edge.

Row 2: Hdc1 flo into every stitch of the previous row.

Row 3: Hdc1 into every hdc of the previous row.

Row 4: Sl-st 1 into the bar in back of the stitch in every hdc of the previous row.

Finally, along the edge of the neckband, surface crochet sl-st (> *page 193*).

With a row of **SLIP STITCHES** on the wrong side of the band, slight imperfections and loose spots can be compensated for.

ABBREVIATIONS can be found on page 344.

How to shape **BANDS**, see also pages 165–167.

For the different ways to insert the hook, please refer to pages 37–42.

Decorative Elements

Crochet projects are made unique by finishing details such as fringe, pom-poms, tassels, cords, embroidery, or crocheted buttons. All these decorative elements are created with much love for detail and provide ample space for creative freedom. No doubt—these ornamental extras will earn your work attention and admiration.

FRINGE

On hearing the word "fringe," knotted-on fringe most often comes to mind first, but the options are a lot more wide ranging than that. Fringe can be crocheted as plain crocheted chains, it can curl in a spiral, or it can be incised into the edge of the crocheted fabric. For attaching the fringe, too, there are a variety of ways.

X Spiral fringe is in many cases a great **ALTERNATIVE** to ruffled edges, but it requires plenty of time and yarn.

SPIRAL FRINGE

The spirally twisted fringe, due to its appearance, is also called curly fringe or corkscrew fringe, and can be worked in single crochet but also in taller stitches. To work a spiral fringe, begin with a crocheted chain plus the appropriate number of height-adjustment chains according to the height of the stitch (> page 64). Then crochet along the chain, working 2 stitches into every chain. Because of the higher number of stitches worked over a shorter beginning length, the band of stitches curls into a spiral. The examples show a spiral in single crochet and a spiral in double crochet. The finished spiral is about 25% shorter than the beginning chain.

When 3 stitches are crocheted into every chain, the band curls more and the finished length will be even shorter. When working this fringe, the groups of stitches should always be worked only into one strand of the beginning chain (> page 58) so the edge won't be too tight.

At the end of the row, for single crochet, leave the last 2 chains (for double crochet, the last 3 chains) unworked. Finish the row with 1 slip stitch into the last chain. To attach the fringe to an edge, anchor the spiral with a slip stitch. Move along the edge to the attaching point for the next fringe with slip stitches.

CHAIN LOOP FRINGE

Loops from crocheted chains also create fringe. How close they are depends on their distribution along the edge of the crocheted piece. In between fringes, single crochets are worked into the edge. In the pictured example, the chain loops beginning at the left edge are spaced 1 single crochet apart, the ones to the right have been crocheted with 2 single crochets in between.

To make a loop, crochet a chain twice as long as the desired length of the fringe and close the fringe loop with 1 slip stitch into the first chain. Then work single crochets into the edge up to the spot for the next fringe.

FLAT CROCHETED FRINGE

This flat fringe from 1 row of double crochet each looks cut into the edge of the crocheted piece. It can be crocheted onto the main piece as you go if the crocheted piece is being worked sideways (i.e., the fringe begins at the side edge). The fringe can be either worked into a foundation chain or crocheted onto the main piece with base loops (> page 59). In the example, the main pattern alternates 1 row of double crochet and 1 row single crochet. The rows worked in single crochet are always shortened to the end of the "incision," where a new fringe begins. After this, a new chain is crocheted from the edge out, which on the return pass is worked into with a double crochet.

Flat fringe worked in double crochet or single crochet can also be crocheted onto the main piece afterward. After having crocheted along the foundation chain, the fringe is attached to the main piece with a slip stitch. If necessary, work another slip stitch at the edge, and then begin the next fringe.

KNOTTING ON FRINGE

Whether in the same color as the crocheted piece or in an array of several colors, knotted-on fringe highlights and embellishes edges on items such as scarves, triangular scarves, ponchos, or bags.

1 First, cut strands of yarn for the fringe. For the length of the strands to cut, calculate 2 times the finished length of the fringe plus 0.8–1.6 in (2–4 cm) allowance for knotting. For each fringe, bundle 4 strands (or other desired number) of yarn and fold in the middle. Insert the crochet hook into the edge of the crocheted piece from the right side of the fabric at the attaching point of the fringe and pull the closed end of the bundled strands 1.2–2 inches (3–5 cm) through.

2 Hold the loop with your left hand and pull all strands through the loop with the help of the crochet hook.

3 Pull at the bundled strands until the loop sits close to the edge of the crocheted piece and securely encloses all strands. Finally, trim all finished fringes to the same length.

X If a lot of fringes need to be created, 2 or 3 chain loops can be crocheted at the same attaching point, one after another. Another VARIATION is fringe in different lengths.

X Individual fringes can be decorated very nicely by threading BEADS onto them and knotting to secure.

X It's worth the effort to prepare a **TEMPLATE** for cutting the individual fringes. Cut a rectangle from sturdy cardboard with a side 0.8 inches (2 cm) longer than the planned fringe length. Wind the yarn not too tightly around the cardboard and cut open one end of the bundle of strands. Separate the cut strands into individual bundles, each containing as many strands as to be knotted on in one spot.

X If net-look fringe is to have **ONLY ONE ADDITIONAL KNOT**, make the first and last fringe bundle with only **HALF THE USUAL NUMBER OF STRANDS,** and knot this with half the strands of the adjoining bundle. Otherwise, half the bundle of strands would later hang down unattached. If more knots are to be worked further down, this is not necessary since the half bundle will be knotted again later.

Both sides of the knotted-on fringe look presentable. If the tightened loop of the bundle is supposed to end up on the **right side of the crocheted piece**, insert the crochet hook into the edge of the crocheted piece from the **wrong** right side of the fabric at the attaching point of the fringe, and pull the closed end of the bundled strands through the edge (the strands will here be on top of the main piece). After this, pull the strands through the loop and tighten the knot.

To create a **net look**, the fringe is first knotted onto the edge, and then fringes are knotted with each other. For this, the strands have to be cut approximately 1.6 inches (4 cm) longer for each additional knot. Separate the knotted-on bundle of strands in half, and then hold together 2 adjacent half-bundles of strands; knot one of the two half-bundles around the other. Make sure that the new knots are located centered between the knot-in spots at the edge, and at equal distance to the edge of the crocheted piece.

If you want to additionally accentuate and embellish the fringe edge, add a simple, **narrow edging with chain arcs.** Into these chain arcs, the bundled strands for the fringe can be knotted.
Example: Stitch count a multiple of 5.
Attach the working yarn to the edge at the first stitch, * skip 1 stitch at the edge, [dc2, ch2, dc2] into the next st, skip 1 stitch at the edge, 1 sl-st each into the next 2 sts of the edge. Repeat from * continuously, after the last spike, work only 1 sl-st into the edge. Knot the fringe into the chain arc.

When **individual fringes** are **very thick**, or the crocheted piece has a **solid stitch pattern**, it is recommended to first work a row of single crochet at the attaching edge, adding loops of 2 or 3 chains at convenient intervals, skipping 1 or 2 stitches at the attaching edge where chains are worked. This prevents the edge from curling after the fringe has been knotted onto it.

POM-POMS

The classic version of a pom-pom, **wound from yarn,** still works perfectly for the pom-pom hat. Additional colorful accents are created when multiple colors are used. Sphere-shaped pom-poms **worked in single crochet** are also very decorative and can embellish a scarf or triangular shawl. Novelty and textured yarns can also be used for this type of embellishment.

▪▪▪ ABBREVIATIONS can be found on page 344.

CROCHETED POM-POM

Small spheres in single crochet can be used for decorating the ends of cord-like fringe crocheted onto the main piece. Here is one example for how these pom-poms can be used to their advantage.

Instructions

Begin the sphere with 1 chain in the center *(> page 67),* and work sc in spiral rounds *(> page 71).*
Round 1: Work sc6.
Round 2: Double every st around—that is, work sc2 each into every st (= 12 sts).
Rounds 3–5: Sc1 into each st without increases.
Round 6: [Crochet 2 sts together] 6 times (= 6 sts). Stuff the ball with fiberfill before this round has been completed.
Round 7: Work sc1 into each st (= 6 sts).
Break the working yarn, leaving a long tail, thread the end into a tapestry needle, and thread it through the front loops of the sts of the last round. Pull taut to close the remaining opening in the center.

To work the pictured edging, proceed as follows:
Stitch count at the edge is a multiple of 8 + 3 or 2 or 1 st extra.
Row 1: Work 1, 2, or 3 sc into the edge, * chain 9, skipping 5 sts at the edge, work 3 sc into the edge, repeat from * continuously, at the end, after a chain arc, work 3, 2, or 1 sc instead of 3 sc into the edge.
Row 2: Work sl-st into all sts (chains and single crochets), working sl-st into sc through the flo *(> page 37),* for the chains, working surface crochet sl-st as explained for slip stitch cord *(> page 180).* In the middle of every chain arc, after the 5th sl-st, continue with ch8 for the fringe. Anchor the finished ball with 1 sl-st, and work back over the fringe chain in sl-st.

WOUND POM-POM

In preparation, cut out two identical **circles of sturdy cardboard** in the desired size of the pom-pom. Using a sharp cutter or nail scissors, cut out a circle from the center of each circle—the larger this opening is, the more densely the yarn can be wound, and the fuller the finished pom-pom will turn out. Place the cardboard rings on top of each other. Wind several strands of yarn held together, first with the help of a crochet hook, around the two cardboard rings. When the opening becomes smaller, use a thick, blunt tapestry needle, until the **hole in the center** has been **filled up.** Insert scissors between the cardboard rings and cut the yarn loops open all around. Carefully pull the cardboard rings apart, place a double strand of yarn between them, wind it tightly around the pom-pom strands 2 times, and knot the ends twice to secure. This strand can later be used for sewing on the pom-pom. Cut the cardboard rings open and remove them. Shake the pom-pom and, if needed, **trim to the desired shape.**

✗ Pom-poms can be produced faster and easier with a **POM-POM TOOL.** These sets contain ready-to-use plastic templates for making pom-poms in different sizes.

TASSELS

Especially when embellishing home decor accessories, tassels come into play. They adorn pillow corners, throw blankets, and curtain ties or serve as decorative pendants on door handles or drawer knobs, and as key fobs.

CROCHETED TASSEL WITH CHAIN LOOP FRINGE

Instructions

For the head of the tassel, crochet a strip in sl-st, 4 sts in width and 14 rows in height, always inserting the hook through the flo only (> *page 37*). Finished strip measurements: 0.8 x 2.2 inches (2 cm x 5.5 cm).

Immediately after the last row of the strip, begin the fringe. For this, crochet a chain twice as long as the desired length of the fringe directly onto the existing piece, and anchor the fringe with 1 sl-st into the first chain, creating a loop. Subsequently work 1 sl-st into the following row at the edge of the strip, and crochet the next fringe from it. In the example fringes of 26 chains for 2.6 inches (6.5 cm) fringe length and 20 chains for 2 inches (5 cm) fringe length have been alternated. Work the chain loops along the whole length of the initial strip.

Roll up the strip and sew stitch by stitch at the narrow end together, using the yarn tail. Cinch the outside edge of the strip with another piece of yarn to form the round shape of the tassel head. For this, thread a piece of yarn into a tapestry needle, thread the needle through one strand of every stitch in every row, and pull the yarn through, which constricts the edge. Weave in the yarn tail, leaving a small loop of yarn sticking out for hanging. Bind off the head of the tassel with a piece of yarn above the spot where the skirt of the tassel emerges, winding it around 3 or 4 times, knotting the ends around each other and pulling through to the inside using a blunt tapestry needle.

CROCHETED TASSEL WITH KNOTTED-ON FRINGE

Instructions

For the head of the tassel, crochet a strip 4 sts in width and 20 rows in height in sl-st, inserting the hook through the flo only (> *page 37*). Finished strip measurements: 0.8 x 3.2 inches (2 cm x 8 cm). Into one long edge, knot fringe strands (> *page 175*).

Attach eight fringes, each one composed of 2 strands, 8 inches (20 cm) long, in every other row, leaving the first or last 4 rows without fringe since the strip will later be rolled up from this end. On the wrong side of the strip, knot on seven more fringes, always set in by 1 stitch from the edge, in the spaces between the outer fringes. Knot on the 2 strands for each fringe, always around one strand of the crocheted stitch.

Roll up the strip and sew together stitch by stitch at the narrow end, using the yarn tail. Cinch the outside edge of the strip with another piece of yarn to form the round shape of the tassel head. For this, thread a piece of yarn into a tapestry needle, thread the needle through one strand of every stitch in every row, and pull the yarn through, constrict the edge. Weave in the yarn tail to secure the shape, and then add a hanging loop made of a crocheted chain of 0.8 inches (2 cm) length in the center of the tassel head.

WOUND TASSEL

Instructions

In preparation, cut a rectangle from sturdy cardboard to the same height as the intended length of the tassel. Wind the yarn around the cardboard 30 to 50 times, depending on the desired thickness of the tassel. At one edge of the cardboard, tie the bundle of yarn strands together using a piece of yarn held double and knotting the yarn twice. At the other edge of the cardboard, cut all yarn loops open. Hold the strands together, with the tied spot at the top of the tassel head, and leave two of the strands used for tying hanging outside, and hide the other 2 strands inside the skirt of the tassel.

Tie off the head of the tassel with an approximately 23.6-inch (60-cm) long piece of yarn, folded in half. Wrap the piece of yarn around the bundled strands 0.6 to 0.8 inches (1.5 to 2 cm) below the first tying spot, thread the two open ends through the closed end, and tighten it. Tightly wrap the tassel with one of the two strands 2 or 3 times more, and then knot the ends. Pull the yarn tails to the inside of the tassel with a blunt tapestry needle so that the knot slips under the wound strands. Trim the strands to the same length.

Using one of the yarn tails, add a hanging loop made of a crocheted chain of 1 inch (2.5 cm) length at the head of the tassel, or leave a small loop of yarn sticking out.

TASSEL WITH CROCHETED BELL

To top the head of the tassel, crochet a sphere-shaped bell cover **in single crochet**. Use a medium-weight yarn (yardage approximately 137 yd/1.75 oz [125 m/50 g]), crochet hook 2.5 mm (US between B-1 and C-2), to achieve a fine crocheted fabric that will be easy to shape. A bell made using the following instructions will be 1 inch (2.5 cm) in diameter and 1 inch (2.5 cm) in height.

Instructions

Begin the bell with a ring of 5 chains (> page 67), and work sc in spiral rounds (> page 71).

Round 1: Work sc8 into the chain ring.

Round 2: Double every st around—that is, work sc2 each into every st (= 16 sts).

Rounds 3–6: Work sc1 in each st without increases. Leave the yarn tail hanging for later use. Make the tassel, but without tying off around the tassel head. Using 2 yarn tails from the tying spot at the top of the tassel, create and sew on a small thread eyelet. Slide the bell over the bundled yarn strands for the tassel head, pulling the sewn-on thread eyelet to the outside through the opening in the center of the bell with the help of a crochet hook.

Round 7: [Crochet 2 sts together] 8 times (= 8 sts).

Round 8: [Sc1, ch1] 8 times, ending with 1 sl-st.

It can also look very nice if the tassel head is tied with a piece of CONTRAST-ING COLOR YARN.

ABBREVIATIONS can be found on page 344.

CORDS, STRINGS, AND RIBBONS

Crocheted cords, strings, and ribbons can be used in many ways in crochet projects: as tie, belt, shoulder strap, or bag handle. A cord can be threaded through a drawstring channel, coiled into fanciful ornaments and sewn on, or formed into a frog closure. Crocheted round cord can be applied very strikingly in jewelry design.

SLIP STITCH STRING

Crochet a **chain** the desired length of the string. Do not break the working yarn yet. Now work slip stitches **into the third loops** in the back of the chain, using new working yarn and beginning in the first chain of the beginning chain. This eliminates the need for attaching new working yarn later in case the string needs to be lengthened.

RIBBON IN SINGLE CROCHET

Instructions

Chain 2, sc1 into the first of these 2 chains. Without turning, for the next sc, insert the hook into the outermost, vertical strand of the post of the stitch, pull a loop through, pull the working yarn through once more, pulling it through the 2 loops on the hook at once. Continue working sc in this manner.

> ! A ribbon in single crochet is the same as **FOUNDATION SINGLE CROCHET** (> page 59).

SLIP STITCH BAND

This stitch pattern is compact and sturdy, and is appropriate for items like shoulder straps, bag handles, or belts.

Instructions

Chain 5, and work sl-st in rows to the desired length, always inserting the hook through the flo of the stitches only (> page 37). The long edges can be additionally crocheted around: For this, * sc1 around the single strand at the edge, and then skip 1 row, bridging it with 1 chain, repeat from * continuously.

ROUND CORD IN SINGLE CROCHET

Instructions

Chain 8, and close to a ring shape with 1 sl-st into the first chain. Work sc in spiral rounds (> page 71) on the inside of the tube.

●●● ABBREVIATIONS
can be found on page 344.

BOW RIBBON

Instructions

Chain 3. * Work dc1 (incomplete) into 3rd ch from hook, leaving the last loop of the stitch on the hook. Place a yarn over onto the hook, insert the hook once more into the same chain, and pull the working yarn through the fabric. Place a yarn over onto the hook, only crochet 1 loop off the hook, place another yarn over onto the hook, and crochet the 2 loops off the hook together. Yarn over once more and pull yarn through all 3 loops on the hook at once. To work the next group of stitches, chain 3, and continue, repeating from *. Following the established pattern, continue the band to the desired length. After this, the long side that doesn't have any chains can be crocheted into. For this, alternate working ch4 and 1 sl-st between the round shapes.

CHAIN LINK BAND

Instructions

Chain 3, dc1 in the 3rd chain from the hook. Then work sc4 along the side of the dc, ch1, continue on the other side, working sc4 around the 3 chains, ch1, and work 1 sl-st into the first sc. The first shape has been completed.
* Chain 3, turn work, and work dc1 into the chain of the previously crocheted around shape. Chain 1 and turn work. Work sc4 in the ch-sp.
Work ch1 to transition to the other side, work sc4 around the dc, ch1, and work 1 sl-st into the first sc on the other side. Repeat from * continuously to the desired length.

ROUND CORD IN SINGLE CROCHET

Instructions

Chain 4 or 5, and close to a ring shape with 1 sl-st into the first chain. Work sc in spiral rounds (> page 71) on the inside of the tube/work, always inserting the hook through the outermost loop of the stitch only. Do not work too tightly, so the hook can be easily inserted into the stitches.

⚠ A cord with 4 stitches circumference appears rather edgy and, because of the small circumference, special attention has to be paid to **INSERTING THE HOOK** in the **CORRECT SPOTS**.

If the **way of inserting the hook** is changed, the stitch appearance changes visibly. Crochet 5 chains, and close to a ring shape with 1 sl-st into the first chain. Work single crochets in spiral rounds (> page 71) on the inside of the tube. From the second round on, for every single crochet, always insert the hook through the outermost loop of the stitch together with the horizontal strand below it.

If a round slip stitch cord is to be used for a **BAG HANDLE**, the edges need to be left **OPEN** over about 1.2 inches (3 cm) at the beginning and end. The flat ends of the cord are sewn on.

ROUND SLIP STITCH CORD

When slip stitches are worked in rows, always working through the front loop of the stitch only (> page 37), a stitch appearance with small horizontal ridges is created—a dense texture, which, when crocheted loosely in a thick yarn, has a very striking look.

Instructions

Crochet a beginning chain in the desired length of the cord. In Row 1, insert the hook in the second chain from the hook and work sl-st through the blo of each chain (> page 58), grasping only 1 strand of the stitch.

For Row 2, chain 1 for turning, and turn. Then work sl-st through the flo (upward facing) of the stitches. Work the following rows the same way, until a total of 6 rows have been worked. Do not crochet too densely so that you will be able to easily insert the hook for the sl-sts of the next row. After Row 6, chain 1, and turn.

Now crochet the long edges together in sl-st. For this, fold the beginning edge upward. * Insert the hook at the same time through one loop of the stitch of the beginning chain and the loop of the sl-st from the previous row facing it. Grasp the working yarn, pull it through the fabric and immediately through the working loop. Repeat from * continuously until the edges of the strip have been crocheted together.

SEMICIRCULAR SLIP STITCH CORD

Work with yarn held double or single. Besides the ridged texture, a color change creates an additional effect.

Instructions

In color 1, crochet a chain corresponding to the length of the cord. At the end, do not break the working yarn. Now pull the working yarn in color 2 through the working loop, and work Row 1 in color 2, working

sl-st blo (> page 58), grasping only 1 strand of the stitch. To work Row 2, take up the yarn at the end of the beginning chain (in color 1) and work another RS row of sl-st blo of the chains. The stitch pattern is created on the wrong side of the fabric (see photo).

SPIRAL CORD

Instructions

Make three crochet chains of the same desired finished cord length. Hold the three chains together and insert the hook into the respective first chain of all three chains one after another and work 1 single

crochet very tightly so that the beginning point is fixed and the following stitches won't slide off. Now you will enclose the chains held together in single crochet, always bringing the working yarn to the front of work underneath the three chains and leading it up to the height level of the working loop. Twist the finished cord around itself, so that the top loops of the single crochets spiral around the cord. Secure the opposite end with 1 very tight single crochet through all three chains.

FLAT CORD

This flat, sturdy cord is also known as "macramé cord."

Flat cord looks especially beautiful as raised embellishment along bands or arranged into a curlicue ornament and sewn on. An example for this is the frog closure (see below).

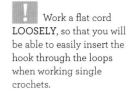 Work a flat cord **LOOSELY**, so that you will be able to easily insert the hook through the loops when working single crochets.

1 Crochet 2 chains, work 1 single crochet into the first one of these 2 chains. Rotate the crocheted piece toward the front and directed to the left (clockwise).

2 Insert the hook into the unused chain (see arrow in photo), and pull the working yarn through the fabric. Place a yarn over onto the hook and crochet the two loops off the hook together. 1 single crochet has been completed. The bracket marks the 2 loops for the next step.

3 Rotate the crocheted piece as before, do not work an additional turning chain. At left, 2 loops are now stacked atop each other. Insert the hook through these 2 loops together and work 1 single crochet.

Repeat **Step 3** all the time. At the end of the cord, work 1 slip stitch instead of 1 single crochet.

FROG CLOSURE

A frog closure consists of **two parts** and is created of a cord or band arranged into decorative curlicues and then sewn on. The two pieces of the frog closure are **symmetrical** to each other and most often closed with a **toggle button**, which joins the two parts of the closure to each other.

To make this closure, crochet two flat cords of equal length (see above). In the pictured example, each flat cord is 20 inches (50 cm) long and 3.2 inches (8 mm) wide. Each finished closure part is 4.1 inches (10.5 cm) in height and 5 inches (12.5 cm) in width, 2.8 inches (7 cm) of which account for the fastening loop.

FANCIFUL ORNAMENTS can be designed with cords and strings, whose typical features are curlicues arranged into looped shapes similar to the pictured frog closure. Different sizes of curlicues can also be combined. Sewn on in a straight line, cords can also be used to accentuate the transition from main part to front bands and borders.

The **TOGGLE BUTTON** for a frog closure can also be crocheted (> page 188).

It is recommended to first sketch the planned ornament on graph paper to have references for general size and crossing points when arranging the cord. Place the cord on the drawing in the appropriate loop shapes, and temporarily fix the crossing points with tailor pins. The ends of the cords should always meet under a crossing point. Sew the cords together at the crossing points to fasten the ornament. If needed, the size of the fastening loop can be reduced by sewing the cords together in this spot with a few stitches. Sew a toggle button onto the button side, either at the turnaround point (in which case, this loop stays round) or at some distance from the end (which shapes the two cords more parallel to each other). To close, pull the loop of the counterpart over the button.

More pretty **EDGE FINISHINGS** can be found beginning on page 155.

ABBREVIATIONS can be found on page 344.

DECORATIVE EDGE FINISHINGS

Curling fringe made of single crochet embellished with flowers threaded onto it or ribbons in double crochet attached in a bow shape with additional floral ornaments are examples for how spectacular effects can be achieved through creative use of basic components.

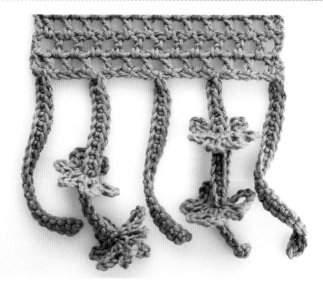

FRINGE WITH FLOWER EMBELLISHMENT

Instructions

For the **fringe**, chain 20–23, and crochet 1 row of sc along the chain, working the sc only through 1 strand of each chain (*> page 58*). The finished fringe will be 4.1–4.7 inches (10.5–12 cm) long. Using the yarn tails, attach the fringe to the edge of the crocheted piece, making sure to space evenly with 5 sts (approximately 1.2 inches [3 cm]) between fringes. Weave in the yarn tails.

To work a **flower**, chain 5, and close to a ring shape with 1 sl-st into the first chain. Now alternate working sc1 into the chain ring and, for the petals, [chain 5] 4 times, and [chain 6] 2 times, finally, sc1 into the chain ring. Knot the yarn tails with each other. Pull a fringe through the centers of two flowers, sew the flower to the fringe using the yarn tails, knot the yarn tails twice, and break the working yarn. For variety, thread only one flower to some of the fringes, and between fringes with flower decoration occasionally leave 1 or 2 fringes unadorned.

ARCHED RIBBON WITH FLORAL ORNAMENTS

Instructions

For the **Band**, chain 13 + 2 height-adjustment chains, and work 1 row of hdc. At the end of the row first, ch2, and then work sl-st along the beginning edge, so that the long sides look the same. The finished length of the band in the example is 3.5 inches (9 cm). At the edge of the crocheted piece, mark the joining spots for the ribbons, spaced 2 inches (5 cm) apart. Pin the ends of the ribbon to the edge of the crocheted piece, twisting the second end of the ribbon to face the other side, and place the ends of the ribbon atop each other. Sew on the ribbons using the yarn tails.

For a **petal**, chain 6, dc1 into the 4th chain from the hook, and then work hdc1, sc1. Crochet a total of 7 interconnected petals. At the end, for the

center of the flower, ch2, and work a flat bobble from hdc3 (*> page 52*) in the post of the last sc, ending with ch1. Break the working yarn and pull it through the working loop. Arrange five petals into a circular shape and sew, on top of those, the remaining two petals together with the center of the flower. Now the finished flower can be sewn on.

CROCHETED BUTTONS

Crocheted buttons not only are functional closures but also serve as an eye-catcher on clothing and bags. In addition, they can be used as cufflinks, pendants, or decorative elements or to embellish home decor accessories, such as pillows. Either a suitable base shape is enveloped in a crocheted cover or the whole button is crocheted in the desired shape and size. A non-traditional shape, colorful accents, and interesting details such as incorporated beads, crocheted chain loops, or embroidery turn buttons into fanciful little pieces of art.

CROCHETING AROUND A BASE SHAPE

Ordinary flat or domed buttons serve as **inserts** for the crocheted cover. They determine the **size** and support the **shape** of the finished button. The inserted button can also be equipped with an eye or shank, which allows for directly sewing on the crochet-covered button. Beads are incorporated into sphere-shaped buttons. The following examples show the working steps for simple flat or domed shapes and for a sphere-shaped button.

FLAT BUTTONS

Flat buttons can be worked in different shapes and various stitch types.

FLAT BUTTON IN SINGLE CROCHET

Finished size of the button: 1 inch (25 mm)
Button insert: 0.08 inches (20 mm)

Instructions

Work top and bottom part separately as circular shapes.
Begin the circle with 1 chain in the center (> page 67), and work sc in spiral rounds (> page 71).
Round 1: Work sc6.
Round 2: Double every st around—that is, work sc2 each into every st (= 12 sts).
Round 3: Double every other st around, work sc1 in all other sts (= 18 sts), and additionally work 1 sl-st.

Break the working yarn and pull the working loop long until the tail has been pulled through. Work a second circle the same way.
The **edges of the button** can now be sewn together in one of two different ways.

To work a **pronounced edge**, place the two discs together so that the wrong side of the single crochets is on the outside and seam with a ladder stitch (> page 145) using a dull tapestry needle and always catching only the 2 innermost loops of the stitches of the last round. Slide the button insert between the two layers before the seam has been completely closed.

For a rounded **edge**, the two discs are sewn together in whipstitch (> page 142) using a dull tapestry needle and always catching only the 2 outermost loops of the stitches of the last round. The edge of the button appears curved.

If the two discs of the button are to be crocheted in one piece, when the top has been finished, individual stitches are decreased in regular intervals until the bottom part completely covers the button insert. The decreases are worked in opposite order to the previous increases. Depending on the size of the button insert, the number of rounds for the bottom part might need to be adjusted: working 1 fewer round than for the topside, until finally only a small opening of about 0.2 inches (5 mm) diameter remains.

FLOWER-SHAPED buttons accentuate a romantic style. Make them by surrounding a half-sphere shape with short chains for petals.

It is best to work with a **THIN YARN** (yardage approximately 137 yd/1.75 oz [125 m/50 g], crochet hook 2.5 mm [US between B-1 and C-2]) to create a fine crocheted fabric, which allows for easily developing the desired shape. Sock yarn can be used, too. If you want to experiment, use a thinner novelty or textured yarn.

The button insert should preferably be made of **PLASTIC** to eliminate the need for removing the button before washing.

This button can be additionally padded with a small amount of **FIBERFILL**, giving it an even plumper appearance. Thanks to its identical sides, it can also serve as a decorative element in form of a "disc bead" for jewelry making.

> **!** If the **BACK** of the single crochets is supposed to appear on the outside of the button, as for the button in the photo, the crocheted button has to be turned after the first decrease round.

> **X** Large buttons practically offer themselves for being additionally embellished—when used as a **BROOCH**, abundance is called for!

Finished size of the button: 1.4 inches (35 mm)
Button insert: 1.2–1.3 inches (30–33 mm)

Instructions

Work the topside as described on page 185, and then continue as follows:

Round 4: Double the 1st and every 3rd stitch after it, work sc1 in all other sts (= 24 sts).

Round 5: Work 24 sc around. Round 5 will place itself later around the edge of the button

insert. Now begin decreases as follows:

Round 6: Crochet together the 1st and 2nd, and every 3rd and 4th stitch, work sc1 in all other sts (= 18 sts). Place the button

insert inside.

Round 7: Crochet together every 2nd and 3rd stitch, work sc1 in all other sts (= 12 sts).

Round 8: [Crochet 2 sts together] all around (= 6 sts).

The crocheted cover should fit tightly around the base shape. Cinch the stitches of the last round as described for domed button (see at right). If the button insert is equipped with an eye or a shank, it should be left uncovered for sewing on later.

FLAT BUTTON WORKED IN DOUBLE CROCHET

Finished size of the button: 0.9 inches (23 mm)
Button insert: 0.7 inches (18 mm)

Instructions

Begin the circle with 1 chain in the center (> page 67) and work 3 additional height-adjustment chains. Into the 4th chain from the hook, work dc13. Close the round with 1 sl-st into the topmost chain. Make two circles and join them using a

contrasting color yarn. For this, place the circles together wrong sides facing each other and crochet together in sl-s in a contrasting color, catching the two innermost loops of the

stitches only. Don't forget to place the button insert inside. This way of joining produces a decorative ornamental edge that looks different at the topside and underside.

> **X** This method is well suited to creating a button cover for **ASYMMETRICAL SHAPES** or with **STRANDED COLORWORK PATTERNS** (> page 218). However, the base shape should not be larger than about 1.4 inches (35 mm), so that the corners of the square can be gathered conveniently, without the underside of the button becoming knobby. The finer the project yarn, the better it is suitable for covering a large button.

COVERING A SPHERE-SHAPED BUTTON

1 Crochet a square-shaped piece in single crochet in two or three colors in the desired colorwork pattern. The size is calculated as follows: diameter of the button insert + ½ diameter of the button insert (rounded up). This yields, for instance, for a button insert diameter of 0.9/1.1/1.3 inches (23/28/33 mm), a square with a side length of 1.4/1.7/2 inches (35/42/50 mm). Place the button onto the wrong side of the crocheted square. Using one of the yarn tails, first sew the diagonally opposed corners together with 2 stitches, leaving the yarn tails hanging. Treat the other two corners the same way.

2 After that, join the still open edges now opposite each other. For this, thread the yarn tail from the center out through the edge, lead it back along the adjoining side, and again, end in the center; then, using the yarn tail, cinch the edges to pull the protruding corners inward so the cover will fit closely to the curvature of the insert. Close the remaining three openings the same way.

SQUARE-SHAPED BUTTON

Crochet a tube shape in the round, in 2 or 3 colors, striped or in color blocks. Work single crochet through the back loop (> page 37). Begin with a ring of chains (> page 67), calculating the required number of chains as follows: [stitch count for the width of the button] times 2, plus 2 stitches extra for the depth of the button. Work the tube shape to the same height as the width. If you don't have a button insert in the required size, you can substitute a cardboard insert. For this, cut two squares from thin, sturdy cardboard that are 0.08 inches (2 mm) smaller than the crocheted cover. Glue the pieces together. Trim the corners. Join the open edges of the tube using the yarn tails and working in whipstitch (> page 142), placing the insert inside before closing the last seam.

! Buttons with inserts of wood, metal, and especially cardboard, should be REMOVED BEFORE WASHING.

X It is best to work with a THIN YARN (yardage approximately 137 yd/1.75 oz [125 m/50 g], crochet hook 2.5 mm [US between B-1 and C-2]) to create a fine crocheted fabric, which allows for easily developing the desired shape. Sock yarn can be used, too. If you want to experiment, use a thinner novelty or textured yarn.

••• ABBREVIATIONS can be found on page 344.

THREE-DIMENSIONAL BUTTONS

Three-dimensional buttons make for pretty accents on crocheted pieces and are easy to grip and button. For this reason, they are very well suited for children's clothing.

DOMED BUTTON

Finished size of the button:
1 inch (25 mm)
Button insert: 0.08 inches
(20 mm)

Instructions

Begin the circle with 1 chain in the center (> page 67), and work sc in spiral rounds (> page 71).

Round 1: Work sc6.

Round 2: Double every st around—that is, work sc2 each into every st (= 12 sts).

Round 3: Double every 3rd st around, work sc1 in all other sts (= 16 sts).

Round 4: Work 16 sc. Work 1 more sl-st, and chain 1, and then turn the piece inside out so the back of the sc is on the outside.

Round 5: Work 16 sc, inserting the hook from the inside out though the top loops of the sts of the last round, to create a prominent line (cylinder > page 124).

Round 6: [Crochet 2 sts together] 8 times (= 8 sts).

Before beginning the next round, insert a small amount of fiberfill or yarn clippings into the button cover, and place the button insert on top of it.

Round 7: Work sc8. Now the bottom of the button has been completely covered.

Break the working yarn, leaving a tail of 8 inches (20 cm), and pull the tail through the working loop. Weave the yarn tail with a tapestry needle through the outermost loops of the stitches of the last round and use it to cinch the stitches to close the opening. Weave in the end.

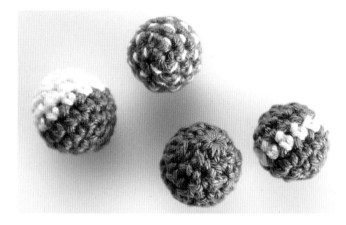

Subtle colorful accents can be created with embroidered **BACK STITCHES** (> page 189), each spanning 1 single crochet, following the course of the spiral rounds.

A crocheted sphere-shaped button can also be shaped with a dense ball of **FIBERFILL**. Prerequisite is a **TIGHTLY CROCHETED** opaque **COVER**, so that the core is not visible from the outside and no fiberfill can escape through the gaps between stitches. Another option are yarn remnants, with which the crocheted ball is packed tightly.

It is best to work with a **THIN YARN** (yardage approximately 137 yd/1.75 oz [125 m/50 g], crochet hook 2.5 mm [US between B-1 and C-2]) to create a fine crocheted fabric, which allows for easily developing the desired shape. Sock yarn can be used, too. If you want to experiment, use a thinner novelty or textured yarn.

A toggle button is the typical button shape for **FROG CLOSURES** (> page 183).

ABBREVIATIONS can be found on page 344.

SPHERE-SHAPED BUTTON

Finished button sizes: 0.7 inch (18 mm) and 0.08 inch (20 mm) Button insert is a sphere-shaped bead of 0.5 inch (13 mm) or 0.6 inch (15 mm) diameter.

Instructions

Begin the circle with 1 chain in the center (> page 67), and work sc in spiral rounds (> page 71).

Round 1: Work sc4.

Round 2: Double every st around—that is, work sc2 each into every st (= 8 sts).

Round 3: Double every other st around, work sc1 into all other sts (= 12 sts).

Rounds 4 and 5: Work 12 sc. To make a smaller size, work only 1 round of 12 sc before working the shaping decreases.

Round 6: * Crochet 2 sts together, sc1, repeat from * 3 times more (= 8 sts). Before the round has been finished, insert the sphere-shaped bead.

Round 7: Work 8 sc. Now the sphere-shaped core has been completely covered.

Break the working yarn, leaving a tail of 8 inches (20 cm), and pull it through the working loop. Weave the yarn tail with a tapestry needle through the outermost loops of the stitches of the last round, and use it to cinch the stitches to close the opening. Weave in the end.

For a **half-sphere-shaped button**, work to the 4th or 5th round as described for the sphere-shaped button. Then, as described in Round 5 of the domed button, work the single crochets below the top loops of the stitches—an important working step for achieving a crisp half-sphere shape. Stuff the button cover with yarn remnants tightly wound into a tiny ball. In the next round, which will be the last round, [crochet 2 sts together] 6 times.

TOGGLE BUTTON

Finished size of the button: 1.7 inches (43 mm) long
Button insert: paper clip, 1.3 x 0.4 inches (32 mm x 10 mm)

Instructions

Begin the shape with ch1 in the center (> page 67), and work sc in spiral rounds (> page 71).

Rounds 1 and 2: Work 8 sc.

Round 3: Double the first st (i.e., work sc2 into this stitch), 3 sc, double the next st, 3 sc (= 10 sts).

Round 4: Work 10 sc.

Round 5: * Sc2in1, 4 sc, repeat from * once more (= 12 sts).

Rounds 6 and 7: Work 12 sc.

Round 8: * Sc2tog, 4 sc, repeat from * once more (= 10 sts).

Round 9: Work 10 sc.

Round 10: * Sc2tog, 3 sc, repeat from * once more (= 8 sts).

Rounds 11 and 12: Work 8 sc. At the end of Round 12, work 1 sl-st more, and then break the working yarn, leaving a tail of 8 inches (20 cm), and pull it through the working loop. Use a paper clip as insert to reinforce the button. Sew around the paper clip with yarn and wind a second layer around it. Put the so-camouflaged insert together with some fiberfill into the crocheted cover, and carefully shape the button. Finally, weave the yarn tail with a tapestry needle through the

outermost loops of the stitches of the last round and use it to cinch the stitches to close the opening.

EMBROIDERY, SURFACE CROCHET, AND APPLIQUE

Embroidery and applique add interest to a crocheted piece whether made in a colorful accent yarn or in the same yarn and color as the main pattern.

DECORATIVE EMBROIDERY STITCHES

Embroidery stitches can fulfill a decorative as well as a practical purpose. Choose a smooth yarn with a fiber content matching that of the crocheted piece. If you want to combine different yarns, it is recommended to make a swatch and wash it to make sure that the yarns are colorfast and don't shrink. The tool for embroidering is an **embroidery or tapestry needle.** The size of the needle's eye should be chosen to match the yarn to ensure the needle with the thread can be effortlessly pulled through the crocheted base. With a **dull needle**, the yarn used for the embroidery can be easily passed through between the stitches of the crocheted fabric so that it remains moveable and yields to stretching. When embroidering along a row of crocheted stitches, **evenly spaced insertion and exit points** must be maintained so that the embroidery runs in a straight line. When embroidering curves or placing stitches selectively without being tied to the existing gaps between stitches, a **sharp needle** is suggested, as it will puncture the crocheted fabric. However, areas embroidered over in this way are less stretchy.

RUNNING STITCH

The running stitch, also called basting stitch, is a simple stitch that is easy to work. It is worked **from right to left.** After having inserted the needle from back to front through the fabric, * insert the needle one stitch length further left on the path of embroidery from front to back, and then again from back to front another stitch length further left. Pull the working yarn through. Repeat from * all the time.

BACKSTITCH

The backstitch is used for closing seams (> page 143) but also as a decorative stitch for **lines and outlines.** It is worked **from right to left.**
Insert the needle from back to front one stitch length to the left of the intended beginning of the path of embroidery, and then insert it from front to back at the beginning of the path. Lead
the needle two stitch lengths to the left, insert the needle from back to front, and pull the working yarn through. Insert the needle again at the exit point of the last stitch, and insert the needle two stitch lengths to the left. Continue the line of back stitches this way.

STEM STITCH

In stem stitch, **fines lines** can be embroidered, which can follow **any desired shape.** A stem stitch line is worked **from left to right.**
After having made a first straight stitch, insert the needle from back to front at half the stitch length beside the initial straight stitch. Insert the needle at whole stitch length to the right, and exit the needle the same way as before, always exiting over (or always under) the respective previous stitch.

There are multiple ways to transfer a motif or a detailed template onto crocheted fabric:

DRAWING, IRONING, EMBROIDERING: Draw the motif mirror-inverted onto parchment paper with an iron-on transfer pencil, and iron it onto the crocheted base fabric. Make sure to use a washable iron-on transfer pencil.

EMBROIDERING OVER TEAR-AWAY FABRIC: Transfer the motif onto organza fabric, not too tightly woven linen, or fine-mesh needlepoint canvas, cut it out with about 0.8 inch (2 cm) allowance, and pin it to the crocheted piece. Embroider with a sharp needle through the tear-away fabric and the crocheted background. Trim excess tear-away fabric close to the finished embroidery, and then pull out the embroidered-over threads individually using tweezers (moisten the tear-away fabric beforehand).

⊠ When long ROWS of CROSS STITCHES are embroidered in the same color, first make a series of half cross stitches in one direction, and then complete the crosses in the next working step on the return pass.

⊠ CROSS STITCH is especially well suited for embroidering onto base fabric crocheted in KNOT STITCH (> page 221) and BASIC TUNISIAN CROCHET STITCHES (> page 230), since these stitches are nearly square-shaped.

⊠ Embroidering in chain stitch yields a HARMONIOUS PATH since it does not depend on the gaps between stitches for insertion points as for a line of crocheted slip stitch.

❗ The SIZE OF THE KNOTS depends on the number of coils.

CROSS STITCH

Crocheted base fabric in single crochet makes a very good background to be embroidered in cross-stitch. Using a dull embroidery needle, each cross-stitch is embroidered over 1 single crochet. The described working steps produce a horizontal row of stitches, which begins at right, and continues to the left.

1 To work the first cross, embroider the initial diagonal stitch from bottom left to top right. To begin the top stitch, exit the needle at the bottom right corner point and pull the yarn through.

2 Complete the top stitch, inserting the needle at the top left, and for the second cross, exiting it at the corner point bottom left (= starting point for the next initial diagonal stitch).

CHAIN STITCH

Embroidered chain stitch visually resembles a line of surface-crocheted slip stitches (> page 193). Work embroidered chain stitches from right to left, using a sharp needle.
After having inserted the needle from back to front through the fabric, arrange the yarn into a loop, insert the needle again into the exit point, and insert again at stitch length, placing the yarn

loop under the tip of the needle. When pulling at the yarn, a loop will place itself around the last exit point. The exit point is located within the loop. * For the next stitch, insert the needle within the loop into the exit point of the working yarn, and insert the needle again at stitch length, with one loop of the working yarn located under the needle tip. Pull the working yarn through, and then repeat from * continuously to the end of the path of embroidery. Finally, insert the needle with a short straight stitch outside of the loop, and pull the working yarn through to the wrong side.

LAZY DAISY STITCH

A lazy daisy stitch is basically embroidered like an individual chain stitch. After having made a chain stitch, anchor the loop of working yarn with a short straight stitch by inserting the needle closely outside of the loop and pulling the working yarn through to the wrong side. To work a small blossom, embroider 5 or 6 lazy daisy stitches around a center.

FRENCH KNOT

The French knot, as its name implies, forms tiny, raised knots on the surface.
1 Insert the needle from back to front in the desired spot and place the needle tip close to the exit point. Wind the working yarn around the needle 1 to 3 times, tighten, slide the coils toward the base fabric, and hold the working yarn.

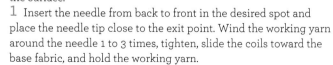

2 Insert the needle close to the exit point and exit the needle again at the desired distance for the next French knot. Pull the working yarn through but continue holding the coils until the working yarn has been pulled all the way through. The knots should sit close to the base fabric.

BULLION KNOT

The bullion knot is raised over the base fabric over a certain length.

1 Insert the needle from back to front in the desired spot, and then insert the needle from front to back a little distance (= length of the finished bullion knot) from the exit point, lead the needle back to the first point, and insert the needle there. Leave the needle inserted in the fabric in this position. Wind the working yarn around the needle 4 to 6 times and, using your left hand, push the coils together toward the base fabric, and hold them in place.

2 Pull the needle and the yarn through, while continuing to hold the coils until the working yarn has been pulled all the way through. The coils will flip over toward the insertion point. Don't tighten the working yarn too much—the stitch should arch and the coils sit side by side, loosely encompassing the stitch. Pull the working yarn through to the wrong side close to the beginning point and insert the needle to begin the next stitch.

> ✕ If the coils are supposed to lie **CLOSELY** on top of the base fabric, the initial stitch has to be sufficiently **LONG**. Adjust the number of coils according to the stitch length. For coils that **STAND OUT** from the base fabric, make the initial stitch rather **SHORT** and work a larger number of coils.

STRAIGHT STITCH

Stitch length and direction of the straight stitch are variable. It is placed individually and connects two points but is most often arranged into groups to create a motif. For a straight stitch, first insert the needle from back to front, and then at the desired stitch length insert the needle from front to back. Make sure that the connecting stitches on the wrong side of the fabric are not too long.

SATIN STITCH

Closely spaced straight stitches placed parallel to one another to cover an area are called satin stitches. The stitch length is determined by the outline of the area to be embroidered. Here, it is important to work with a sharp needle!

BLANKET STITCH

Blanket stitch is also known as festoon stitch or open buttonhole stitch. Open edges can be hemmed in blanket stitch, adding colorful accents as desired. For an even stitch appearance, it is important to evenly space the stitches in width and height along the crocheted stitches and rows, and to embroider at uniform stitch length or depth from the outside edge.

Work with a dull needle from left to right along the bottom edge of the crocheted piece. Insert the needle from back to front directly at the edge, and then move the working yarn to the right. Insert the needle from the front of work at the desired distance from the edge and at the level of the first exit point, and lead the tip of the needle toward the edge over the working yarn. Pull the working yarn through—the first stitch has been completed. Move the working yarn to the right. For the second stitch, insert the needle from the right side of the fabric at the desired distance to the first stitch, keeping the same distance to the edge. Move the tip of the needle over the working yarn and pull the working yarn through. Continue embroidering around the whole edge in this manner.

WHIPSTITCH

Whipstitch can also be used for hemming edges in regular stitch and row intervals.

Work with a dull needle, going from **left to right**. These are simple straight stitches, placed diagonally, and leading around an outside edge (i.e., the needle is always inserted from **back to front**). Whipstitch can also be used to join crocheted pieces (*> page 142*).

SEWING AROUND POSTS

Decorative sewing can be done around the posts of taller crochet stitches such as double crochet, treble crochet, and taller stitches.

Using working yarn in a contrasting color or the same color as the base fabric, enclose a group of 2 or 3 double crochets, pulling them closer together, causing small gaps in the fabric. Wind the working yarn around a group of stitches 2 or 3 times, and secure every group of wraps with a short stitch before moving the working yarn to the next spot.

X IRISH CROCHET MOTIFS (*> page 269*) provide an extensive fundus for applique ideas.

APPLIQUÉ

An appliqué of **flowers and leaves,** artfully entwined with delicate cords, embellished with **embroidery and beads,** provides great opportunity for creative design. From which elements the motifs are composed and how they are arranged can follow a playful, folkloristic, or purist style. The appliqué can either appear understated or opulently play the starring role. Motif parts can lie flat or be prominently raised, and they can be sewn on either all around the outside edges or only in a few spots, leaving the edges of the motif parts to stand out from the background.

SURFACE CROCHET IN SLIP STITCH

While the slip stitch itself looks unpretentious, it is very versatile: Not only can whole items be worked in the slip stitch crochet technique (> page 261), as well as crocheted rounds joined (> page 70) and the working yarn moved to a different spot (> page 105), but slip stitch can also be employed for **decorative purposes**. A solid stitch pattern worked in single crochet is the perfect background for surface crocheting a **line of slip stitch**. In slip stitch, freeform motifs can be shaped or words lettered. Rows of slip stitches can also form a pattern element when crocheted in several colors into a mesh background or run in horizontal and vertical lines to create a plaid pattern.

SLIP STITCH LINE

The method of working is the same as for a single slip stitch crocheted as part of a stitch pattern (> page 33), the only difference being that it is not worked in a current row but directly **on top of an existing surface**.

1 At the beginning point, insert the crochet hook from front to back through the crocheted fabric, and pull the first loop through with the help of the crochet hook. The working yarn is located behind work. To work the first slip stitch, insert the hook at a short distance, and pull another loop through. For a background fabric in single crochet, an appropriate spacing is 1 stitch or 1 row.

2 Continue pulling the working yarn immediately through the first loop. The first slip stitch has been completed. Continue in this manner, crocheting one slip stitch after another, following a line of any shape. Always insert the hook in the gap between stitches. At the end point of the path, break the working yarn leaving an end of 59 inches (15 cm) and pulling it through to the right side. Pull it through to the wrong side again closely beside the last slip stitch, and weave in the end.

SLIP STITCHES AS A PATTERN-BUILDING COMPONENT

For a plaid pattern, **horizontal and vertical rows of slip stitches** are surface-crocheted onto a base fabric of **double crochet**.

To work horizontal lines, crochet the slip stitches into the base points of the double crochets. For vertical lines of slip stitch, plan ahead while crocheting the base fabric, replacing a double crochet with a chain in all rows in the same spot. In the chain spaces of those chains, the slip stitches will be worked, with an additional chain in between to bridge. As an alternative, vertical rows of slip stitches can also be run between 2 double crochets, in which case advance planning is not necessary. Plaid patterns will look especially sophisticated if lines go alternatingly over and under a crossing line at intersecting points, as if **woven** into each other.

! For every new row of slip stitches, place a **BEGINNING SLIPKNOT** onto the crochet hook (> page 30), securely anchoring the attaching point of the working yarn.

Care and Finishing

When all parts of crocheting and embellishing a crocheted item have been finished, two more important steps to perfection lie ahead. The finished item should be washed for the first time to remove any residue from the manufacturing process of the yarn and to let wool yarns "bloom." Some items, especially those worked in lace patterns, must be additionally blocked to shape to develop their full splendor.

WASHING, DRYING, FOLDING

After having invested time and expense to create a precious crocheted item, special attention should be paid to the care of this new favorite piece to keep it enjoyable for a long time. A lovingly handmade item can quickly lose its shape or even suffer damage when not properly cared for.

The most important facts about the care of a certain yarn can always be found on the yarn label. If a crocheted item has been made using two or more different yarns, care instructions for the most delicate yarn should be followed.

WASHING

Wool should always be handled gently. It will not tolerate hot water, rubbing, and friction, which would make it felt and shrink. While wool should be washed by hand if possible, most modern washing machines are equipped with a special wool cycle, which treats wool gently.

Suds should always be rather lukewarm or cold, and the piece agitated as little as possible. Suitable laundry detergents are special liquid wool detergents without optical brighteners. If using powdered detergents, residue can remain after washing, which can turn the crocheted item hard and rough. Here, a splash of vinegar in the last rinse cycle helps to render the crocheted piece soft and fluffy again.

After hand washing, gently lift the crocheted piece out of the water, and press out excess water—never wring. Rinse the crocheted item at least three more times with clear, cold water, and press out excess water. Finally, place the wet piece onto a terrycloth towel, roll it up, and press out the remaining water.

In washing machines without wool cycle, wool should only be washed when care instructions expressly permit it. Many wool blends or yarns of synthetic fiber can be washed in the washing machine; always following the instructions on the ball band. Sock yarns (most often of 75% pure new wool, 25% polyamide) are particularly hard-wearing, and nowadays specially treated to be able to be laundered in the washing machine using the delicate cycle. They won't felt and will keep their shape. After washing, items from these yarns can even be dried in the delicate cycle of the clothes dryer. However, in this case, too, it is much safer to spread out the crocheted item flat for drying.

For cotton yarn as well, always heed the care instructions on the yarn label. Many crocheted pieces from pure cotton are easy-care and can be washed in the washing machine at 140°F (60°C) using a detergent for delicates without optical brighteners. Many dyed and printed cotton yarns, however, do require lower temperatures! If

Small, not too heavy crocheted items can also be carefully spun in a **SALAD SPINNER.**

the yarn label is missing but you believe the yarn is a pure cotton yarn, washing at 104°F (40°C) in the **delicate cycle** is suggested. With **cotton blend yarns**, in most cases, the fiber content determines whether they are washable at 86°F (30°C) only; always follow the instructions provided by the yarn's manufacturer. For the first washing, the crocheted item should in every case be washed **separately** to avoid discoloration on other laundry items. **Small pieces and lace items** must be enclosed in a laundry net or a pillowcase of pure cotton for washing to avoid damage. Pieces from cotton yarns should only be spun at low revolutions.

An overview over the most important **CARE SYMBOLS** and their explanations can be found on page 345.

DRYING

Crocheted pieces should be **gently pulled in shape** after washing and left to dry **horizontally** on a towel. They should, if possible, be placed in the shade to avoid discoloration and sun damage, especially during the summer. Never hang crocheted items on a clothesline—they are very heavy when wet and will lose their shape; this is especially true for items worked in cotton yarns.

IRONING AND STEAM IRONING

Once dry, most crocheted pieces will be in good shape. Should it nonetheless become necessary to iron the crocheted item, here, too, the specifications and instructions from the **yarn label** must be followed. Many synthetic yarns may not be ironed; wool and sensitive yarn blends do not tolerate **high temperatures**. When ironing cannot be avoided, cover the crocheted piece with a wet cloth, and do not press the iron directly onto the crocheted fabric but hover over the cloth. The resulting steam straightens the fabric. This task is most easily done with a steam iron, which is guided easily and without touching down over the cloth, so that the steam penetrates and straightens the crocheted fabric. Yarns of synthetic fiber are not subject to steam blocking.

RAISED and **TEXTURED PATTERNS** should not be ironed under any circumstances, as otherwise the textured stitches would be pressed flat and the stitch pattern loose its appeal. It is preferred to move a **STEAM IRON** over the surface at a distance and operate the steam burst.

STORING

Crocheted garments should **not** be stored hanging **on clothes hangers**, since they sag due to their weight and can permanently lose their shape. For this reason, it is recommended to carefully fold crocheted items and **store** them **horizontally**. Garments must rest loosely on top of each other to be able to "breathe." It should also be ensured that the fabric has **not** retained any **moisture**. Delicate wool pieces can be stored **in newspaper** since moths do not like printer's ink. A further effective way of mothproofing are **essential oils**. The most natural and convenient option are small sachets filled with lavender, cloves, or orange peel, which can very easily be home-made. It also helps to hang small bouquets of sweet clover in the closet or to put small pieces of cedarwood between the woolen items.

If you regularly have to block larger pieces, you can cover a **SHEET OF PLYWOOD** in an appropriate size with batting from the roll or a sheet of foam approximately 1.2 inches (3 cm) thick and somewhat larger than the plywood board and top it with two layers of a tightly woven white (if possible) cotton fabric. This allows the upholstery and cover fabric to be folded over to the back of the plywood board on all four sides and be tacked on there.

When a **SQUARE GRID** is needed for blocking, top the blocking mat with grid-printed fabric. The advantage of such a blocking board is that it can be put away upright until the piece has thoroughly dried.

When steam ironing, always follow the **MANUFACTURER'S CARE INSTRUCTIONS** on the yarn label!

Pieces crocheted from **YARNS** of entirely **SYNTHETIC FIBERS** should not be steam ironed.

"COLD BLOCKING" is a very gentle method for all pieces, especially those that have not become much distorted during crocheting or those made of yarns with a **HIGH PERCENTAGE OF SYNTHETICS**. Pin down the dry crocheted piece and cover it with a cold moistened cloth. Gently press on the cloth to lightly moisten the crocheted fabric. Let it dry overnight while covered, and then remove the cloth and the blocking pins.

BLOCKING AND STARCHING

By blocking, individual crocheted parts are given their **final shape**, since some stitch patterns constrict during crocheting and only show their full potential after having been blocked. Parts are pinned onto a blocking surface according to the **measurements** as listed in the pattern instructions or shown in the schematic. After the blocking, individual pieces can also be sewn together much easier and better.

BLOCKING FLAT PIECES

Special **blocking mats** with printed grids as guide for evenly pinning are available in stores. Other suitable alternatives are a large-format ironing pad, a rigid foam or Styrofoam sheet, or foam rubber puzzle mats, as found in toy stores. These surfaces, if necessary, can be topped with a mat with printed square grid, onto which the crocheted piece is pinned, placing tailor pins in **evenly spaced intervals** of a maximum 2 inches (5 cm) apart from each other. Pin down corners and any openwork edges of the crocheted piece especially well. In **delicate lace**, stitch patterns will only unfold their full beauty if every individual chain arc, every picot, or every filet pattern corner are pinned down individually. The base mesh of filet crochet pieces receives its even grid structure through blocking.

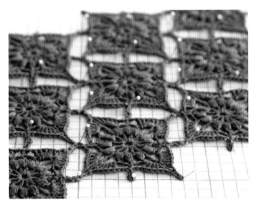

Then **moisten** the pinned crocheted piece **and let it dry**. This procedure is suggested for delicate crochet lace, such as lace shawls, or crocheted pieces with heavily textured stitch patterns.

If the fiber content of the yarn permits, the pinned crocheted piece can also be **lightly steamed** with a clothes iron: For this, moisten a cotton or linen cloth with cold water and cover the crocheted piece with it.

Place the iron on top gently and, without pressing, move it back and forth as little as possible, instead placing it on anew several times, until the complete area has been steam blocked. Remove the cloth and let the still damp item thoroughly dry.

After the parts have been sewn together, it is worth the effort to quickly steam all **inside seams** once more. Doing so will flatten the seams and make them less rigid.

BLOCKING THREE-DIMENSIONAL PIECES

Pieces crocheted in the round show a much more even stitch appearance when blocked wet and let dry. For **socks**, ready-to-use sock blockers are offered in a range of shoe sizes. Matching templates from sturdy cardboard can also be easily made at home. Those need to be encased in plastic film so that they cannot absorb moisture. **Hats** can be pulled over small bowls, lampshades, or pails for blocking. You can also block crocheted **containers** over appropriate vessels in a fitting shape (for instance, bulbous vases or bowls). **Cozies** should preferably be placed in a wet state over the same glass for which they are intended, pulled into shape, and let dry.

STARCHING—LACE AND OBJECTS

Individual filigree-like motifs used as hanging ornaments or window decoration, lace edgings on curtains, and delicate doilies should be able to keep their shape for longer periods and stand or lie flat on their own. To make this possible, these pieces are starched. The most uncomplicated method is to moisten the crocheted item with **spray starch** after having pinned it to a blocking surface and let it dry thoroughly.

Small decorative objects, such as flowers, butterflies, or baskets, can be shaped the same way. Various agents on a chemical basis, which harden the yarn so the item can no longer collapse, are commercially available.

A few simple starch solutions that you can also **prepare on your own**:

Starch: Mix liquid starch with warm water at a ratio of 4:3.

Sugar water: Mix water and household sugar at a ratio of 1:1, let it come to a boil, and then let cool.

Wallpaper paste: Stir the paste into cold water. The result should have a viscous consistency.

Place the crocheted piece to be shaped into the starch solution and wait until the yarn is fully saturated with the solution. Then press out excess liquid and place or block the crocheted item over an appropriately shaped vessel to shape it. Vessels to be used for wet shaping crocheted pieces need to be covered with **clear food wrap** beforehand so the crocheted piece can be easily removed later. Let everything dry thoroughly.

Crocheted pieces that have been stiffened with starch, sugar water, or wallpaper paste should be **protected from moisture** since otherwise the starch will dissolve again, causing the shape to collapse. However, solubility in water has the advantage that the starch can be **washed out** again.

A shape becomes **PERMANENTLY STIFFENED** if it is treated with a **LIQUID WOOD GLUE** solution: Combine 2.1 oz (60 g) wood glue with 4.2 fl oz (125 ml) water and stir well. Moisten the crocheted piece thoroughly with the solution, press out excess liquid, and place or block over an appropriately shaped item. This glue-based starch is **NOT** removable by **WASHING**!

●●● More interesting facts about blocking can be found in the chapter **CROCHETED LACE** (> *page 300*).

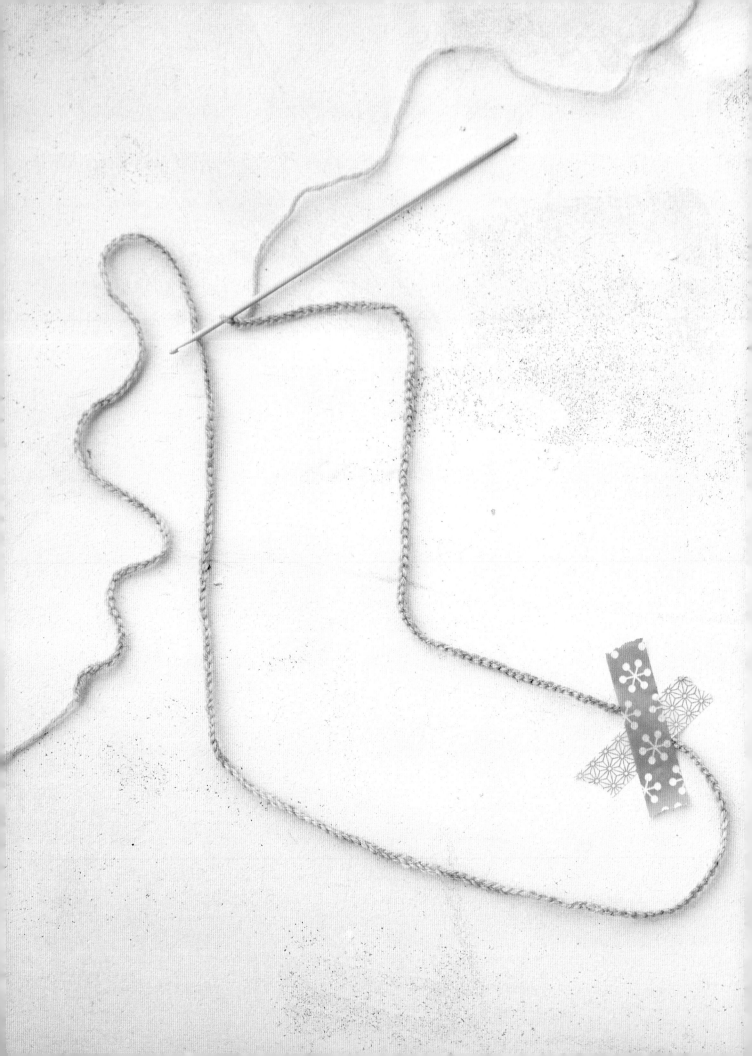

Hats, Socks, and Mittens

Crocheted hats are always in. The same can be said about crocheted socks and mittens, even if they are not as widely known as their knitted counterparts. Crocheted accessories will keep one especially warm and cozy!

Crocheting Socks

Creating warm socks by hand is not exclusively reserved for those who have mastered the art of knitting and are familiar with using a set of double-pointed needles. Wonderfully cozy foot coddlers can also be conjured up with a single crochet hook!

MATERIALS AND GAUGE

Just as is customary with knitted socks, crocheted socks are worked in **4–ply sock yarn** with a yardage of approximately 230 yd/1.75 oz (210 m/50 g) and a fiber content of 75% pure new wool and 25% polyamide/nylon. This yarn is thin enough to not add too much bulk, and also durable because of the addition of polyamide. Socks are worked using a **crochet hook 3.5 mm (US E-4)** or any other appropriate size to match the appropriate gauge. Additionally, **2 stitch markers** or a **piece of contrasting color yarn** of 23.6 inches (60 cm) length are needed.

> ! A GAUGE SWATCH made in fingering weight sock yarn with a crochet hook 3.5 mm (US E-4) should yield 22 elongated single crochets and 19 rows/rounds in a 4 x 4-inch (10 x 10 cm) square.

Total Yarn Amount Needed

Shoe size	Approx. amount needed
4T–8T	230 yd (210.3 m)
9T–7M/8.5W	460 yd (420.6 m)
7.5M/9W–13M/14.5W	690 yd (631 m)

SOCKS WORKED FLAT AND SEAMED

Seamed socks are **crocheted** flat in rows and only at the end **sewn together** into a sock. They are worked mainly in extended single crochet (> page 34), since it is especially stretchy and therefore makes a good fit possible, similar to that of knitted socks. For seamed socks, the main parts are especially well recognizable since they are crocheted one after another. Standard stitch counts for specific **shoe sizes** are provided in a table (> page 204).

> X CONTRASTING COLORS for toe and heel look pretty, and make ORIENTATION easier when crocheting a sock for the first time.

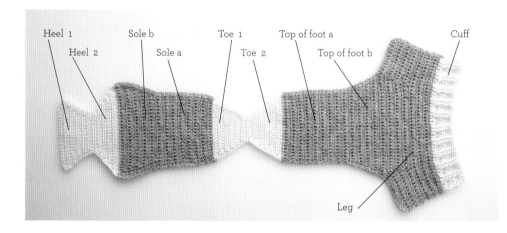

Heel 1 · Heel 2 · Sole b · Sole a · Toe 1 · Toe 2 · Top of foot a · Top of foot b · Cuff · Leg

HEEL

A seamed sock begins with the upper part of the heel, which consists of two interconnected trapezoid shapes. After having been sewn together later, they resemble a knitted **short row heel**.

For **Heel 1**, chain the required number of chains according to the table, plus 1 additional height adjustment chain. Now, beginning into the 2nd chain from the hook, work in regular single crochet in rows, always working through the front loop of the stitch only (> page 37). Continue working in rows, replacing the first single crochet of every row by 1 turning chain (> page

64). For every size, work the number of rows stated in the table, at the same time decreasing stitches as follows in rows marked in bold font: Crochet together the 2nd with the 3rd stitch, as well as the next-to-last stitch of the row with the preceding stitch (> page 102).

When all rows for the **Heel 1** part have been worked, begin with **Heel 2**. Continue to work single crochets through the front loop of the stitch in rows and double the second and the next-to-last stitch of the row as listed in rows printed in bold in the table (> page 98) to increase stitches.

SOLE

Now crochet the sole in **extended single crochet** worked in rows, replacing the first stitch of every row with 2 turning chains.

For **Sole b**, decrease the number of stitches listed in the table, crocheting together the second with the third stitch, and the next-to-last with the preceding stitch in every row

Then, for **Sole a**, work even without decreases over the remaining stitches, until the required length according to the table has been reached.

> **!** To **CROCHET TOGETHER** 2 elongated single crochets, complete the two stitches up to the last step, leaving the last loop of each stitch on the hook (= 3 loops on the hook), and then pull working yarn through all 3 loops on the hook at once.

> **X** In this part, the sock can be **ADAPTED TO INDIVIDUAL SIZE** by working **A LONGER OR SHORTER SOLE**. Just make sure that the measurement for "Top of foot a" matches the adjusted length.

TOE

The toe is, just like the heel, **worked in regular single crochet**, always working through the front loop of the stitch only.

For **Toe 1**, at both ends of the row, in every other row, crochet together the second with the third stitch, and the next-to-last stitch with the preceding stitch, until only 3 decrease rows are left to reach the "stitch count toe" listed in the

table (i.e., until you still have 6 sts more than listed). For the last 3 decrease rows, work decreases in every row. For **Toe 2, work** these decreases in opposite order as the increases: first [increase 2 stitches each in every row as described for the heel] 3 times in all, and then continue, increasing in every other row until the stitch count for **Sole a** has been reached again.

TOP OF FOOT

For **Top of foot a**, work again even in extended single crochet without increases or decreases in rows, replacing the first stitch of every row with 2 turning chains. Work **Top of foot b** mirror-inverted to **Sole b**, increasing 2 stitches each in every row until the stitch count for **Top of foot b** according to the table has been reached, ending with a wrong-side row.

LEG

For the Leg, **add additional stitches.** For this, at the end of a right-side row, first chain the required number of chains for the first half plus 2 turning chains. Turn work and work 1 elongated single crochet into the third chain from the crochet hook. Continue working **extended single crochet** into all newly added chains. Place a marker. Continue working extended single crochet across the stitches of the row. Place the work aside for a short time and chain the stitches for the increase for the second side (half of the total stitches to be increased). Continue, working extended single crochet over the new chains (> page 101), placing a marker in the transition spot. Work one row over all stitches. In Row 2, begin decreases as follows: In every row, at both ends of the row, crochet together 2 stitches each in the transition spots from the side parts to the middle part. For a more even appearance of the decrease line, alternate between working the decrease before and after the marked spot. When the stitch count for the **Leg** according to the table has been reached, work even without increases or decreases to the **desired leg height.**

> **X** Leg decreases can be **INDIVIDUALLY CUSTOMIZED**. While crocheting, it can be checked from time to time whether the width of the leg fits over foot and heel. Should the leg become too narrow, work only as many decreases as needed to reach the required width.

> **X** Decreases can also be worked by decreasing **4 STITCHES IN EVERY OTHER ROW**. For this, always crochet 2 stitches together before and after the marked stitches.

! If the stitch count is **NOT A MULTIPLE OF 4**, immediately after the turning chain work 2 raised stitches and end with 1 double crochet.

X "Right sides facing each other" means that the two **BETTER-LOOKING SIDES OF THE PIECES** are placed together on the inside. Which side is the right side of work can be determined by looking at the **RIBBED TEXTURE** of the ribbing pattern.

X When the **BEGINNING AND ENDING TAILS** of the sock parts are left long enough, they can be used to **SEAM THE SOCK**.

X At the **BEGINNING OF THE ROUND**, for Marker A, use a **MARKING THREAD OR STITCH MARKER IN A DIFFERENT COLOR** than for Marker B to keep track of the beginning of the round.

CUFF

Row 1: Work dc (*> page 35*) over all stitches, turn work.
Row 2: Work 2 turning chains (replacing the first dc), work 1 double crochet, * 2 front post double crochets (*> page 42*), 2 double crochets, repeat from * continuously.

Row 3: Work 2 turning chains and skip 1 double crochet, work bpdc into all raised stitches (*> page 42*), work dc into all double crochets. Repeat Rows 2 and 3 until the cuff has reached the desired length.

FINISHING

Weave in all ends. Place **Heel 1 and Heel 2** together with **right sides facing each other** and join the two slanted sides with a **ladder stitch seam** (*> page 145*) each.
Place **Sole and Top of foot** together with **right sides facing each other** and join with a ladder stitch seam, and then seam the slanted sides of the toe continuously. Place the two open edges of **Leg and Cuff** together with **right sides facing each other**, and seam continuously. Finally, close the open horizontal seam between Heel and Leg, and then turn the sock. Work the second sock the same way.

SOCKS CROCHETED IN THE ROUND

Socks crocheted in the round are worked directly according to their later shape in **seamless rounds**. This method produces a **more even stitch appearance** similar to that of knitted socks. Seaming parts together can be omitted, the fit is improved, and there are no seams that could rub later in the shoe.

A sock worked in the round **begins at the toe** and is worked toe-up to the cuff. The heel is worked separately in turned rows. To be able to work increases and decreases correctly, it is necessary to mark the beginning of the round as well as the opposite half of the round with a **piece of contrasting color yarn or a stitch marker.**

TOE

Crochet the number of chains required for the toe according to the table (*> page 204*), plus work 1 height-adjustment chain. Now **crochet all around the beginning chain on both sides** (*> page 69*). For this, work **regular single crochet in spiral rounds** (*> page 71*), always working **through the back loop of the stitch only** (*> page 37*). Work the first single crochet into the second chain from the crochet hook. Then work 1 single crochet each into every chain, and work 2 single crochets into the last chain. After that, work into the unused loops on the other side of the initial chain the same way. After the first round, you should have **twice the number** of the initially cast-on stitches (the height-adjustment chain is not included in the stitch count).
Place a stitch marker or a marking thread between the last and first stitch of the round (**Marker A = begin of round**). Continue working in spiral round and after half of the stitches, opposite of Marker A, place another marker (**Marker B**).
To work the toe shaping, now increase stitches as follows: From the beginning of the round, work 1 single crochet, double the next stitch (*> page 98*), work single crochet to 1 stitch before Marker B, double 1 stitch, work 2 single crochets, double 1 stitch, work single crochet to 1 stitch before Marker A, double 1 stitch, work 1 single crochet. With every increase, the stitch count increases by 4 sts. Increase at first in every round, 3 times in all, and then increase in every other round until the stitch count for the Foot according to the table has been reached. Carry Markers A and B, moving them up every few rows.

FOOT

For the Foot, work elongated single crochets *(> page 34)* even **without increases in spiral rounds** until the foot has reached the length for "tip of toe to gusset" according to the table.

Then begin increases for the **gusset**. First, check the placement of Markers A and B once more and correct if necessary: Marker A is located at the beginning of the round, Marker B exactly opposite after half of the total stitch count.

Now, in every other round, work increases as described for the toe until the required stitch count according to the table has been reached. Then work half a round to Marker B (= top of foot), secure the working loop, and place work on this piece aside. The last stitch before the marker stays unworked.

HEEL

The heel is now worked in **increasing rows** in regular single crochet over the other half of the stitches (= Sole). Always work the single crochets through the **front loop of the stitch only** *(> page 37)*.

First mark the **middle of the sole** with a stitch marker or piece of contrasting color yarn. Then begin at this marked spot, and join the rows getting longer with every row with slip stitches to the Sole as follows:

Row 1: Attach new working yarn 1 stitch to the right of the center stitch. Chain 1 and work 2 single crochets into the same stitch. Then, into the next stitch, work 2 single crochets, in the following stitch, work 1 slip stitch (= 4 single crochets in all). Turn work.

Row 2: Work in single crochet, working 2 sts each into the first and the last stitch, and 1 stitch into every stitch in between (= 6 single crochets in all), work 1 slip stitch into the next stitch of the sole.

Repeat Row 2 continuously, increasing 2 stitches in every row this way, until the required stitch count for the heel width according to the table has been reached. Continue working even in **rows without increases** until all sole stitches have been crocheted into, always joining the end of every row as before with 1 slip stitch into the sole, ending with a wrong-side row. Break the working yarn and pull it through the working loop. Place the formerly set aside working loop before Marker B on the hook again.

LEG

Over the heel stitches, work half a round of elongated single crochets until Marker A has been reached. Continue **working elongated single crochet in spiral rounds,** carrying the markers and working decreases until the required stitch count according to the table has been reached. For a more even appearance of the decrease line, alternate between working the decrease before and after the marked spot. After the end of the decreases, work the **leg even without increases or decreases** to the desired leg height. As an alternative, you can also decrease 4 stitches in every other round. For this, always before and after the market spots, crochet 2 stitches together. Continue working to the center back, so that the ribbing pattern will start in this spot.

CUFF

Round 1: Work double crochet.

Round 2: * 2 front post double crochets *(> page 42)*, 2 double crochets, repeat from * continuously.

Repeat Round 2 all the time, until the cuff has reached the desired length. Break the working yarn and pull it through the working loop. Weave in all ends.

Work the second sock the same way.

! The SLIP STITCH is not counted, and in the following row NOT CROCHETED INTO!

X Especially for larger sizes, work the increases not always at the same spot but **DISTRIBUTED EVENLY** to achieve a nice, round heel shape.

! TO CROCHET 2 elongated single crochets **TOGETHER**, complete the two stitches up to the last step, leaving the last loop of each stitch on the hook (= 3 loops on the hook), and then pull the working yarn through all 3 loops on the hook at once.

X While working the decreases, frequently **CHECK** whether the width of the leg fits over foot and heel. Should the leg become too narrow, work only as many decreases as needed to reach the **REQUIRED WIDTH.**

! If the stitch count is NOT A MULTIPLE OF 4, work "1 front post double crochet, 1 double crochet" into the remaining stitches.

SEAMED SOCK IN FINGERING WEIGHT SOCK YARN

Yarn weight should be approximately 230 yd/1.75 oz (210 m/50 g); (see table on page 200 for approximate yardage needed per size).

Gauge: In extended sc with 3.5 mm (US E-4) hook, 22 sts and 19 rnds = 4 x 4 inches (10 x 10 cm)

Shoe size	Beginning chains	row count Heel 1 and Heel 2	stitch counts Heel 1	stitch counts Heel 2	# of decreases Sole b/remaining # of sts for Sole a	length Sole a/Top of foot a in in/cm	stitch count toe	stitch count Top of foot b	chains to add for Leg right and left	stitch count Leg after decreases
4T/5T	13	7	13-13-11-11-9-9-7	7-9-11-11-13-13-15	[2 sts] 4 times / 7	1.6/4	5	15	6+7	14
6T/7T	15	7	15-15-13-13-11-9-7	7-9-11-13-15-15-17	[2 sts] 4 times / 9	2/5	5	17	7+8	18
8T	18	7	18-16-16-14-14-12-10	10-12-14-16-18-18-20	[2 sts] 5 times / 10	2/5	6	20	9+9	20
9T/10T	18	7	18-16-16-14-14-12-10	10-12-14-16-18-20-22	[2 sts] 5 times / 12	2.4/6	6	22	9+9	24
11T/12T	19	8	19-17-17-15-15-13-13-11	11-13-15-17-19-21-23-23	[2 sts] 5 times / 13	2.4/6	7	23	9+10	26
12.5T/13.5T	21	10	21-19-19-17-17-15-15-13-11	11-13-15-17-19-21-23-23-25-25	[2 sts] 6 times / 13	2.75/7	7	25	10+11	26
1.5Y/2Y = 2.5W/3.5W	22	10	22-20-20-18-18-16-16-14-14-12	12-14-16-18-20-22-24-24-26-26	[2 sts] 6 times / 14	3.1/8	8	26	11+11	28
3Y/4Y = 4.5W/5.5W	22	10	22-20-20-18-18-16-16-14-14-12	12-14-16-18-20-22-24-24-26-26	[2 sts] 6 times / 14	3.1/8	8	26	11+11	28
4.5Y/5Y = 6W/6.5W	24	11	24-22-22-20-20-18-18-16-16-14-14-12	12-14-16-18-20-22-24-26-28-30-30	[2 sts] 7 times / 16	3.5/9	8	30	12+12	32
6M/7M = 7.5W/8W	24	11	24-22-22-20-20-18-18-16-16-14-14-12	12-14-16-18-20-22-24-26-28-30-32	[2 sts] 8 times / 16	3.5/9	8	32	12+12	32
7.5M/8.5M = 9W/10W	25	13	25-23-23-21-21-19-19-17-17-15-15-13-13	13-15-17-19-21-23-25-27-29-31-31-33-33	[2 sts] 8 times / 17	3.9/10	9	33	12+13	34
9M/10M = 10.5W/11.5W	26	14	26-24-24-22-22-20-20-18-18-16-16-14-14-12	12-14-16-18-20-22-24-26-28-30-30-32-32-34	[2 sts] 8 times / 18	4.3/11	9	34	13+13	36
10.5M/12M = 12W/13.5W	27	15/14	27-25-25-23-23-21-21-19-19-17-17-15-15-13	13-15-17-19-21-23-25-27-29-31-31-33-33-35	[2 sts] 8 times / 19	4.7/12	9	35	13+14	38
12.5M/13M = 14W/14.5W	27	15	27-25-25-23-23-21-21-19-19-17-17-15-15-13	13-15-17-19-21-23-25-27-29-31-33-33-35-35-37	[2 sts] 9 times / 19	5.1/13	9	37	13+14	38

SOCK WORKED IN THE ROUND IN FINGERING WEIGHT SOCK YARN

Yarn weight should be approximately 230 yd/1.75 oz (210 m/50 g); (see table on page 200 for approximate yardage needed per size).

Gauge: In extended sc with 3.5 mm (US E-4) hook, 22 sts and 19 rnds = 4 x 4 inches (10 x 10 cm)

Size	stitch count toe	increase in every round	increase in every other round	stitch count foot each half / total	tip of toe to gusset in in/cm	gusset increase	stitch count end of gusset	stitch count heel width	stitch count Leg after decreases	total foot length in in/cm
4T/5T	5	3	-	11/22	2.4/6	2x4 = 8	30	14	22	5.3/13.5
6T/7T	5	3	1	13/26	2.4/6	2x4 = 8	34	14	26	5.7/14.5
8T	6	3	1	14/28	2.8/7	3x4 = 12	40	18	28	6.3/16
9T/10T	6	3	2	16/32	3.1/8	3x4 = 12	44	18	32	6.9/17.5
11T/12T	7	3	2	17/34	3.5/9	3x4 = 12	46	20	34	7.3/18.5
12.5T/13.5T	7	3	3	19/38	3.9/10	3x4 = 12	50	20	36	7.9/20
1.5Y/2Y = 2.5W/3.5W	8	3	3	20/40	4.3/11	3x4 = 12	52	22	40	8.5/21.5
3Y/4Y = 4.5W/5.5W	8	3	3	20/40	4.3/11	4x4 = 16	56	22	40	8.9/22.5
4.5Y/5Y = 6W/6.5W	8	3	4	22/44	4.7/12	4x4 = 16	60	24	44	9.4/24
6M/7M = 7.5W/8W	8	3	4	22/44	5.1/13	5x4 = 20	64	24	44	10/25.5
7.5M/8.5M = 9W/10W	9	3	4	23/46	5.5/14	5x4 = 20	66	26	46	10.4/26.5
9M/10M = 10.5W/11.5W	9	3	4	23/46	5.9/15	5x4 = 20	66	26	48	11/28
10.5M/12M = 12W/13.5W	9	3	5	25/50	6.3/16	5x4 = 20	70	28	50	11.6/29.5
12.5M/13M = 14W/14.5W	9	3	6	27/54	6.7/17	5x4 = 20	74	28	54	11.8/30

Crocheting Mittens

Nothing warms so pleasantly in chilly cold winters like a pair of wooly mittens—which are all the more beautiful if they are also homemade with love! Worked in a hard-wearing sock yarn and in a stretchy stitch pattern, these crocheted mittens are in no way inferior to their knitted peers.

MATERIALS AND GAUGE

For crocheted mittens, a **4-ply sock yarn** with a yardage of approximately 230 yd/1.75 oz (210 m/50 g) and a fiber content of 75% pure new wool and 25% polyamide/nylon is a good choice. Crocheted in a yarn like this, the mittens will be very durable. Mittens are worked using a **crochet hook 3.5 mm (US E-4)** or any other size to match the appropriate gauge. Additionally, a **piece of contrasting color yarn** about 23.6 inches (60 cm) long is needed.

Total Yarn Amount Needed

Refer to measurements in chart on page 206 to determine size.

Size	Approximate Total Needed
3–5	230 yd (210.3 m)
6–8	460 yd (420.6 m)
8.5–9.5	690 yd (630.9 m)

! A GAUGE SWATCH made in fingering weight sock yarn with a crochet hook 3.5 mm (US E-4) should yield 22 elongated single crochets and 19 rows/rounds in a 4 x 4 inch- (10 x 10 cm) square.

INSTRUCTIONS

The mittens are begun at the cuff and worked **in the round** in extended single crochet (> page 34) from bottom to top. This stitch worked in the round produces an **even stitch appearance** similar to that of knitted fabric and is very stretchy.

! To determine the **CORRECT MITTEN SIZE**, measure hand circumference and hand length, and compare to the numbers in the table on page 206.

CUFF

Work the required stitch count according to the table as **foundation single crochet** (> page 59). Join into the round with 1 slip stitch and mark the beginning of the round with a long **piece of contrasting color yarn**. In the next round, first work 1 single crochet, and then work 1 double crochet; join into the round with 1 slip stitch.
Now continue the cuff in **spiral rounds** (> page 71), alternating "2 double crochets and 2 front post double crochets" (> page 42) until the cuff has reached the desired height, keeping the marker for the beginning of the round. For this, move the marking thread to the front and to the back of work every few rounds.

HAND

Continue, now working **elongated single crochets** (> page 34) in spiral rounds and still carrying the marker for the beginning of the round. During Round 1, work three-quarters of the stitches, and then, before the last quarter, insert a marking thread for the thumb. Now, in every round, double the stitch after the marking thread (> page 98) until the required number of stitches for the **thumb gusset** according to the table has been increased. Always after 3 increases, move the increase spot 1 stitch to the right. When all increases have been worked, for sizes 3 through 6, work 1 more round without increases, for sizes 7 through 9.5, 2 **more rounds without increases**.

! TO CROCHET 2 elongated single crochets TOGETHER, complete the two stitches up to the last step, leaving the last loop of each stitch on the hook (= 3 loops on the hook), and then pull the working yarn through all 3 loops on the hook at once.

In the next round, work to 4 stitches before the thumb marker. Chain as many stitches as stated in the table for the **thumb stitches to add**. Skip the stitches increased for the thumb gusset on the body of the mitten and, after this, again work elongated single crochet to the end of the round.

Continue in spiral rounds, working elongated single crochet, also crocheting across the **new thumb chains**. For sizes 6 and 8.5 to 9.5, continue directly over the number of stitches stated in the table. For all remaining sizes, in the first round, before and after the newly cast-on stitches, crochet together 2 stitches each, to reach the number stated in the table for "hand circumference in sts." Continue, crocheting the hand in the round, until the required **length to tip** given in the table has been reached.

TIP

Before beginning the tip decreases, count from the beginning of the round half of the stitches, and place **another marker**. Continue working spiral rounds in elongated single crochet and, over the number of rounds stated in the table, **decrease 2 stitches per round** as follows: Always crochet together the 2 stitches before the marker.

In the following rounds, always **before and after the marker** crochet 2 stitches each together (= 4 stitches decreased per round), until only 12 stitches remain in all. Break the working yarn leaving a long tail, place the mitten flat in front of you, and **seam** the opening using your preferred method (> page 142). Weave in the yarn tail on the wrong side.

THUMB

At one side of the thumb opening, attach **new working yarn** and work **regular single crochet** across the opening, working through the back loops of the stitches only (> page 37). Into the extended single crochet to the right and left of the thumb opening, work 2 single crochets each. For this, rotate work by 90° and crochet into the sides of the rows, until the required stitch count for the thumb according to the table has been reached. For sizes 3 and 4, during Round 1, 2 stitches have to be crocheted together for this.

Continue working **regular single crochet** through the **back loops of the stitches only** in spiral rounds until the thumb length to the beginning of the tip decreases according to the table has been reached. Now, in every round, continuously crochet 2 single crochets together, until only **8 stitches total remain**. Break the working yarn leaving a long end, and pull the tail through the working loop. Using a tapestry needle, pull the tail through the last 8 stitches, cinch these, and weave in the yarn tail on the wrong side.

FINISHING

Use the beginning tail from the cuff to close the small remaining gap. Weave in the beginning tail at the thumb on the inside of the mitten.
Crochet the second mitten the same way.

MITTENS IN FINGERING WEIGHT SOCK YARN

Yarn weight should be approximately 230 yd/1.75 oz (210 m/50 g); (see table on page 205 for approximate yardage needed per size).
Gauge: In extended sc with 3.5 mm (US E-4) hook, 22 sts and 19 rnds = 4 x 4 inches (10 x 10 cm)

Size	3	4	5	6	7	7.5	8	8.5	9	9.5
hand circumference in in/cm	5.5/14	5.9/15	6.3/16	6.3/16	6.7/17	7.3/18.5	7.9/20	8.3/21	8.7/22	9.3/23.5
hand length in in/cm	5.1/13	5.7/14.5	6.3/16	6.7/17	7.1/18	7.5/19	7.7/19.5	8/20	8.3/21	8.7/22
sts to chain for the cuff	28	32	36	36	40	40	44	44	48	48
increase for thumb gusset	6	6	6	8	8	8	8	10	10	10
thumb sts to add	4	4	4	4	5	5	5	5	6	6
hand circumference in sts	30	34	38	40	43	43	47	49	54	54
length to tip in in/cm	4/10	4.5/11.5	4.9/12.5	5.3/13.5	5.5/14	5.7/14.5	5.7/14.5	5.7/14.5	5.9/15	6.1/15.5
# of rounds with 2-stitch-decreases	-	-	3	3	5	5	5	6	6	6
stitch count thumb	14	14	16	16	17	17	17	17	18	18
thumb length to begin of tip decreases in in/cm	1/2.5	1.2/3	1.2/3	1.4/3.5	1.4/3.5	1.6/4	1.6/4	1.8/4.5	1.8/4.5	2/5

Crocheting Hats

Crocheted hats are very trendy, and the craft world and everyday life are hard to imagine without them. They can be crocheted in various shapes, stitch patterns, and techniques—the variety is nearly endless, and whole books are filled with instructions for crocheted hats alone.

Hats can be worked **from top to bottom** or the other way around **from bottom to top**. They can be crocheted in **seamless rounds** or **worked in rows** and later **seamed.** Using a variety of basic stitches and stitch patterns, every crocheted hat will be a most unique accessory.

This chapter provides a short overview of the **most common basic shapes** for crocheted hats: beret, close-fitting beanie, and slouchy hat.

All three hat types come with instructions for working in the round from the top down. This has several advantages: No long beginning chain must be wrestled with—work starts conveniently with a **magic circle and just a few stitches.** Furthermore, no guesswork for the head circumference is needed right at the beginning—the hat can be **tried on as needed anytime** during work, and customized.

All hats shown in this chapter are worked in **half double crochets**. This stitch is fast and easy to work and produces a tighter fabric than double crochet but is more elastic than single crochet. Using a hook size of 7.0–8.0 mm (US L-11), the hat is finished very quickly.

BERET

A beret receives its distinctive shape by first increasing more stitches than for a regular hat. This makes the top part plate-shaped and flat, and the hat becomes wider overall. After a few rounds without increases, the extra stitches are decreased, returning to a close fit at the brim.

Materials
Wool blend yarn, 60 yd/1.75 oz (55 m/50 g)
Crochet hook, 7.0 mm (US K-10.5 or L-11)

Gauge
In hdc with hook 7.0 mm (US K-10.5 or L-11): 10 sts and 9 rnds = 4 x 4 inches (10 x 10 cm)

WOMEN'S BERET
Head circumference: approximately 21.3–22.8 inches (54–58 cm)
The hat is worked from the center top down to the brim. For this hat, work in hdc (> *page 34*), beginning every round with ch2 to replace the first hdc and ending with 1 sl-st into the second chain to join the round. Make a magic circle (> *page 68*) and work the first round into it.
Round 1: Work ch2 and hdc8 into the ring. Join the round with 1 sl-st (= 9 sts).
Round 2: Work hdc2 in every stitch around (> *page 98*), (= 18 sts).
Round 3: Work hdc2 in every other stitch around, work hdc1 in all other sts (= 27 sts).
Round 4: Work hdc2 in every 3rd stitch around, work hdc1 in all other sts (= 36 sts).

Round 5: Work hdc2 in every 4th stitch around, work hdc1 in all other sts (= 45 sts).
Round 6: Work hdc2 in every 5th stitch around, work hdc1 in all other sts (= 54 sts).
Round 7: Work hdc2 in every 6th stitch around, work hdc1 in all other sts (= 63 sts).
Rounds 8–13: Work 63 hdc per round.
Round 14: Crochet every 6th and 7th hdc together (> *page 102*), work hdc1 in all other sts (= 54 sts).
Rounds 15 and 16: Work 54 hdc per round.
Round 17: Crochet every 5th and 6th hdc together, work hdc1 in all other sts (= 45 sts).
Round 18: Work 45 hdc.
Weave in all ends.

ABBREVIATIONS
can be found on page 344.

X The size of the hat can be easily customized. To achieve a **LARGER HEAD CIRCUMFERENCE**, after the fifth round, keep increasing at the same pace. To make a **LONGER HAT**, work more rounds without increases.

ABBREVIATIONS can be found on page 344.

CLOSE-FITTING BEANIE

This hat is the most classic of all the basic shapes. It fits the head snugly and covers the ears.

Materials

Wool blend yarn, 60 yd/1.75 oz (55 m/50 g)
Crochet hook, 7.0 mm (US K-10.5 or L-11)

Gauge

In hdc with hook 7.0 mm (US K-10.5 or L-11): 10 sts and 9 rnds = 4 x 4 inches (10 x 10 cm)

WOMEN'S BEANIE

Head circumference: approximately 21.3–22.8 inches (54–58 cm)
The hat is worked from the center top down to the brim. For this hat, work in hdc (> page 34), beginning every round with ch2 to replace the first hdc and ending with 1 sl-st into the second chain to join the round. Make a magic circle (> page 68) and work the first round into it.
Round 1: Work ch2 and hdc8 into the ring. Close the round with 1 sl-st (= 9 sts).
Round 2: Work hdc2 in every stitch around (> page 98) (= 18 sts).
Round 3: Work hdc2 in every other stitch around, work hdc1 in all other sts (= 27 sts).
Round 4: Work hdc2 in every 3rd stitch around, work hdc1 in all other sts (= 36 sts).
Round 5: Work hdc2 in every 4th stitch around, work hdc1 in all other sts (= 45 sts).
Rounds 6–17: Work 45 hdc.
Weave in all ends.

MEN'S BEANIE

Head circumference: approximately 22–23.6 inches (56–60 cm)
The hat is worked from the center top down to the brim. For this hat, work in hdc (> page 34), beginning every round with ch2 to replace the first hdc and ending with 1 sl-st into the second chain to join the round. Make a magic circle (> page 68) and work the first round into it.
Round 1: Work ch2 and hdc9 into the ring. Join the round with 1 sl-st (= 10 sts).
Round 2: Work hdc2 in every stitch around (> page 98) (= 20 sts).
Round 3: Work hdc2 in every other stitch around, work hdc1 in all other sts (= 30 sts).
Round 4: Work hdc2 in every 3rd stitch around, work hdc1 in all other sts (= 40 sts).
Round 5: Work hdc2 in every 4th stitch around, work hdc1 in all other sts (= 50 sts).
Rounds 6–17: Work 50 hdc.
Weave in all ends.

CHILDREN'S BEANIE

Head circumference: approximately 20.1–20.9 inches (51–53 cm)
The hat is worked from the center top down to the brim. For this hat, work in hdc (> page 34), beginning every round with ch2 to replace the first hdc and ending with 1 sl-st into the second chain to join the round. Make a magic circle (> page 68) and work the first round into it.
Round 1: Work ch2, and hdc7 into the ring. Join the round with 1 sl-st (= 8 sts).
Round 2: Work hdc2 in every stitch around (> page 98) (= 16 sts).
Round 3: Work hdc2 in every other stitch around, work hdc1 in all other sts (= 24 sts).
Round 4: Work hdc2 in every 3rd stitch around, work hdc1 in all other sts (= 32 sts).
Round 5: Work hdc2 in every 4th stitch around, work hdc1 in all other sts (= 40 sts).
Rounds 6–16: Work 40 hdc.
Weave in all ends.

BABY BEANIE

Head circumference: approximately 18.5–20 inches (47–50 cm)
The hat is worked from the center top down to the brim. For this hat, work in hdc (> page 34), beginning every round with ch2 to replace the first hdc and ending with 1 sl-st into the second chain to join the round. Make a magic circle (> page 68) and work the first round into it.
Round 1: Work ch2 and hdc6 into the ring. Join the round with 1 sl-st (= 7 sts).
Round 2: Work hdc2 in every stitch around (> page 98) (= 14 sts).
Round 3: Work hdc2 in every other stitch around, work hdc1 in all other sts (= 21 sts).
Round 4: Work hdc2 in every 3rd stitch around, work hdc1 in all other sts (= 28 sts).
Round 5: Work hdc2 in every 4th stitch around (= 35 sts).
Rounds 6–15: Work 35 hdc.
Weave in all ends.

SLOUCHY HAT

A slouchy hat is a close-fitting beanie with added height, which is casually scrunched at the back of the head or can even hang down. For this reason, it is often also called "long beanie" or "slouchy beanie."

Materials

Wool blend yarn, 60 yd/1.75 oz (55 m/50 g)
Crochet hook, 7.0 mm (US K-10.5 or L-11)

Gauge

In hdc with hook 7.0 mm (US K-10.5 or L-11): 10 sts and 9 rnds = 4 x 4 inches (10 x 10 cm)

X The size of the hat can be easily customized. To achieve a **LARGER HEAD CIRCUMFERENCE**, after the fifth round, keep increasing at the same pace. To make a **LONGER HAT**, work more rounds without increases. The taller the slouchy hat, the more it will later hang down from the head.

WOMEN'S SLOUCH

Head circumference: approximately 21.3–22.8 inches (54–58 cm)

The hat is worked from the center top down to the brim. For this hat, work in hdc (> page 34), beginning every round with ch2 to replace the first hdc and ending with 1 sl-st into the second chain to join the round. Make a magic circle (> page 68) and work the first round into it.

Round 1: Work ch2 and hdc8 into the ring. Join the round with 1 sl-st (= 9 sts).

Round 2: Work hdc2 in every stitch around (> page 98) (= 18 sts).

Round 3: Work hdc2 in every other stitch around, work hdc1 in all other sts (= 27 sts).

Round 4: Work hdc2 in every 3rd stitch around, work hdc1 in all other sts (= 36 sts).

Round 5: Work hdc2 in every 4th stitch around, work hdc1 in all other sts (= 45 sts).

Rounds 6–23: Work 45 hdc.

Weave in all ends.

MEN'S SLOUCH

Head circumference: approximately 22–23.6 inches (56–60 cm)

The hat is worked from the center top down to the brim. For this hat, work in hdc (> page 34), beginning every round with ch2 to replace the first hdc and ending with 1 sl-st into the second chain to join the round. Make a magic circle (> page 68) and work the first round into it.

Round 1: Work ch2 and hdc9 into the ring. Join the round with 1 sl-st (= 10 sts).

Round 2: Work hdc2 in every stitch around (> page 98) (= 20 sts).

Round 3: Work hdc2 in every other stitch around, work hdc1 in all other sts (= 30 sts).

Round 4: Work hdc2 in every 3rd stitch around, work hdc1 in all other sts (= 40 sts).

Round 5: Work hdc2 in every 4th stitch around, work hdc1 in all other sts (= 50 sts).

Rounds 6–23: Work 50 hdc per round.

Weave in all ends.

CHILD'S SLOUCH

Head circumference: approximately 20.1–20.9 inches (51–53 cm)

The hat is worked from the center top down to the brim. For this hat, work in hdc (> page 34), beginning every round with ch2 to replace the first hdc and ending with 1 sl-st into the second chain to join the round. Make a magic circle (> page 68) and work the first round into it.

Round 1: Work ch2, and hdc7 into the ring. Join the round with 1 sl-st (= 8 sts).

Round 2: Work hdc2 in every stitch around (> page 98) (= 16 sts).

Round 3: Work hdc2 in every other stitch around, work hdc1 in all other sts (= 24 sts).

Round 4: Work hdc2 in every 3rd stitch around, work hdc1 in all other sts (= 32 sts).

Round 5: Work hdc2 in every 4th stitch around, work hdc1 in all other sts (= 40 sts).

Rounds 6–20: Work 40 hdc.

Weave in all ends.

BABY SLOUCH

Head circumference: approximately 18.5–20 inches (47–50 cm)

The hat is worked from the center top down to the brim. For this hat, work in hdc (> page 34), beginning every round with ch2 to replace the first hdc and ending with 1 sl-st into the second chain to join the round. Make a magic circle (> page 68) and work the first round into it.

Round 1: Work ch2 and hdc6 into the ring. Join the round with 1 sl-st (= 7 sts).

Round 2: Work hdc2 in every stitch around (> page 98) (= 14 sts).

Round 3: Work hdc2 in every other stitch around, work hdc1 in all other sts (= 21 sts).

Round 4: Work hdc2 in every 3rd stitch around, work hdc1 in all other sts (= 28 sts).

Round 5: Work hdc2 in every 4th stitch around, work hdc1 in all other sts (= 35 sts).

Rounds 6–18: Work 35 hdc.

Weave in all ends.

Creative
Crochet

There are so many fascinating ways to
crochet beyond the basics! Here you'll
learn plenty of special effects that can
be magically conjured with a crochet
hook and often look completely
different from traditional crochet.
On to new shores!

Crocheting in Color

Crocheting with different colors opens up a variety of possibilities for customizing projects—beginning with simple stripes, through pattern variations with selective color changes, incorporating small color accents or motifs in intarsia, up to large color blocks. The final appearance of the finished crocheted item depends to a large part on whether the colors combined are starkly contrasting ones or hues of the same color as the base fabric.

WORKING WITH MULTIPLE SKEINS

Working with multiple skeins in different colors requires continuous control to prevent the strands from twisting or tangling. If it can be arranged, the skeins should not be able to roll away. It helps to start the skein from the inside end, causing the skein to unwind from the center while crocheting. If working at home, individual skeins can be placed into clean glass jars to keep them in place. Nevertheless, the strands can become twisted—therefore they need to be frequently checked and untangled in time, before becoming inextricably jumbled.

CROCHETING STRIPES IN COLOR

One of the easiest and most popular ways to create a multicolored crochet project is to crochet stripes in different colors. Options are manifold, ranging from wide block stripes in two colors to stripes of different widths in all colors of the rainbow. A few points should be considered, however, to produce a neat and professional-looking finished object.

CARRYING UNUSED COLORS

Carrying the strand in the currently not used color at the edge of the crocheted piece to the spot where used next saves the need for frequent breaking and weaving in the yarn.

CARRYING YARNS LOOSELY

The easiest method is to loosely carry the strand in the unused color. It will at first stay visible at the edge of the crocheted piece but will later be hidden in the seam or border.

For this, the last stitch of the last row of a stripe in one color (a wrong-side row, since an even number of rows is needed) needs to be completed except for the last 2 loops. Then drop the strand in the current color, and let it hang, bring the strand in the new color up to the current row, and crochet the last two loops of the last stitch using this new color. Make sure to bring up the yarn at the proper tension, not too loosely but not too tight, so it will arrange itself in a straight line along the edge of the just-finished color stripe.

! The working yarn in the old color can be placed either **IN FRONT OF OR BEHIND** the newly taken-up current color, which crosses the strands. It does not matter which direction the crosses go as long as it is always the same one.

CROCHETING STRANDS INTO INDIVIDUAL CHAIN STITCHES OF A CHAIN

In this technique, the working yarn can be carried best if the new rows begin with turning chains. The color change at the edge of the crocheted piece is hardly noticeable this way and does not need to be hidden or woven in later.

1 Work the last wrong-side row of a stripe in color A except for the last 2 loops of the last stitch. Change to color B and crochet the last two loops of the last stitch using this new color. Place the strand in color A from front to back over the new working yarn in color B.

2 Then work the first turning chain in color B.

3 Now place the strand in color A from back to front over the working yarn, and work the next turning chain. This way, before every chain, move the yarn alternatingly to the back or front, and work the required number of turning chains.

The working yarn has now been moved up to the beginning of Row 1 of the stripe in the new color.

COLOR STRIPES WORKED IN ROWS

In color stripes in rows, a distinction must be made between colorwork patterns for which every color stripe consists of an even number of rows and those for which an odd number of rows is needed, for the strand in each color has to be always picked up exactly in the spot in which it had been left after the last row.

STRIPES WITH AN EVEN NUMBER OF ROWS

Stripes in two colors over 2 rows each are the easiest stripe version, since after a right-side and wrong-side row, one always again arrives at the side where both colors are available to continue. This way, the unused color can be carried at the edge. Generally, stripes over 2 rows each with more than two colors or stripes of more than 2 rows in height—but always having an even number of rows—can be worked in this manner. However, the more colors used and the broader each individual stripe, the more strands have to be carried over a longer stretch. Depending on the yarn weight, this can cause unsightly bulk. Therefore, it may be advisable to cut the working yarn after every stripe and to join it anew. For this, all methods for attaching new working yarn at the beginning of a row are suitable: with or without beginning slipknot, with provisional knot and height-adjustment chains, or "false stitch" or standing stitches (> pages 76–79).

⊠ This method of carrying the yarn is also especially well suitable for **BROADER STRIPES IN TWO COLORS**. When the working yarn is in this manner crocheted in during every other row, long floats can be avoided.

⊠ When, for broader stripes or lots of different colors, yarn tails are immediately **CROCHETED IN** (> page 154), the need for time-consuming weaving in at the end is eliminated.

⊠ Those numerous **BEGINNING** and **ENDING TAILS** in different colors can also be used **AS DECORATIVE FRINGE**. For this, just leave the beginning tail long enough, and at the end of the row cut the ending tail to the same length.

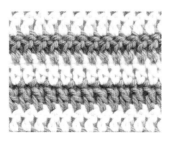

STRIPES WITH AN ODD NUMBER OF ROWS

Stripes with an odd number of rows are somewhat more complex, since close attention must be paid to where a color remains and can later be picked up again. For this, it might be, for instance, necessary to work 2 right-side rows or 2 wrong-side rows directly one after another. This way, the strands can likewise be carried at the edge and don't have to be cut.

Example: Stripes over 1 row of double crochet each

1 To work the first RS row, work 1 row of double crochet in color A. Using the crochet hook, pull a length of the yarn from the working loop of the last double crochet in color A large enough to pull the skein of yarn through that loop. To secure the loop, pass the skein through it, and then pull at the working yarn until the loop has been secured. Heads up! Do not turn.

2 To work the second RS row, attach the working yarn in color B at the right edge (i.e., insert the hook into the topmost turning chain and pull the working yarn in color B through). This can be done with a beginning slipknot (> page 76). Work ch3 for height adjustment.

3 Continue, working double crochet to the end of the row, completing the last double crochet of the row in color B except for the last 2 loops. Move the strand in color A from further down to the top row and finish the double crochet in this color. To work the first WS row, chain 3, turn work, and continue, working double crochet in color A to the end of the row. Secure the working loop of the last double crochet as done in the first RS row. Do not turn.

4 To work the second WS row, insert the hook into the topmost turning chain at the right edge, move the working yarn in color B up to the top, and pull a loop through. Work ch3 for height adjustment. Continue, working double crochet to the end of the row. Complete the last double crochet of the row except for the last 2 loops, move the working yarn in color A to the top, and finish the double crochet. Chain 3 and turn work.

In this manner, alternate working 2 right-side rows and 2 wrong-side rows.

5 Work again 2 right-side rows and 2 wrong-side rows. Work the first RS row as described in Step 1, but for the second RS row, the working yarn does not need to be joined anew but is pulled through the turning chain as described in Step 4.

In this way, stripes with an odd number of rows and more than two colors can also be worked. For this, one after another, in every one of the colors, 1 right-side row must be worked and then, in the same order in every one of the colors, 1 wrong-side row. For three colors, it would accordingly be 3 right-side rows, 3 wrong-side rows, 3 right-side rows, and so forth.

Also possible are stripes with more than 1 row but always with an odd number of rows. For these, in the color change spots 2 right-side rows or 2 wrong-side rows must always follow each other; within the individual stripes, regular RS and WS rows are worked. Stripes with 3 rows, for instance, are worked as follows:

Color A: 1 right-side row, 1 wrong-side row, 1 right-side row
Color B: 1 right-side row, 1 wrong-side row, 1 right-side row
Color A: 1 wrong-side row, 1 right-side row, 1 wrong-side row
Color B: 1 wrong-side row, 1 right-side row, 1 wrong-side row

••• Different options to join a **NEW COLOR** are explained on pages 76–79.

X The loop at the end of every first right- or wrong-side row can also be **PULLED LONG** instead of securing by passing the skein through. When the respective color is needed again, completely finish the last stitch of the old color, and then pull the long loop through to use as a new **WORKING LOOP**.

COLOR STRIPES IN THE ROUND

When crocheting stripes in the round, the color can be changed without problems as well after an even as after an odd number of rows without having to break the yarn all the time, since at the end of every round the unused color is arrived at again and can be taken up to proceed crocheting. The strands are either carried or crocheted in as described for crocheting in rows.

Carried floats

Floats enclosed within stitches

CRISPLY DELINEATED COLOR STRIPES

A clear, linear demarcation for simple color stripes can be achieved when working the stitches of the first row after a color change, not through both, but only through one of the loops of the stitch: for a color change on the right side of the fabric, insert the hook through the back loops, for a color change on the wrong side of the fabric, through the front loops of the stitches only (> page 37). If the stitches of a row after a color change are worked through both loops of the stitches of the previous row, the strands interlock and the color transition appears slightly distorted.

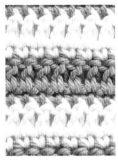

Regular way of inserting the hook through both top loops

Worked through one loop of the stitch only

STRIPES OF IRREGULAR WIDTH

If the color change happens within a row and the colors are always changed in different spots within a row, as well as after a different number of rows, a dynamic color and stripe pattern is created that breaks up the linear stripe structure and disperses the color.

To save on weaving in yarn tails, they are crocheted in as they occur: After the color change, place the beginning tail in the new color onto the stitches of the top row, and crochet it into the next 4 or 5 stitches (> page 154), cut the excess end. In the following row, work up to the color change spot, place the other hanging end onto the stitches of the current row—the colors are the same—and likewise crochet it into the next 4 or 5 stitches and cut the excess end.

X If you want to leave the color change to chance, you can knot **STRANDS OF ANY LENGTH** onto each other, and just start working. Join the strands with a **REEF KNOT**: Wrap the strands around each other once, and then wrap them around each other in the opposite direction, so that 2 loops of working yarns interlock. Pull the knot tight and trim the yarn tails.

PATTERN VARIATIONS WITH COLOR

If a stitch pattern, is worked with two or several colors instead of just one, an entirely new stitch appearance is created. The effect also depends on the rhythm of the color change. Generally, within each row, only one color is used.

MULTI-COLORED SHELL PATTERN

A selective color change after every 1 or 2 rows creates a stitch pattern in which the simple striped look is loosened up or completely broken up.

DOTTED PATTERN

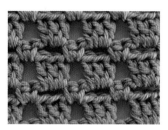 

When a stitch pattern contains chain spaces into which the alternate color stitches are worked, the continuous color flow of the row is interrupted. Instead of stripes, the stitch pattern features a dot-like look.

CHECKERBOARD PATTERN AND VERTICAL STRIPES

This multi-colored pattern looks much more complicated than it actually is, since every row is crocheted only with a single color, which is easy to keep track of. Both stitch patterns—the three-colored one as well as the two-colored one—are worked the same but have a completely different look.

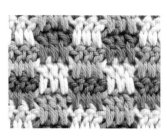 

To work the Checkerboard pattern, alternate "1 right-side row, 1 wrong-side row;" for the vertical stripes, work "2 right-side rows, 2 wrong-side rows" (> *page 214*).

1 In Row 1 (RS), work single crochet in color A and, in regular intervals, skip a certain number of stitches (3 in the example), bridging them with chains. Turn work. Attach new working yarn in color B at the right edge, and for Row 2 (WS) shift the stitch pattern. Work chains atop the crocheted stitches of the previous row and work double crochets encasing the chains of the previous row within the new stitches. Turn work.

2 To work Row 3 (RS), shift the stitch pattern once more and work in color A. Work another wrong-side row in color B.

To work the three-colored stitch pattern, work 3 right-side rows one after another in colors A, B, and C as described above, and then work 3 wrong-side rows in colors A, B, and C.

WAVE AND CHEVRON PATTERNS

Wave and chevron patterns look particularly charming with stripes, which accentuate the direction of the rows.

The example in the photo has been worked as follows: 2 single crochets into the same stitch, * 4 single crochets, crochet 2 single crochets together skipping 1 stitch in the middle, 4 single crochets, 3 single crochets in the same stitch, repeat from * all the time, ending with 2 single crochets into the same stitch.

The result will look different depending on the number of rows between color changes.

COLORFUL BOBBLES

Individual contrasting-color bobbles on a solid-colored background make for especially pretty accents for children's garments. Bobbles of double-crochet clusters, worked on a background fabric in single crochet, stand out three-dimensionally from the background fabric.

1 Work the bobbles in a wrong-side row. In the main color, crochet to the spot where the bobble is to be placed and work the last step of the last single crochet in bobble color. The working yarn in main color and the beginning tail of the bobble are located on the wrong side of the fabric (i.e., current front of work). Hold both strands with your thumb.

2 To work the bobble, work 5 double crochets through the back loop of the next stitch, keeping the last loop of every stitch on the hook. Crochet the 6 loops together in bobble color. Pull the working yarn taut—the finished bobble bulges toward the back of the fabric and therefore ends up on the right side of work.

3 Take up the working yarn in main color again, and pull it through the working loop (= in the bobble color), which creates a single chain. Pull the working yarn taut, and then continue in main pattern, incorporating more bobbles at the desired spacing in the colors of your choice, each one from a separate piece of working yarn.

4 Before the next right-side row is worked, tighten the yarn tails of every bobble and secure with a double knot. Above the individual bobbles, 2 colored top loops each are visible.

5 When crocheting over the bobbles, work 1 single crochet into the first colored top loop, skipping the second. Continue in main pattern to the next row featuring colored bobbles.

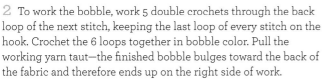

X Go for the REMNANT BASKET! Combining different yarns creates pretty effects.

···· How BOBBLES IN DOUBLE CROCHET are worked is explained on page 52.

X Individual color bobbles can create a pattern when placed CLOSELY TOGETHER, creating simple shapes or motifs, such as diamonds. When worked in rows, bobbles can be either placed ATOP EACH OTHER or STAGGERED. Bobbles arranged in irregular groups create flower motifs.

X Colorful bobbles can also be CROCHETED ONTO THE SURFACE AFTERWARD. Attach new working yarn in bobble color either at the beginning point between 2 stitches of the base fabric or around the post of the stitch, chain 2, and then make a bobble in double crochet. After having completed the stitch, chain 1 to secure all loops. Break the working yarn and pull the tail through the working loop to secure it. Pull the beginning and ending tails through to the wrong side with the help of a crochet hook and secure with a double knot.

! CHOOSING THE RIGHT TECHNIQUE: THE LARGER THE COLORED SECTIONS are, the more convenient is the intarsia technique (> page 222). NARROW PATTERN REPEATS, which are repeated multiple times within a row or round, are worked in the JACQUARD TECHNIQUE. For small motifs, a combination of both techniques can also be used (> page 223).

JACQUARD TECHNIQUE

In the Jacquard, or Norwegian, technique, patterns using multiple colors and decorative bands with small pattern repeats as well as small colored sections only a few stitches wide are worked—a challenging and laborious way of color design. The allocation of the colors is shown in counting charts (> page 94).

Basic stitches such as single crochets, half double crochets, and double crochets are well suited for stitch patterns in color. The best choice is single crochet, which also allows for incorporating smaller motifs. However, if the colored sections become too small, their outlines are not clearly enough delineated for the motif to be recognized. Double crochet, thanks to the linear shape of the stitches, is very well suited for geometric colorwork patterns such as checkerboard patterns or vertical stripes. In the jacquard technique, most often only two strands in different colors are used within a single row. Since only one color is used at a time, the respective unused color must be carried to the spot where it will be used next. After a color change, the unused strand is carried, loosely tensioned, in back of work behind the already-worked stitches in the other color. These so-called floats always run on the wrong side of the crocheted fabric. Unused strands can also be carried within the current stitches.

CROCHETING FROM COUNTING CHARTS

Stranded colorwork patterns are often shown in charts. These consist of a square grid in which every box represents 1 stitch. Colors or symbols within the boxes show in which color every stitch has to be worked. Numbers to the side of the chart stand for the row number. At the bottom, the pattern repeat is noted. The stitch pattern is shown as it will look from the right side of the fabric. This means: Right-side rows are to be read from right to left and wrong-side rows (where the back of work is facing the viewer) from left to right.

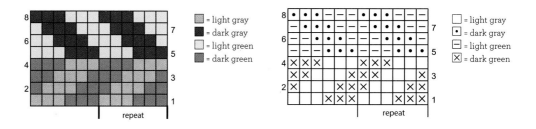

= light gray
= dark gray
= light green
= dark green

repeat

☐ = light gray
⊡ = dark gray
⊟ = light green
☒ = dark green

repeat

! When working in HALF DOUBLE CROCHET, for the last half double crochet before the color change, make a yarn over onto the hook, insert the hook, and pull the working yarn through the fabric. Crochet the 3 loops on the hook together in the new color.

COLOR CHANGE WITHIN A ROW

An essential feature of the color change is that the change to the new color happens during the last stitch in the old color. The last loop of this last stitch is worked off the hook in the new color. For single crochet, crochet the 2 loops on the hook together in the new color, a double crochet is completed except for the last 2 loops and then finished in the new color (color change within a row during the last step of the stitch > page 79).

CARRYING AND CROCHETING IN FLOATS

Floats created when working patterns in several colors can be either loosely carried or enclosed within the current stitches.

CARRYING FLOATS LOOSELY

 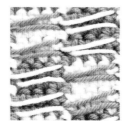

For a small pattern repeat that is repeated multiple times throughout the row with stretches in one color never wider than 5 stitches, the currently unused color can be carried loosely to the next color change. In right-side rows, the floats run in back of work, in wrong-side rows, in front of work. This way carried strands are not visible from the right side of the fabric.

After the first color change in the first right-side row, lead the beginning tail in the new color over the foundation chain and enclose it within the next 4 to 6 stitches. Trim excess ends. Keep the unused strand in the other color in back of work.

In all right-side rows, before a color change move the working yarn in the old color down behind work, and then take up the working yarn in the new color and work the color change. Keep this order in all rows, so that the wrong side of the fabric looks neat, too.

In wrong-side rows, after a color change move the working yarn in the old color to the front and hold it with the thumb of the left hand until the first stitch in the new color has been crocheted.

! Carried strands in unused colors should be kept EVENLY TENSIONED in back of work. They should neither constrict the crocheted fabric nor hang about too loosely. If the floats are too long, the stitch pattern can become distorted. Moreover, one can get caught in them when the finished item is in use. With A LITTLE PRACTICE, an even tension of the working yarn often sets itself up on its own

At the end of every row, also move the tail from the last color change from within the row to the edge and, before crocheting the turning chain, move it from front to back over the working yarn, catching it. When all floats throughout the whole piece are led up to the side edges, drape and thickness of the crocheted fabric will be identical over the whole area.

ANCHORING LONG FLOATS

If spacing between color changes is more than 5 stitches, in these longer stretches, loosely carried floats should be anchored in a spot (i.e., enclosed within a stitch, every 4 or 5 stitches).

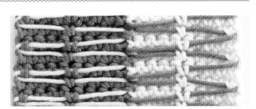

For this, before inserting the hook to work the stitch, move the unused strand to the edge of the crocheted piece, and enclose it in the stitch when working it. After that, carry the working yarn loosely—in right-side rows, behind work, in wrong-side rows, in front of work.

Lead the floats to the side edges, too, and before working the turning chain, place them from front to back over the working yarn, embedding them, and additionally enclose them within the first stitch of the following row.

! Crocheting in the floats is suggested for yarns of even thickness throughout. For **THIN YARNS**, the enclosed strands could become **VISIBLE** between the stitches. This looks especially unsightly if colors high in contrast are used together. For this reason, work a **SWATCH**, if possible, and try out both methods—crocheting in and loosely carrying the floats. This helps to decide on the best method.

✗ When working with 2 **COLORS**, the strands are prone to twist around each other. It makes work easier if the strands are **DETANGLED** every 2 rows.

✗ Compared to single crochet, floats enclosed in double crochet are **LESS FIRMLY EMBEDDED**. For this reason, before the color change, especially after a long stretch in one color, check the **LENGTH** of the enclosed floats: gently tighten the floats, and then slightly stretch the top edge of the crocheted piece.

! **TAPESTRY CROCHET** is worked in the round in single crochet using 2 or 3 colors, as described for the jacquard technique. The **TYPICAL GRAPHIC SHAPES** and stylized animal figures originate in the ornate patterns of the Mayas in Central America.

EMBEDDING FLOATS

The floats in colorwork patterns can also be crocheted in. In this method, when working the stitches, the currently unused color is enclosed within every stitch worked over the whole stretch in the other color. Front and back look identical.

In the current row, place the unused strand on top of the top loops of the row worked last. Insert the hook as usual into the stitch, pull the working yarn through the fabric, and through the loops on the hook. During this process, the carried strand is enclosed, and will be embedded within the post of the stitch.

Even if at the beginning of the row the color is not changed again, it is recommended to crochet in the unused floats to the end of the row and, before crocheting the turning chain, to place them from front to back over the working yarn, catching them. This ensures an even thickness and appearance of the crocheted fabric throughout.

EMBEDDING MULTIPLE COLORS

Double crochet, owing to the linear shape of the stitches, is very well suited for geometric colorwork patterns. The example shows a three-colored stitch pattern with step-like stripes.

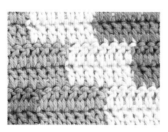

During the color change, finish the last step of the last double crochet in the old color with the new color. Place both unused strands across the top of the top loops of the row worked last and enclose them within the double crochets of the current row. At the side edges, catch the two unused strands before the first and second turning chain, which carries them up to the spot where they will be enclosed within a stitch and at the same time anchors them.

DECORATIVE BANDS IN ROWS AND ROUNDS

Two-colored stranded colorwork patterns can look different depending on whether they are worked in rows or rounds.

Rows and Rounds Compared

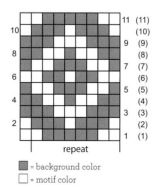

■ = background color
□ = motif color

Numbers in parentheses refer to crocheting in the round.

Single crochets worked in turned rows produce a grainy texture. With slanted lines in which the stitches are staggered by 1 stitch in every row, this can cause the outlines to appear distorted and blurred.

Single crochets worked in the round or worked on the right side only (> page 66), produce a steady, clear stitch appearance. Due to the slight offset of the stitches, the stitch pattern maintains a twist to the right.

Color Shift in Every Other Row

If, as for this border in 3 colors, the colors are shifted in every other row, in turned rows a clear outline of the pattern is likewise achieved. For this, first work 2 right-side rows one after another according to the chart; then, in the wrong-side row, keep the color arrangement of the previous right-side row. Always enclose the two unused colors in the current stitches (> page 220).

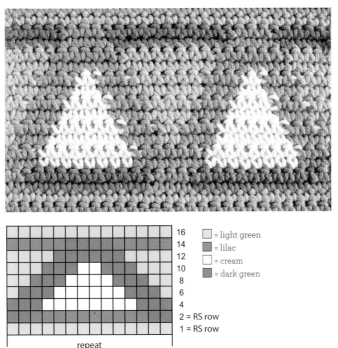

16
14
12
10
8
6
4
2 = RS row
1 = RS row

☐ = light green
▨ = lilac
☐ = cream
▨ = dark green

repeat

✂ For stranded colorwork, charts for knitting or cross-stitch patterns can often also be used as **TEMPLATES**. An actual gauge swatch is, however, needed to check in advance whether the desired appearance will be achieved in crochet.

MOTIF BANDS IN KNOT STITCH

A two-colored stitch pattern can also be worked very conveniently in a so-called knot stitch. It is exclusively worked in right-side rows or in the round. The advantage of this stitch type is that the stitches sit exactly atop each other and therefore crisply show a crocheted-in colorwork motif. Knot stitches produce a dense fabric.

To make a knot stitch, insert the hook into 2 adjoining stitches one after the other, pulling through 1 loop for each stitch. Make a new yarn over onto the hook and pull the working yarn through all 3 loops on the hook. * For the next knot stitch, insert the hook first into the second insertion point of the previous stitch, and then into the next stitch, pulling through 1 loop for each stitch. Then crochet all 3 loops off the hook together. Repeat from * continuously.

❗ The **COLOR CHANGE** happens within the last stitch of the old color, the second insertion point of which already falls in the area of the new color. All 3 loops of old color are worked off the hook in the new color. Old and new color sections share an insertion point.

✂ If the band is to be worked in **RIGHT-SIDE ROWS**, 2 additional green stitches need to be added to the last pattern repeat at the left edge for a symmetrical ending.

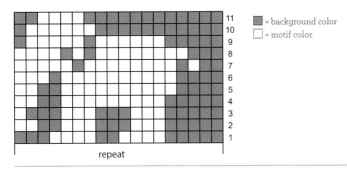

11
10
9
8
7
6
5
4
3
2
1

▨ = background color
☐ = motif color

repeat

INTARSIA TECHNIQUE

Large adjoining colored sections or extensive color motifs surrounded by a background in one color are worked in the intarsia technique. Every area of color is worked from a separate ball or bobbin, even when the background color before and after a motif is the same. Depending on the size of the color block, the yarn is pre-wound onto bobbins or into tiny balls. At the color change, the unused working yarn is kept hanging and is taken up again in the following row. There are no floats, and nothing to crochet in!

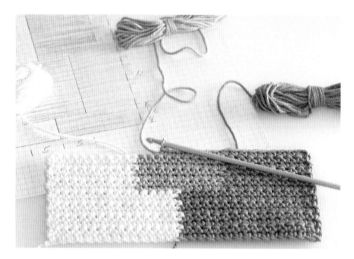

X There are **SPECIAL BOBBINS** designed for winding small amounts of yarn (> *page 22*).

SETUP

If only one area of a color is to be worked, it can be crocheted directly off the skein. When, however, more areas of color are to be worked in the same color than individual skeins are available, suitable amounts of yarn are wound onto bobbins or into tiny balls.

ESTIMATING THE YARN AMOUNT

X For **LARGE AREAS OF COLOR** it is prudent to calculate the total yarn amount needed based on a larger stitch count to avoid running out of yarn prematurely.

To determine how much yarn is needed for an area of color, the stitch count is estimated on the basis of the chart and rounded up to the next multiple of ten. Make a small swatch in the main pattern; in the pictured example, single crochet was used. Immediately after a single crochet, mark the yarn with a short, tied-on piece of yarn. Then work 10 single crochets and, immediately after, place another marker. Dissolve the stitches just worked and

measure the marked length. This is how much yarn you need per 10 single crochet. Go back to your previously calculated stitch count of the whole area of color and determine yardage needed. Add a buffer of 20 inches (50 cm) and wind the yarn in portions.

WINDING A MICRO SKEIN (A.K.A. BUTTERFLY)

X Crocheting in the intarsia technique is much easier if the strand from the crocheted piece to the bobbin is kept **AS SHORT AS POSSIBLE**. Shorter lengths can be kept hanging in back of work without getting tangled.

1 Hold the beginning tail with ring and middle finger of the left hand, and wind the required yarn amount in a figure 8 shape around index finger and thumb until about 7.9 inches (20 cm) of the yarn are left.

2 Remove the loops from thumb and index finger, holding them together in the middle. Wind the yarn tail around the middle of the bundle, and secure with a simple knot. Make sure that the beginning tail is uncovered.

When crocheting, pull the working yarn out of the middle of the skein, only as little as needed to work the next few stitches of the row so the remainder of the skein hangs down the back of work on a short leash.

COLOR CHANGE IN THE INTARSIA TECHNIQUE

The arrangement of the areas of color is shown in a chart as for the jacquard technique (> page 94 and 218). The color change, too, always happens in the last stitch of an area of color by crocheting the loops off the hook in the new color (> page 79).

When a crocheted piece begins with two areas of color, the beginning chain for the left half must be worked first. To work a width of 15 stitches, 14 chains in color B (here: cream) are crocheted, the working loop on the hook is marked for the 15th stitch in the same color. Then 15 chains for the other area of color are worked in color A (here: dark green).

In right-side rows in color A (dark green), work up to the color change spot, and then move the working yarn to the back. Take up color B (cream) and use it to complete the last step of the last stitch in color A from this section. Do not cross the strands. Work the stitches of the new area of color in color B.

In wrong-side rows, work up to the color change spot, and then move the strand in color B to the front and hold it with the thumb of the left hand. Take up color A and use it to complete the last step of the last stitch of this area in color B. Continue the row, working over the new area of color. The position of the required color changes in the following rows can be derived from the chart.

When a third area of color is located atop the two previously worked areas of color, work up to the color change spot and complete the last step of the last stitch in the first background color with the new color from a separate skein. Work the stitches of the new area of color. Carry the working yarn in the second background color within the stitches up to the spot where used next. This eliminates joining a new color and weaving in the tails later. Continue the areas of color according to the chart and work the color change as previously described.

! When a LARGE AREA OF COLOR is worked into an otherwise ONE-COLORED BACKGROUND, the section before (to the right of) and after (to the left of) the color block are treated as separate areas of color, each being worked from its own skein. Floats would turn out too long in this case, and strands carried within stitches would unnecessarily increase yarn use.

X If desired, the BEGINNING TAIL in color A, hanging from the middle, can be crocheted into the stitches of Row 1, eliminating the need for weaving it in later.

X This method can also be used when an existing area of color is extended TO THE LEFT.

SMALL MOTIFS WITHIN AN AREA OF COLOR

When only small individual motifs are crocheted within an area, a combination of Jacquard and intarsia technique can be used. Multiple small motifs in different colors can also be combined in this manner, with every motif being worked from a separate ball or bobbin. The required yarn amount can also be calculated as described on page 222.

For a one-colored background, likewise only one skein is used. The working yarn in the background color is enclosed in the stitches (> page 154) while the stitches of the motif are being worked. Floats are not created. This method can only be used for small color motifs with a width of only a few stitches. The total number of skeins used in each row is smaller than for the "pure" intarsia technique, for which each area in background color is worked from a separate ball.

front of work

![chart]

☐ = background color
☒ = motif color

> ⚠ Always weave in the **YARN TAILS** in an area of the same color (> *page 154*).

back of work

> ⚠ In right- and wrong-side rows, stitches are **NOT** located **EXACTLY ATOP EACH OTHER**, but staggered. For this reason, the outline of a motif looks **RATHER UNEVEN**, especially with staggered stitches. The larger a motif in a contrasting color, the less noticeable is this shortcoming.

COLOR CHANGE WITH SLANTED LINES

Generally, areas of color with slanted sides are worked the same way as those with straight sides. When an area of color shifts by 1 stitch, attention should be paid to how the yarn is carried in wrong-side rows to create a neat color transition.

In wrong-side rows with color area extending to the right: Complete the last loop of the last stitch before the motif in motif color, and then enclose the strand in background color within the stitches in motif color.

In wrong-side rows with color area extending to the left: Complete the last loop of the last stitch of the motif in background color and only after this move the working yarn in motif color above the strand in background color to the front of work. Continue the row in background color.

Tunisian Crochet

Tunisian crochet, also called afghan crochet, is a very pretty specialty form of crochet that creates appealing textures and pattern effects. It creates a dense but still stretchy fabric with a woven-like look.

CROCHET HOOKS

Since for Tunisian crochet, in every right-side row, all stitches of a row are taken up one after another and at the end of the row remain on the hook together, this technique uses long and smooth hooks without thumb rest. The length of the hook determines the maximum width of the crocheted piece. There are rigid hooks, resembling knitting needles, and flexible ones, where the stitches farther back slide onto a cord, as well as interchangeable systems in which a flexible cord in the required length can be connected to tips in different hook sizes.
Double-ended crochet hooks expand the pattern options and make working in the round possible.

! Crochet hooks for Tunisian crochet should generally be chosen one **HOOK SIZE LARGER** than those for traditional crochet, since the crocheted piece would otherwise very quickly become **TOO DENSE**.

TUNISIAN BASIC TECHNIQUE

In Tunisian crochet, every completed row consists of two working steps: a forward pass, in which individual stitches/loops are picked up one after another from right to left, and a return pass, in which they are crocheted off from left to right one after another. Tunisian crochet is worked on the right side of the fabric only; work is not turned.

FOUNDATION STITCHES AND FIRST ROW

Begin with a loosely crocheted chain (> page 32) with the required stitch count as for regular crochet. The working loop on the hook counts as the first stitch of Row 1 and is located in front of the first chain. To work the next stitch, insert the hook into the second chain from the crochet hook, through the third loop in back of the chain (> page 58) and pull up a loop.
Continue to pick up stitches this way to the end of the foundation chain.

! To work the first row of stitches, you can also insert the hook **UNDER 2 STRANDS** of the chain (> page 58). The method described here, however, produces a neater edge, which can later be easily finished by adding a border or an edging.

When all stitches of the beginning chain have been picked up, they are then crocheted off during the return pass. Do not turn work for this.

1 Make a yarn over, grasp the working yarn, and pull it through the first stitch on the left to form the left edge stitch.

2 Make a new yarn over, pull the working yarn through the fabric, and through the first 2 stitches on the hook at once.

Repeat Step 2 until the end of the row—which is the right edge of the piece here—has been reached, and the working loop is the only loop remaining on the hook.

The first row as base of the crocheted piece has been completed.
Individual stitches with vertical and horizontal loops, which form a kind of grid, are created. Through these vertical loops, the hook is inserted for most Tunisian stitch types.

CROCHETING IN ROWS

After the end of the first return pass, only the working loop—which at the same time is also the right edge stitch—is still on the hook. During the next forward pass, all stitches are picked up again.

X It is recommended to **TIGHTEN THE WORKING YARN** at the beginning and the end of the row to keep the edge stitches tight.

1 Insert the crochet hook from right to left under the second vertical loop. The first vertical loop stays unused, since atop it the working loop is already located as the first stitch.

2 Make a yarn over and pull the working yarn through behind the vertical loop.

3 Continue in this manner until only the last vertical loop stays not crocheted into.

! Sometimes it is recommended to insert the hook for the left edge stitch **ONLY UNDER THE VERTICAL STRAND**. The method shown here, however, creates a significantly **STURDIER EDGE**.

4 To work the left edge stitch, insert the hook not only under one vertical loop but under 2 strands, and pull the working yarn through the fabric.

Now, for the return pass, as described previously for the first row, first crochet off a single stitch on its own and then all other stitches in pairs.

DECREASING STITCHES

In Tunisian crochet, stitches can be decreased as with regular crochet. Here, decreases are worked differently depending on whether the decrease is located at the beginning, within, or at the end of a row.

AT THE BEGINNING OF THE ROW

If an individual stitch is to be decreased at the beginning of the row, then, at the end of the previous return pass, 3 instead of 2 stitches are worked off together.

When picking up the stitches during the subsequent forward pass, the first two vertical loops close together are skipped, the second stitch is picked up from the next solitary loop.

If multiple stitches are to be decreased at the beginning of the row, the appropriate number of stitches is bound off (> page 229) immediately at the beginning of the forward pass. Then the row is continued as usual.

AT THE END OF THE ROW

To decrease a single stitch at the end of the row, during the forward pass, insert the hook at the same time under the vertical loop of the next-to-last stitch and into the edge stitch, and pull the working yarn through both.

If multiple stitches are to be decreased at the end of the row, the appropriate number of stitches is left unworked at the end of the forward pass, not picking up new loops from these stitches. The now last stitch at the left edge turns into the new edge stitch.

WITHIN A ROW

If an individual stitch is to be decreased within a row, the hook is inserted in the appropriate spot during the forward pass under 2 vertical loops at the same time, a yarn over is placed onto the hook, and the working yarn pulled through.

During the return pass, the stitches are worked off the regular way.

If multiple stitches are to be decreased within a row, individual decreases are worked evenly distributed over the row.

Up to 4 stitches can also be decreased as described for a single decrease by combining MULTIPLE VERTICAL LOOPS into one decrease. For larger stitch counts, decreases should be distributed evenly to avoid unsightly holes.

INCREASING STITCHES

Increasing stitches is also possible in the Tunisian crochet technique. Here, too, different methods are used depending on whether increases are located at the beginning, within, or at the end of a row.

AT THE BEGINNING OF THE ROW

To work a single increase at the beginning of the row, an additional stitch is taken up during the forward pass. For this, insert the hook under the first vertical loop of the row, which is normally skipped, and pull a loop through to form a stitch.

The next stitch is picked up as usual from the second loop. During the return pass, crochet the loops off the hook as usual; the stitch count has been increased by 1.

If multiple stitches are to be increased at the beginning of a row, at the end of the previous return pass, work as many chains from the working loop as stitches to be increased.

After that, pick up new stitches as described for the cast-on (> page 225), beginning into the second chain from the crochet hook. At the transition to the edge of the main piece, also pick up 1 stitch from the first vertical loop, which is an edge stitch in regular rows and normally not crocheted into.

AT THE END OF THE ROW

A single increase at the end of a row is worked by picking up 1 additional stitch. For this, in the forward pass, insert the hook into the horizontal upper loop before the left edge stitch and pull a loop through to form a stitch. Work the last edge stitch as usual, and in the return pass work off the stitches the regular way in pairs.

If multiple stitches are to be increased at the end of a row, an additional regular crochet hook of the same size is needed as an auxiliary hook.

1 Complete the forward pass to and including the left edge stitch. Turn work, hold the auxiliary hook in your right hand and insert the auxiliary hook from left to right through the first stitch on the main hook.

2 Make a yarn over and pull the working yarn through this stitch.

3 Move the working yarn behind the Tunisian crochet hook, bring it over the hook to the front of work, and pull it through the loop on the auxiliary hook.

! Long cords for Tunisian crochet hooks (up to 60 inches [150 cm]) make it possible to work GARMENT FRONT AND BACK WITH INCORPORATED SLEEVES in one piece over the whole width. This construction involves extending the beginning and end of the row for the sleeves.

4 Repeat step 3 until the desired number of additional stitches minus 1 have been placed onto the Tunisian hook. The working loop on the auxiliary hook forms the last increased stitch and is also placed onto the Tunisian hook.

5 Turn work again and work the return pass as usual.

WITHIN A ROW

If a single stitch is to be increased within a row, during a forward pass insert the hook at the appropriate spot between 2 vertical loops under the horizontal loop in front, which is located at the top, and pull the working yarn through. During the return pass, crochet the loops off the hook as usual.

If multiple stitches are to be increased within a row, work this type of increase evenly distributed within the row, the appropriate number of times.

BINDING OFF AND CROCHETING AROUND THE EDGES

Before a piece in Tunisian crochet can be finished, the top edge of the last row must be reinforced by binding off. Most often, this is done with slip stitches.

1 Insert the hook under the next vertical strand.

2 Make a yarn over onto the hook and pull the working yarn through the vertical loop and the loop on the hook at once.

3 Repeat Steps 1 and 2 until all stitches are bound off and only 1 loop remains on the hook. Then finish the crocheted piece as described for a piece worked in regular crochet (> page 80).

For binding off, single crochet can also be used. First, chain 1, and then insert the hook as for increasing a single stitch into the horizontal top loop of the stitch in front and pull the working yarn through to form a loop. Then pull the working yarn through both loops on the hook at once.

After binding off the last row, single crochet can be worked all around the whole crocheted piece. For this, at the side edges, always insert the hook into the edge stitches through the 2 outer loops of the stitch and work 1 single crochet (> page 33) for each row. Into the corners, work "1 single crochet, chain 1, 1 single crochet." Along the bottom edge work 1 single crochet into every stitch.

✗ Binding off in this manner results in a top edge that exactly mimics the CAST-ON EDGE, provided the hook has been inserted through the THIRD LOOP IN BACK OF THE STITCH.

✗ Depending on yarn weight, it is recommended to use a SMALLER CROCHET HOOK for a sturdier edge when binding off.

✗ The VERTICAL LOOPS of single crochets are not crocheted into.

BASIC TUNISIAN STITCHES

In addition to the basic Tunisian simple stitch, numerous other stitch types can be worked in the Tunisian crochet technique. During the forward passes, the insertion point as well as the way the working yarn is placed vary. The edge stitches (i.e., the first and last stitch of the row) are always worked as for the basic technique, to achieve a neat edge. Return passes are always worked the same as described for the basic technique (i.e., the first loop on its own) and then working off the remaining loops in pairs.

TUNISIAN SIMPLE STITCH

The Tunisian simple stitch is the basic stitch of Tunisian crochet and creates a woven look. It can also serve very well as a base for colorwork patterns (> page 232).

Pick up all stitches by pulling the working yarn through the vertical loop.

TUNISIAN KNIT STITCH

This stitch produces a fabric that looks knitted but is notably thicker.

1 To create a stitch, insert the hook under the vertical loop and below the horizontal loops at top of stitch.

2 Pull the working yarn through the fabric.

TUNISIAN PURL STITCH

The stitch appearance of this stitch resembles that of fabric knitted in garter stitch but is significantly thicker.

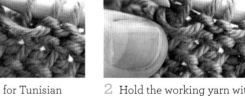

1 Move the working yarn to the front of work. As for Tunisian simple stitch, insert the hook under the vertical loop, and lead the working yarn across in front of the hook.

2 Hold the working yarn with your thumb, make a yarn over and pull the working yarn through under the vertical loop.

X For this stitch, the working yarn can also be pulled through SOME-WHAT EASIER if the crochet hook is turned with the hook to the back, and the YARN OVER is placed onto the hook FROM FRONT TO BACK.

! Since the stitch, after having pulled the working yarn through for the first time, often turns out TOO LOOSE, pull a little at the working yarn once more before crocheting the next stitch.

TUNISIAN REVERSE STITCH

Tunisian reverse stitch forms a stitch pattern of small raised bumps.

For this, insert the hook under the vertical loop at the back of the work and pull the working yarn through.

TUNISIAN STITCH PATTERNS

Through further variations of hook insertion points or using a combination of different stitches, a variety of stitch patterns can be created in Tunisian crochet. Here, only a small selection of basic patterns are introduced.

For the beginning of the stitch pattern, either a first row can be worked in the Tunisian simple stitch or the stitch pattern can be started directly when picking up stitches from the foundation chain. When binding off, the same applies: either insert the hook as required for the stitch pattern or finish work with a row of Tunisian simple stitch.

CROSSED STITCH PATTERN

Instructions
Stitch count: an even number.
Forward pass: 1 selv st, * pick up 1 st from the vertical loop after the next one (at the beginning of the row = 3rd loop from the right), pick up 1 st from the next (previously skipped) vertical loop, repeat from * to last st, 1 selv st.
Return pass: First crochet off the first st individually and then all others in pairs.

••• ABBREVIATIONS
can be found on page 344.

STAGGERED CROSSED STITCH PATTERN

Stitch count: an even number.
Forward pass 1: 1 selv st, * pick up 1 st from the vertical loop after the next one (at the beginning of the row = 3rd loop from the right), pick up 1 st from the next (previously skipped) vertical loop, repeat from * to last st, 1 selv st.
Return pass 1: First crochet off the first st individually and then all others in pairs.
Forward pass 2: 1 selv st, pick up 1 st from the second vertical loop of the row, * pick up 1 st from the vertical loop after the next one, pick up 1 st from the next (previously skipped) vertical loop, repeat from * to last 2 sts, pick up 1 st from the next-to-last vertical loop, 1 selv st.

Return pass 2: Crochet off the first st individually and then all others in pairs.
Repeat these 4 forward/return rows continuously.

FILLED STITCH PATTERN

Instructions
Stitch count: an even number.
Forward pass: 1 selv st, * before the next vertical loop, insert the hook under the horizontal top loop in back of work, pull the working yarn through the fabric, keep the vertical loop unused, repeat from * to last st, 1 selv st.
Return pass: First crochet off the first st individually and then all others in pairs.

! Make sure that IMMEDIATELY BEFORE THE EDGE STITCH, no stitch is pulled through under the horizontal loops, otherwise you would create an unintended INCREASE.

••• ABBREVIATIONS
can be found on page 344.

MESH PATTERN

Instructions
Stitch count: an even number.
Forward pass: 1 selv st, * pick up 1 st from under the next vertical loop, 1 yo, skip 1 vertical loop, repeat from * to last st, 1 selv st.
Return pass: Crochet off the first st individually and then all others in pairs, treating each yarn over as a stitch.

STAGGERED MESH PATTERN

Stitch count: an even number.
Forward pass 1: 1 selv st, * pick up 1 st from under the next vertical loop, 1 yo, skip 1 vertical loop, repeat from * to last st, 1 selv st.
Return pass 1: Crochet off the first st individually and then all others in pairs, treating each yarn over as a stitch.
Forward pass 2: 1 selv st, * 1 yo, skip 1 vertical loop, pick up 1 st from under the next vertical loop, repeat from * to last st, 1 selv st.
Return pass 2: Crochet off the first st individually and then all others in pairs, treating each yarn over as a stitch.

Repeat these 4 forward/return rows continuously.

MOSS STITCH

Forward pass 1: 1 selv st, * pick up 1 st from under the next vertical loop, with yarn in front of work pick up 1 st from under the next vertical loop (*Tunisian purl stitch > page 230*), repeat from * to last st, 1 selv st.
Return pass 1: First crochet off the first st individually and then all others in pairs.
Forward pass 2: 1 selv st, * with yarn in front of work pick up 1 st from under the next vertical loop, pick up 1 st from under the next vertical loop, repeat from * to last st, 1 selv st.
Return pass 2: First crochet off the first st individually and then all others in pairs.

Repeat these 4 forward/return rows continuously.

TUNISIAN CROCHET IN COLOR

In Tunisian crochet, artful effects with color that cannot be recreated with any other crochet technique can be achieved—from simple color stripes in woven-look fabric up to crocheted-in stranded color-work patterns.

SIMPLE STRIPES

The easiest option for working with color is to work each forward and return pass in the same color, and to change the color for the next pair of forward and return rows. Stripes over only 1 row can also be easier worked than in traditional crochet, since the working yarn after the return row always ends up back at the starting point and can be picked up there when needed next.

! Strands can be
CARRIED UP THE EDGE
loosely as for regular crochet
(> page 212).

The color change always happens at the end of the return pass, where the last two stitches should be crocheted off in the color of the following forward pass.

WOVEN-LOOK STRIPES

A special feature of Tunisian crochet is that the color can also be changed within a row, with the beginning of crocheting off loops in the return pass. This produces an especially pleasing pattern, which looks like woven fabric.

If you want to create even stripes, color changes in forward and return passes need to be worked in a certain manner.

FOR TWO
COLORS

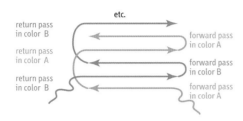 

FOR THREE
COLORS

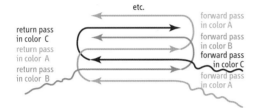 

FOR FOUR
COLORS

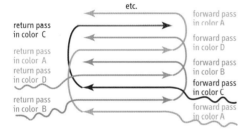 

X Before a color is taken up again, SLIGHTLY TIGHTEN the last loop worked in this color, to give it its proper size, so it won't turn out too loose. However, DON'T TIGHTEN IT TOO MUCH, so the side edges won't curl.

X In addition, numerous other COLOR PATTERN VARIATIONS are also possible: MORE COLORS can be used, or forward and return rows can be worked in other COLOR SEQUENCES, including IRREGULAR ones, or color fading can be worked. The only restriction is that only that color can be used which is AVAILABLE AT THAT TIME at the current edge and that the strands carried up along the edges should not be too long. Of course, the colors for forward and return pass can also be cut every time and joined anew in any spot.

STRANDED COLORWORK PATTERNS

In Tunisian crochet, just as in traditional crochet, stranded colorwork patterns can be worked in different colors, following charts. This yields especially pretty effects and crisp lines since Tunisian stitches are nearly square-shaped.

1 Before beginning the colorwork pattern, pick up the stitches during the forward pass in the respective color according to the chart.

2 Now begin crocheting off in the return pass. The color in which 2 stitches must be crocheted off together depends on the color of the stitches: When the first 2 stitches on the hook are of the same color, they are crocheted off together in this same color. If the first 2 stitches on the hook have different colors, they are always crocheted off in the color of the rightmost stitch of the two (= color change spot).

3 Continue in this manner, following the colorwork chart in the forward passes and crocheting off the stitches according to their respective colors during the return passes.

A detailed overview of **TUNISIAN CROCHET HOOKS** can be found on page 20.

WORKING WITH A DOUBLE-ENDED CROCHET HOOK

Tunisian crochet hooks with hooks at both ends come in a short version about the length of a regular crochet hook, in a longer variety about the length of a straight single-pointed knitting needle, as well as in form of two hook tips connected through a flexible cord resembling a circular knitting needle. These special Tunisian crochet hooks, which resemble a circular knitting needle, can be used in two ways: for working in rows, which creates a special effect, and for working Tunisian crochet in the round.

In preparation, it is important that the different tips of the double-ended crochet hook are easy to distinguish. One end might bear an imprinted mark, which can be used to tell them apart, or you can mark them yourself using a permanent marker.

Double-ended hooks can be used for working in one or two colors. In the example shown, two colors were used for better orientation. However, even when working in only one color, two separate skeins are needed.

IN ROWS

Tunisian stitch patterns worked in rows with a double-ended crochet hook acquire a completely new look. Work is turned during crocheting, so that unlike usual, front and back of the stitches are alternatingly visible.

1 Work the foundation chain and the first forward pass as described for Tunisian basic technique from skein A (here: dark green), using hook tip 1. Turn work.

2 Now, with skein B (here: cream), using hook tip 2, crochet off the stitches during the return pass as described for a basic Tunisian return pass. Do not turn work.

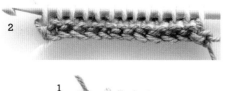

3 With hook tip 2 and skein B, pick up stitches as for Tunisian simple stitch (> page 230). Turn work.

4 With hook tip 1 and skein A, crochet off the stitches as usual during the return pass. Do not turn work. After that, with hook tip 1 and skein A, again pick up stitches in Tunisian simple stitch. Turn work.

Repeat Steps 2–4 continuously.

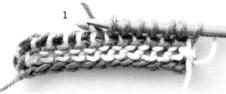

IN ROUNDS

Since the Tunisian crochet hook is rigid, and cannot be bent for working in the round, rounds must be worked in sections using double-ended crochet hooks.

CROCHETING IN ROUNDS

1 With hook tip 1 and skein A, work a foundation chain the length of the desired circumference of the circular piece. Arrange the chain into a ring-shape without twisting. Insert the hook into the first chain. Pull the working yarn through the first chain and through the working loop at once, making 1 slip stitch (> page 33) to join into the round. Mark this stitch with a stitch marker.

2 With hook tip 1 and skein A, keep picking up stitches from the beginning chain until either approximately ⅔ of the hook has been filled with stitches or the work feels too taut. Turn work.

3 With hook tip 2 and skein B, crochet off the stitches as described for the standard return pass, until 3 loops remain on the hook. Turn work again. Repeat Steps 2 and 3, until only a few stitches before the marked stitch have not yet been crocheted into.

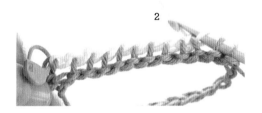

4 With hook tip 1 and skein A, pick up stitches from the remaining chains of the round. Finally, insert the hook into the marked stitch, and pick up a new stitch from this stitch. Do not turn work.

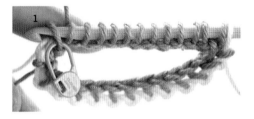

5 Continuing from right to left, pick up stitches from the already-crocheted stitches as for a basic Tunisian simple stitch until either approximately ⅔ of the hook has been filled with stitches or the work feels too taut. Turn work and with hook tip 2 and skein B, crochet off the stitches as described for a basic return pass, until 3 loops remain on the hook. Turn work.

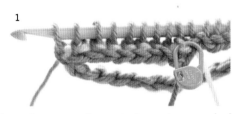

Repeat Step 5 continuously. The exact turning point is not important since spiral rounds are worked without a defined transition spot.

BINDING OFF IN THE ROUND

In the last forward pass, pick up stitches to before the marked stitch. Turn work, and crochet off all stitches as usual in pairs, until only 1 remains on the hook, and then turn work. Then, with hook tip 1 and skein A, going from right to left, bind off all stitches around as

described for Tunisian basic bind-off (> page 229). Finish off as described for regular crochet (> page 80).

! This STITCH, when crocheted in the round in one color, resembles a regular Tunisian simple stitch. Working it in two colors produces VERTICAL STRIPES, which cannot be achieved when working in turned rows.

! The MARKER IN THE FIRST STITCH, if possible, should be carried up after every round, preferably immediately AFTER HAVING PICKED UP the new stitch.

X With a short double-ended crochet hook, ANY DESIRED CIRCUMFERENCE can be worked. The advantage of LONGER HOOKS is only that the work can be turned less frequently.

Filet Crochet

Filet crochet is a very old technique that emulates knotted filet lace. Knotted filet lace is very laborious to make, since it consists of a knotted net background into which patterned areas are embroidered in a weaving technique. With filet crochet, a very similar look can be achieved much more easily.

TECHNIQUE BASICS

Filet crochet is always worked using only two basic stitches: chains and double crochets. Using these two stitches, a mesh background of small boxes is crocheted, into which patterns or motifs are worked by "filling in boxes." The result is a transparent crocheted fabric resembling lace.

The boxes of the mesh background should be square-shaped so that the incorporated ornament or motif does not become distorted. In most cases, the boxes are composed of "1 double crochet and 2 chains" for an empty box or "3 double crochets" for a filled box (i.e., in a stitch ratio of 1:2). If the height to width ratio does not match, first try to achieve evenly square-shaped boxes through changing the tension of the working yarn. In case of large discrepancies in the height to width ratio, the shape of the box can be adapted through the number of chain stitches worked between the double crochets. Boxes in a stitch ratio of 1:1 (= 1 double crochet and 1 chain or 2 double crochets) turn out narrower and the filet crochet piece turns out narrower overall. Boxes in a stitch ratio of 1:3 (= 1 double crochet and 3 chains or 4 double crochets) become wider, and the filet crochet piece turns out wider overall.

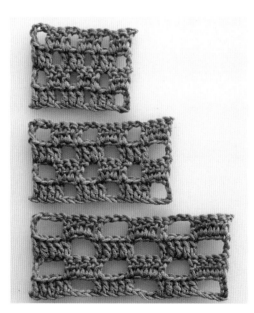

To illustrate what influence the shape of the individual box has on the overall outcome, samples in three different stitch ratios are shown here: at the top, a swatch in a stitch ratio of 1:1, in the middle, in a stitch ratio of 1:2, at the bottom, in a stitch ratio of 1:3.

When working filet crochet, it is important to note whether the next working step requires an empty or a filled box. The necessary distribution of empty and filled boxes is visualized in a chart (> page 94). If boxes must be increased or decreased at the edge, or when crocheting even in turned rows without increases or decreases—when turning, the type of the first box determines the number of chains and double crochets.

X Always crochet the chains between the double crochets EVENLY LOOSELY, so the hook can be easily inserted into the chain and all boxes turn out a UNIFORM SHAPE.

! In patterns, it is also often said that a double crochet worked atop an empty box should be worked not into individual chains, but in the chain space AROUND THE CHAINS (see chain arc > page 43). However, this has an impact on the stitch appearance.

Into individual chains   In the chain space

FOUNDATION CHAIN AND BEGINNING OF THE ROW

At the beginning of a filet crochet piece, the correct stitch count for the foundation chain has to be calculated, which in turn depends on the chosen stitch ratio. For crocheting in turned rows, it is then further important whether the row begins with an empty or a filled box.

CALCULATING THE STITCH COUNT

The number of chains is determined by the number of boxes needed for the first row. In the following explanations all working steps are explained for boxes with a stitch ratio of 1:2, since this mesh background is the most commonly used one. Modifications for other stitch ratios can be found in the notes in the margins.

The base of a box consists of 3 chains. Added to this is 1 additional chain to conclude the box later. The stitch count for the beginning chain therefore has to be a multiple of 3 + 1 stitch extra.

Into the foundation chain, the boxes of Row 1 are crocheted. Empty boxes consist of "1 double crochet and chain 2," while skipping 2 chains of the beginning chain; filled boxes consist of 3 double crochets. At the beginning of the row, the first double crochet is always replaced by 3 chains. These 3 chains are located atop the last chain of the beginning chain. This is of advantage if an edging will be later worked all around the crocheted piece since the corner stitches can be used as the base for smartly shaped corners. The last box is always concluded with a double crochet at the edge.

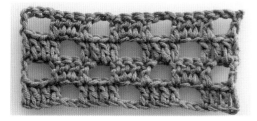 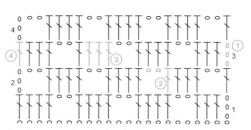

① 3 chains to replace the first double crochet
② 1 double crochet, 2 chains to create an empty box
③ 3 double crochets for a filled box
④ double crochet edge stitch as conclusion for the last box

BEGINNING WITH AN EMPTY BOX

When the row begins with an empty box, the beginning chain is extended by an additional 2 chains to replace the first double crochet and another 2 chains for the top edge of the box—so altogether 5 additional chains.

The first double crochet is now crocheted into the 9th chain from the hook.

Then continue working boxes into the beginning chain, whereas the 2 chains of every empty box bridge the skipped 2 chains of the beginning chain.

The STITCH KEY for the crochet symbols can be found on pages 340–343.

The stitch count for the beginning chain for boxes in a STITCH RATIO of 1:1 has to be a multiple of 2 + 1 stitch extra; for a STITCH RATIO of 1:3, it needs to be a multiple of 4 + 1 stitch extra.

Some patterns list the number of chains for the beginning chain as a MULTIPLE OF 3. In this case, the first double crochet of Row 1, replaced by turning chains, is not located atop the last chain of the crocheted chain but is arched at the outer edge. If the crocheted piece is later finished with an all-around edging, the lowermost chain of the replaced double crochet will be the corner stitch.

For boxes in a STITCH RATIO of 1:1, for the first empty box of the row, work 2 additional chains to replace the first double crochet + 1 chain extra, and work the first double crochet into the 7TH CHAIN from the hook. Additionally, with every chain, skip only 1 chain of the base chain.

For boxes in a STITCH RATIO of 1:3, for the first empty box of the row, work 2 additional chains to replace the first double crochet + 3 chains extra, and work the first double crochet into the 11TH CHAIN from the hook. Additionally, with the 3 chains, skip 3 chains of the base chain.

238

! NO MATTER WHAT THE STITCH RATIO of the mesh background is, the first filled box always begins the same: 3 chains replace the first double crochet, which serves as edge stitch. The following double crochet is always worked into the 5th chain from the hook. At a STITCH RATIO of 1:1, 1 double crochet fills a box; with a STITCH RATIO of 1:3, 3 double crochets fill the box.

... The STITCH KEY for the crochet symbols can be found on pages 340–343.

! For boxes in a STITCH RATIO of 1:1, the row is turned with 5 CHAINS (= 1 chain for the base of the new box + 3 chains for the first double crochet + 1 chain for the top edge of the new box).

For boxes in a STITCH RATIO of 1:3, the row is turned with 9 CHAINS (= 3 chains for the base of the new box + 3 chains for the first double crochet + 3 chains for the top edge of the new box).

BEGINNING WITH A FILLED BOX

When the row begins with a filled box, in addition to the beginning chain, 3 more chains are worked for the first double crochet.

Work the first double crochet into the 5th chain from the hook.

Then continue working boxes into the beginning chain, whereas the 2 chains of every empty box bridge the skipped 2 chains of the beginning chain, and for filled boxes 2 double crochets, worked one after another into 2 subsequent chains, fill a box.

INCREASING BOXES

To extend a piece worked in filet crochet at the sides, whole boxes are usually increased at the side edges as shown in the pattern. Extensions are worked differently, depending on whether the box is empty or filled.

INCREASING EMPTY BOXES

One or more empty boxes can be increased at the beginning or end of the row.

A SINGLE BOX AT THE BEGINNING OF THE ROW

When a single empty box is to be increased at the beginning of the row, the previous row is turned with 7 chains (= 2 chains for the base of the new box + 3 chains for the first double crochet + 2 chains for the top edge of the new box). Complete the box with 1 double crochet into the first double crochet of the previous row.

 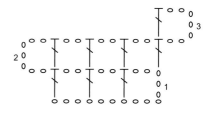

MULTIPLE BOXES AT THE BEGINNING OF THE ROW

The increase of multiple empty boxes must be prepared at the end of the previous row by working additional chains.

For every empty box to be increased, crochet 3 chains, and for the box at the edge, crochet 7 chains. If for instance, 3 boxes are to be increased, 3 chains each per box for the first and second box (3 chains, 2 times) + 7 chains once for the box at the edge (= 13 chains total) need to be crocheted. The first double crochet for the first empty box is worked into the 8th chain from the hook, the remaining boxes are worked as described in the pattern instructions.

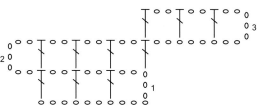

> ! For boxes in a **STITCH RATIO** of **1:1**, for every box, add on 2 chains, and for the box at the edge, add on 5 chains.
>
> For boxes in a **STITCH RATIO** of **1:3**, for every box, add on 4 chains, and for the box at the edge, add on 9 chains.

A SINGLE BOX AT THE END OF THE ROW

When a single empty box needs to be increased at the end of the row, first 2 chains are crocheted. Then, as for a double treble crochet, make 3 yarn overs onto the hook.

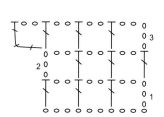

Now work 1 double treble crochet (> page 48) into the insertion point of the last double crochet of the row. The two chains create the top edge of the new box and the double treble crochet forms the base and the outside edge of the box.

> ! For boxes in a **STITCH RATIO** of **1:1**, for the new box, work 1 chain and 1 double crochet (> page 35).
>
> For boxes in a **STITCH RATIO** of **1:3**, for the new box, work 3 chains and 1 triple treble crochet (> page 48).

MULTIPLE BOXES AT THE END OF THE ROW

If more empty boxes need to be increased, again chain 2 and make 3 yarn overs onto the hook. To work the double treble crochet, insert the hook into the middle horizontal loop of the previously worked double treble crochet, and finish the double treble crochet as usual. In this manner, any number of boxes can be increased.

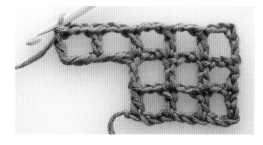

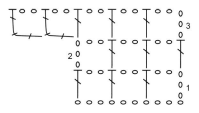

> ! For boxes in a **STITCH RATIO** of **1:1**, for every additional box, work 1 **CHAIN AND 1 TREBLE CROCHET**, inserting the hook for the new treble crochet between the two diagonally placed loops of the previous treble crochet.
>
> For boxes in a STITCH RATIO of **1:3**, for every additional box, work 3 **CHAINS AND 1 TRIPLE TREBLE CROCHET**, inserting the hook for the new triple treble crochet between the 2nd and 3rd diagonally placed loops of the preceding triple treble crochet.

> For boxes in a **STITCH RATIO** of 1:1, turn the row with **4 CHAINS** (= 1 chain for the base of the new box + 3 chains for the first double crochet), and then work the following double crochet into the 4th chain from the hook.
>
> For boxes in a **STITCH RATIO** of 1:3, turn the row with **6 CHAINS** (= 3 chains for the base of the new box + 3 chains for the first double crochet), and then work the following 3 double crochets into the 4th–6th chain from the hook.

INCREASING FILLED BOXES

One or more filled boxes can be increased at the beginning or end of the row.

A SINGLE BOX AT THE BEGINNING OF THE ROW

When a single filled box is to be increased at the beginning of the row, the previous row is turned with 5 chains (= 2 chains for the base of the new box + 3 chains for the first double crochet). Then, into the 4th and 5th chain from the hook, work 1 double crochet each, and finish the box with a double crochet into the first double crochet of the previous row.

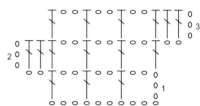

MULTIPLE BOXES AT THE BEGINNING OF THE ROW

The increase of multiple filled boxes must be prepared at the end of the previous row through additional chains.

> For boxes in a **STITCH RATIO** of 1:1, for every box add 2 chains, and for the box at the edge, 4 chains. The first double crochet is worked into the 4th chain from the hook.
>
> For boxes in a **STITCH RATIO** of 1:3, for every box add 4 chains, and for the box at the edge, 6 chains. The first double crochet is worked into the 4th chain from the hook.

For every box, add on 3 chains, and for the box at the edge, 5 chains. If, for instance, 3 filled boxes need to be increased, 3 chains each per box for the first and second box (3 chains, 2 times) + 5 chains once for the box at the edge (= 11 chains) need to be worked. Then work 1 double crochet each into every chain of the beginning chain, beginning in the 5th chain from the hook.

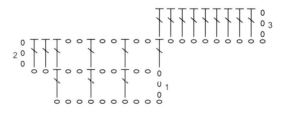

A SINGLE BOX AT THE END OF THE ROW

> For boxes in a **STITCH RATIO** of 1:1, for the new box work only **2 TREBLE CROCHETS** one after another.
>
> For boxes in a **STITCH RATIO** of 1:3, for the new box work **4 TREBLE CROCHETS** one after another.

When a single filled box needs to be increased at the end of the row, after the last double crochet of the row, make 2 yarn overs onto the hook as for a treble crochet.

Now work 1 treble crochet (> page 35) into the insertion point of the last double crochet.

Then work another treble crochet into the base of the previous treble crochet

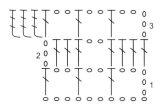

Finally, work a third treble crochet the same way.

MULTIPLE BOXES AT THE END OF THE ROW

If more filled boxes need to be increased, 3 treble crochets must be worked for every box. For every treble crochet, make 2 yarn overs onto the hook, insert the hook as described into the base of the last treble crochet. Then complete the treble crochet as usual.

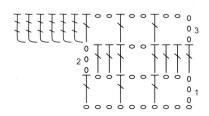

! For boxes in a
STITCH RATIO of 1:1, for
every additional filled box,
work 2 TREBLE CRO-
CHETS.

For boxes in a STITCH
RATIO of 1:3, for every
additional filled box, work
4 TREBLE CROCHETs.

DECREASING BOXES

To make a piece in filet crochet narrower, whole boxes are usually decreased at the side edges as stated in the pattern. Since it doesn't matter whether the box no longer worked would have been empty or filled, there are fewer spots in which the directions differ.

DECREASING BOXES AT THE BEGINNING OF THE ROW

To decrease boxes at the beginning of the row, any number of boxes of the previous row can be skipped with slip stitches (> page 33).

A SINGLE BOX AT THE BEGINNING OF THE ROW

To work a decrease of an individual box, move with 4 slip stitches (= 1 slip stitch each into every stitch of the box of the previous row) to the beginning of the new box, move up and continue the row, replacing the first double crochet with 3 chains.

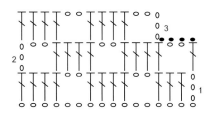

••• The STITCH KEY for
the crochet symbols can be
found on pages 340–343.

! For boxes in a **STITCH RATIO** of **1:1**, for decreasing boxes, work 3 slip stitches to move to the beginning of the new row across the first box to be decreased; across every additional box to be decreased, work 2 slip stitches each.

For boxes in a **STITCH RATIO** of **1:3**, for decreasing boxes, move to the beginning of the new row across the first box to be decreased with 5 slip stitches, and across every additional box to be decreased, work 4 slip stitches each.

! The first one of the 4 slip stitches for the first box tightens very much and is later **BARELY VISIBLE**. If the edge is later to be crocheted into, keep an eye out for this stitch.

✕ A variation of the decrease **ATOP A FILLED BOX**: At the end of the previous row, complete all double crochets of the filled boxes that need to be decreased only **TO THEIR RESPECTIVE LAST LOOP** (i.e., in addition to the working loop, for every double crochet, 1 additional loop each will be on the hook). Crochet off these loops in pairs, until 3 loops remain on the hook. Crochet the last 3 loops together. Then turn work with 3 chains to replace the first double crochet, and work the new row.

DECREASING MULTIPLE BOXES AT THE BEGINNING OF THE ROW

To decrease multiple boxes, over the first box work 4 slip stitches to the beginning of the new row, and over every further box to be decreased work 3 slip stitches each, and then replace the first double crochet by 3 chains and start the new row there.

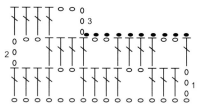

DECREASING BOXES AT THE END OF THE ROW

To decrease boxes at the end of the row, leave the appropriate number of boxes to be decreased unworked. This applies to all mesh backgrounds, no matter what the stitch ratio is.

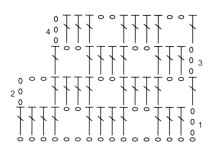

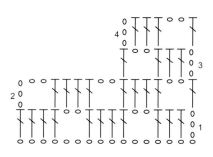

DIPS AND CONNECTIVE BARS

Airy openwork patterns created from dips and connective bars expand the design possibilities of filet crochet pieces many times over. Dips are created from chains and 1 single crochet; connective bars are crocheted chains. Here, too, the stitch ratio plays an important role for the appearance of the stitch pattern.

1 To work a dip, work up to the 2 boxes atop which the dip is to be located. First chain 3, work 1 single crochet into the double crochet between the boxes, and then chain 3. Proceed with the double crochet for the next regular box.

2 In the following row, chain 5 as connective bar atop the two boxes of the dip. Proceed with the double crochet for the next box.

3 When in the following row, boxes are worked on top of the connective bar, for empty boxes the middle double crochet between the two boxes is worked into the middle chain of the connective bar. Alternatingly, further dips and connective bars can also be worked.

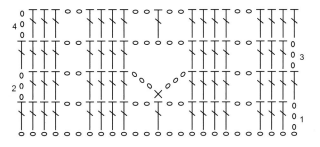

! Dips in a STITCH RATIO of 1:1 are created from "chain 2, 1 single crochet, chain 2;" for connective bars, chain 3.

Dips in a STITCH RATIO of 1:3 are created from "chain 4, 1 single crochet, chain 4;" for connective bars, chain 7.

••• The STITCH KEY for the crochet symbols can be found on pages 340–343.

FILET CROCHET IN THE ROUND

Squares worked from the center out can be divided into squares with an even number and an odd number of boxes per side. The principle is the same as for crocheting in rows: chains and double crochet create the side edges of the box. Since when crocheting in the round, the boxes join differently than when crocheting in turned rows, it must be carefully planned where the transition of the round will be located, and in which manner the corner boxes will be constructed.

SQUARES WITH AN EVEN NUMBER OF BOXES PER SIDE

Squares with an even number of boxes per side always feature a block of 4 boxes in the center.

BEGINNING WITH EMPTY BOXES

ABBREVIATIONS can be found on page 344.

1 Chain 9 (= 1st ch as center-st, chain 3 for the 1st dc, and ch5 for the side edges of the 1st box), * dc1 into the center-st, ch5, rep from * 2 times more. Join into the round with 1 sl-st into the 3rd ch of the 1st dc. A square of 4 empty boxes has been created.

2 Begin every subsequent round with chain 3 to replace the 1st dc, and work 1 box each atop every existing box. At corners with empty boxes, into the middle chain of the previous rnd work 1 corner box each (= dc1, ch5, dc1). Join every round with 1 sl-st into the 3rd ch of the 1st dc. After every round worked, the square has turned wider by 2 boxes each in length and width.

3 In all following rounds, at the side edges, atop every box, work 1 box each, and at corners with empty boxes, work 1 corner box each into the middle chain of the previous rnd.

The STITCH KEY for the crochet symbols can be found on pages 340–343.

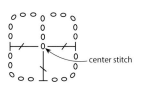 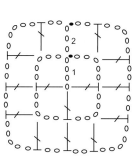 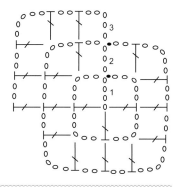

center stitch

BEGINNING WITH FILLED BOXES

1 Chain 7 (1st ch as center-st), and work dc1 each into the 5th–7th ch from the hook, * rotate work 90°, chain 3, dc2 around the post of the last dc (now lying across), dc1 into the center-st, repeat from * once more, rotate work 90°, chain 3, dc2 around the post of the last dc (now lying across). Join into the round with 1 sl-st into the 3rd ch of the 1st dc. A square of 4 filled boxes has been created.

2 Begin every subsequent round with chain 3 to replace the 1st dc, and work 1 box each atop every existing box. At corners with filled boxes, always chain 3, dc2 around the post of the last dc (now lying across), and work dc1 into the 3rd ch of the side edge of the box of the previous rnd. Join every round with 1 sl-st into the 3rd ch of the 1st dc. After every round worked, the square has turned wider by 2 boxes each in length and width.

3 In all following rounds, at the side edges, work 1 box each atop every existing box, and for corners with filled boxes, work 1 corner box each of "chain 3, dc2."

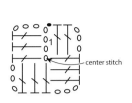 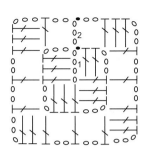 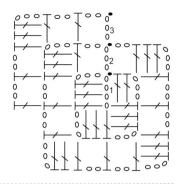

center stitch

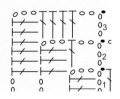

X When a FILLED BOX is located ABOVE a FILLED CORNER BOX OF THE PREVIOUS ROUND, the double crochets are worked into individual chain stitches of the chain of the previous round.

SQUARES WITH ODD NUMBER OF BOXES PER SIDE

Squares with an odd number of boxes per side have 1 box in the center, around which all subsequent boxes are crocheted.

BEGINNING WITH AN EMPTY BOX

1 To work the center box, chain 9 (1st ch as center-st, ch8 for the side edges of the 1st box), and work dc1 into the center-st.

2 In the next round, begin with ch8 (= ch3 to replace the 1st dc, and ch5 for the chain arc at the corner), and at the sides, work 1 box each, at the corners 1 empty corner box each (= dc1, ch5, dc1) as shown in the crochet chart. The square now consists of 9 boxes.

3 In all following rounds, at the side edges, atop every box, work 1 box each, and for corners of empty boxes, work 1 corner box each into the middle chain. After every round worked, the square has turned wider by 2 boxes each in length and width.

X MANY MOTIFS from other crafts can be converted to filet crochet—from geometric patterns over floral ornaments to animal shapes.

Even if grandmother's crocheted doilies first come to mind, there are many more POSSIBLE USES for filet crochet. The classic café curtain, large bedspreads, place mats, bags, decorative bands, and wall hangings are in most cases worked in rows. Doilies worked in the round are not just a table decoration; they can also be sewn onto plain, one-colored pillows and bags as decorative "centerpieces."

 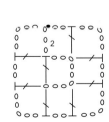 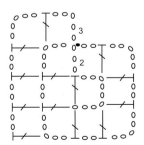

center stitch

> The mesh back-grounds obtain their **ACCURATE SHAPE** only through diligent **BLOCK-ING** of the finished piece (> page 196).

ABBREVIATIONS can be found on page 344.

The **STITCH KEY** for the crochet symbols can be found on pages 340–343.

BEGINNING WITH A FILLED BOX

1 To work the middle filled box, chain 7 (1st ch as center-st, chain 3 as bottom edge of box, chain 3 to replace the 1st dc), and work dc1 each into the 5th–7th chain from the hook.

2 In the next round, chain 6 (= ch3 to replace the 1st dc, and ch3 for the side edge of the box), and at the sides, work 1 box each, at the corners, 1 filled corner box each as shown in the crochet chart. The square now consists of 9 boxes.

3 In all following rounds, at the side edges, atop every box, work 1 box each, and for corners with filled boxes, work 1 corner box each of "chain 3, dc2." After every round worked, the square has turned wider by 2 boxes each in length and width.

center stitch

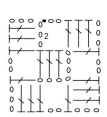 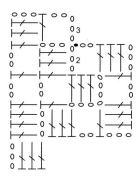

SHAPING CORNERS IN FILET CROCHET LACE

Filet crochet pieces are often used as inserts or as decorative borders. In most cases, this requires shaping corners. To transition the stitch pattern of a decorative border as seamlessly as possible from one side into the next, a clever technique for corner formation has been developed.

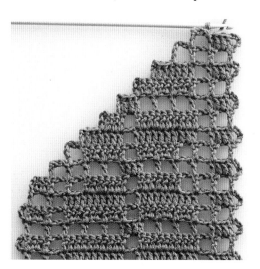

Work the border to the beginning of the corner. Then continue the border, but from the inside corner on, shorten every row by 1 box each (i.e., in right-side rows, leave the last box unworked, not crocheting into it, and before beginning the wrong-side row, move forward across 1 box with slip stitches). Repeat this maneuver until the last box of the outer corner has been reached. When the outer corner has been reached, rotate work 90° and continue, extending the rows. For this, in right-side rows, work the box to the peak, and join the last stitch with 1 slip stitch to the box of the diagonal. In wrong-side rows, do not turn work right away, but first always increase 1 box each, taking note of whether this is an empty or filled box.

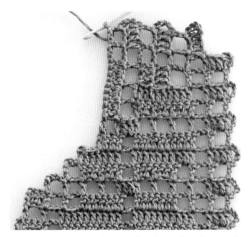

For empty boxes, chain 2 for the side edge, and work 1 double crochet into the upper right corner of the following box of the diagonal. The double crochet forms the top edge of the box. Then turn work, and work the wrong-side row.

For filled boxes, first work 3 double crochets into the stitches of the box on the diagonal, and then turn work and work the wrong-side row.

For filet crochet lace where instructions are given only for a straight border without corner solutions, a **CORNER** can also be **CREATED VERY EASILY**. Place a frameless **POCKET MIRROR** onto the pattern chart exactly on the diagonal and move it around until a suitable corner solution presents itself. Transfer this corner solution onto a piece of **GRAPH PAPER**. Then mark the row in which the diagonal needs to be started.

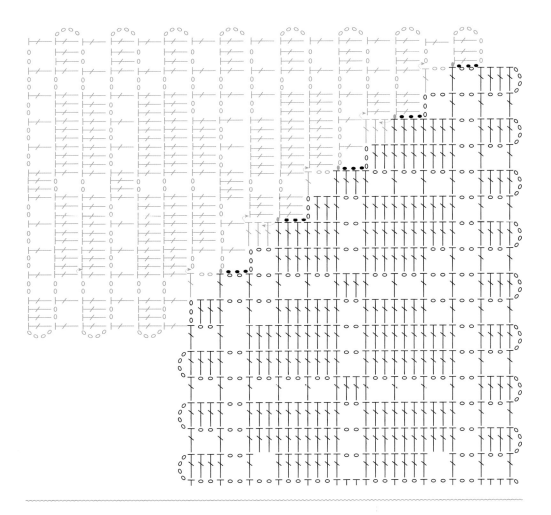

Double-Sided
Crochet

Double-sided crochet is an especially clever technique producing a thick crocheted fabric with two right sides. Both sides are permanently joined together during crocheting, but each one of them can nevertheless be designed independently.

X Because of the thickness of the crocheted fabric, the double face technique is especially well suited for POTHOLDERS. The best choice is COTTON YARN.

BASIC DOUBLE-SIDED TECHNIQUE

A piece crocheted in double-sided technique consists of paired rows that are always composed of an odd-numbered row and a companion even-numbered row. First, an odd-numbered row is worked, into which an even-numbered row is worked at the same height level. All odd-numbered rows together form one face of the crocheted fabric, the even-numbered ones together the other.

During work, both sides are joined together in every row and at every stitch, for every stitch is, in fact, generally worked not through both loops of the stitch as for regular crochet but only crocheted through the back loop of the stitch. The unused loops of the stitches are crocheted into while working the following row, which joins the pieces.

It is always worked on the inside of the crocheted piece, so that later, the backs of the stitches form the outsides of the crocheted piece. For this reason, it is easier to hold the crocheted piece "upside down" from the second row on as demonstrated in the photos.

DOUBLE-SIDED DOUBLE CROCHET

Double crochet is especially well suited for double-sided crochet, since the height of the stitches makes joining easier than for single crochet. The crocheted fabric does not turn out as dense as in single crochet, which can be of advantage, depending on the intended use. At the beginning of every odd-numbered row, 2 height-adjustment chains are worked, at the beginning of every even-numbered row, 1 height-adjustment chain. However, these never count as a stitch, but only are located next to the edge.

BEGINNING ROW (ODD-NUMBERED ROW)

1 In color A (dark green), work a beginning chain of the required stitch count plus 2 additional height-adjustment chains, to reach the appropriate height for the first double crochet. Then, in color A, work double crochet through the back loop of the stitch only (> page 37).

2 Always finish the last 2 loops of the last double crochet of a row in the color of the following row, here color B (cream). After that, work 1 height-adjustment chain, since the even-numbered row is located slightly higher than the odd-numbered one.

ROW 2 (EVEN-NUMBERED ROW)

To work the second row, rotate work 180°, so that the last double crochet is now located at right. For all subsequent even-numbered rows, work is later turned. Now work an even-numbered row on the right side of the fabric of the already-completed odd-numbered row. First, place the working yarn in color A onto the already-worked row. The working yarn in the unused color is always carried between the two layers and crocheted in while working, so that it will end up in the required spot, ready to be used when needed again.

1 Now, to work a double crochet in the even-numbered row, first insert the hook into the upper front loop of the stitch, facing the viewer, of the just worked, odd-numbered row (in color A), to join both layers. Then, in color B, make a yarn over onto the hook. Insert the hook through the still unused front loop of the chain. Make sure that crochet hook and yarn over are located above the carried strand.

2 Pull the working yarn in color B through the fabric, and pull it through the bottom loop on the hook.

3 Yarn over and pull the yarn through the front loop on the hook, the yarn over, and the double crochet of the odd-numbered row.

4 Yarn over and and pull the working yarn through the last 2 loops on the hook at once.

Repeat Steps 1–4 until the even-numbered row of double crochet in color B has been completed. Complete the last double crochet with the color of the following row, here color A. Before this, place the working yarn in color B over the working yarn in color A onto the narrow groove that has formed between odd- and even-numbered rows. With this, the first pair of an odd- and an even-numbered row has been completed.

! The correct insertion points at the beginning and end of a row are not always very easy to spot. At the BEGINNING OF AN ODD-NUMBERED ROW, the upper insertion falls together with the stitch from which the height-adjustment chains emerge, too. At the bottom, make sure to insert the hook not into individual chain stitches of the chain, but into the first actual stitch.

At the BEGINNING OF AN EVEN-NUMBERED ROW, the upper insertion point falls together with the emerging spot of the height-adjustment chain, and at the bottom, the hook needs to be inserted not into individual chain stitches of the chain, but into the first actual stitch.

At the END OF A ROW, the last insertion point is often easily overlooked, since it pulls inward. For this reason, slightly stretch the edge, which makes the last stitch visible.

! Always make sure that the double crochets of the even-numbered row run VERTICALLY, and not diagonally: The insertion points should always be located EXACTLY ATOP EACH OTHER.

! Because the crocheted piece is held differently during work than in regular crochet, and the fronts of the stitches are actually located on the inside, the distinction between **FRONT AND BACK LOOPS OF THE STITCHES** can be confusing. When both loops of the stitch have not yet been crocheted into, the hook is inserted into the loop that points to the interior side of work. If only one loop is unused, crochet into this one.

! Before inserting the hook, always briefly consider whether the **YARN OVER** has to be made already before first inserting the hook (in odd-numbered row) or only after this (in even-numbered row).

ROW 3 (ODD-NUMBERED ROW)

1 Turn work, and work 2 height-adjustment chains to reach the appropriate height for the first double crochet.

2 Now, to work the double crochet in the odd-numbered row, make a yarn over in color A onto the hook. Then insert the hook first through the front loop of the stitch, facing the inside, of the just worked even-numbered row (in color B), lead the hook over the carried strand, and insert the hook through the still unused back loop of the stitch of the previous odd-numbered row (in color A). The carried strand emerges between the loops of the stitches. Now pull the working yarn in color A through, and pull it at the same time through the two loops of the stitch and over the carried strand. Then finish the double crochet as usual.

3 Work the whole odd-numbered row this way.

4 Finish the last double crochet of the row in the color of the following row, here color B, but before that, first place the working yarn in color A over the working yarn in color B onto the already-worked odd-numbered row. After this, work 1 height-adjustment chain, and turn work.

After this, again work an even-numbered row the same way as Row 2. Instead of into the unused loops of the chain, work into the unused loops of the stitches of the previous even-numbered row. From here on, alternate working odd- and even-numbered rows.

DOUBLE-SIDED SINGLE CROCHET

With single crochets, too, a very sturdy and dense crocheted fabric can be created using the double-sided technique.

BEGINNING ROW (ODD-NUMBERED ROW)

1 In color A (dark green), work a beginning chain of the required stitch count plus 1 additional height-adjustment chain to reach the appropriate height for the first single crochet. Then, in color A, work single crochet through the back loop of the stitches only (> page 37).

2 Always finish the 2 loops of the last single crochet of a row with the color of the following row, here color B (cream). After that, work 1 height-adjustment chain, since the even-numbered row is located slightly higher than the odd-numbered one.

ROW 2 (EVEN-NUMBERED ROW)

For the second row, rotate work 180°, so that the last single crochet is now located at right. For all subsequent even-numbered rows, work will later be turned. Now work an even-numbered row on the right side of the fabric of the already-completed odd-numbered row. First, place the working yarn in color A onto the already-worked row. The working yarn in the unused color is always carried between the two layers and crocheted in while working, so that it will end up in the required spot, ready to be used again when needed.

For double-sided single crochet, use a **LARGER HOOK SIZE** if needed, since otherwise the crocheted fabric could easily become too dense and tight.

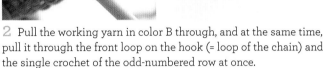

1 Now, to work a single crochet in the even-numbered row, first insert the hook into the back loop of the stitch of the just worked odd-numbered row (in color A), and through the still unused back loop of the stitch of the crocheted chain. Make sure the hook is located above the carried strand.

2 Pull the working yarn in color B through, and at the same time, pull it through the front loop on the hook (= loop of the chain) and the single crochet of the odd-numbered row at once.

3 Grasp the working yarn again, and pull it through both loops on the hook at once.

Repeat Steps 1–3 until the even-numbered row in single crochet in color B has been completed. Always complete the last single crochet with the color of the following row, here color A. Before this, place the working yarn in color B over the working yarn in color A onto the narrow groove that has formed between odd- and even-numbered rows. With this, the first double row of single crochets has been completed.

ROW 3 (ODD-NUMBERED ROW)

1 Turn work, and work 1 height-adjustment chain to reach the appropriate height for the first single crochet.

2 Now, to work a single crochet of the odd-numbered row, first insert the hook through the front loop of the stitch, facing the inside, of the just worked even-numbered row (in color B), lead the hook over the carried strand, and insert the hook through the still unused back loop of the stitch of the previous odd-numbered row (in color A). The carried strand emerges between the loops of the stitches. Now pull the working yarn in color A through, and pull it at the same time through the two loops of the stitch and over the carried strand. Then complete the single crochet as usual.

Finish the last single crochet of the row with the color of the following row, here color B, but before that, first place the working yarn in color A over the working yarn in color B onto the already-worked odd-numbered row. Now work 1 height-adjustment chain, and turn work.
After this, again work an even-numbered row the same way as Row 2. Instead of into the unused loops of the crocheted chain, insert the hook into the unused loops of the stitches of the previous even-numbered row. From here on, alternate working odd- and even-numbered rows.

CROCHETING AROUND THE EDGES

Pieces worked in double-sided technique can be very nicely crocheted around in double-sided single crochet. This can be done either in the same color or in a contrasting color. Bottom and top edge are worked the same for crocheted pieces in both single and double crochet; the side edges are worked differently, depending on the stitch type.

FRONT OF WORK
When crocheting around the front, the back is facing.

TOP EDGE
Insert the hook through the back loops of the stitches of the last row worked on the pieces in back and front. Now, through both loops together, work 1 single crochet. The working yarn in the other color can be carried between the loops of the stitches.

> ! Inserting the hook under the single crochets of the front piece is not always easy, especially if crocheted tightly. If necessary, use a **SMALLER CROCHET HOOK** to pull the stitch through.

CORNERS
At each corner, work 3 single crochets each into the last stitch at the edge.

SIDE EDGES
At the side edges, for double crochet, insert the hook under the outermost double crochet of a row in front, and work 3 single crochets around the post of every double crochet.
For single crochet, work 1 single crochet around the stitch at the side edge of every row of the piece in front.

BOTTOM EDGE
Here, work 1 single crochet each into the still unused third loops in back of the crocheted chain. Break the working yarn in color A, and weave in the end.

BACK OF WORK
Turn the crocheted piece. When crocheting around the back, the front is facing.

TOP EDGE
Insert the crochet hook through the back loops of the just worked single crochets and the last row worked of the back piece and work 1 single crochet through both loops together.

SIDE EDGES

At the side edges, for double crochet, insert the hook through the back loops of the just-worked single crochets and under the respective outermost double crochet of a row of the back piece. Into every single crochet, work 1 single crochet, and likewise 3 single crochets per double crochet.

For single crochet, insert the hook through the back loop of the just worked single crochet, and under the respective outermost single crochet of a row of the back piece, and work 1 single crochet.

BOTTOM EDGE

At the bottom edge, first insert the hook through the back loop of the just worked single crochets. Then the loops of the crocheted chain must be slightly pulled out between the stitches of Row 1. After that, work 1 single crochet each into every spot.

X When **CHANGING COLORS OR JOINING A NEW SKEIN,** just pull overhanging yarn tails **BETWEEN THE LAYERS.** For this, pull them between the layers a few inches in from the edge, and exit again at the end of the tail. Pull the working yarn through, slightly tighten, and then break the working yarn. The **YARN TAIL** disappears between the layers.

DOUBLE-SIDED CROCHET IN THE ROUND

Double-sided crochet can also be worked in the round from the center out. This allows for working all kinds of colorwork motifs (> page 116). It is recommended to work in double crochet, since the crocheted fabric would otherwise turn out very dense, and it would be harder to insert the hook. The double-sided technique is here, too, worked in rows, always joining into the round with a slip stitch. Since when crocheting from the center out, increases are being worked, it is important to remember the basic rule for even-numbered rounds: When multiple stitches had been worked into the same stitch in an odd-numbered round, these will be worked in the even-numbered round at the top always through the individual stitches, but at the bottom, always into the same insertion point.

.... How **TO INCREASE STITCHES** is described on page 98.

BEGINNING ROUND (ODD-NUMBERED ROUND)

Chain 6, and join into the round with a slip stitch. In color A (dark green), through the third loop in back of the chain, work 3 double crochets into every chain. Close the round with a slip stitch in the color of the following even-numbered round, here color B (cream), and work 1 height-adjustment chain.

ROUND 2 (EVEN-NUMBERED ROUND)

Work the round the same as Row 2 of the basic technique. Here, too, work 3 double crochets into the same stitch, but at the top, insert the hook one after another through the individual double crochets of the odd-numbered round. For even-numbered rounds, join the round with 1 slip stitch in the same color.

Turn work, work 2 height-adjustment chains, and again, work an odd-numbered round like an odd-numbered row. Close the round with a slip stitch in the color of the following even-numbered round, and then chain 1. Then continue, alternating odd- and even-numbered rounds, and working the increases for the desired motif.

 When contemplating a multi-colored stitch pattern, always keep in mind: **THE MORE COLORS** used, the more strands must be carried between the layers and **THE THICKER AND LESS PLIABLE** the crocheted piece will turn out.

 Before the **COLOR CHANGE**, slightly **TIGHTEN** the working yarn that will be used next. However, not too hard, as this would cause the crocheted piece to curl.

CROCHETING IN MULTIPLE COLORS

In the double-sided technique, colorwork patterns with several colors can be incorporated. Ingenious is that both sides can be worked in different patterns and even colors. The unused colors can be carried between the layers.

At the end of a row, note in which color the next row is supposed to begin. Complete the last stitch, except for the last two loops. Now place the two unused colors onto the already-crocheted row (no matter whether even- or odd-numbered), finish the last stitch in the next color, and work the required number of height-adjustment chains.

For a color change within the row, finish the last stitch of the previous color block except for the last 2 loops. Retrieve the new color from underneath the current color and complete the last stitch in this color.

Move the no longer required color down and carry it.

Knooking

Knooking is a technique in which a knitted result is produced with a crochet hook. The word is composed of the words "knitting" and "hook." Knooking is suitable for all who crochet but can't knit traditionally, and nevertheless don't want to miss out on knitted items.

KNOOKING HOOK AND CORD FOR HOLDING STITCHES

For Knooking, a special knooking hook is needed. This tool has a hook at one end like a conventional crochet hook and a large eye as in an embroidery or tapestry needle at the other. Through this eye, a cord for holding stitches in a color contrasting to that of the yarn is threaded at the beginning of work. The length of the cord for holding stitches is determined by the width of the piece to be produced. It should be calculated very generously, but at least twice as long as the intended width of the project. Since the cord for holding stitches is threaded through the stitches all the time during work, it should be made of a very smooth material. Since it is heavily stressed, it should also be sturdy, and not fray, so that it does not catch at the stitches or the knooking hook, nor fall apart.
The size of the knooking hook should always be chosen somewhat smaller than stated on the yarn label, since knooked stitches are rather loose.

! Knooked fabric is **SOFTER AND STRETCH-IER** than crocheted fabric, due to its different stitch formation than regular crochet.

! As with every new craft technique, knooking requires some **PRACTICE**. For some, it might seem harder at first to produce evenly knooked stitches. Take your time, and work slowly.

! The **DIRECTION OF WORK** for knooking is the same as for crochet: Right-handed crocheters work from right to left, left-handed crocheters from left to right (*Left-handed crochet > page 310*).

X Hold the knooking hook preferably from above like a **KNITTING NEEDLE OR A KNIFE** (*> page 29*).

FOUNDATION ROW

 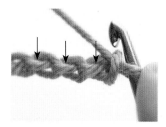 

> When making your foundation row, make sure that all loops are of the **SAME HEIGHT**, so that the stitches will also turn out the same size, and look even later on.

1 As for crochet, begin with a loosely crocheted chain (> page 57). From this crocheted chain, stitches will be picked up. The loop on the hook counts as the first stitch.

2 Tilt the crocheted chain toward the front, so that the horizontal third loops on the wrong side of the chain are on the top.

3 To work the second stitch, insert the hook in the second horizontal bar. Place the yarn from bottom to top over the hook to make a yarn over . . .

4 . . . and pull it through. The yarn sits on the hook in the form of a loop.

5 Then continue inserting the hook into all other back loops and pulling up a loop until all stitches sit on the hook in form of loops. Inserting the hook in back of the beginning chain has formed a neat beginning edge. Now thread the cord for holding stitches (see below), turn work, and knook the first row.

KNOOKING IN TURNED ROWS—CORD FOR HOLDING STITCHES

The cord for holding stitches is an auxiliary thread, which, in a sense, replaces the second knitting needle. It bears all stitches that are to be knooked. Every time at the beginning and the end of a row, the cord for holding stitches must be moved. With every new row, it is alternately inserted and again removed.

CORD FOR HOLDING STITCHES BEFORE THE BEGINNING OF A ROW

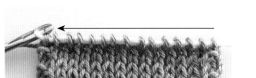

> The **CORD FOR HOLDING STITCHES** may loosen during work and emerge from between individual stitches. To make work easier, always **RETIGHTEN** the cord for holding stitches.

Before the beginning of a row, place all stitches onto the cord for holding stitches (i.e., thread the cord for holding stitches in the direction of the arrow from right to left through the loops). Then turn work and knook the next row.

CORD FOR HOLDING STITCHES AT THE END OF A ROW

At the end of a row, all stitches have been knooked and sit on the knooking hook. The cord for holding stitches passes below the hook. Now pull the cord for holding stitches out of the loops in the direction of the arrow from left to right. Now rethread the cord for holding stitches for the new row, and then turn work.

STITCH TYPES

As in knitting, knit and purl stitches are the two basic stitches of which every knooked piece is composed. The manner in which a stitch is being knooked determines the look of the stitch. When working the stitches, always make sure that for every stitch the hook is inserted the same way, and the working yarn grasped in the same manner and pulled through the loop on the hook.

KNIT STITCHES

 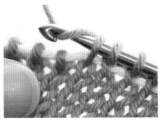 

1 Hold the working yarn in back of work. To work the next stitch, insert the hook into the stitch in front of the working yarn from right to left.

2 Place the working yarn from back to front over the hook to make a yarn over . . .

3 . . . and pull it through the loop.

X When knooking a stitch, the **FOLLOWING STITCH** is often pulled smaller. To prevent this, work should be held near the holding cord so that the stitch can be secured with the fingers of the left hand.

TWISTED KNIT STITCHES

1 Under the cord for holding stitches, grasp the back loop of the stitch from behind with the hook and pull the loop up onto the hook and slightly to the right.

2 Place the working yarn from back to front over the hook to form a yarn over . . .

3 . . . and pull it through the stitch. The stitch twists below the hook.

! The work-in-progress of a knooked piece is held **IN YOUR LEFT HAND** as for a regular crochet project (> page 29).

PURL STITCHES

1 Hold the working yarn in front of work. Hold the crochet hook so that the hook points down. Do not insert the hook into the next stitch but grasp it from left to right with the hook. Make sure to grasp all the stitch.

2 Pull the stitch lightly to the back right while turning the head of the hook . . .

3 . . . so that it eases into the stitch, and the stitch sits on the hook. The working yarn is still located in front of work.

4 Place the working yarn from back to front over the hook to form a yarn over . . .

5 . . . and pull it through the stitch.

TWISTED PURL STITCHES

1 Hold the working yarn in front of work. Insert the hook from right to left into the next stitch.

2 Place the working yarn from back to front over the hook to form a yarn over . . .

3 . . . and pull it through the stitch.

EDGE STITCHES

The first and last stitch of a row are called edge stitches or selvedge stitches. Depending on how they are treated, a side edge is created that can have different functions.

The double knotted edge creates a sturdy edge. It is well suited for sewing knooked parts together and for picking up new stitches from the side edge. For this, the first and last stitch of every row are always knooked in knit stitch.

The chained edge is a loose, stretchy edge. Along the side edge runs a V-shaped stitch, which looks very decorative at edges that are not subsequently seamed.

There are two options to work a chained edge. Either in both right- and wrong-side rows always slip the first stitch knit-wise (with working yarn in front of work) and knook the last stitch in knit stitch or, the other way around, knook the first stitch in knit stitch and slip the last stitch knit-wise with yarn in front of work

X Always work edge stitches EVENLY LOOSELY or slip them to prevent the edge from constricting.

! When SLIPPING, THE HOOK IS INSERTED into the stitch as for knooking the appropriate stitch type, but the working yarn is NOT PULLED THROUGH.

BASIC STITCH PATTERNS

A few common basic stitch patterns are created by combining different stitch types.

 Fabric knooked in **STOCKINETTE** appears on the **WRONG SIDE OF THE FABRIC** as **REVERSE STOCKINETTE**, and the other way around.

REVERSE STOCKINETTE/ STOCKINETTE

Alternate knooking "1 row in knit, 1 row in purl." For reverse Stockinette (at left in picture) begin with a purl row; for Stockinette (at right in picture), begin with a knit row.

GARTER STITCH

In right- and wrong-side rows, knook all knit stitches.

TWISTED STOCKINETTE

Alternate knooking "1 row knit all stitches twisted, 1 row purl all stitches twisted."

RIBBING PATTERN

For a 1x1 ribbing pattern (at left in picture), alternate knooking "knit 1, purl 1."
For a twisted 1x1 ribbing pattern (at right in picture), alternate knooking "knit 1 stitch, purl 1 stitch twisted."

CROCHETING STITCHES OFF

To secure the top edge, all stitches must be bound off at the end of work.

 When binding off, the stitches can all be either **KNOOKED IN KNIT** or worked according to their **STITCH TYPE** in the stitch pattern.

1 Work the edge stitch as usual, and then insert the hook into the next stitch, pull the working yarn through . . .

2 . . . and, at the same time, pull it through the two loops on the hook so that only 1 loop remains on the hook.

3 Insert the hook into the next stitch, pull the working yarn through the fabric once more . . .

4 . . . and pull it through both stitches on the hook at once.

5 Repeat Steps 3 and 4 until only 1 last loop remains on the hook. Finish off as for regular crochet (> page 80) and remove the cord for holding stitches.

X A VISIBLE INCREASE is created when inserting the hook below the cord for holding stitches from FRONT TO BACK under the bar between stitches and pulling the working yarn through. This creates a small hole under the new column of stitches, which can be decoratively integrated into the stitch pattern.

! The stitch immediately AFTER THE INCREASED STITCH often turns out VERY SMALL from pulling at the bar between stitches. Make sure to not accidentally miss this stitch later.

INCREASING STITCHES

With an increase, the number of stitches on the hook becomes higher and the piece being knooked becomes wider or larger.

When increasing from the bar between stitches, a new column of stitches is formed between two existing stitches. Since the bar between stitches provides only a relatively short strand of yarn for the new stitch, this stitch is tighter than all other stitches, and the increase fits in invisibly between the surrounding stitches.

Invisible increase

Visible increase

1 Knook up to the spot where a stitch is to be increased. The bar between stitches is the short horizontal strand between 2 stitches.

2 Below the holding cord, grasp the bar between stitches with the hook from above, and pull it to the front and top, so that it sits on the hook.

3 Place the working yarn from back to front over the hook to form a yarn over ...

4 ... and pull it through. The bar between stitches twists below the hook. On the hook, there is 1 loop more for the new stitch row.

DECREASING STITCHES

With a decrease, the number of stitches on the hook becomes lower and the piece being knooked becomes narrower or smaller. Decreases are easiest to work with knit stitches.

1 Knook up to the spot where a stitch is to be decreased. Here, insert the hook into the following two stitches together from right to left ...

2 ... and pull the working yarn through both stitches. The two stitches have been combined below the hook, and on the hook only one loop remains for both stitches together

Slip Stitch
Crochet

While slip stitch crochet is an old crochet technique, it has been historically established only in a few geographic areas and had not been universally known in the past. It is also called Bosnian crochet. Bosnian crochet produces a dense crocheted fabric that resembles knitting.

SLIP STITCHES AND THEIR VARIATIONS

Slip stitches have no post and practically consist only of one single loop. Since this loop tends to constrict while being worked, slip stitch crochet should be worked very loosely. It is also recommended to use a larger hook size than usual: The crochet hook should be 1.0 to 1.5 mm (about 4 US sizes) larger than what would be used for regular crochet with the same yarn, or even more if crocheting very tightly.

Slip stitches can be worked in a variety of ways. By changing the insertion point and the way of inserting the hook, a total of 9 different stitch types can be produced, which in turn make a wide variety of stitch patterns possible.

The term "slip stitch" always means the common slip stitch, as it is known from traditional crochet. Inverse slip stitches are all mirror-inverted slip stitches (i.e., these stitches are so crocheted that on the right side of the fabric, the actual back of the stitch appears). As the name indicates, twisted slip stitches twist while being crocheted, creating a new, other kind of stitch with its very own stitch appearance.

Further variations can be achieved by inserting the hook only through the back or the front loop of the stitch. The naming convention for the stitches also contains the insertion point. An inverse front loop only slip stitch stands for a mirror-inverted slip stitch that is worked through the front loop of the stitch only. A twisted back loop only slip stitch is a slip stitch for which the hook is inserted through the back loop of the stitch only, and which is worked twisted.

X The more loosely the slip stitches are crocheted, the easier it is to insert the hook into the loops of the stitches and to crochet new stitches. Additionally, in **FABRIC WORKED MORE LOOSELY,** individual stitches are much better shown to their advantage.

MIRRORED STITCHES AT A GLANCE

Within the stitch types for slip-stitch crochet, there are pairs of stitches that always mirror each other and thus allow the creation of symmetrical stitch patterns.

slip stitch ⟷ inverse slip stitch

front loop only slip stitch ⟷ inverse back loop only slip stitch

back loop only slip stitch ⟷ inverse front loop only slip stitch

SLIP STITCHES THROUGH BOTH LOOPS OF THE STITCH

Slip stitches, like traditional crochet stitches, can be worked through both loops of the stitch (> page 33). This way of inserting the hook can create three variations.

REGULAR SLIP STITCHES

The crocheted fabric features rows of V-shaped loops, which point to the left. The resulting ridges create a three-dimensional texture.

1 Insert the hook under the two V-shaped loops of the next stitch, and pull the working yarn through the insertion point . . .

2 . . . and immediately through the working loop.

X ESPECIALLY LOOSE STITCHES are produced when the WORKING LOOP is pulled SLIGHTLY LONGER after having completed a stitch. After having inserted the hook for the new stitch, make sure that this loop does not get pulled smaller again through inherent tension of the yarn.

INVERSE SLIP STITCHES

This crocheted fabric features rows of V-shaped loops just like with regular slip stitches, which, however, here are pointing to the right. The stitches are textured just the same, but mirror-inverted.

1 Insert the hook from back to front under the two loops of the next stitch, with working yarn in front of work.

2 Now make a yarn over and grasp the working yarn and . . .

3 . . . pull it through the insertion point and through the working loop.

TWISTED SLIP STITCHES

The twisted slip stitch looks mesh-like and with a cord-like texture.

1 Insert the hook from back to front through both loops of the next stitch with working yarn in back of work.

2 Now make a yarn over, grasp the working yarn, and pull it through the insertion point . . .

3 . . . and immediately after through the working loop. The stitch twists below the hook.

SLIP STITCHES THROUGH THE FRONT LOOP OF THE STITCH ONLY

The top loops of the stitch can be used independently of each other to serve as insertion points (> page 37). Regardless of whether the front or the back of work is presently facing up (i.e., whether a right- or a wrong-side row is being worked), the part of the stitch that faces the viewer is called front loop of stitch, the loop behind it back loop of stitch.

FRONT LOOP ONLY SLIP STITCH

Slip stitches through the front loop of the stitch only are also called "rugged Bosnian stitch" since the fabric with the ridges and crosswise loops resembles garter ridges.

1 Insert the hook from front to back through the front loop of the stitch, make a yarn over, grasp the working yarn, and pull it through the insertion point . . .

2 . . . and through the working loop.

INVERSE FRONT LOOP ONLY SLIP STITCH

The crocheted fabric features rows of V-shaped loops, which point to the right. Its stitch appearance is similar to that of back loop only slip stitches, but not as three-dimensional.

1 Insert the hook from back to front through the front loop of the stitch only, with working yarn in front of work. Make a yarn over, grasp the working yarn, and pull it through the insertion point . . .

2 . . . and through the working loop.

TWISTED FRONT LOOP ONLY SLIP STITCH

The stitch appearance of twisted front loop only slip stitch features rows separated by ridges as well as by crosswise and diagonal loops.

1 Insert the hook from back to front through the front loop of the stitch, with working yarn in back of work. Make a yarn over, grasp the working yarn, and pull it through the insertion point . . .

2 . . . and through the working loop. The stitch twists below the hook.

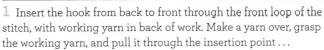
Crocheted fabric in twisted front loop stitches is overall **TIGHTER AND DENSER**, since the loops are smaller on account of the stitches being twisted. For this reason, it is especially important here to crochet the stitches **AS LOOSELY AS POSSIBLE.**

SLIP STITCHES THROUGH THE BACK LOOP OF THE STITCH ONLY

The back loop of the stitch is always the part of the stitch that faces away from the viewer, no matter whether the front or the back of the fabric is currently facing.

BACK LOOP ONLY SLIP STITCHES

For how to **INSERT** the hook through the front/back loop of the stitch, see also page 37.

Back loop only slip stitches have the stitch appearance of mirror-inverted inverse front loop only slip stitches (i.e., the stitches look the same but are pointing to the left).

1 Insert the hook from the front through the back loop of the stitch, make a yarn over, grasp the working yarn, pull it through the insertion point . . .

2 . . . and through the working loop.

INVERSE BACK LOOP ONLY SLIP STITCHES

 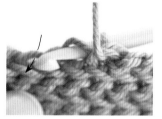 

Inverse back loop only slip stitches have the stitch appearance of mirror-inverted front loop only slip stitches (i.e., the stitches look the same, but the V-shaped loops are pointing to the left).

1 Insert the hook from back to front through the back loop of the stitch with working yarn in front of work. Make a yarn over, grasp the working yarn, pull it through the insertion point . . .

2 . . . and through the working loop.

TWISTED BACK LOOP ONLY SLIP STITCHES

The **TOP EDGE OF THE CROCHETED PIECE** of twisted front or back loop only slip stitches is looser than the whole piece. To finish work, work a last **ROW OF REGULAR SLIP STITCHES**, which constricts the top edge somewhat.

The crocheted fabric features markedly three-dimensional, horizontal ridges.

1 To work a twisted back loop only slip stitch, insert the hook from back to front through the back loop of the stitch with working yarn in back of work. Make a yarn over, grasp the working yarn, pull it through the insertion point . . .

2 . . . and through the working loop. The stitch twists below the hook.

SELVEDGE STITCHES

Edge stitches, or selvedge stitches, are the first and last stitch of every row. These stitches should be given special attention to achieve a clean edge.

At the beginning of the row, a row can be turned without turning chain without any problems, since slip stitches are shallow, however, the working loop should then be pulled slightly longer. This creates room to be able to easily insert the hook into the first stitch of the row.

Furthermore, the stitch won't constrict this way, and remains at the top edge of the crocheted piece as a clearly visible loop, so that in the following row, the hook can be again easily inserted. A top row worked without turning chains appears as a tight, uniformly closed edge.

When at the beginning of every row, a turning chain is worked, the edge will be loose and stretchy. Owing to the loop of the chain at the edge, the edge appears slightly serrated. This effect can be used as a decorative edge finishing.

Turning chains should in any case be worked for increases or decreases to prevent the crocheted piece from constricting.

Depending on the type of stitch worked, the **LOOP OF THE FIRST STITCH** can become **SMALLER** or tilt to the back. For this reason, at the end of a row, always make sure you have not forgotten to crochet into the last loop. In case of doubt, **RECOUNT** the stitches of the row.

SLIP STITCHES IN THE ROUND

Slip stitches are always crocheted in spiral rounds, since thanks to the low height of the stitches, there is no significant height difference between the individual rounds *(crocheting in spiral rounds > page 71)*. In rounds, front and back loop only slip stitches as well as twisted front and back loop slip stitches are usually worked.

In this example, 2 rounds of front loop only slip stitch and 2 rounds back loop only slip stitches have been crocheted. In front loop only slip stitches, the loops of the stitches align themselves in back of work. The surface appears rough and resembles garter stitch ridges. In back loop only slip stitches, in every round, the unused loops of the stitches arrange themselves toward the front. This creates delicate ridges, positioned horizontally.

In spiral rounds, the beginning of the round should preferably be marked with a piece of contrasting color yarn, and the marker be moved over the stitches from front to back and back again in every round or in every other round. This way, the beginning of the round is always noticeable. As the name indicates, the beginning of a new round is not located directly above that of the just-finished round but shifts slightly to the right with every new round and then spirals upward.

INCREASING STITCHES

When working increases, over 2 adjoining stitches, a total of 3 stitches are crocheted. Increases are worked the same for all slip stitch types.

Increase on the example of front loop only slip stitches

1 Work up to the spot where a stitch is to be increased. Now first work 1 front loop only slip stitch into the next stitch.

2 Then insert the hook once more into the same stitch just crocheted into and pull the working yarn through the fabric. There are 2 loops on the hook now.

3 Insert the hook into the next stitch, pull the working yarn through the fabric . . .

4 . . . and through both loops on the hook at once.

5 Now insert the hook once more into the second stitch, which had already been crocheted into, and work 1 front loop only slip stitch. There are now 3 top loops atop 2 stitches; the middle one of the 3 stitches has been increased and can be crocheted into the regular way in the following row.

DECREASING STITCHES

In MIRROR-INVERTED STITCH TYPES, stitches are decreased according to their mirrored stitches: inverse back loop only slip stitches are decreased like front loop only slip stitches, and inverse front loop only slip stitches like back loop only slip stitches (*mirrored stitches > page 261*).

Stitches are decreased differently depending on whether they are front or back loop only slip stitches and whether worked in rows or rounds.

DECREASING FRONT LOOP ONLY SLIP STITCHES WORKED IN ROWS

1 Work up to the spot where a stitch is to be decreased. Now insert the hook through the front loop of the stitch after the next one and pull the working yarn through the fabric. There are 2 loops on the hook.

2 Then insert the hook through the front loop of the skipped first stitch . . .

3 . . . pull the working yarn through the fabric (for a short time, there are 3 loops on the hook) . . .

4 . . . and immediately through both loops on the hook at once.

DECREASING FRONT LOOP ONLY SLIP STITCHES WORKED IN ROUNDS

1 Work up to the spot where a stitch is to be decreased. Now insert the hook through the front loop of the next stitch and pull the working yarn through the fabric. There are 2 loops on the hook now.

2 Then insert the hook through the front loop of the stitch after the next one, pull the working yarn through the fabric . . .

3 . . . and immediately through both loops on the hook at once.

DECREASING BACK LOOP ONLY SLIP STITCHES WORKED IN ROWS

1 Work up to the spot where a stitch is to be decreased. Now insert the hook through the back loop of the following stitch and pull the working yarn through the fabric. There are 2 loops on the hook now.

2 Then insert the hook through the back loop of the second stitch, pull the working yarn through the fabric . . .

3 . . . and through both loops on the hook at once.

DECREASING BACK LOOP ONLY SLIP STITCHES WORKED IN ROUNDS

1 Work up to the spot where a stitch needs to be decreased. Now insert the hook through the back loop of the stitch after the next one and pull the working yarn through the fabric. There are 2 loops on the hook now.

2 Then insert the hook through the back loop of the skipped first stitch, pull the working yarn through the fabric (for a short time, there are 3 loops on the hook) . . .

3 . . . and through both loops on the hook at once.

X When decreasing back loop only slip stitches worked in the round, the hook is always inserted **FIRST INTO THE STITCH AFTER THE NEXT ONE** and then **INTO THE FIRST STITCH**. The result looks much better this way.

COLOR CHANGE

Slip stitches crocheted in different colors create charming effects. The color change works differently than for traditional crochet.

COLOR CHANGE AT THE BEGINNING OF THE ROW

1 Work the last row before the color change except for the last slip stitch in the current color, and then complete the last step of the last slip stitch already in the new color. A working loop in the new color for the beginning of the new row is now on the hook.

2 Then turn work and work the new row in the new color.

COLOR CHANGE WITHIN A ROW OR ROUND

1 Within the row or round, work to 1 slip stitch before the color change, and then complete the last step of the last slip stitch already in the new color. A working loop in the new color is now on the hook.

2 Then continue, working slip stitches in the new color.

TRADITIONAL AND MODERN SLIP STITCH CROCHET

The traditional Bosnian crochet technique is used to crochet mainly bands and edgings. Modern slip stitch crochet greatly expands the options by using additional stitch variations. This makes it possible to create decorative accessories such as cowls, mitts, or bags.

With the help of **MIRROR-INVERTED STITCHES**, stitch patterns normally worked in the round can **ALSO** be worked **IN ROWS**. For this, in right-side rows, work the stitches in the stitch pattern listed in the instructions, in wrong-side rows, always work the respective mirror-inverted stitch.

ABBREVIATIONS can be found on page 344.

TRADITIONAL PATTERN BAND IN THE ROUND

Instructions
Stitch count: a multiple of 3.
Rounds 1–3: Work back loop only sl-st.
Rounds 4 and 5: Work front loop only sl-st.
Rounds 6–12: Alternate "3 front loop only sl-sts and 3 back loop only sl-sts ," shifting the stitch pattern in every round 1 stitch to the left.
Rounds 13–17: Work as rnds 1–5, but in opposite order.
Finally, work 1 round of regular sl-sts into the top edge.

STITCH PATTERN WITH INVERSE SLIP STITCHES

Instructions
Stitch count: a multiple of 5 + 3 sts extra. Begin with a WS row.
Row 1 (WS): 3 front loop only sl-sts, * 2 inverse back loop only sl-sts , 3 front loop only sl-sts, repeat from * to end of row.
Row 2 (RS): * 3 inverse back loop only sl-sts, 2 front loop only sl-sts, repeat from *, ending with 3 inverse back loop only sl-sts.
Repeat Rows 1 and 2 to desired height.

Irish Crochet

Irish crochet or crochet gipure (from French "guipure") belongs to the more sophisticated lace crochet techniques. This technique imitates the patterns of bobbin lace or embroidered needle lace. Artfully crocheted flat or three-dimensional flowers, leaves, and ornaments are arranged into motifs and connected by a filigree-like net background. It is traditionally worked using tightly plied, fine cotton yarns, and a very small crochet hook.

MOTIFS

The appeal of Irish crochet lies in its almost inexhaustible treasure trove of motifs. Besides classic motifs such as the Irish rose or the ridged leaf, there are simpler motifs that can complement an Irish crochet project. Additionally, this technique also leaves much freedom for one's own imaginative creations.

FLOWERS

Simple flowers are crocheted in the round. Around the center of a flower, rounded, oval, or serrated petals are worked that define the look of the flower. The number of petals also has an influence on the appearance of a flower.

The center of a flower consists of a crocheted chain that is joined into the round with a slip stitch or started from a magic circle or adjustable magic ring, into which the stitches of the first round are crocheted (crocheting in rounds > page 67). The magic circle has the advantage that the center of the flower can be cinched tightly to create an evenly shaped course of rounds.

FLAT FLOWERS

Flat flowers enrich every Irish crochet project with their wealth of shapes. The imagination knows no boundaries.

 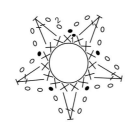

Small Flower

Round 1: Begin the flower with a magic circle (> page 68) and work sc15, join with 1 sl-st into the first sc.

Round 2: Work the petals according to the chart.

! Some flowers in Irish crochet BRING TO MIND MOTIF CROCHET, but the two techniques have not much in common. In motif crochet, usually many of the same motif, such as flowers or squares, are crocheted and then joined by being either sewn together or crocheted together. For Irish crochet, however, ENTIRELY DIFFERENT INDIVIDUAL MOTIFS are combined imaginatively with each other. In the hands of creative crochet artists, pieces that resemble a flower garden or flower arrangements are created this way.

X Worked in EXTRA FINE THREAD, Irish lace garnishes christening or wedding gowns and other high-end textiles.

X Irish crochet requires MUCH TIME and a HIGH DEGREE OF PRACTICE. Newcomers to this technique should plan a rather simpler piece for their first project.

∙∙∙ The STITCH KEY for the crochet symbols and the ABBREVIATIONS can be found on pages 340–344.

●●● How to **INCREASE** by **DOUBLING STITCHES** is explained on page 98.

Six-petal Flower

Round 1: Begin the flower with a magic circle (> page 68), and work sc16, join with 1 sl-st into the first sc.

Round 2: Work in dc, doubling every other stitch.

Round 3: Work the petals according to the chart.

Small Star Flower

Round 1: Begin the flower with a magic circle (> page 68), and work sc18, join with 1 sl-st into the first sc.

Round 2: Work sc and chain arcs according to the crochet chart.

Round 3: Work all petals according to the crochet chart into the chain of the previous rnd, inserting the hook into individual chains (not the chain space).

❗ When the hook is supposed to be inserted **INTO INDIVIDUAL CHAIN STITCHES OF THE CHAIN ARCS**, always insert so that 2 loops of each individual chain sit on the hook (> page 58).

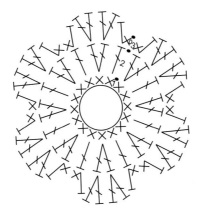

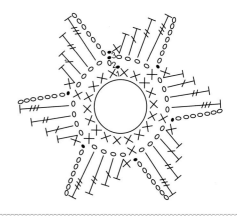

Filigree Flower

Round 1: Begin the flower with a magic circle (> page 68), and work sc16, join with 1 sl-st into the first sc.

Round 2: Work dc and chain arcs according to the crochet chart.

Round 3: Work the petals according to the crochet chart into the chain spaces of the previous rnd.

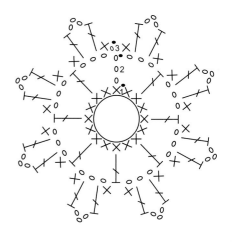

Large Sunflower

Round 1: Begin the flower with a magic circle (> *page 68*), and work sc16, join with 1 sl-st into the first sc.

Round 2: Work dc and chain arcs according to the crochet chart.

Round 3: Work sc according to the crochet chart, inserting the hook into individual chains (not the chain space).

Round 4: Work sc and ch4-arcs according to the crochet chart.

Round 5: Work every petal in the chain space of the previous rnd according to the crochet chart.

••• **ABBREVIATIONS** can be found on page 344.

Baroque Blossom

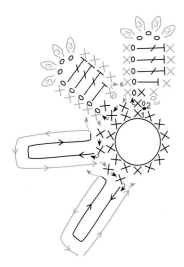

••• The **STITCH KEY** for the crochet symbols can be found on pages 340–343.

Round 1: Begin the blossom with a magic circle (> *page 68*), and work sc14, join with 1 sl-st into the first sc.

Round 2: Work the petals, one after another, each one over 2 sts widthwise, according to the crochet chart as follows:

1 Chain 1, sc1, ch8, along the chain dc3, hdc1, sc1, inserting the hook for the 1st dc into the 4th chain from the hook.

2 Ch1 for turning, turn, and work sc edging all around the petal, working sc1 each into the 5 sts of the previous row, at the tip of petal [sc 1, ch3, sc1] 4 times, moving onto the opposite side, and work sc5 along the loops of the chain.

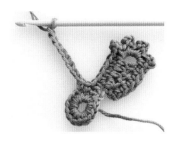

3 Turn only the center of the flower, so that the right side is facing up again (while holding the petal to leave it unturned). Sc1 each into the next 2 sc of the flower center, and then begin the next petal as described with a chain. After having crocheted along the chain, turn the center of the flower, sc1, 1 sl-st into the 2nd sc of the previous petal (while the petal turns), and then continue to work sc and chains into the petal as shown in the crochet chart.

Work all other petals the same way. After the last petal, sc1 into the last sc, and join the round with 1 sl-st. Use the ending tail to join the first and last petal.

THREE-DIMENSIONAL FLOWERS
Three-dimensional crocheted flowers are created by crocheting multiple rounds of petals placed behind each other like the petals of filled flowers. This effect can be achieved in different ways.

X Flower arrangements of combined **THREE-DI-MENSIONAL AND FLAT FLOWERS** look particularly lively. With leaves in different sizes, whole fabric gardens can be created.

●●● How to **INCREASE** by **DOUBLING STITCHES** is explained on page 98.

Small, Closed Blossom
Round 1: Begin the blossom with a magic circle (> page 68), and work sc10, join with 1 sl-st into the first sc.
Round 2: Work sc1 into every sc.
Round 3: Work hdc, doubling every stitch.
Round 4: Work the petals in dc and ch according to the chart, always inserting the hook through the front loop of the stitches only (> page 37).

Round 5: Work the petals in tr and ch according to the chart through the unused back loops of the stitches of rnd 4.
For this, after rnd 4, fold the petals toward the front, ch1 to move to the back of work, and work 1 sl-st each into each of the following 2 unused loops of the stitch, and then work the second round of petals, always inserting the hook through the unused loops of the stitch.

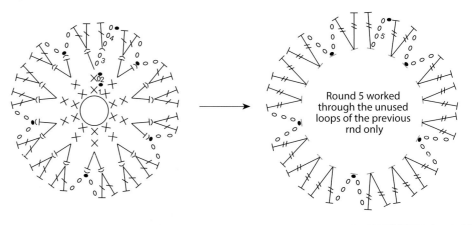

Round 5 worked through the unused loops of the previous rnd only

Daffodil

Round 1: Begin the blossom with a magic circle (> page 68), and dc16, join the round with 1 sl-st into the topmost ch of the height-adjustment chain.

Round 2: Work sc and chain arcs according to the crochet chart.

Round 3: Work all petals according to the chart above the chain arcs of the previous rnd, and anchor with sc1.

Round 4: In the chain spaces of Rnd 2, work the smaller front petals.

For this, after rnd 3, work 1 sl-st in the 1st ch-sp of rnd 2, fold the larger petals to the back, and crochet in the chain space.

ABBREVIATIONS can be found on page 344.

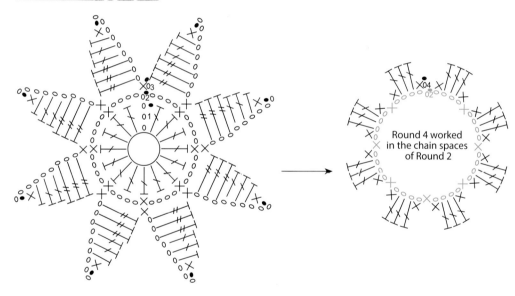

Round 4 worked in the chain spaces of Round 2

The STITCH KEY for the crochet symbols can be found on pages 340–343.

Irish Rose

The Irish rose is the best-known flower in Irish crochet. Depending on how many petals are placed behind each other, the finished size of the flower varies. In round 1 and all other odd-numbered rounds, chain arcs are worked, into which the petals are crocheted in Round 2 and all following even-numbered rounds. Every round is joined with 1 slip stitch into the first stitch.

Center Petals

Round 1: Begin the blossom with a magic circle (> page 68), and work dc and chain arcs according to the crochet chart.
Round 2: Work petals of sc, ch, and dc3 each in the chain space according to the crochet chart.

Second-tier Petals

Round 3: Chain 1 to move to the back of work, and at the beginning, work sc1 around the post of the dc of the previous rnd, inserting the hook from back to front around the post of the dc as for a bpdc (> page 42) . . .

. . . * ch5, sc1 around the following dc of the previous rnd, repeat from * to end of rnd, ending with ch5.
Round 4: Work petals in the ch-sp of rnd 3 according to the crochet chart. Chain 1 to move to the back of work.

ABBREVIATIONS can be found on page 344.

Third-tier Petals

Round 5: Work sc1 around the sc of the previous rnd, inserting the hook from back to front around the post of the sc as for a bpsc, * ch6, sc1 around the post of the following sc of the previous rnd, repeat from * to end of rnd, ending with ch6.
Round 6: Work petals in ch-sp of rnd 5 according to the crochet chart. If more tiers of petals need to be worked, ch1 to move to the back of work.

Additional tiers of petals

For every additional tier, work as described for rnd 3, and in every odd-numbered round ch1 more for chain arc, in every even-numbered round, work dc2 more into every chain space.

X The **DIFFERENT COLORS** of the crochet symbols for each round are for better orientation only—the actual example shown has been worked in one color only. However, a splendid effect can also be created if the Irish rose is worked in two hues of the same basic color, or even in multiple different colors.

LEAVES

Leaves complement Irish crochet flowers in many ways.

OBLONG LEAF

A leaf with a midrib is formed by crocheting into a beginning chain from both sides.

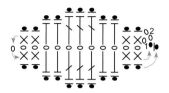 

Round 1: Begin with ch11, and work all around the beginning chain from both sides as shown in the chart.

Round 2: Work 1 sl-st each through the back loop only in every chain.

OPENWORK LEAF

A leaf with an openwork center is created from a crocheted chain into which alternatingly "1 double crochet, chain 1" are worked.

Round 1: Begin with ch11, and work sc, dc, and chains into it as shown in the chart.
Round 2: Work sc all around the leaf.
Round 3: Work sl-sts all around the leaf, inserting the hook through the back loop of the stitches only.

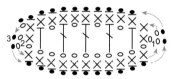

RIDGED LEAF

A ridged leaf is made of single crochets that are worked through the back loop of the stitch only in all rows. This creates the characteristic three-dimensional texture. The size of the leaf is determined by the number of rows worked.

Work sc onto a beginning chain (chart shows 12 chains), whereas the chain at the beginning of the row will be the corner stitch. Then work sc in rows, working every stitch through the back loop of the stitch of the previous row only (> page 37). From Row 2 on, at the beginning of every row, always move across the first 2 sts with 2 sl-sts, at the end of every row, leave the last 2 sts unworked. Into each one of the corner sts, work sc3 into the same insertion point. The middle sc will always be the corner st for the next row.

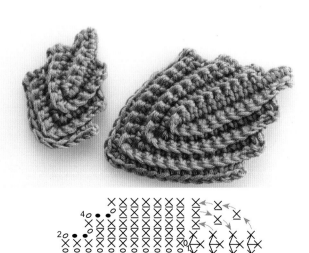

X SYMMETRICAL
LEAVES with midrib are created when crocheting into the same stitches on both sides of the center spine chain. The vein shifts away from the middle if taller stitches are crocheted on one side than on the other.

The STITCH KEY for the crochet symbols can be found on pages 340–343.

For how to insert the hook through the BACK LOOP OF THE STITCH ONLY, see page 37.

> ! These interconnected leaves can also be **WORKED SEPARATELY**, with and without stalk.

Larger leaves are created by using taller stitches. Instead of every listed stitch, work the next taller one and, if needed, work 3 instead of 2 stitches into 1 insertion point. A variety of options can be used for shaping the leaves.

> X Not only leaves and flowers but also smaller or larger **ORNAMENTS**, such as stylized shamrocks or drops, can be integrated into an Irish crochet project since they can be resourcefully combined with traditional motifs. In crocheted pieces with a modern touch, **GRAPHIC SHAPES** such as simple circles, squares, or triangles can also be found.

> ... **ABBREVIATIONS** can be found on page 344.

> ... The **STITCH KEY** for the crochet symbols can be found on pages 340–343.

> X If you want to produce **VERY THREE-DIMENSIONAL FLOWER CENTERS**, combine multiple inlay threads to the desired thickness, and crochet around them.

INTERCONNECTED LEAVES

Connected leaves are advantageous if flower motifs need to be joined in freeform work (crocheting motifs onto existing pieces > page 278). Depending on the length of the crocheted chain forming the leaf stalk and midrib, as well as the type and number of stitches worked at the sides of the leaf, every leaf can be designed individually.

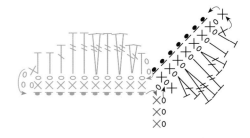

Work sc onto a beginning chain, leaving a few chains unworked at the beginning of the chain for the stalk. At the end of the leaf, ch1 over the stalk to move to the opposite side of the beginning chain, and then work sc, hdc, dc, and tr as shown in the chart (or other sts as desired) along the chain. Due to the different height of the stitches, the leaf is shaped. Change again to the other side of the leaf, and work sl-sts into the sc.
After the last sl-st, make a short chain of ch2, and work as described for the first leaf, first in sc and then in sts of different height and sl-sts. After the last sl-st, work sc1 each into the remaining unused chains of the leaf stalk.

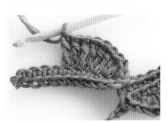

WORKING OVER AN INLAY THREAD

A typical feature of Irish crochet is the three-dimensional character of individual elements. To additionally enhance the three-dimensional effect of motifs, work is often started not with a crocheted chain, but over an inlay thread. The inlay thread is much thicker than the project yarn and should be of the same color. If yarn of sufficient thickness is not available, you can just use the working yarn held double or triple. In the pictured examples, inlay thread in a contrasting color has been used to better show the concept.

1 Make a beginning slipknot (> page 30) and place the inlay thread over the hook to the left of it.

2 Make a yarn over, pull the working yarn through, and pull it through underneath the inlay thread. There are 2 loops on the hook now.

3 Make another yarn over and pull the working yarn through both loops. The inlay thread has been held in place with a single crochet.

4 Then continue working single crochets very close to each other around the inlay thread.

5 To work the center of the flower, join the round as usual with 1 slip stitch, and push the stitches closely together on the inlay thread.

! Weave the ENDS OF THE INLAY THREAD within the motif by threading the tails within the stitches for approximately 0.8 inches (2 cm), and then trim excess.

SPIRAL AROUND AN INLAY THREAD

A popular motif is the spiral, which can be well integrated into motif groups. Sewn to the centers of large flowers, the spiral lends a playful, light touch to the composition.

1 Around an inlay thread, work, for instance, 20 single crochets close to each other. The size of the individual spiral is determined by the number of stitches worked.

2 Join the first curl of the spiral with 1 single crochet into the first stitch on the inlay thread. This stitch needs to be likewise worked around the inlay thread itself. Pull at the inlay thread, so that the stitches move close to each other and form a circle.

3 After this, work 25 single crochets more (= 5 stitches spacing to the first spiral + 20 stitches for the second spiral) around the inlay thread.

! The SPACING between the curls of the spiral can be increased or decreased by working MORE OR FEWER SINGLE CROCHETS accordingly between the individual curls of the spiral.

! When PULLING THE INLAY THREAD TAUT, always make sure that the individual curls of the spiral turn out the same size.

4 Now join the second curl of the spiral with 1 single crochet into the 5th single crochet after the first curl of the spiral, likewise working this stitch around the inlay thread itself. Again, move the stitches closer together by pulling at the inlay thread.

5 For additional curls of the spiral, repeat steps 3 and 4 all the time.

X The STEM OF THE CLOVER LEAF can also be WIDENED by working single crochet into the beginning chain.

WORKING A CLOVER LEAF OVER AN INLAY THREAD

The principle of the spiral can also be easily applied to make a clover leaf.

1 Chain 1 very loosely as center, loop on an inlay thread, and work, for instance, 27 single crochets around the inlay thread. Join the first coil of the leaf with 1 slip stitch into the center point, but do not enclose the inlay thread within this stitch.

2 Work the second and third coils of the leaf the same way. Make sure the leaves are evenly sized.

3 Crochet a chain for the stalk, and work slip stitches along the chain. Finally, anchor the stalk with a slip stitch into the center point. Weave in all ends.

X If you plan to venture into freeform lace design as a BEGINNER, you can prepare a PRELIMINARY DRAWING from which it can be seen how the individual motifs should be joined.

JOINING MOTIFS BY CROCHETING THEM ONTO EXISTING PIECES

Crocheting motifs onto existing ones allows a great flexibility in the configuration of lacework. Motifs, such as various flowers, can be arranged arbitrarily and according to one's own design choices. Resulting free spaces between stitches are later filled with smaller motifs such as leaves. All motifs are joined together during the last round with slip stitches, double crochet, Y-stitches, and so forth (*joining motifs > page 146, Y-stitches > page 50*).

In the pictured crocheted lace, small flowers (*> page 269*) and small star blossoms (*> page 270*) have been chosen as main motifs. Together with oblong leaves of different sizes (*> page 275*) and connective bars worked in double crochet, treble crochet, and Y-stitches (*> pages 35 and 50*), the motifs were joined to form lace fabric.

CLONES KNOT

Clones knots are slipknots that can be crocheted within flowers or mesh backgrounds as prominent elements. A clones knot has to be always worked loosely.

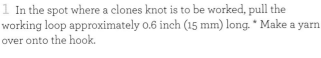

1 In the spot where a clones knot is to be worked, pull the working loop approximately 0.6 inch (15 mm) long. * Make a yarn over onto the hook.

2 Now rotate the hook horizontally in a counterclockwise direction until the hook end is again located to the left of the working loop. The working yarn will place itself below the hook around the working loop pulled long, there are 2 loops on the hook.

3 lead the crochet hook from left to right under the working yarn . . .

4 . . . rotate it back again in a clockwise direction. There is one more loop on the hook now.

5 Repeat steps 1–3 from * 3–4 times more, making sure that the loops are loosely aligned side by side.

6 Grasp the working yarn and pull it through all loops on the hook at once. Finally, lock in the knot by working 1 single crochet into the adjoining chain.

> X Into mesh backgrounds, picots (> page 280) can also be incorporated (> page 280), but clones knots are more compact and more voluptuous, and give the mesh more **STRUCTURE AND STRENGTH.**

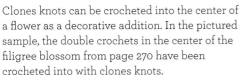

Clones knots can be crocheted into the center of a flower as a decorative addition. In the pictured sample, the double crochets in the center of the filigree blossom from page 270 have been crocheted into with clones knots.

Clones knot in a regular, open mesh background.

THE MESH BACKGROUND

To turn individual ornaments or groups of motifs into a lace fabric, they are incorporated into a fine mesh background, the background net. Depending on type and size of the motifs, a uniformly sized or irregular mesh background is worked. All uniform mesh backgrounds are crocheted; for irregular mesh backgrounds, options are to either crochet the motifs into the background or join them with wrapped connective bars.

UNIFORMLY SIZED MESH BACKGROUND

A uniformly sized mesh background is especially well suited for simple flowers, graphic shapes, and individual ornaments with symmetrical construction, since these in most cases form a contiguous area so the spaces between motifs are easy to fill in.

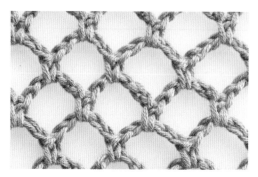

A dense mesh background is created with simple chain arcs, which are worked staggered in every row. The shorter the chain arcs, the denser the mesh background turns out.

An open mesh background is created with chain arcs into which additional small, picot-like chain arcs are crocheted. The longer the chain arcs, the more open the mesh background becomes.

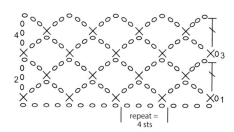

repeat = 4 sts

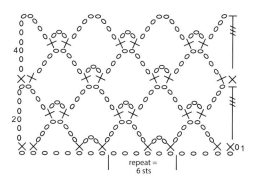

repeat = 6 sts

IRREGULAR MESH BACKGROUND

An irregular mesh background is suitable for more complicated projects such as compositions of multiple groups of motifs, which are placed unconnected on a background surface. This mesh background also offers itself for freeform crochet projects.

CROCHETED IRREGULAR MESH BACKGROUND

For an irregular mesh background, chain arcs in different lengths are crocheted. Additionally, work is always rotated and turned at will and sentiment, creating a pattern of irregular shapes.

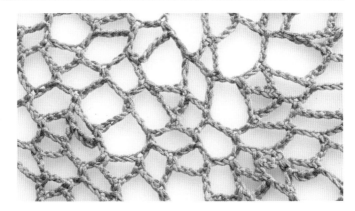

MESH BACKGROUND WITH WRAPPED CONNECTIVE BARS

A mesh background with wrapped connective bars can be produced very well on a flat work surface.

First, draw the motifs and framing edging in original size onto thin cardboard. Then crochet up individual parts and pin them to the cardboard according to the design. Now use a pen to draw in connec-

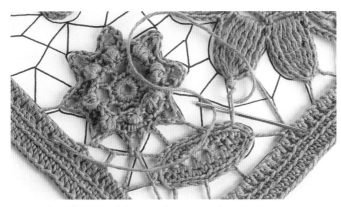

tive bars between the motifs, making sure that all parts of the motifs are joined.

For a connective bar, stretch the working yarn at the marked spot from one motif to the next once, and on the return pass, wrap it. When a connective bar forks, the working yarn is first spanned to one end point and wrapped up to the fork point. Now the working yarn is stretched to the next end point and wrapped back to the junction. Finally, the connective bar is wrapped back to the starting point. Move on to the next connective bar on the wrong side of work.

Lace of large sunflowers (> page 271), filigree flowers with clones knot, (> page 279) and openwork leaves (> page 275), joined with wrapped connective bars.

X If possible, practice the irregular mesh background beforehand with a **PRACTICE PIECE** to develop a sense for the construction of freeform textures.

! Adding in the connective bars requires **SOME PRACTICE** to place them evenly distributed but not too close to each other. Too densely spaced connective bars can distort the motifs; too loosely stretched bars don't give the motifs enough support and the whole lace can lose its shape.

! WHEN THE BAR FORKS SEVERAL TIMES, individual partial bars are worked one after another, until you arrive back at the first fork point. Then wind the yarn around the bar back to the starting point. Long, straight connective bars with one or more crossing points can also be wound first over their whole length. Then work the transverse round connective bars. For these connective bars, stitch through the already-wound bar at the crossing points, so that the new connective bars are anchored in these spots.

! Motifs should be pinned on **NOT TOO CLOSE TO THE EDGE**, so the connective bars can be mounted without any problems. It will also be easier to move to the position of the next bar on the wrong side of work this way.

INCORPORATING MOTIFS INTO A MESH BACKGROUND

If motifs are to be worked into a mesh background, a little pre-planning is required.

INCORPORATING MOTIFS INTO A UNIFORM BACKGROUND

X For better orientation, the right- and wrong-side rows of the mesh background drawing can be rendered in **DIFFERENT COLORS.**

Draw the desired mesh background in original size onto paper (= size of the mesh background after blocking). Now place the motif on the preliminary drawing and transfer the outlines onto the paper. Then, on the motif, mark the spots in which the motif abuts the mesh background with a piece of contrasting color yarn.

Crochet the mesh background and in the marked spots attach the mesh background to the motif with 1 slip stitch. When turning at the edge of the motif, if necessary, move up to the next attaching point with chains, anchor the chains with 1 slip stitch, and then work the next row of the mesh background.

Irish rose in a uniform mesh background.

X The mesh background can also be **CROCHETED SEPARATELY.** The motifs are then **SEWN ONTO** the finished mesh background. This approach comes very close to the original guipure technique and is a good alternative if crocheting in the motifs should prove difficult.

Irish rose with leaves in an irregular mesh background.

INCORPORATING MOTIFS INTO AN IRREGULAR MESH BACKGROUND

Working the mesh background freeform style makes the motif look lively. When working, always make sure that the mesh background around the motif is evenly tensioned. To check during work, repeatedly spread out the motif flat together with the mesh background.

Hairpin Lace Crochet

Hairpin lace crochet is a very old crochet technique, for which in addition to a regular crochet hook yet another tool—the hairpin lace loom—is used. In hairpin lace crochet, airy strips of loops are created, which can be joined in a variety of ways into a finished item—straight, undulating, or even in a circular shape.

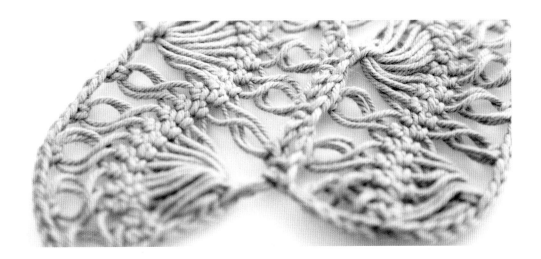

THE HAIRPIN LACE LOOM

Hairpin lace looms come in two different basic types, which are also slightly different to operate, as will be explained further on.

The easiest type to use is shaped like the letter "U," the shape of a hairpin, hence the name "hairpin lace." The two parallel rods are connected at the bottom by a horizontal spacer and are open at the top. In this type of hairpin lace loom, the spacing between the rods and thus also the length of the loops is fixed and cannot be changed.

The more complex type of loom also consists of two long rods, which, however, have one connecting part at the bottom, and another one at the top. Through holes in the connecting parts, the spacing between the rods can be adjusted, so that loops of different length and therefore strips in different widths can be crocheted. In some hairpin lace looms of this kind, the spacer at the top is also removable, so the loom can be used like a U-shaped hairpin lace tool.

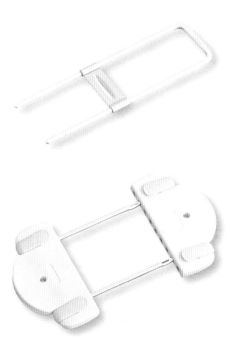

! In the **NINETEENTH CENTURY,** hairpin lace crochet was used to produce mainly ribbons for decorating curtains, but also whole curtains, belts, stoles, and scarves.

The delicate bands can also be joined very nicely to create **MODERN ACCESSO-RIES AND GARMENTS.**

When working with a hairpin lace loom that is joined at both ends and **CANNOT BE OPENED**, work needs to be **STARTED A DIFFERENT WAY**. For this, place a beginning slipknot onto the crochet hook and lead the working yarn around the right rod to the back. Hold the working loop in the middle between the rods and pull the working yarn through the loop from the back. Then continue from step 5. During turning, the crochet hook must be briefly released.

With some hairpin lace looms, the **TOP SPACER** must **STAY REMOVED** during crocheting, since otherwise the crochet hook would not fit through.

The **BEGINNING TAIL** can at the start be fastened to the hairpin lace loom with a piece of adhesive tape so the center of the strip does not shift. Some hairpin lace looms have a special **HOLE** in the bottom connector for this purpose, through which the yarn tail can be threaded.

BASIC HAIRPIN LACE CROCHET TECHNIQUE

For adjustable hairpin lace looms, first the desired width of the strip must be set up by adjusting the spacing of the rods.

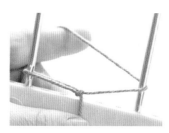

1 Then make a beginning slipknot (> page 30) and pull it to half the length of the spacing between the rods. Thread the loop onto the left rod (if needed, briefly removing the top connector beforehand). Place the beginning slipknot in the middle between the rods, and hold the yarn tail with the thumb of your left hand. Move the working yarn from front to back around the right rod, and behind the slipknot.

 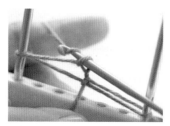

2 Hold the hairpin lace loom in your left hand, take up a crochet hook appropriate for the yarn weight in your right hand, and insert the hook under the top strand through the beginning slipknot. Pull the working yarn through the loop.

3 Then make a yarn over, and pull the working yarn through through the loop on the hook.

4 The first stitch of the loop strip has been completed. There is one loop each around the left and the right rod. The working yarn is located behind the hairpin lace loom, the crochet hook is in the middle between the rods.

5 Now move the crochet hook to the back over the tip of the right rod. If the hairpin loom has a closed top, the crochet hook might need to be briefly removed and reinserted.

6 Rotate the hairpin lace loom once horizontally in a clockwise direction, so that the working yarn winds itself around the left rod (after rotating the loom, the left rod is now at the right). During this, the crochet hook moves again toward the front. Now insert the hook under the front strand of the loop that goes around the left rod. Pull the working yarn through.

7 Yarn over and pull the working yarn through the two loops on the hook. A single crochet has been completed.

8 Repeat steps 5–7 until the loop strip has reached the desired length. To finish work on the loop strip, ch1 to secure, break the working yarn, and pull it through the working loop.

When too many loops are crowded on the hairpin lace loom but still more need to be worked, release loops from the hairpin lace loom (> page 286) in between then continue making more loops.

STITCH PATTERNS FOR HAIRPIN LACE LOOM STRIPS

The hairpin lace crochet base strip as just described can be modified in various ways by changing the insertion point, the stitch type, or the length of the loops. The first two loops are always worked as described in the base technique, and the stitch pattern always starts from the 3rd loop on only.

DIFFERENT BASIC STITCHES

Just as single crochet has been worked in the base technique, other stitch types or combinations of different stitches can be worked around the working yarn of the left loop.

single crochet per loop

2 single crochets per loop

1 single crochet, 1 half double crochet, and 1 single crochet per loop

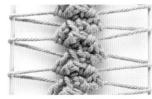

3 double crochets per loop

> **!** The **DIAMETER OF THE ROD** does not matter for the length of the loops, which is exclusively determined by the distance of the rods.

CHANGING THE INSERTION POINT

Instead of inserting the hook under the front strand of the loops only to work the center stitch or group of stitches, the hook can also be inserted under both strands (i.e., the whole loop). This method creates a denser middle stitch, and the whole strip will be accordingly less airy.

1 single crochet around both strands

CHANGING THE INSERTION POINT AND A COMBINATION OF STITCHES

Interesting variations of the pattern are also created if different stitches and changed insertion points are combined. For the pictured stitch pattern, first 1 single crochet had been worked around a single strand and then 2 double crochets crocheted together around both strands. This creates a wide stitch pattern resembling a dense leafy vine.

> **X** At the end of a loop strip, the **NUMBER OF LOOPS** around the left and the right rod should be **IDENTICAL**. To avoid unexpected surprises at the end, make sure to count along while working. Mark the side of the hairpin lace loom on which you've started, for instance, by tying the working yarn to it. The last stitch of the band should always be worked on the other side. This ensures that you have crocheted an even stitch count, and thus an equal number of loops on each side.
>
> You can also thread a **STITCH MARKER** onto one of the rods after a certain number of loops to aid in counting.

VARYING THE LENGTH OF THE LOOPS

It is also possible to produce strips in which the loops on either side are of different lengths. For this, position the beginning slipknot not centered, but shifted to one side. This will create a shorter and a longer loop. A strip like this can, for instance, be used as a decorative border when the shorter loops are crocheted onto the edge of a crocheted piece, and the longer ones are decorated with further crochet work (*crocheting onto the strips > page 286*).

X The loops themselves are secured by the stitches along the middle and **CANNOT BECOME UNDONE.** Gathering them only serves the purpose of getting them out of the way while continuing to work.

X Some hairpin lace looms have **INCORPO-RATED EYES** at the bottom of the rods through which a piece of contrasting color yarn can be threaded. This allows for pulling the rods upward out of the loops while inserting the auxiliary thread at the same time.

X The **PIECE OF CONTRASTING COLOR YARN** can be temporarily left in the loops, just make sure to not accidentally crochet it into the following stitches.

RELEASING THE LOOPS

While the strip is being worked, finished loops travel to the bottom and accumulate there. They later must be removed from the hairpin lace loom when the space there becomes tight but the loop strip still needs to be worked longer or when the loop strip has been finished.

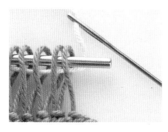

TO WORK ADDITIONAL LOOPS

When the bottom loops need to be removed from the hairpin lace loom to make room for new loops, the next steps depend on the type of loom being used.

The easiest method is when the bottom connector can be detached. In this case, all finished loops except for about 5 of them can be pushed off the rods, and the connecting part reinserted. When the bottom connector is non-removable, first all loops need to be removed from the hairpin lace loom and then only the 5 ones worked last remounted.

The loops freed this way can be threaded onto a piece of contrasting color yarn with a tapestry needle and rolled up to save space while continuing to work. Alternatively, they can also be fastened with large safety pins or clothespins.

AFTER THE STRIP HAS BEEN FINISHED

When the loop strip has been finished, secured, and you have checked that the number of loops is the same for both sides, it can simply be pulled up or down off the rods in its entire length. To do this, open the hairpin lace loom at the top.

For especially slippery yarns, before releasing the loops, it is recommended to thread a long piece of contrasting color yarn through the loops at both sides, as shown above. When the strips are later joined or crocheted into, this way, all loops will be mounted in correct orientation.

CROCHETING ONTO THE STRIPS

When hairpin lace loom strips are used on their own, the sides with the open loops are crocheted into. The finished strip is placed on an even surface. It is crucial that all loops are oriented in the same direction (i.e., always with the front or back strand to the right or left, so that the hook is always inserted into the loops the same way).

The edges of the strips can be crocheted into in different ways. Various stitch types can be used, the way of inserting the hook can be changed, or you can experiment with the number of loops bundled together.

In all cases, a new strand of yarn needs to be attached at the beginning of the strip.

A SINGLE CROCHET IN EVERY LOOP

Place a beginning slipknot (> page 30) onto the hook, and then work 1 single crochet each into every loop. Depending on whether the hook is inserted into the loops from the front or from the back, the loops will appear either twisted or open.

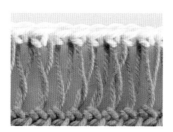  

ONE STITCH IN MULTIPLE LOOPS

The hook can also be inserted into several loops at the same time. Important is that the total number of loops must be a multiple of this number. The spacing between individual stitches then needs to be bridged with chains.

To recreate the pictured example, work 1 single crochet into a single loop, * chain 2, 1 single crochet in 2 loops together, repeat from * all the time, ending with "1 single crochet into the last individual loop."

You can also combine even more loops; for this, however, always insert the hook from the back, and crochet more chains between the individual stitches.

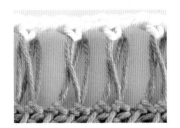

! For an even edge, if needed, for the **FIRST AND THE LAST STITCH,** only bundle half the number of loops as in the other spots.

PICOTS AT THE EDGE

Instead of chains, between joining multiple loops, picots *(> page 158)* can also be crocheted. To work the pictured example, work as follows: * 1 single crochet in 2 loops together, chain 3, 1 single crochet in the second chain, 1 half double crochet into the third chain, 1 double crochet through the post of the single crochet in the loops, repeat from * to the end of row or round.

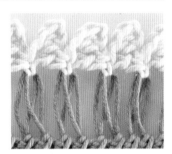

JOINING STRIPS

When multiple strips are combined into a larger crocheted piece, they need to be joined together. For this, the strips can either be first crocheted into separately and then joined *(> page 138)* like regular crocheted pieces or, instead of being first crocheted into, be joined in a special way. Just as when being crocheted into, here, too, the loops need to be oriented in the same direction so that the hook is always inserted the same way.

WITH ADDITIONAL CROCHET WORK

In this method, with new working yarn, basic stitches or stitch combinations are crocheted between the loops of the bottom and the top strip. Here, too, the number and type of the stitches worked as well as the number of loops bundled with each stitch can be modified.

WITH SINGLE CROCHET

Attach new working yarn at the first loop of the top strip. Work 1 single crochet into the first loop of the bottom strip, 1 single crochet into the first loop of the top strip, * 1 single crochet into the next loop of the bottom strip, 1 single crochet into the next loop of the top strip, repeat from * continuously.

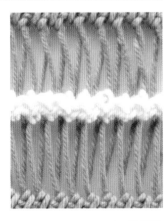

⊠ At the end, weave in the **YARN TAILS** within the stitches carefully and as inconspicuous as possible.

❗ If **STRIPS NEED TO BE CONTINUED**, choose a number of loops that is a multiple of 20, and then add 22 loops to this number. Repeat the pattern repeats between * and * continuously.

❗ When **BROADER STRIPS** need to be worked, adjust the number of chains at the narrow ends accordingly.

❗ When joining long strips, it is recommended to regularly check whether **ALL LOOPS** have been **GRASPED**. If a loop has been left out, the join back to the spot where the loop is missing must be taken out and reworked.

WITH SINGLE CROCHETS AND CHAINS

For this join, several loops are combined and chains worked in between.

The number of loops in each strip is a multiple of 3 + 2 loops extra. Attach new working yarn at the first loop of the top strip. Work "chain 1 and 1 single crochet" into the first loop of the bottom strip, * chain 1, insert the hook from the back into the next 3 loops of the top strip (starting into the 2nd loop at the beginning of the strip), and work 3 single crochets, chain 1, 3 single crochets into the next 3 loops of the bottom strip, repeat from * continuously, ending with "chain 1 and 1 single crochet" in the last loop of the top strip, 1 single crochet in the last loop of the bottom strip.

UNDULATING JOIN

To work this join, which is very characteristic for hairpin lace crochet, the number of loops bundled together is played with. To both sides of the joining line, small, staggered fans appear. The longer the strips are, the more loops from which each fan can be formed, and the fuller the fans appear.

Instructions

Work two strips (A and B) with a spacing of 2.4 inches (6 cm) and 42 loops per side as described on page 284. Now crochet along strip A separately, beginning in the upper right corner. For this step, insert the hook into the first 6 loops and pull the working yarn through, and then yarn over and pull the working yarn through the loop on the hook. Then * [ch3, combine 2 loops with 1 single crochet] 5 times, chain 3, crochet 10 loops together *, [ch3, crochet 2 loops together] 5 times, chain 3, crochet 6 loops together.

Rotate work by 90°, and crochet into the narrow bottom edge of the strip as follows : ch5, sc1 into the middle of the strip, ch5. Rotate work by 90° again, and work along the other long side as follows:

[crochet 2 loops together, chain 3] 3 times, * crochet 10 loops together, chain 3, [crochet 2 loops together, chain 3] 5 times *, crochet 10 loops together, chain 3, [crochet 2 loops together, chain 3] 2 times, crochet the last 2 loops together. Rotate work once more by 90°, and crochet into the narrow end as described above, join the edging with 1 sl-st into the first sc.

To join strip B to strip A, on Strip B first crochet along the top edge and one narrow end as described above. Then crochet along the bottom edge as described for strip A, but instead of "chain 3," always work as follows: ch1, sc1 into the opposite ch3-arc of strip A, ch1. This way, additional strips can also be joined.

WITHOUT ADDITIONAL CROCHET WORK

This way of joining produces a kind of herringbone pattern.

Crochet two strips and lay them flat next to each other, loops onto loops. To prevent the finished crocheted piece from slanting, place the beginning of one strip to the left, of the other, to the right.

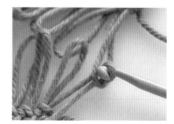

1 Insert the crochet hook into the first loop of the top strip. Pull the first loop of the bottom strip through this loop.

2 Now, with the help of the crochet hook, pull the next unused loop of the top strip through the loop on the hook (first loop of the bottom strip).

3 Grasp the next unused loop of the bottom strip with the crochet hook and pull it through the loop on the hook.

4 Repeat steps 2 and 3 until all loops of the strips are connected and 1 loop remains on the hook. Secure it with a stitch marker.

In this method, multiple loops can also be grasped together. The only thing to keep in mind is that the total number of loops must be a multiple of this number.

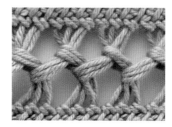

FINISHING OUTER EDGES

When multiple strips are joined into a whole piece, finally, the outer edges of the piece must be finished, too.

TOP AND BOTTOM EDGE

The top and bottom edges of a piece of multiple strips can be crocheted into as shown above. The loops can also be turned into a decorative edge without additional crochet work.

For this, begin at the upper right corner, and first insert the hook into the first 2 loops. Grasp the next 2 loops and pull through the first 2 loops. * Grasp the next 2 loops and pull through the two-stranded loop on the hook. Repeat from * continuously. Secure the last 2 loops with a stitch marker.

X The LOOPS of an edging can also be turned into FRINGE just by CUTTING THE LOOPS OPEN.

SIDE EDGES

How the side edges of a piece can be finished depends on the way the strips were previously joined. In all cases, after finishing the top edge, new working yarn is joined at the right-side edge. Then crochet chains to the centerline of the first strip, work 1 single crochet centered onto it, crochet chains to the join of the first with the second strip, 1 single crochet into the beginning of the join or into the final stitch that had been secured with a stitch marker. This way, always work single crochets in the middle of the band or into the join, and bridge the stretches in between with chains. These should form a straight line and be worked neither too loosely nor too tightly.

X A decorative crocheted ornament like this one also looks very appealing if worked in a **METALLIC CROCHET THREAD**.

HAIRPIN LACE CIRCLE

Lesser known are circular ornaments in the hairpin lace technique. They are based on strips that are joined into the round and then, depending on how they are crocheted into, turned into either a star or a flower.

Crochet a strip with a center-line in the stitch of your choice and break the working yarn, leaving an end of 5.9 inches (15 cm). Before releasing the loops from the hairpin lace loom, thread a piece of yarn in the same color through all left or right loops. Then release the loops from the hairpin lace loom. Gather the new thread, and knot the ends together, which forms the center of the circle. Sew beginning and end of the middle strip together with a few stitches. Crochet an

edging in the stitch of your choice around the outer loops. In the example, a strip with 60 loops on each side has been crocheted. For the edging, 3 loops each have been crocheted together with 1 single crochet and then the distance bridged with 6 chains. The round was joined with 1 slip stitch, then crocheted around the circle with 8 single crochets each for every chain arc, and finally joined with 1 slip stitch.

Bruges Crochet

This crochet technique is named for the town of Bruges in Belgium, which is famous for its traditional lace. Bruges crochet imitates this fine bobbin lace by much less elaborate crochet work. A band worked in double crochet called a Bruges "tape" or "ribbon" is bent into various shapes with the help of joined chain arcs.

BASIC TECHNIQUE

The base of Bruges crochet are ribbons of double crochet rows with 4 double crochets each with chain arcs at the sides. Instead of ch3 for height adjustment as usual for double crochet, every row of double crochet is turned with 6 chains. This creates a ribbon with chain arcs at alternating ends.

1 Chain 10. Work 1 double crochet into the 7th chain from the hook, and 1 double crochet each into the next 3 chains.

2 Turn work. Chain 6, and then work 1 double crochet in every double crochet of the previous row.

3 Repeat step 2 continuously.

To bring the ribbon into the desired shape, a specified number of chain arcs is always joined at certain intervals using stitches of different height. Typically, at a connection point, first half a chain arc is crocheted (i.e., 3 chains), and then the already-finished chain arcs are joined; next, the current chain arc is completed by working the remaining 3 chains. After that, the tape of double crochet is continued as usual.

WAVY RIBBON

The wavy ribbon is the easiest shape in Bruges crochet. To shape it, always the same number of chain arcs is joined alternatingly on the right and left edge of the ribbon, which creates the wave shape.

1 In basic technique, work 6 rows of double crochet. The last row is a wrong-side row; the back of work is facing up. There are 3 chain arcs at each one of the two edges. Without turning work, chain 3. Then insert the crochet hook from front to back into each one of the 3 chain arcs below and pull the working yarn through all 3 chain arcs at the same time.

> **!** Bruges crochet is **IN MOST CASES** worked with bands **4 DOUBLE CROCHETS** wide, but the number can also vary, depending on stitch pattern and pattern instructions.
>
> **X** When working with wider bands, patterns in **FILET CROCHET** (> page 236) can also be incorporated.

292

2 Yarn over and pull the working yarn through the two loops on the hook.

3 Finish the started chain arc, working 3 additional chains, turn work, and work the next row of double crochet (= 7th row as counted on the right side of the fabric).

4 Work 6 more rows of double crochet with chain arcs. The last (13th) row is a right-side row; the front of work is facing up. Now join the 3 chain arcs at the left edge as described in steps 1–3.

5 After the end of the chain arc used for joining, work 7 more rows of double crochet, and again work another join at the other side. Repeat step 5 until the ribbon has reached the desired length.

In the finished wavy ribbon, on every side, 3 freestanding chain arcs alternate with 4 joined chain arcs.

CROCHET CHARTS FOR BRUGES CROCHET

To depict Bruges crochet in crochet charts, the same symbols as for regular crochet are generally used. However, since the whole ribbon is worked in double crochet and chains through-out, this is often visualized only schematically as a ladder-like structure with chain arcs at the edges. Usually only the first rows and the stitches used for joining chain arcs are shown in detail. The joins are often symbolized by arrows.

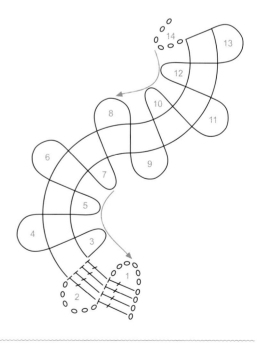

The STITCH KEY for the crochet symbols can be found on pages 340–343.

PARALLEL RIBBONS

In this stitch pattern, very tight bends are worked into the ribbon, causing it to make 180° turns, with ribbon sections parallel to each other. In the parallel sections, the ribbons are joined together at every other chain arc.

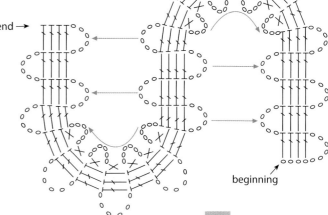

end →

beginning

Instructions

Work 5 rows of dc with chain arcs as described in basic technique (> page 291). * To work a bend, work 6 shortened rows of dc with chain arcs as follows:

Row 1: Ch6, sc1, hdc1, dc2.
Row 2: Ch6, dc2, hdc1, sc1.
Rows 3–6: Repeat Rows 1 and 2 another 2 times.

Work the first 3 chains of the next chain arc and gather the 3 previous chain arcs at the left edge with a sc as described for

the Wavy Ribbon, and then complete the missing ch3 of the current chain arc. Work 1 row of "sc1, hdc1, dc2, ch6" and 1 regular row of dc.

Now, for joining the parallel section, ch3 for the next chain arc, sc1 into the opposite chain arc, and finish the current chain arc with ch3. Work 1 row of dc, one chain arc and 1 row of dc, and join the next chain arc the same way. Complete the last ch3 of the current chain arc and work 1 more row of dc.

When the parallel section is supposed to be longer, after every join, work 2 rows of dc with 1 chain arc, and after the last join, work 1 more row of dc. For the next bend, work from * as described, but switch the first and second row in the short row section and join the chain arc at the right edge.

.... ABBREVIATIONS can be found on page 344.

! The short rows described in these instructions are recommended when MORE THAN 3 CHAIN ARCS are combined or if VERY THICK YARN is being used. This way, not too much fabric accumulates at the joins, which would later add bulk.

LARGER CIRCLES

To create larger circles with Bruges ribbons, the chain arcs at the edges are combined with a Y-stitch in double or treble crochet. Owing to its shape, this pattern is also called "spider."

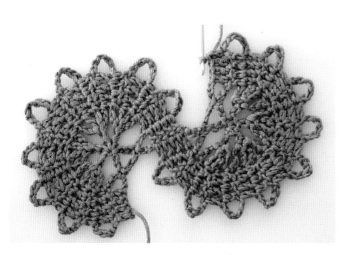

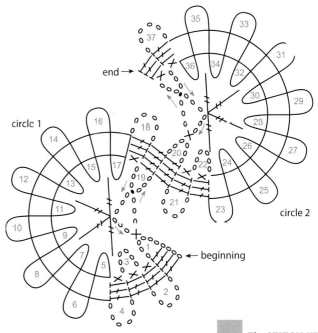

end →

circle 1

circle 2

← beginning

.... The STITCH KEY for the crochet symbols can be found on pages 340–343.

●●● **ABBREVIATIONS** can be found on page 344.

Instructions

For the first circle, chain 10, work dc4, working the first dc into the 7th chain from the hook. Work 17 short rows with chain arcs as follows:

Row 2: Ch6, dc2, hdc1, sc1.

Row 3: Ch6, sc1, hdc1, dc2.

Rows 4–17: Repeat Rows 2 and 3 another 7 times.

Row 18: Work as Row 2.

Now, for the large circle, combine the 3rd–17th chain arcs with a "spider," and join the 19th chain arc to the first one. For this, work as follows:

After the last sc of Row 18, ch6 and * make 2 yarn overs, and then, one after another, pull the working yarn through the 17th and 15th chain arcs. There are 5 loops on the hook now. Now yarn over and pull the working yarn through the first 3 loops (3 loops on the hook), and then yarn over and pull the working yarn through the first 2 loops on the hook. The working loop plus 1 additional loop remain on the hook. Repeat from * continuously, joining all chain arcs in pairs up to the third

chain arc. Finally, 5 loops remain on the hook—make a yarn over and crochet these loops off the hook together. Now chain 3, sc1 into the first chain arc, chain 3, 1 sl-st into the middle of the ch6-arc from the beginning, and complete the 19th chain arc with ch3. Work Row 19 in 4 regular dc. For the second and all further circles, repeat Rows 1–19.

BRUGES DOILIES

Bruges crochet can also be combined very nicely with regular crochet. For the doily shown here, for the center, a round motif with 16 chain arcs around the outside edge has been worked. To these, a Bruges crochet ribbon has been joined in every other row.

●●● The **STITCH KEY** for the crochet symbols can be found on pages 340–343.

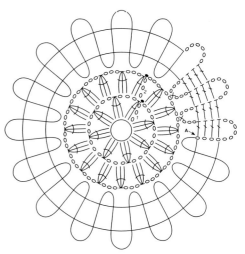

Instructions

Begin with a magic circle or adjustable magic ring (> page 68), and then work the center motif over 2 rounds according to the chart. Break the working yarn and weave in the end.

In Point A, begin the Bruges ribbon, and join every other chain arc of the ribbon with a chain arc of the central motif. For this, chain 3 each, sc1

into the appropriate chain arc of the motif, and complete the chain arc with ch3. To finish, break the working yarn, leaving an end of 4–8 inches (10–20 cm), and use it to sew or crochet the edges of the last row and the first row together (> pages 138 and 142). Weave in the yarn tail.

Loop Stitch Crochet

Loop stitch crochet encompasses various techniques used to create a patterned area featuring long loops of yarn. As with many other crochet techniques, working in loop stitches opens up a variety of pattern possibilities. The loops can be worked loose and close to each other over a compact crochet fabric, for a fur-like effect. Or the yarn loops can be integrated into the stitch pattern, spread out individually over an area, or crocheted around in groups, creating decorative holes.

LOOP STITCHES OVER A FINGER

The base fabric for this stitch pattern should be worked in single crochet to provide a solid base. The loops are formed in wrong-side rows, where for every loop the working yarn is wrapped around the index finger. Worked this way, it is unavoidable that the loops end up being of different lengths. But exactly this irregularity makes these "freestyle" loops interesting and loosens up the overall appearance. The working yarn runs over the index finger of the left hand and is additionally held with the ring finger and pinky finger.

1 First, work a row of single crochet without loops. In the following row, first sc1, and then work the first loop stitch. For this step, insert the hook as for a regular single crochet, pick up the working yarn from behind the finger, and pull it through. Adjust the loop length according to your taste.

2 Now finish up the single crochet to anchor the loop. For this, lead the crochet hook behind the loop …

3 … pick up the working yarn from behind the loop …

4 … and pull it through the 2 loops on the hook.

5 Remove the finger from the loop, and move the loop to the back of work, so it is no longer in front of the working yarn.

The **FURRY LOOK** of the loop stitch pattern looks particularly striking and decorative. The tousled stitch pattern is suitable for **COLLARS AND BORDERS** on jackets, for fashionable accessories such as **BAGS**, as well as for **STUFFED TOYS, PILLOWS**, and so forth.

When purchasing materials, keep in mind that this stitch pattern uses **LARGE AMOUNTS OF YARN**.

The loopy fringe can also be decorated **WITH BEADS** that have already been threaded onto the working yarn **PRIOR TO CROCHETING** (> page 306).

Sometimes it is recommended to finish the single crochet **IN FRONT OF THE LOOP** instead of behind the loop. However, pieces crocheted this way can turn out very floppy, since the loops can be pulled into the crocheted fabric.

This way, work a whole row of loop stitches, ending with a regular single crochet stitch. In right-side rows, work regular single crochet. Work rows of loop stitches and regular single crochet alternatingly.

LOOP STITCHES OVER AN AUXILIARY STRIP

As the main pattern work single crochet; the loops are formed during wrong-side rows. As an aid, a strip of thin, sturdy cardboard or a strip of paper folded several times can be used. The working yarn is always wrapped around the auxiliary strip, creating evenly sized loops in the length of the strip's width. The working yarn is wrapped once around the index finger, for tensioning the yarn, and held in place with the ring finger and pinky finger.

1 First, work a row of single crochet without loops. In the following row, first sc1, and then work the first loop stitch. Hold the paper strip behind work. Now insert the hook as for a regular single crochet, and place the working yarn from front to back onto the hook. (Please note! Different from a yarn over for regular crochet.)

2 With a finger of the right hand, hold the strand on the hook, lead the working yarn from back to front around the paper strip, and place it in front of the hook.

3 Pull the two strands that are in front of and on the hook, respectively, together through the stitch. On the hook are now a "double loop," plus the working loop.

4 Pull the double loop to the height of a single crochet, yarn over and crochet the 3 loops off together.

This way, work a whole row of loop stitches, ending with a regular single crochet stitch. In right-side rows, work regular single crochet. Alternate rows of loop stitches and single crochets.

CROCHETING LOOPS ONTO AN EDGE

Loops can also be worked as decorative finishing edging during the last row or round. Irregularities in loops length are welcome here. Loops of even length need to be worked over a ruler or a strip of sturdy cardboard.

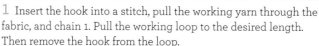

1 Insert the hook into a stitch, pull the working yarn through the fabric, and chain 1. Pull the working loop to the desired length. Then remove the hook from the loop.

2 Tighten the loop by hand.

Repeat steps 1 and 2 continuously along the whole edge.

LOOP STITCHES OVER A FLAT STICK

In this way of creating loop stitches, the stitch pattern is achieved through loops of equal length placed flat next to each other, which are anchored by rows of single crochet. The loops for the all-over pattern are formed by crocheting around an inserted flat stick.

The working yarn is wrapped once around the index finger and additionally held in place between ring finger and pinky finger. Hold the crochet hook from above (> page 29). During crocheting, the flat stick stands rather vertically instead of the regular way of holding for crocheting in a horizontal direction.

Loop stitch pattern, front of work | Loop stitch pattern, back of work

! For the FLAT STICKS for this crochet technique, you can use WOODEN CRAFT STICKS, TONGUE DEPRESSORS from the pharmacy, strips of cardboard cut to size, or rulers.

1 First, work a row of single crochet, before starting the loops in the second row. * Pull the working loop of the last single crochet of Row 1 as long as the width of the flat stick. Turn work. Place the craft stick behind this long loop.

2 Bring the working yarn up behind the stick, and pull it through the long loop, and then chain 1—this chain must be exactly at the top edge of the stick.

3 Insert the hook into the next single crochet and pull the working yarn through. Pull the loop up to the top edge of the stick.

4 Bring the working yarn up behind the stick and just grasp it with the hook end of the crochet hook, without placing a yarn over onto the hook! Now pull the working yarn through the long loop and further through the working loop.

X For LONGER ROWS, use MULTIPLE STICKS one after another, and to crochet into, remove only the one in front.

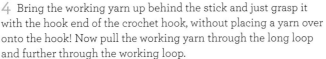

5 Repeat steps 3 and 4 all the time, until a whole row's worth of loops has been crocheted. The top loops should sit close to the edge of the stick; the other edge sits directly on the stitches of the previous row. Finally, ch1 for turning.

6 Remove the stick and turn work.

7 Now again work single crochet. For each single crochet, insert the hook below the top loop of every stitch, and at the same time through the group of loops, to secure the still loose loop. At the end of the row, pull the working loop to the height of the last single crochet.

Repeat steps 1–7 from * continuously, always alternating "1 row of loops, 1 row of single crochet."

X The loop rows can also be combined with OTHER CROCHET STITCHES or with narrow DECORATIVE BANDS between two loop rows.

The DIAMETER of the auxiliary needle, as well as the YARN WEIGHT, are key for the size of the yarn loops and consequently for the stitch appearance. Combining thinner yarn with a large-diameter auxiliary needle creates a lace pattern with a more pronounced openwork effect than when using a thicker yarn.

Knitting needles with a large diameter are sold in lengths up to 16 inches (40 cm). The length of the auxiliary needle determines the MAXIMUM WIDTH of the crocheted piece. However, the loops on the auxiliary hook can also be pushed tightly together for more width.

The first row of loops can also be worked over a BEGINNING CHAIN (> page 57).

If possible, always place the loops onto the auxiliary needle THE SAME WAY (i.e., with left leg in front of and right leg behind the auxiliary needle, or the other way around). This makes crocheting together easier, but is NOT ABSO-LUTELY NECESSARY since the loops can still be turned later on.

When crocheting the loops together, place the THICK AUXILIARY NEEDLE vertically in front of you in the crook of your legs and, if needed, additionally lean it against the edge of a table.

BROOMSTICK CROCHET

A "broomstick" is the large diameter auxiliary needle used to crochet a loop pattern—the namesake for this type of loop crochet. As an auxiliary needle, knitting needles in sizes 15 mm, 20 mm, or 25 mm (US sizes 19, 35, or 50), depending on the desired length of the loops, or similar tools from housewares or home improvement stores can be used. To work the pictured stitch pattern, a birchwood knitting needle in size 20 mm (US size 35) has been used as an auxiliary needle. The crochet hook size is chosen according to the yarn weight.

Broomstick crochet pattern, front of work

Broomstick crochet pattern, back of work

Essential for the broomstick technique are two working steps: First, crocheted-in loops are led around the auxiliary needle, and during the next step crocheted around in groups, creating a lace pattern.

BASIC BROOMSTICK TECHNIQUE

Work begins with a base row of single crochet. The stitch count must be a multiple of the number of loops that will later be combined into groups, in this example, 5 loops.

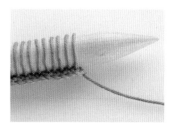

1 After the end of the base row, do not turn work. Pull the working loop of the last stitch long. Hold the thick auxiliary needle in your left hand and lift the long loop onto the auxiliary needle.

2 To work the next loop, insert the crochet hook in the next-to-last single crochet, make a yarn over, pull the working yarn through, and place the loop onto the hook, pull the loop long, and likewise lift it onto the auxiliary needle. Tighten the working yarn so the loop sits tight on the auxiliary needle but not too tight.

3 Continue, working from left to right, pulling a loop out of every stitch of the base row and placing it onto the auxiliary needle.

4 When loops have been picked up from all stitches, do not turn work. Now, working from right to left, grasp as many loops at the same time with the crochet hook as need to be crocheted together according to the pattern instructions (here: 5 loops). During work, the working yarn is located behind the loops. At the same time, note that the loops need to be grasped the same way, without twisting them.

5 Grasp the working yarn with the crochet hook and pull it through all 5 loops on the hook at once, and then chain 1. Make sure that the working yarn is carried loosely, to prevent the edge from constricting.

6 After that, work as many single crochets around all loops together as loops had been combined, here 5 stitches.

7 Place the next group of loops onto the auxiliary needle, again pick them up from right to left with the crochet hook, and then directly crochet together with the appropriate number of single crochets. No chain is worked here since there is already a working loop on the hook. Continue, always joining the same number of loops in the same manner, to the end of the row. When the last group of loops has been crocheted together, chain 1 to secure the end of the row—pull the single chain tight. Do not turn work.

8 Pull the working loop of the last stitch of the last row long with the help of the crochet hook. Lift the pulled-long working loop onto the auxiliary needle. Continue, working from left to right, picking up one yarn loop each from all single crochets of the previous row and lifting it onto the auxiliary needle.

Repeat steps 4–8, ending with a row of regular single crochet.

X The SIDE EDGES can be framed with height-adjustment chains at the beginning of the row, which are worked into the last loop on the auxiliary needle, plus a stitch of matching height at the end of the row. The appropriate height should be found out by trial and error.

PATTERN VARIATIONS FOR BROOMSTICK CROCHET

Besides the length of the loops, which is determined by the diameter of the auxiliary needle, the broomstick pattern can also be modified by the type of crochet stitches worked as well as number and direction of the joined loops.

Just by blocking (> page 196) alone, a stitch pattern is changed. The lace pattern effect is amplified even more. The only basic parameters remaining are the diameter of the auxiliary needle and the yarn weight.

In this stitch pattern, the groups of loops have been twisted alternatingly to the left and to the right. This minimal change creates a new stitch appearance.

Here, for crocheting together, double crochet has been used instead of single crochet.

In this swatch, only 3 loops have been crocheted with 3 single crochets each. Its stitch appearance appears more delicate.

Crocheted Lace

The word "lace" means "openwork." Lace fabric can be created in numerous craft techniques. Bobbin lace, knitted or crocheted lace—all of them are unique, and the sheer, delicate structures are fascinating small works of art. Traditionally, especially shawls, scarves, and stoles are worked in lace crochet.

! Lace work can look artistic and highly complicated without actually being it. Many STITCH PATTERNS are created with simple and very SHORT WIDTHWISE AND HEIGHTWISE PATTERN REPEATS.

THIN YARN AND THICK HOOKS

Lace crochet projects are crocheted with very fine yarn. Used are wool or mohair yarns with yardages of 328–547 yards per 1.75 oz (300–500 m per 50 g). As a rule, the crochet hook is significantly thicker than customary for the respective yarn weight. Generally, hook sizes of 3.0 to 5.0 mm (US C/2 to H/8) are used for this purpose.

Often, yarn labels contain the manufacturer's recommendations for hook sizes to be used with the respective yarn weight. For special lace yarns, the larger hook size has already been considered. When using other yarn weights, the recommended hook size will apply to regular crocheted fabric. If you plan to use these yarns for lace work, the hook size must be accordingly larger.

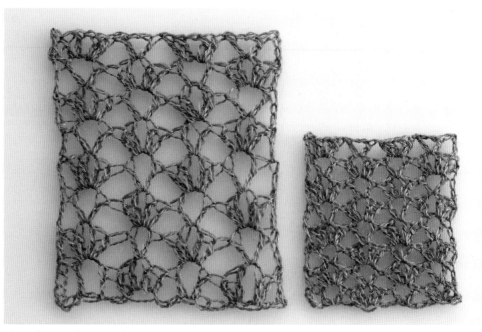

The influence the ratio of yarn weight to hook size has on the outcome of the crocheted fabric can be seen in the photo. The recommended hook size for the yarn is between 2.0 and 4.0 mm (US B/1 and G/6). The smaller swatch has been worked with a hook size of 2.5 mm (US between B/1 and C/2), the larger one with a hook size of 4.0 mm (US G/6). The smaller piece appears dense and compact, while the larger one shows the typical delicate sheer lace look.

For choosing the correct hook size, one should take time and prepare gauge swatches with different hook sizes (> page 95). The appearance of a stitch pattern can vary significantly with a difference in hook size of just 0.5 mm (one step in US sizes). Which hook size to choose depends on whether one prefers a denser crocheted fabric or the loose and airy look that almost dissolves the stitch structure. One should also consider that larger hook sizes result in a larger crocheted piece, and the total yarn amount needed will increase.

GENERAL INFORMATION ABOUT LACE PATTERNS

Crocheted lace at first sight looks difficult and complicated. If delving into this topic more in detail, one soon discovers that a few well-known basic stitches form the groundwork for this technique. Used are mainly chain stitches, single crochet, double and treble crochet and taller stitches, as well as slip stitch. Stitch patterns for lace and openwork crochet are also called openwork patterns, lacework patterns, or eyelet patterns, as there are large and numerous free spaces between the stitches, which give the piece an open look and a light and airy drape.

These open spaces are often created by chain arcs bridging skipped stitches. Often, multiple stitches are worked into the same stitch, too, or worked off together, which creates fan-like patterns. For stitches increased or decreased in this way, usually a certain number of stitches are being skipped, not being crocheted into. When a special shape needs to be created—for instance, a triangle—in some spots, stitches are increased without skipping stitches to compensate.

Crochet lace patterns are also often portrayed by crochet charts (> page 91), since specifics like special insertion points can be much better visualized this way than in written-out form.

BLOCKING

A just-completed lace project looks wrinkled and crumpled. It is also much narrower than the eventual size of the finished project, since the stitch patterns often pull in heavily. Only through blocking will these crocheted pieces achieve their final shape and size, and the stitch pattern be shown to its full advantage.

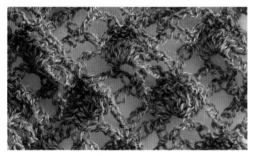 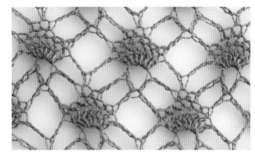

After completion, the crocheted piece is pinned to a blocking surface in a wet state and left to dry while pinned. Wet blocking evens out the stitches. While drying, the fibers of the lace yarn interlock, which retains the new stitch definition and keeps the crocheted piece in the blocked shape until the next wash (blocking and starching > page 196).

In the lace crochet technique, most often rectangular and triangular shapes are worked. The item is blocked in steps, always working over the whole area of the complete crocheted piece. For shawls with narrow crocheted edgings, blocking begins at the outside edge of the border. Shawls with wide filigree border edgings, which often contain peaks and chain arcs, are pinned beginning at the outside edge of the center part (minus the border edging). Only after this, the individual peaks and chain arcs of the edging are pinned down separately, so they will later show their whole beauty.

! COTTON YARNS or blends with LOW WOOL CONTENT behave differently during blocking than wool yarns. They should be SLIGHTLY STARCHED for reinforcement while drying, to prevent the crocheted piece from constricting again.

✗ Lace pieces should be LEFT TO DRY FOR 2 OR 3 DAYS, so the fibers of the yarn can align with the new shape.

! After EVERY WASH, a lace shawl must be re-blocked and left to dry while pinned.

•••• For help choosing a **BLOCKING MAT,** see page 196.

BLOCKING RECTANGULAR PIECES

1 On the blocking mat, mark the finished size of the lace shawl. Then pin the lace shawl at the corners with rust-proof stainless steel pins. The pins are inserted diagonally against the traction into the shawl and the blocking mat, like tent-pitching pegs.

2 Then, on all sides, between the corners, place more pins in evenly spaced larger intervals, always bisecting the distance between two pins with a new pin.

3 Now, between the inserted pins, in evenly spaced intervals, place more pins in smaller intervals, until the shawl has been pinned around all sides.

BLOCKING TRIANGULAR PIECES

1 On the blocking mat, first mark the finished size of the triangular shawl and, after this, pin down the shawl at the corners and once each in the middle between the corners. Then pin the center spine in a straight line so that the shawl will be blocked evenly.

2 Now, on all three sides, centered between the two existing pins, place another pin.

3 Now, between the already-inserted pins, place more pins in evenly spaced smaller intervals until the shawl has been pinned around all sides. This way, the triangular shawl will be blocked to an exact triangular shape.

X When blocking triangular shawls, they can also be formed in a **CERTAIN SHAPE.** For this, the outside edges are pinned in a light curve, creating a wing shape. Before blocking, the intended shape should here, too, be marked as exactly as possible on the blocking mat.

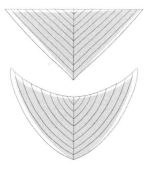

JOINING NEW WORKING YARN AND WEAVING IN ENDS

When a new skein needs to be started in crocheted lace, this should for thin yarns always be done at the beginning of a new row to avoid having to weave in beginning and ending tail in the middle of the row, which could cause the woven-in ends to stay visible as noticeable unsightly bulges in the delicate lace.

•••• For how to **JOIN A NEW SKEIN,** see pages 76–79.

WASHING

Delicate lace requires thorough and gentle care. After having been crocheted, but also after having been in use for some time, the lace shawl should be washed. For this, a mild wool detergent and lukewarm water are used. Place the shawl into the suds and agitate as little as possible. Then wrap the shawl in a towel and carefully press out excess liquid—do not wring—or spin it in a salad spinner specially reserved for this purpose to remove all excess water and reach the correct level of moisture for blocking.

THE PINEAPPLE PATTERN

The pineapple pattern is a traditional stitch pattern that exists in countless variations. Typical for this stitch pattern is the drop-like shape of the "pineapple," which highly resembles knitted lace leaves.

For lace crochet projects, pineapple patterns are especially popular. Crocheted in thin yarn with a thicker hook, the motifs appear wonderfully delicate like filigree. A shawl made of fine mohair or angora yarn either with individual pineapple motifs or crocheted in an all-over pineapple pattern also looks very elegant and sophisticated.

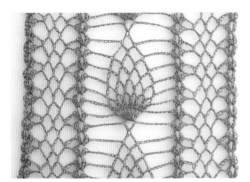

PLANNING YOUR OWN LACE PROJECTS

While for more complex shapes such as triangular shawls, it is prudent to rely on ready-to-use crochet patterns, straightforward rectangular stoles and scarves can, with a little practice and careful planning, also be very well custom-designed by yourself.

THE PLANNING STAGE

When attempting a simple shawl with lace pattern, two components must be taken into account during planning: the pattern repeat of the desired stitch pattern and the intended size of the finished shawl. Since the shawl will grow considerably in size through blocking, a gauge swatch (> page 95) in the desired stitch pattern should be made and subsequently blocked. Based on the dimensions after blocking, the required stitch and row counts can then be calculated. During work, stitch and row counts might need to be rounded up or down to match those of the pattern repeat.

If a lace shawl shall later be finished with additional lace edging, the overall size of the shawl needs to account for the width of the ADDED border. In addition to the gauge swatch of the lace pattern itself, another gauge swatch for the border must be rendered. Both swatches need to be blocked and placed onto each other.

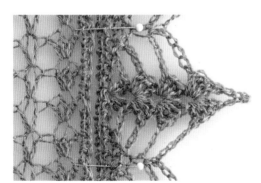

Sideways crocheted border

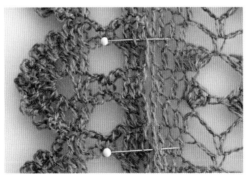

Lengthwise crocheted border

••• For further details on the topic of **DECORATIVE BORDERS,** see page 160.

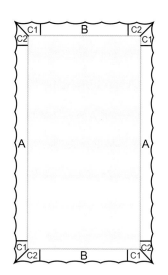

For planning, it is useful to keep a PROJECT JOURNAL in which all important numbers for gauge swatches, regular pattern repeats, pattern repeats at the corners, and so on, are recorded. Small sketches are very helpful, too, for additionally visualizing the project (*project journal > page 24*).

At the border edging, one pattern repeat is marked. Now it can be calculated how many stitches of the lace pattern in width or rows in height correspond to one pattern repeat of the border. The number of pattern repeats per side, however, is not all that determines the height and width of the lace shawl. Added to this are additional stitches or rows needed for the corners of the border edging. The number of these stitches must be considered as well.

For the width of the lace shawl, the length of the border edging is calculated from the number of widthwise pattern repeats for the short side B + the number of pattern repeats or stitch count for the corners C1 and C2.

For the height of the lace shawl, the length of the border edging is calculated from the number of heightwise pattern repeats for the long side A + the number of pattern repeats or row count for the corners C1 and C2.

From the number of pattern repeats in width and height and on the basis of the gauge swatch, the stitch count for the beginning of the lace pattern and the number of rows to be worked can be calculated.

A = pattern repeats at the long sides
B = pattern repeats at the short sides
C1 and C2 = corner halves, which together form the whole corner

BORDER EDGINGS

When the shawl has been completed with the calculated numbers in main lace pattern, wide border edgings of filigree lace motifs can be crocheted onto the outside edges in two different ways.

CROCHETING BORDER EDGINGS ONTO THE OUTSIDE EDGES

Add 1 round of single crochet at the outside edges. Then crochet a border (> *page 161*) worked in the round directly into the top loops of the single crochets. Begin the border edging at the bottom right, above the corner (see schematic), and work in the direction of the arrow with right side of work facing up. Border edgings crocheted directly onto outside edges usually come with a corner solution, which is shown in a separate crochet chart.

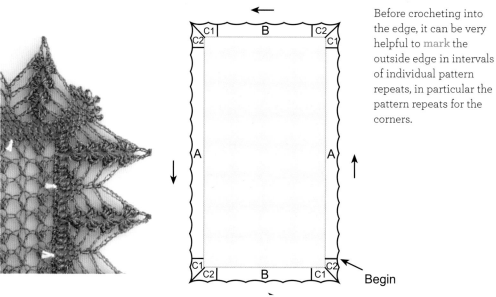

Before crocheting into the edge, it can be very helpful to mark the outside edge in intervals of individual pattern repeats, in particular the pattern repeats for the corners.

CROCHETING BORDER EDGINGS ONTO OUTSIDE EDGES

Border edgings crocheted sideways or borders (> page 160) with a straight edge can be directly joined with the outside edge while being crocheted like facings (sideways crocheted ridged edgings > page 171). Border edgings with a straight edge at the left edge of the border start at the bottom right above the corner (black in the schematic), with the right side of the shawl facing up. For this, join the working yarn and work a beginning chain of as many chains as needed for the width of the edging as base for the border. Onto this foundation chain, work the edging, and join it in every row with the outside edge of the main part.

Border edgings with a straight edge at the right edge of the border start at the bottom left above the corner (blue in the schematic), with the wrong side of the shawl facing up. For this, join the working yarn and work a beginning chain of as many chains as needed for the width of the edging as base for the border, attach the crocheted chain with 1 slip stitch at the outside edge of the main part and then work the edging, and join it in every row with the outside edge of the main part.

Crocheted-on decorative bands don't have special corner solutions. Instead, the band is "gathered" around the corner. Depending on the width of the border, 3 or more pattern repeats of the border are worked over a certain number of stitches or rows at the corner. For this, when crocheting the border to the main part, the hook is usually inserted into the same insertion point 2 times, in the corner stitch 3 times.

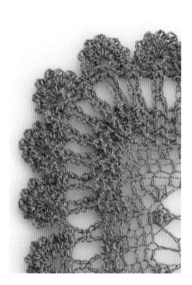

Before crocheting into the edge, it can be very helpful to mark the outside edge in intervals of individual pattern repeats, in particular the pattern repeats for the corners.

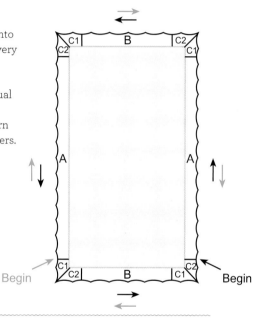

When the border edging has been crocheted onto the main piece on all four sides, BREAK THE WORKING YARN and SEW the beginning edge TOGETHER with the last row.

Beads and Sequins

To add a glamorous touch to crocheted pieces, shimmering beads and sequins can be cleverly crocheted into the fabric. Depending on whether beads of the same color as the base fabric or a contrasting color are used, entirely different effects are created.

SETUP

To prepare for crocheting in beads or sequins, there are two basic methods. Either the entirety of beads or sequins required for the project can be threaded onto the working yarn before beginning work on the crocheted piece, and subsequently gradually crocheted into the fabric, or the beads can be placed directly onto the stitches during crocheting with the help of a fine crochet hook or a thread loop.

THREADING BEADS IN ADVANCE

If the hole in the bead is sufficiently large, the working yarn can just be threaded into a tapestry needle and the beads transferred to the yarn over the needle. For rocailles (Native American beads) and similar small beads, and also for sequins, the hole of which is often not large enough to accommodate a thicker needle, a sewing needle and sewing thread can be used for the purpose.

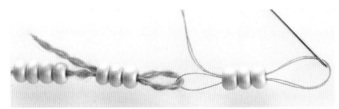

Take up a piece of sewing thread approximately 8 inches (20 cm) long, fold it in half, and thread the loop through the eye of the sewing needle. Pull the working yarn through the loop of the sewing thread and double it up. Now pick up the beads or sequins with the sewing needle, and slide them onto the working yarn over the loop of the sewing thread, where they remain until being crocheted in as required for the pattern. While crocheting, continually push the string of beads back on the working yarn toward the skein.

When beads are threaded onto the working yarn before crocheting, the last bead to have been threaded will be the one to be crocheted first. This is important to remember if beads in different colors or shapes must be crocheted in in a certain order.

X When not quite sure about the number of beads needed for a crocheted piece, it is better to thread **A FEW BEADS MORE**. These can be easily removed later when breaking the working yarn after the piece has been completed. Threading beads as an afterthought is only possible if only a few stitches or rows remain to be worked. In this case, break the working yarn at sufficient length for working the remaining stitches, and thread the missing beads onto the working yarn from its end.

X If crocheting in beads seems too tedious, they can instead be **SEWN ON** afterward, using sewing thread in a color matching that of the working yarn: The beads and sequins are threaded onto the sewing thread and appliqued with more or fewer easy stitches onto the crocheted item.

CROCHETING IN BEADS

The procedure for crocheting in beads is different depending on whether the beads have been threaded previously or are being added during work.

CROCHETING IN PREVIOUSLY THREADED BEADS

With this method, beads can be incorporated in any arrangement, over the whole area or for individual motifs. The beads appear raised on the background fabric and are attached with a single thread.

> If beads and sequins incorporated using this method are supposed to later appear on the right side of the fabric, they must be crocheted in WRONG-SIDE ROWS.

1 In a wrong-side row, work in the main pattern—here, single crochet—up to the spot where the next bead is to be placed. Slide the bead as close as possible toward the last crocheted stitch on the working yarn . . .

2 . . . and work the next single crochet as usual in the next stitch of the previous row. During work, hold the working yarn taut so the bead does not hover too loosely over the surface of the crocheted fabric.

3 The bead has now been secured and is located on the back side (right side) of the fabric.

ADDING BEADS WHILE CROCHETING

In this method, the beads are embedded in the background fabric and are attached with a double strand of yarn. Beads can be added either with a fine crochet hook or with the help of a thread loop.

WITH A CROCHET HOOK

This method is most easily worked with an additional very fine crochet hook that fits through the hole of the bead. The hook end, however, must be large enough to grasp the crochet thread. For rocailles with a diameter of 4 mm (0.16 inches), a steel crochet hook in size 1 to 1.25 mm (US steel hook 12/8 to 9/4) is suitable. For some patterns, for instance if 3 beads need to be crocheted in at once for edge embellishments, an even smaller crochet hook can be of advantage. A longer throat is convenient, too, since multiple beads can fit on it, and "refilling" needs to be done less frequently.

1 Work in pattern up to the spot where the next bead is to be added. Remove the crochet hook from the working loop. First, pick up a bead with the tip of the tiny crochet hook, and then place the working loop onto this crochet hook.

In a **SINGLE CROCHET** stitch pattern, in the next row above the bead, the single crochet is replaced by **A SINGLE CHAIN**. In subsequent rows, the stitch pattern can be continued in the regular manner.

2 Slide the bead from the crochet hook onto the working loop. Place the working loop onto the regular crochet hook again.

3 To make room for the bead in the crocheted fabric, skip 1 stitch in the stitch pattern. After this, continue working as stated in the pattern.

WITH A THREAD LOOP

When a fine crochet hook in a suitable size is not available, the beads can also be incorporated during work with the help of a sewing needle and a loop of sewing thread.

For this, thread a piece of sewing thread held single through the eye of the sewing needle, and then knot both ends. Now push the first bead onto the double-layered thread, and knot the bead to the bottom end of the thread as a stopper. String a small supply of beads.

When the bead needs to be incorporated into the crocheted piece, remove the crochet hook from the working loop, insert the sewing needle through the loop, bring up a bead, and insert the sewing needle back through the bead. Then push the bead over the working yarn onto the working loop. Remove the sewing needle and continue working with the crochet hook.

DECORATING EDGES

Incorporating beads during crocheting is especially well suited for embellishing edges of crocheted items with multiple beads, since in this case the working yarn is doubled in the beads, thus reinforcing the edge embellished with beads. When threading beads before the beginning of work, however, the working yarn goes through the beads only single.

As described above, thread the desired number of beads onto the working loop in the intended spot with the help of a thin crochet hook, pulling the working loop long. After that, continue, working 1 single crochet into the next stitch of the previous row.

CROCHETING IN SEQUINS

For crocheting in sequins, both methods as described for beads can be used. When sequins are threaded onto the project yarn before beginning work, the working yarn ends up going single through the sequins, whereas if they are added during work with the help of a thin crochet hook, it is doubled.

CROCHETING IN PREVIOUSLY THREADED SEQUINS

In this method, the sequins are attached to the surface with a single strand of working yarn.

1 In a wrong-side row, work in main pattern—here, single crochet—up to the spot where the next sequin is to be placed. Slide the sequin as close as possible toward the last crocheted stitch on the working yarn. Then work the next single crochet as usual in the next stitch of the previous row, grasping the working yarn behind the sequin.

2 Continue working single crochet as usual—the sequin will place itself onto the back side (right side) of the fabric. In the next row, work single crochets without sequins, working 1 single crochet each into every stitch of the previous row.

ADDING SEQUINS WHILE CROCHETING

In this method, the sequins are attached to the crocheted piece by a double strand of yarn.

1 In a right-side row, work in pattern up to the spot where the next sequin is to be placed. Remove the crochet hook from the working loop. Pick up a sequin with the tip of the tiny crochet hook (paying attention to the correct direction of the curvature), and then place the working loop onto this crochet hook. Slide the sequin over the needle onto the working loop.

2 Place the working loop onto the regular crochet hook again and work the next stitch into the following stitch of the previous row.

In the next wrong-side row, work 1 single crochet each into every single crochet of the previous row, and skip every sequin with 1 chain, making sure that the working yarn is located in front of work and the sequin in back of work (i.e., on the right side of the fabric).

In the next right-side row, work 1 single crochet each into every single crochet of the previous row and in the chain space of every ch1. After this, the stitch pattern can be continued as usual in single crochet. At the end, all sequins will appear on the right side of the fabric.

! If the sequins are to later appear on the right side of the fabric, remember that they must be crocheted in during WRONG-SIDE ROWS.

✗ As with crocheting in beads, the SEQUIN THREADED LAST will be the first to be integrated into the crocheted fabric. Unlike beads, which in most cases look the same from all sides, for sequins, the shape is also an important factor: When, as here, the concave (inward curved) side of a sequin is to appear on the outside of the fabric, the hook is inserted from the back into the sequin for threading from the back. Make sure to thread all sequins in the SAME DIRECTION.

! Since sequins generally have very SMALL HOLES, a VERY THIN ADDITIONAL CROCHET HOOK must be used; shown in the example is a 0.60 mm (US steel hook 12) crochet hook.

Left-Handed
Crochet

For left-handed crocheters, it can be just as with writing—impossible or difficult to get used to working with your non-dominant hand. Even though right-handed crochet looks easy and straightforward, left-handed crocheters have a hard time working in that way. With a few simple tips, however, crocheting will no longer be a problem for left-handed crocheters.

X Almost all illustrations and photos in crochet books describe right-handed crochet. If placing a **HAND-HELD MIRROR** at the right angle to the right or left next to the photo, the now mirror-inverted image shows the direction for left-handed crochet.

YARN POSITIONING AND CROCHET TECHNIQUE

Movements for left-handed crochet are exactly mirror-inverted to right-handed movements. The result is basically the same, with the difference that all stitches and stitch patterns crocheted left-handed appear in reverse to right-handed ones. Top loops of the stitches in the last row of the crocheted piece are likewise oriented in the reverse direction: the V-shaped loops point to the right.

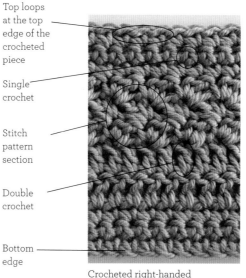

Top loops at the top edge of the crocheted piece

Single crochet

Stitch pattern section

Double crochet

Bottom edge

Crocheted right-handed

Top loops at the top edge of the crocheted piece

Single crochet

Stitch pattern section

Double crochet

Bottom edge

Crocheted left-handed

X It is also possible to scan the images for personal use, mirror them on a vertical plane with the help of **IMAGE PROCESSING SOFTWARE**, and print them out. These photos can then be pasted into a project journal or placed over the original images in the book with a paper clip or with removable adhesive.

Left-handers hold the crochet hook in their left hand. As for right-handers, the crochet hook can be held either from below like a pen or from above like a knife (*Holding the crochet hook > page 29*). Either way works well; the chosen hook hold is a matter of personal preference.

The working yarn is led over the fingers of the right hand so that an even tension of the yarn is attained. At the same time, the right hand holds the crocheted piece during crocheting.

Yarn overs for half double crochets, double or treble crochets or taller stitches as well as for crocheting loops off the hook are placed around the crochet hook from back to front as for right-handed crochet.

FROM RIGHT-HANDED TO LEFT-HANDED CROCHET

All steps of the project (beginning chain, crocheting the loops of a stitch off the hook, turning with turning chains, etc.) are worked the same as for right-handed crochet. Every right-handed pattern can be easily translated into left-handed crochet by considering a few rules.

• Left-handed crocheters always hold the crochet hook in the left hand and work in the opposite direction (i.e., in rows from left to right).
• Direction of work or instructions establishing a direction are translated into the opposite direction. An example: To work a stitch for which, according to instructions, the hook needs to be inserted "3 rows below and going back 3 stitches (3 stitches to the right)," left-handed crocheters have to insert the hook 3 rows below and 3 stitches to the left.
• Crab stitch is worked by left-handed crocheters from right to left.
• Crochet charts always must be read in the opposite order. Right-side rows with the row number to the right of the chart are read and crocheted by left-handed crocheters from left to right. In wrong-side rows, it is the other way around. They have the row number to the left of the chart but are to be read and crocheted from right to left.
• When crocheting in the round, left-handed crocheters work in a clockwise direction (i.e., in the crochet chart, going from left to right).

• For crossing stitches: When 2 stitches are to be crossed for right-handed crocheters to the right, after crossing, the first stitch is located behind the second stitch. When they are crossed to the left, however, after crossing, the first stitch is located in front of the second stitch. Left-handed crocheters work mirror-inverted (i.e., they cross the stitches exactly the other way around). If for instance, instructions state to cross 2 stitches to the left, and then left-handed crocheters work 2 stitches crossed to the right.
• For crocheting cables: For cables that are to be cabled to the right (for right-handers), first, the second group of stitches is worked, and then the first group of cable stitches crocheted; for cables that are to be cabled to the left, it is the other way around. Left-handed crocheters work here, too, exactly opposite (i.e., for a cable that needs to be cabled to the right, the first group of stitches is worked first, and then the second group of stitches is crocheted).

! Translating "left" as "right" and the other way around is only applicable to directions or actions, such as "going from left to right" or "crossing to the right." It does NOT apply TO THE NAMES FOR PARTS OF CROCHETED GARMENTS, such as "left shoulder" or "right front."

Crocheting and Felting

Untreated wool fibers are covered by a layer of scales whose cells overlap each other. Friction and heat can cause individual scales to raise and interlock with each other. On the surface, lint is formed, and finally small knots, both of which can be easily removed again. Suds cause wool fibers to expand considerably. If wool fibers are additionally exposed to heavy mechanical stress, such as friction or agitation in the wash, the scales become so interlocked that they can no longer be disentangled, and a soft, dense felted fabric is created. A similar effect can be achieved by washing and drying with significant changes in temperature or at too-high temperatures.

BEGINNING CROCHETERS can rejoice: The crochet felting technique "forgives" small mistakes and irregularities.

FELTING IN THE WASHING MACHINE

To cause felting, the finished and seamed crocheted pieces are washed twice at 104°F (40°C) in the washing machine with detergent and ten to twelve laundry balls or four massage balls. The crocheted item should be given enough time to dry after the first wash, and it should be checked whether one wash cycle has not already shrunk the stitches to the intended size, because the result, unfortunately, depends not on yarn and hook size alone. It can be seen time and again that every washing machine delivers different results. Determining the individual shrinkage factor, in addition to a gauge swatch, cannot be avoided. The crocheted piece is pulled into the desired shape while still wet, and, if necessary, pinned with blocking pins, and left to dry.

FELTING IN THE CLOTHES DRYER

It is also possible to produce wool felt from loosely crocheted wool yarn fabric with the help of a clothes dryer. For this, briefly hand wash the finished crocheted piece and begin to felt it at a high temperature in the clothes dryer. Do not let the crocheted piece dry completely, but interrupt the drying process again and again to check the size of the piece. When the intended size has been reached, the crocheted piece can be left to air dry, pinned at light tension.

SHRINKAGE FACTOR AND GAUGE

The shrinkage factor indicates by how much a crocheted piece shrinks during felting. Determining it is thus an essential part of swatching for gauge.

To find out the shrinkage factor, crochet a swatch in single crochet at least 8 x 8 inches (20 x 20 cm) large. To be able to experiment a little, it is recommended to crochet three of these testing pieces at once. Beginning and ending tails should be woven in to prevent them from getting tangled during washing.

When felting multiple testing swatches at the same time, they should be additionally marked, for instance, with marking threads in different colors threaded through a corner with the help of a tapestry needle, knotted together, and kept in during felting. Make a note of the color of the marking threads.

X This technique of crochet felting is ideally suited for SLIPPERS, BAGS, AND ACCESSORIES, for which exact size and fit are not important. For garments, this method is less advisable.

1 Before felting, the stitch count and row count of every swatch in single crochet per 4 inches (10 cm) are counted and written down together with the color of the marking thread. Additionally, (a) the complete width and (b) the complete height of each testing swatch are measured and recorded.

2 Felt all testing swatches either in the washing machine or in the clothes dryer. After having completely dried, note (c) the complete width and (d) the complete height for each felted swatch. Make sure to assign each set of measurements to the appropriate swatch with the help of the color markings.

The widthwise shrinkage factor in stitches is calculated from:
total width before felting (a) ÷ total width after felting (c).

The heightwise shrinkage factor in rows is calculated from:
total height before felting (b) ÷ total height after felting (d).

Since the crocheted piece shrinks during felting, the shrinkage factor is always larger than 1. Often, it is approximately 1.25 to 1.35. This means that the crocheted piece measures only approximately 75% to 80% of the original size after felting. In this state, individual stitches in the felted fabric are no longer recognizable, but the texture of the felt is already very dense.

The schematic of the planned felted item is multiplied in width by the widthwise shrinkage factor in stitches, and in height by the heightwise shrinkage factor in rows.

A garment pattern enlarged in this manner is the basis for grading the crochet pattern, which is then calculated using the pre-felting gauge.

Crocheting with Non-Traditional Materials

The range of beautiful and unusual commercially available yarns is continuously growing. But apart from these regular and familiar yarns, there are a number of non-traditional materials with which interesting results can be achieved in crochet. Whether packing twine, raffia, wire, fabric or plastic strips—every flexible material that can be formed into stitches with the help of a crochet hook is suitable. Experimenting is worth it, because it is fun and every crocheted piece is unique.

THE MATERIALS

Non-traditional materials should usually be worked up in single crochet, especially when trying out a new material for the first time. The look of the material itself is the effect, stitch patterns could even be distracting.

However, you should experiment a little and only decide in the second step which stitch pattern can be used effectively and satisfactorily with the respective material. Raffia or plastic strips, for instance, are well suited for filet crochet (> page 236), packing twine lends itself to mesh patterns with Solomon's knot (> page 55).

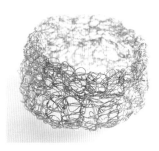

X Many alternative materials are carried by SPECIALIZED CRAFT STORES, but you can also often find what you are looking for in HOME IMPROVEMENT STORES or in the HOUSEWARES DEPARTMENT. Additionally, cast-off clothing can be creatively recycled.

! "Yarn" can be sourced from FABRIC, LEATHER, OR PLASTIC BAGS you cut into STRIPS yourself. You can also purchase READY-TO-USE MATERIAL, such as precut strips from leftover textile manufacturing material wound into skeins or onto cones, and start crocheting right away.

FINE RAFFIA

Fine raffia is a very fine "thin-skinned" but very sturdy tape made of viscose (rayon), and can be matte or glossy. It is very flexible and easy to crochet with and works well for purses or market bags.

PAPER YARN

This material is produced either in the shape of ribbons of even width or twisted into a cord. Originally, these ribbons were intended for wrapping gifts. The cord type is rather unyielding during crochet and produces a transparent, open stitch pattern when worked with a large crochet hook. Paper yarn is well suited for decorative home decor accessories.

PACKING TWINE AND STRING

Packing twine and string are in most cases made of natural fibers but are also produced in synthetic fibers, and are available in different yarn weights and colors. Since packing twine has hardly any elasticity, it is rather recalcitrant when crocheting. Thick packing twine should be crocheted up relatively loosely. It is especially useful for ball nets or market bags, but could also be used for hammocks, flowerpot hangers, baskets, or other containers.

FABRIC

Cotton fabrics are offered in a wide range of colors and a variety of prints, mostly for quilting. From these fabrics, you can cut strips yourself. For this, either cut individual strips and knot them together in a decorative way or cut a continuous strip (> page 316). Cut the strips freehand or use a ruler. For the first experiment, 0.8 inch (2 cm) wide strips are suitable, which are worked with a crochet hook in size 10.0 mm (US N/P-15). Worked in single crochet, a dense fabric is formed. The fabric strips can be used in many ways, working especially well for home decor items such as rugs and mats, pillows, baskets, containers, and so forth.

JERSEY/KNIT FABRIC

You can make strips of knit fabric yourself from used t-shirts or from newly purchased yardage. Cut strips of 2 to 2.4 inches (5 to 6 cm) width horizontally, so that the cut edges later roll inward by themselves when the strip is stretched lengthwise. Crochet the resulting "yarn" with a 20.0 mm (US S) crochet hook. Nowadays, many suppliers also offer ready-cut strips from jersey remnants of the textile industry, which are already wound into ready-to use skeins or cones. Strips of knit fabric are used to crochet seat cushions, seating pads for garden furniture, rugs and mats, and so forth.

LEATHER

Cut 0.2 to 0.4 inch (5 to 10 mm) wide strips from leather. The softer the leather (nappa or suede), the easier it is to crochet with it. Very soft leather should be cut in not too narrow strips, since it could tear otherwise. Beginning and ending tails in joining spots can also be left hanging—this fits into a casual look and matches the natural character of the material—or knotting and crocheting in are equally suitable. Just as with fabric, a continuous strip (> page 316) can also be cut. The strips should not be cut in a straight line, but follow the shape, to minimize waste and the number of joining spots. It is best to work with a bamboo crochet hook, in which the leather yarn slips better than on a plastic crochet hook. Crocheted in large stitches, this is the perfect look for purses and bags.

PLASTIC BAGS

Thin trash bags come in clear, opaque white, blue, green, yellow, orange, and other colors. These are very pliable and can be crocheted up into unique market bags, cosmetic bags, or pouches. Colorful plastic grocery bags can be used too, which can create unexpected color effects. Combine to your heart's content! How to cut the strips is explained on page 316. Strips should be cut at least 1.2 inches (3 cm) wide, preferably even wider. This strip width should be crocheted with a hook size of 12.0 to 15.0 mm (US P-15 to P/Q).

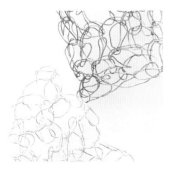

WIRE

With wire, three-dimensionally shaped, malleable structures can be created. For jewelry, jewelry crochet wire should preferably be used, which at 0.3 mm (AWG 28) is very fine. Crocheted up in simple stitches such as single crochet with a thicker crochet hook, size 5.0 mm (US H/8), wire structures with large stitches and amazing effects can be created. If desired, beads (> page 306) can also be incorporated. Medium-size wire is utilized for creating objects of decorative art or bowls, for which a thicker crochet hook should be used.

It is recommended to always prepare a SWATCH FOR EVERY MATERIAL beforehand, since while one material can be very stretchy (such as jersey or knit fabric), others hardly budge (such as wire). The stretch factor should be taken into account for every planned project.

Many of the materials mentioned here can be rather unyielding while being crocheted and are often difficult to slide off the hook. For this reason, always WORK LOOSELY.

PREPARING YOUR OWN MATERIAL

Some materials must be cut into strips and so turned into a "yarn." To avoid having to knot many short strips together, there are special techniques for cutting longer strips.

CUTTING FABRIC STRIPS

Place the fabric double, with the open edges of the two layers at the top, opposite to the closed edge at the fabric fold. Now, starting at the fabric fold (i.e., the bottom edge), begin to cut in a straight line toward the open edge at the desired strip width. End the incision at "strip width minus 0.2 to 0.6 inch (0.5 cm to 1.5 cm)" before the edge—for strips 1.6 inches (4 cm) wide, for instance, leave 1.2 inches (3 cm) before the edge uncut.

 **ROTARY CUTTER, RULER, AND CUTTING MAT** are proven tools to cut strips without great time investment. Strips can also be cut by hand and just by eye.

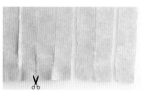

When all incisions have been made, unfold the fabric and place it in one layer. To create a continuous strip, the incisions on every other strip now must be continued to the edge. For this, cut on one edge of the fabric between the 1st and the 2nd strip, and then between the 3rd and the 4th strip, between the 5th and the 6th strip, and so forth.

At the other edge of the fabric, the incisions must be worked staggered (i.e., the first cut between the 2nd and the 3rd strip, the second between the 4th and the 5th strip, etc.).

These transitions are later folded when crocheting, or else the corners are wrapped around the strip, depending on the material. You can also just disregard them and later crochet over these spots without any preliminary work.

CUTTING PLASTIC BAGS OR T-SHIRTS

For **T-SHIRTS, CUT OFF THE** sleeves and neckline below the armpits.

Place the plastic bag spread out onto a blocking mat. Cut off the drawstring channel or handles and the closed bottom seam. This has yielded a tube shape. The folds (for instance, heat-sealed seams) are located at the top and bottom. Flip the bottom fold upward, so that it is spaced 1.6 to 2 inches (4 to 5 cm) from the upper fold edge. Fold the bottom edge two times more up to this point. Now cut the strips at a width of 1.2 inches (3 cm). Make the incisions over the multiple-layer sections only (i.e., end shortly after the point where all folds meet).

Spread out the doubled-up material so that the fold edge or the seam lies flat in the middle. Multiple interconnected strips have been created, each of them in its own closed round.

For a continuous strip, the still-joined strips must be cut in spiral rounds. This allows for crocheting with a "single strand" strip. For the beginning of the strip, cut diagonally, beginning at the seam or the "original" fold line, from bottom right to top left toward the incision between the 1st and the 2nd strip. Continue, always cutting diagonally to the left from the next incision below the seam or the "original" fold line to the next incision above the seam or fold line. Staggering is important so that the strips are later connected. Make further cuts from/to the end point parallel to the first one. Finally, wind the strip into a ball.

Strips of fabric or plastic bags can be **KNOTTED TOGETHER** with ends left sticking out, which creates an interesting **ADDITIONAL EFFECT** on the surface of the crocheted fabric.

Granny Squares

These iconic crochet squares are by no means an invention of the "flower children" of the 1970s, even though they enjoyed widespread popularity at the time. The first granny square was published in 1897 in the English magazine *Weldon's Practical Needlework*. Nevertheless, these crochet classics are not a bit dusty, but are again experiencing a boom in popularity!

THE STAR AMONG ALL MOTIFS

In principle, granny squares are nothing more than motifs worked in the round from the center out (> page 116). Often, therefore, the term "granny squares" is now also used across the board for many types of other motifs worked in this manner. Since the crocheted squares, lovingly called "grannies" by die-hard fans, have meanwhile evolved from squares to numerous other shapes such as circles or hexagons, the distinctions are indeed fluid.

A unique special feature of "genuine" granny squares is their motley mix of colors. In one single motif, a profusion of different colors can often be found, which are in most cases changed again after every, or almost every, round. This accounts for the colorful "hippie" look often associated with granny squares. Depending on the type and combination of the yarns used, calmer and more refined effects can also be achieved. To work the frequently occurring color changes, two of the methods described in this book are especially well suited: the color change with height-adjustment chains (> page 76) and the color change with standing stitches (> page 77).

Most often, individual motifs are combined into a cheerful, colorful, crocheted patchwork, such as in the form of blankets or pillows. For this purpose, all methods described for joining motifs can be used (> page 146). Depending on desired appearance, the join is worked either in the same color as the base fabric or in bright contrasting colors.

PLAYING WITH COLORS

The imagination has no limits when combining colors for granny square projects. Depending on whether flashy bright colors with plenty of contrast, muted colors, or shades of the same color are chosen, the same stitch pattern can create entirely different effects. It looks particularly striking when the colors progress from light to dark from the center out. The color of the join also contributes to the appearance of the completed project.

Once a general color selection has been made, it still must be decided whether all colors are to be used in every granny square, and whether always in the same order or in varying sequences. The color sequence could, for instance, be shifted by 1 round in every granny square, so that the finished project appears uniform in color, but still with variety:

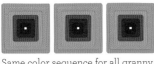

Same color sequence for all granny squares, all colors in every motif

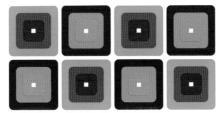

Only three colors in every granny square

All colors in every motif, color sequence shifted

When granny squares are worked separately and only later joined into a larger item, they are an excellent PROJECT for ON THE ROAD. They are also ideally suited for using up ODDS AND ENDS of YARN.

To avoid having to WEAVE IN TOO MANY ENDS from those frequent color changes, the ending tail of the old color and the beginning tail of the new one are CROCHETED IN (> page 154) within the first 6 to 9 stitches of the new round, just placing them along the working edge of the motif while crocheting the new stitches.

When a granny square contains ONLY TWO COLORS that alternate in every round, the strands can also just be carried on the wrong side as FLOATS or CROCHETED INTO the height-adjustment chains (> page 212).

If the granny squares are not to be sewn together in a random ARRANGE-MENT later, sketch the planned project, preferably before starting work, and write down how MANY SQUARES in each color combination will be needed.

With this method of color allocation, the available **YARN AMOUNT** can also be distributed best throughout all granny squares of a project since the rounds in the center of the granny square use up less yarn than the outer rounds.

When turning to the internet for inspiration, appropriate **SEARCH WORDS** are combinations such as "granny square generator" or "random granny squares," "granny squares in colors," and so forth.

Using the same instructions, **ONE-COL-ORED GRANNY SQUARES** can also be crocheted. For this, after Rounds 2 and 4, do not pull the working yarn through but move to the next gap with 1 slip stitch.

This granny square can be **ENLARGED** as desired in the same fashion. In every new round, one **MORE DC3-CLUSTER** is worked per side.

Depending on the yarn used and whether crocheting rather tightly or more loosely, between the double crochet-groups, either one or (as seen here) no chain can be worked, and at the corners, **2 OR 3 CHAINS**.

	Round 1	Round 2	Round 3	Round 4	Round 5	Round 6
1st granny square	color A	color B	color C	color D	color E	color F
2nd granny square	color B	color C	color D	color E	color F	color A
3rd granny square	color C	color D	color E	color F	color A	color B
4th granny square	color D	color E	color F	color A	color B	color C
5th granny square	color E	color F	color A	color B	color C	color D
6th granny square	color F	color A	color B	color C	color D	color E

Specific color combinations can also be used for a square, or colors mixed in a motley and random arrangement. Specialized websites generate random color sequences from colors entered, some of them even producing a schematic for the planned project. You can also draw your planned granny squares by hand and color the respective rounds with colored pencils to get an idea of the completed square.

CLASSIC GRANNY SQUARE

This motif is the most classic of all granny squares. It consists of only double-crochet clusters and chain arcs and is worked from the center out in rounds. The number of rounds can vary. In most cases, it will be between 1 and 10, but in principle the chart can be continued indefinitely, creating a whole blanket consisting of just a single square.

GRANNY SQUARE WITH HEIGHT-ADJUSTMENT CHAINS
Traditionally, this granny square is worked with height-adjustment chains (> page 70).

Instructions
Begin with an adjustable magic ring (> page 68) in the center of the motif, and work in rounds. Begin every rnd with ch3 for height adjustment replacing the first dc, and join into the round with 1 sl-st. Work the color change as described on page 76.
Round 1: In color A, ch3 for height adjustment, dc2, * ch2, dc3 into the ring, rep from * 2 times more, ch2. Join into the round with 1 sl-st into the 3rd height-adjustment chain.
Round 2: In color B, ch3 for height adjustment, in the 3 following corners, work [dc3, ch2, dc3] each, [dc3, ch2, dc2] in the last corner. Join into the round with 1 sl-st into the 3rd height-adjust-ment chain, break the working yarn, and pull it through the working loop.
Round 3: In color C, join new working yarn in any gap between the dc3-clusters of the previous rnd, ch3 for height adjustment and dc2 in the same gap, * [dc3, ch2, dc3] in the following corner, dc3 in the following gap, rep from * 2

times more, [dc3, ch2, dc3] in the following corner. Join into the round with 1 sl-st into the 3rd height-adjustment chain.
Round 4: In color A, ch3 for height adjustment, dc3 in the following gap between the dc3-clusters

of the previous rnd, * [dc3, ch2, dc3] in the following corner, [dc3 in the following gap] 2 times, rep from * 2 times more, [dc3, ch2, dc3] in the following corner, dc2 in the following gap. Join into the round with 1 sl-st into the 3rd height-adjustment chain, pull the working yarn through the working loop to secure.

Round 5: In color B, join new working yarn in any gap between the dc3-clusters of the previous rnd, ch3 for height adjustment and dc2 in the same gap, dc3 in the next gap, * [dc3, ch2, dc3] in the following corner, [dc3 in the following gap] 3 times, rep from * 2 times more, [dc3, ch2, dc3] in

the following corner, dc3 in the following gap. Join into the round with 1 sl-st into the 3rd height-adjustment chain.

Round 6: In color C, work 3 height-adjustment chains, [dc3 in the next gap between the dc3-clusters of the previous rnd] 2 times, * [dc3, ch2, dc3] in the following corner, [dc3 in the next gap] 4 times, rep from * 2 times more, [dc3, ch2, dc3] in the following corner, dc3 in the following gap, dc2 in the next gap. Join into the round with 1 sl-st into the 3rd height-adjustment chain.

GRANNY SQUARE WITH STANDING STITCHES

Standing stitches are a good alternative to the traditional option of changing colors with height-adjustment chains. The standing stitches blend in well with the surrounding fabric. The new round can be started in any of the gaps. Here, the corners have been chosen.

Instructions

Begin with an adjustable magic ring (> page 68) in the center of the motif, and work in rounds. During work, begin every rnd with a standing dc (> page 77), and join with 1 sl-st into the top of the beginning dc. After every round worked, break the working yarn, and pull it through the working loop.

Round 1: Work [ch3 for height adjustment, dc2] into the ring, ch2, * dc3 and ch2 into the ring, rep from * 2 times more. Join into the round with 1 sl-st into the 3rd height-adjustment chain.

Round 2: * Work [dc3, ch2, dc3] into the corner. Repeat from * 3 times more.

Round 3: * Work [dc3, ch2, dc3] into the corner, dc3 in the next gap between the dc3-clusters of the previous rnd, repeat from * 3 times more.

Rounds 4–6: Work as rnd 3, but with every new round worked, 1 more dc cluster is added between the corners.

Different stitch types such as **RAISED STITCHES** or **LACE PATTERNS** can create entirely novel effects for granny squares. An abundance of **BOOKS AND DICTIONARIES** on the topic offer an endless variety of design ideas.

A few granny squares can also be found in the **STITCH PATTERN COLLECTION** beginning on page 329.

ABBREVIATIONS can be found on page 344.

The **STITCH KEY** for the crochet symbols can be found on pages 340–343.

Stitch Patterns

In crochet, the possibilities for patterns are nearly endless. This colorful mix of textures, lace, Tunisian stitch patterns, granny squares and colorwork patterns contains the perfect choice for every project!

Textured Patterns

Snowflake Pattern

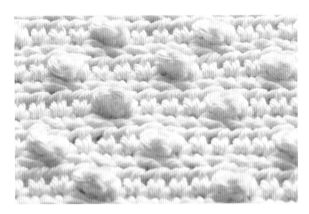

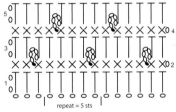

Stitch count: a multiple of 5 + 4 sts extra + 2 height-adjustment chains.

Work in rows according to the crochet chart, beginning with a WS row. In every row, first work the sts before the marked pattern repeat once, repeat the marked pattern repeat continuously, and end with the sts after the marked pattern repeat. Work Rows 1–5 once, and then repeat Rows 2–5 continuously.

Textured Checkerboard Pattern

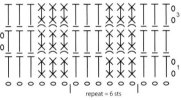

Stitch count: a multiple of 6 + 3 sts extra + 2 height-adjustment chains.

Work in rows according to the crochet chart. In every row, first work the sts before the marked pattern repeat once, repeat the marked pattern repeat continuously, and end with the sts after the marked pattern repeat. Work Rows 1–13 once, and then repeat rows 2 and 3 continuously.

Raised Diamond Pattern

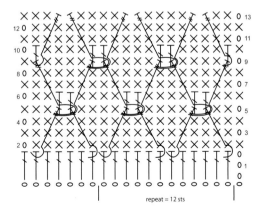

Stitch count: a multiple of 12 + 8 sts extra + ch3 for height adjustment.

Work in rows according to the crochet chart in raised treble crochet. In every row, first work the sts before the marked pattern repeat once, repeat the marked pattern repeat continuously, and end with the sts after the marked pattern repeat. Work Rows 1–13 once, and then repeat Rows 6–13 continuously.

Brick Pattern

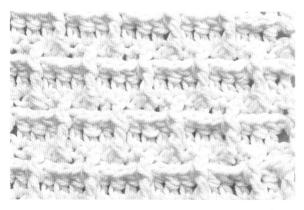

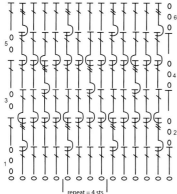

repeat = 4 sts

Stitch count: a multiple of 4 + 3 sts extra + ch3 for height adjustment.
Work in rows according to the crochet chart, beginning with a WS row. In every row, first work the sts before the marked pattern repeat once, repeat the marked pattern repeat continuously, and end with the sts after the marked pattern repeat. Work Rows 1–6 once, and then repeat Rows 3–6 continuously.

Tulip Pattern

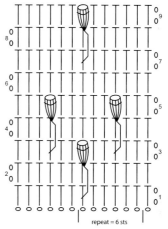

repeat = 6 sts

Stitch count: a multiple of 6 + 1 st extra + 2 height-adjustment chains.
Work in rows according to the crochet chart. In every row, first work the sts before the marked pattern repeat once, repeat the marked pattern repeat continuously, and end with the sts after the marked pattern repeat. Work Rows 1–9 once, and then repeat Rows 4–9 continuously.

Stitch Key

o = 1 chain

✗ = 1 single crochet

⊤ = 1 half double crochet

⊤ = 1 half double crochet through the back loop of the stitch only

† = 1 double crochet

= 1 bobble of 5 chains and 1 slip stitch

✗ = 1 elongated single crochet

✗ = 1 elongated single crochet through the back loop of the stitch only

ʃ = 1 front post double crochet

ʃ = 1 back post double crochet

ʃ = 1 front post treble crochet

 = 1 popcorn worked below

ABBREVIATIONS can be found on page 344.

Rippled Waves

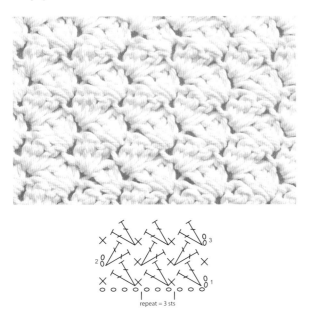

repeat = 3 sts

Stitch count: a multiple of 3 + 1 st extra + 2 height-adjustment chains.
Work in rows according to the crochet chart. In every row, first work the sts before the marked pattern repeat once, repeat the marked pattern repeat continuously, and end with the sts after the marked pattern repeat. Work Rows 1–13 once, and then repeat Rows 2 and 3 continuously.

Side Saddle Shell Stitch

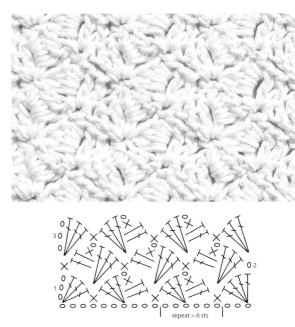

repeat = 6 sts

Stitch count: a multiple of 6 + 1 st extra + ch3 for height adjustment.
Work in rows according to the crochet chart, beginning with a WS row. In every row, first work the sts before the marked pattern repeat once, repeat the marked pattern repeat continuously, and end with the sts after the marked pattern repeat. Work Rows 1–3 once, and then repeat Rows 2 and 3 continuously.

Raised Bobbles on the Bias

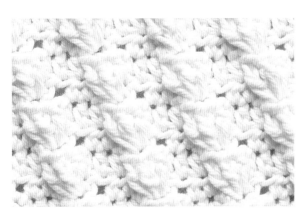

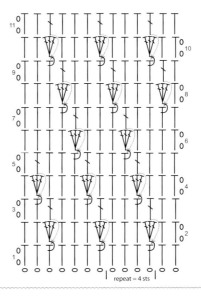

repeat = 4 sts

Stitch count: a multiple of 4 + 1 st extra + 2 height-adjustment chains.
Work in rows according to the crochet chart, beginning with a WS row. In every row, first work the sts before the marked pattern repeat once, repeat the marked pattern repeat continuously, and end with the sts after the marked pattern repeat. Work Rows 1–11 once, and then repeat Rows 3–11 continuously.

Lace Patterns

Trellis Pattern

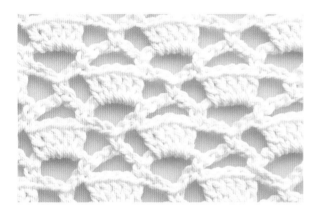

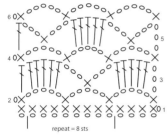

repeat = 8 sts

Stitch count: a multiple of 8 + 5 sts extra + ch1 for height adjustment.

Work in rows according to the crochet chart. In every row, first work the sts before the marked pattern repeat once, repeat the marked pattern repeat continuously, and end with the sts after the marked pattern repeat. Work Rows 1–6 once, and then repeat Rows 3–6 continuously.

Ear Shell Pattern

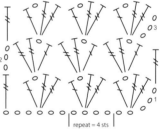

repeat = 4 sts

Stitch count: a multiple of 4 + ch3 for height adjustment. Work in rows according to the crochet chart. In every row, first work the sts before the marked pattern repeat once, repeat the marked pattern repeat continuously, and end with the sts after the marked pattern repeat. Work Rows 1–13 once, and then repeat Rows 2 and 3 continuously.

Stitch Key

o = 1 chain

✕ = 1 single crochet

T = 1 half double crochet

⊤ = 1 double crochet

⊬ = 1 treble crochet

= 3 front post double crochets one after another into the same stitch

ABBREVIATIONS can be found on page 344.

! If symbols converge AT THE BOTTOM, the stitches are worked INTO THE SAME INSERTION POINT.

Zigzag Ladders

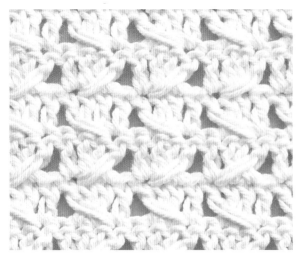

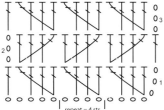

repeat = 4 sts

Stitch count: a multiple of 4 + 1 st extra + ch3 for height adjustment.

Work in rows according to the crochet chart. In every row, first work the sts before the marked pattern repeat once, repeat the marked pattern repeat continuously, and end with the sts after the marked pattern repeat. Work Rows 1–3 once, and then repeat Rows 2 and 3 continuously.

Crossbill Pattern

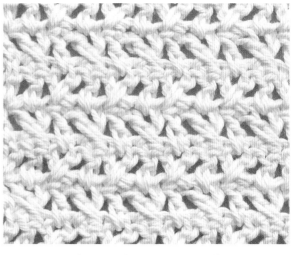

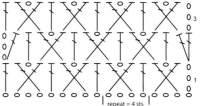

repeat = 4 sts

Stitch count: a multiple of 4 + 1 st extra + ch3 for height adjustment.

Work in rows according to the crochet chart. In every row, first work the sts before the marked pattern repeat once, repeat the marked pattern repeat continuously, and end with the sts after the marked pattern repeat. Work Rows 1–3 once, and then repeat Rows 2 and 3 continuously.

Pyramid Pattern

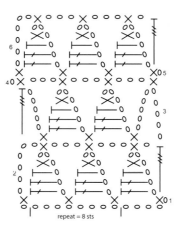

repeat = 8 sts

Stitch count: a multiple of 8 + 5 sts extra + ch1 for height adjustment.

Work in rows according to the crochet chart. In every row, first work the sts before the marked pattern repeat once, repeat the marked pattern repeat continuously, and end with the sts after the marked pattern repeat. Work Rows 1–6 once, and then repeat Rows 3–6 continuously.

Small Pineapple Pattern

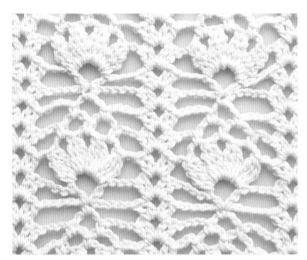

Stitch count a multiple of 14 + 1 st extra + ch3 for height adjustment.
Work in rows according to the crochet chart. In every row, first work the sts before the marked pattern repeat once, repeat the marked pattern repeat continuously, and end with the sts after the marked pattern repeat. Work Rows 1–11 once, and then repeat Rows 7–11 continuously.

repeat = 14 sts

Wavy Block Strips

Stitch count: a multiple of 6 + 3 sts extra + ch1 for height adjustment.
Work in rows according to the crochet chart. In every row, first work the sts before the marked pattern repeat once, repeat the marked pattern repeat continuously, and end with the sts after the marked pattern repeat. Work Rows 1–6 once, and then repeat Rows 3–6 continuously.

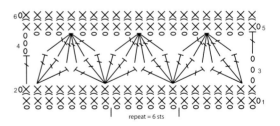

repeat = 6 sts

Stitch Key

o = 1 chain

• = 1 slip stitch

✕ = 1 single crochet

⤬ = 1 single crochet through the back loop of the stitch only

T = 1 half double crochet

† = 1 double crochet

 = 1 double treble crochet

 = 2 crossed double crochets with 1 chain in-between

 = 1 bobble of 3 double crochets

 ABBREVIATIONS can be found on page 344.

❗ If symbols converge **AT THE TOP**, the stitches are crocheted off the hook together. If symbols converge **AT THE BOTTOM**, the stitches are worked **INTO THE SAME IN-SERTION POINT.**

Lacy Bobbles

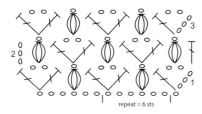

repeat = 6 sts

Stitch count: a multiple of 6 + 1 st extra + ch3 for height adjustment.
Work in rows according to the crochet chart. In every row, first work the sts before the marked pattern repeat once, repeat the marked pattern repeat continuously, and end with the sts after the marked pattern repeat. Work Rows 1–3 once, and then repeat Rows 2 and 3 continuously.

Peacock Tails

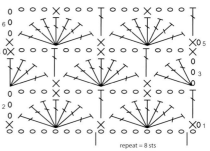

repeat = 8 sts

Stitch count: a multiple of 8 + 1 st extra + ch1 for height adjustment.
Work in rows according to the crochet chart. In every row, first work the sts before the marked pattern repeat once, repeat the marked pattern repeat continuously, and end with the sts after the marked pattern repeat. Work Rows 1–6 once, and then repeat Rows 3–6 continuously.

Chevrons with Bobbles

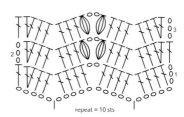

repeat = 10 sts

Stitch count: a multiple of 10 + ch3 for height adjustment.
Work in rows according to the crochet chart. In every row, first work the sts before the marked pattern repeat once, repeat the marked pattern repeat continuously, and end with the sts after the marked pattern repeat. Work Rows 1–3 once, and then repeat Rows 2 and 3 continuously.

Granny Squares

Popcorn Flower

Work in rounds according to the crochet chart. Work Rnds 1–4 once, changing colors after Rnds 1 and 2, and working Rnds 3 and 4 in the same color.

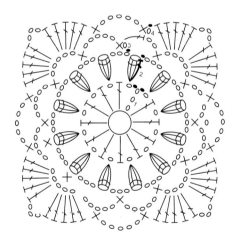

Star with Picots

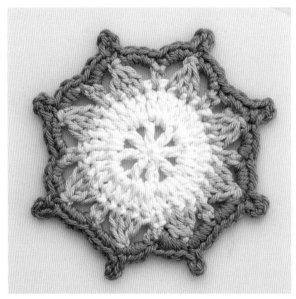

Work in rounds according to the crochet chart. Work Rnds 1–4 once, working Rnds 1 and 2 in the same color, and changing colors before Rnds 3 and 4.

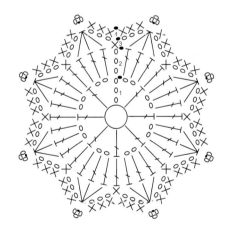

Stitch Key

- o = 1 chain
- • = 1 slip stitch
- ✕ = 1 single crochet
- ⊤ = 1 half double crochet
- ⊤ = 1 double crochet

- ⊤ = 1 standing stitch
- = 1 popcorn of 4 double crochets
- = 1 bobble of 4 half double crochets

- = 1 bobble of 4 half double crochets with 1 chain
- ◯ = 1 magic circle/adjustable magic ring
- = 1 picot of 3 chains and 1 slip stitch back into the first chain

 ABBREVIATIONS can be found on page 344.

! If symbols converge AT THE TOP, the stitches are crocheted off the hook together. If symbols converge AT THE BOTTOM, the stitches are worked INTO THE SAME INSERTION POINT.

Hexagon

Work in rounds according to the crochet chart. Work Rnds 1–5 once, changing colors after Rnds 1, 2, and 3, and working Rnds 4 and 5 in the same color.

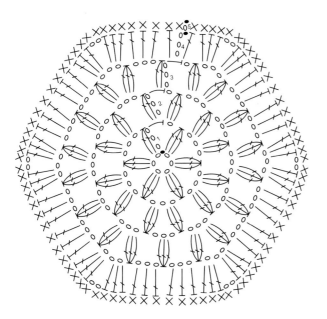

Square with Diagonals

Work in rounds according to the crochet chart. Work Rnds 1–4 once.

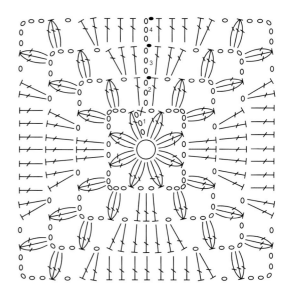

African Flower

Work in rounds according to the crochet chart. Work Rnds 1–5 once, changing colors after Rnd 1, working Rnds 2 and 3 in the same color, and changing colors again before Rnds 4 and 5.

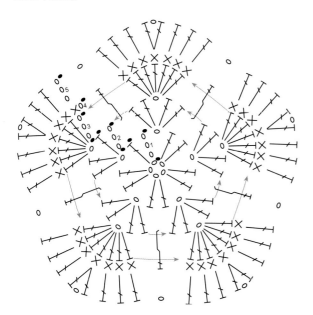

Blossom in a Circle

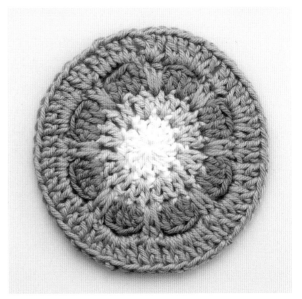

Work in rounds according to the crochet chart. Work Rnds 1–5 once, changing colors after Rnds 1, 2, and 3, and working Rnds 4 and 5 in the same color.

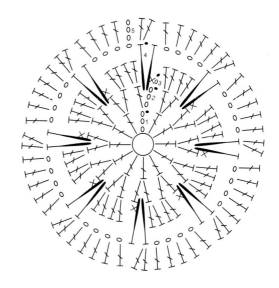

Stitch Key

o = 1 chain

• = 1 slip stitch

✕ = 1 single crochet

┬ = 1 half double crochet

┼ = 1 double crochet

▌ = 1 half double crochet worked below

╽ = 1 double crochet worked below

○ = 1 magic circle/ adjustable magic ring

 = 3 double crochets crocheted together

 = 3 double crochets crocheted together. The first stitch is replaced by 3 chains.

 = 1 double crochet, 1 chain, 1 double crochet into the same stitch

••• ABBREVIATIONS can be found on page 344.

！ If symbols converge AT THE TOP, the stitches are crocheted off the hook together. If symbols converge AT THE BOTTOM, the stitches are worked INTO THE SAME INSERTION POINT.

Four-petal Blossom

Work in rounds according to the crochet chart. Work Rnds 1–4 once, working Rnds 1–3 in the same color, and changing color before Rnd 4.

Flower in a Square

Work in rounds according to the crochet chart. Work Rnds 1–4 once, working Rnds 1 and 2 in the same color, and Rnds 3 and 4 in another color.

Stitch Key

- ○ = 1 chain
- ● = 1 slip stitch
- ✕ = 1 single crochet
- ⊥ = 1 double crochet
- = 1 double crochet worked below

- = 1 standing stitch worked below
- ◯ = 1 magic circle/adjustable magic ring
- = 3 double crochets crocheted together
- = 3 double crochets crocheted together. The first stitch is replaced by 3 chains.

••• **ABBREVIATIONS** can be found on page 344.

! If symbols converge **AT THE TOP**, the stitches are crocheted off the hook together. If symbols converge **AT THE BOTTOM**, the stitches are worked **INTO THE SAME INSERTION POINT**.

Tunisian Patterns

Basket Weave Pattern

Stitch count: a multiple of 8 + 2.
Forward pass 1: Pick up 1 st from every ch of the foundation chain, beginning in the 2nd chain from the hook.
Return pass 1: 1 selv st, crochet off remaining sts in pairs.
Forward pass 2: 1 selv st, * 4 Tunisian knit sts (> page 230), 4 Tunisian purl sts (> page 231), repeat from * continuously, 1 selv st.
Return pass 2: 1 selv st, crochet off remaining sts in pairs.
Rows 3–5: Work as Row 2 forward and return passes.
Forward pass 6: 1 selv st, * 4 Tunisian purl sts, 4 Tunisian knit sts, repeat from * continuously, 1 selv st.
Return pass 6: 1 selv st, crochet off remaining sts in pairs.
Rows 7–9: Work as Row 6 forward and return passes.
Repeat Rows 2–9 continuously.

! For all Tunisian stitch patterns, if not otherwise stated, work the **EDGE STITCHES** as follows: During the **FORWARD PASS**, for the right edge stitch at the beginning of the row, don't pick up a stitch from the first loop, for the left edge stitch at the end of the row, insert the hook under 2 strands. During the **RETURN PASS**, crochet off the left edge stitch individually, the right edge stitch as all other stitches in pairs.

Shell Pattern

Stitch count: a multiple of 4 + 2.
Forward pass 1: Pick up 1 st from every ch of the foundation chain, beginning in the 2nd chain from the hook.
Return pass 1: 1 selv st, crochet off remaining sts in pairs.
Forward pass 1: 1 selv st, pick up 1 st each from every vertical loop, 1 selv st.
Return pass 2: 1 selv st, ch2, * make 1 yo and crochet 5 sts together, ch4, repeat from * continuously, ending with "ch2 and 1 selv st" (crocheting off the last 2 sts together as a pair).
Repeat the Row 2 forward and return passes continuously.

Twisted-stitch Pattern

Stitch count: a multiple of 2 + 2.
Forward pass 1: Pick up 1 st from every ch of the foundation chain, beginning in the 2nd chain from the hook.
Return pass 1: 1 selv st, crochet off remaining sts in pairs.
Forward pass 2: 1 selv st, * insert the hook from right to left under the next vertical loop and pick up 1 st, pull the next vertical loop upward and tilt it to the right, and then insert the hook from left to right and pick up 1 st, repeat from * continuously, 1 selv st.
Return pass 2: 1 selv st, crochet off remaining sts in pairs.
Repeat Rows 1 and 2 (forward and return passes) continuously.

Colorwork Patterns

Woven Pattern

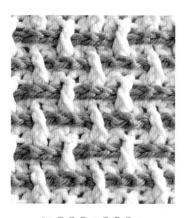

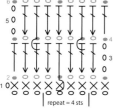

repeat = 4 sts

Stitch count: a multiple of 4 + 1 st extra + ch1 for height adjustment. Work in rows according to the crochet chart, beginning with a WS row. In every row, first work the sts before the marked pattern repeat once, repeat the marked pattern repeat continuously, and end with the sts after the marked pattern repeat. Work Rows 1–6 once, and then repeat Rows 3–6 continuously. During work, alternate working 2 WS rows and 2 RS rows, changing color in every row. At the end of Row 1, secure the working loop. Then, for the color change at the end of Row 2, pull the working loop from Row 1 through the last working loop from Row 2. Crochet in the end from Row 2 at the edge within the height-adjustment chains of Row 3 (> page 213). Continue changing colors this way and carry the unused colors.

Spike Stripes

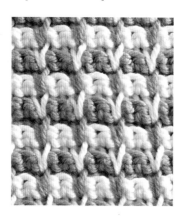

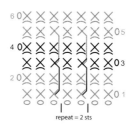

repeat = 2 sts

Stitch count: a multiple of 2 + 1 st extra + ch1 for height adjustment. Work in rows according to the crochet chart. In every row, first work the sts before the marked pattern repeat once, repeat the marked pattern repeat continuously, and end with the sts after the marked pattern repeat. Work Rows 1–6 once, and then repeat Rows 3–6 continuously, changing colors as shown in the chart.

Zigzag Pattern

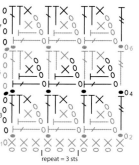

repeat = 3 sts

Stitch count: a multiple of 3 + 1 st extra + ch1 for height adjustment. Work in rows according to the crochet chart, beginning with a WS row. In every row, first work the sts before the marked pattern repeat once, repeat the marked pattern repeat continuously, and end with the sts after the marked pattern repeat. Work Rows 1–7 once, and then repeat Rows 4–7 continuously, changing colors as shown in the chart.

Windblown Pennants

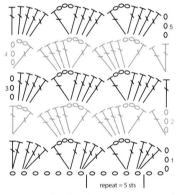

repeat = 5 sts

Stitch count: a multiple of 5 + 4 sts extra + ch3 for height adjustment.

Work in rows according to the crochet chart. In every row, first work the sts before the marked pattern repeat once, repeat the marked pattern repeat continuously, and end with the sts after the marked pattern repeat. Work Rows 1–5 once, and then repeat Rows 2–5 continuously, always working "2 RS rows, 2 WS rows" after one another, and changing colors after every row.

Catherine's Wheel Pattern

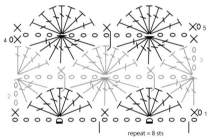

repeat = 8 sts

Stitch count: a multiple of 8 + 1 st extra + ch1 for height adjustment.

Work in rows according to the crochet chart. Work a foundation chain with small picots. For this, for the first time after the first 4 chains, and then always after every 7th chain, make a picot of ch4 and sc1 back into the 4th chain from the hook. While crocheting Row 1, turn the beginning chain with the back of the chain facing, and work the groups of dc into the picots. In every row, first work the sts before the marked pattern repeat once, repeat the marked pattern repeat continuously, and end with the sts after the marked pattern repeat. Work Rows 1–5 once, and then repeat Rows 2–5 continuously, changing colors as shown in the chart.

Stitch Key

o = 1 chain

• = 1 slip stitch

✕ = 1 single crochet

⤬ = 1 single crochet through the back loop of the stitch only

✕ = 1 single crochet worked below

⊤ = 1 half double crochet

⊤ = 1 double crochet

⨏ = 1 treble crochet

⊺ = 1 front post double crochet

⊥ = 1 back post double crochet

⊤↓ = 1 double crochet, worked in right-side rows behind the chain of the previous row, in wrong-side rows in front of the chain of the previous row

⌂ = 1 beginning picot of 4 chains and 1 single crochet back into the first chain

••• ABBREVIATIONS can be found on page 344.

! If symbols converge AT THE TOP, the stitches are crocheted off the hook together. If symbols converge AT THE BOTTOM, the stitches are worked INTO THE SAME INSERTION POINT.

Waves and Wheels

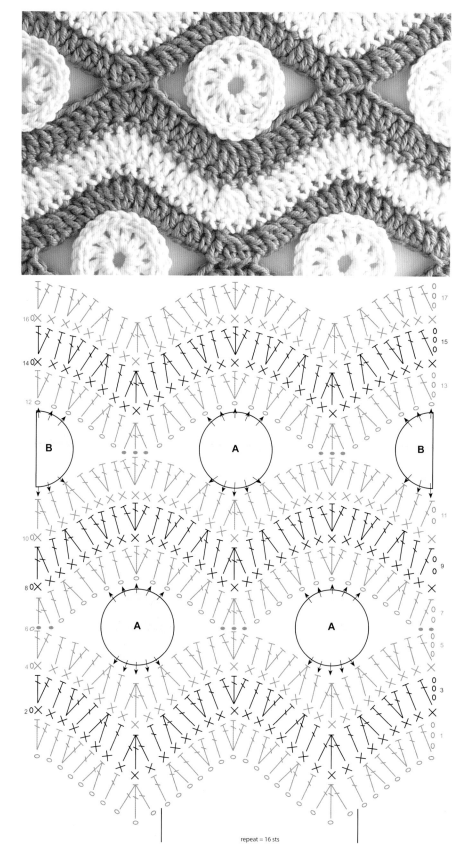

Stitch count: a multiple of 16 + 1 st extra + ch3 for height adjustment. Work the wave pattern in rows according to the crochet chart. In every row, first work the sts before the marked pattern repeat once, repeat the marked pattern repeat continuously, and end with the sts after the marked pattern repeat. Work the beginning chain and Row 1 in the same color, and then change colors after every 2 rows. In Row 6, for the second wave segment, as shown in the chart, work new chains or join with sl-sts to the first segment. With Row 12, the third segment in the wave pattern begins, for this, with new working yarn, ch7, join with 3 sl-sts to the second segment, ch13, join with 3 sl-sts to the second segment, and so forth.

Work Rows 1–17 once, and then repeat Rows 6–17 continuously, changing colors as shown in the chart.

Finally, for every full opening, work Round 1 of a circular motif (Circle A). Then place the motif into the opening, and work a round of sl-st around it, attaching it at the top and bottom as shown in the chart. For the side openings, work half circular motifs (Circle B), leaving a beginning tail of approximately 20 inches (50 cm), and insert all motifs the same way.

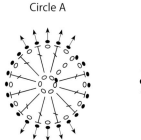

Circle A   Circle B

repeat = 16 sts

Wave Pattern

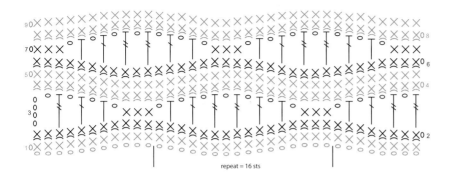

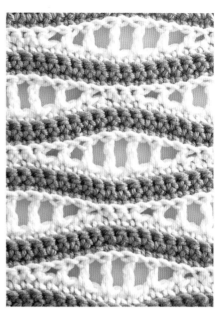

repeat = 16 sts

Stitch count: a multiple of 16 + 3 sts extra + ch1 for height adjustment.
Work in rows according to the crochet chart. In every row, first work the sts before the marked pattern repeat once, repeat the marked pattern repeat continuously, and end with the sts after the marked pattern repeat. Work Rows 1–9 once, and then repeat Rows 2–9 continuously, changing colors as shown in the chart. In the row after a color change, always work the sc through the back loops of the stitches only.

Bridge Arch Pattern

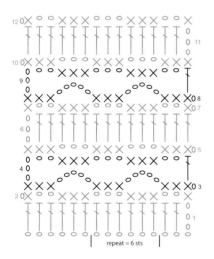

repeat = 6 sts

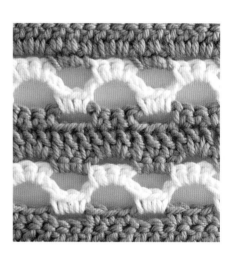

Stitch count: a multiple of 6 + 3 sts extra + ch3 for height adjustment.
Work in rows according to the crochet chart. In every row, first work the sts before the marked pattern repeat once, repeat the marked pattern repeat continuously, and end with the sts after the marked pattern repeat. From Row 3 on, always work sc and dc in the ch-sp of the previous row. Work Rows 1–12 once, and then repeat Rows 3–12 continuously, changing colors as shown in the chart. In Rows 7 and 8, work 2 RS rows one after another, in Rows 9 and 10, work 2 WS rows one after another.

Stitch Key

○ = 1 chain

● = 1 slip stitch

✕ = 1 single crochet

⨉ = 1 single crochet through the back loop of the stitch only

𝖳 = 1 half double crochet

𝖳 = 1 double crochet

𝖳 = 1 treble crochet

●●● ABBREVIATIONS can be found on page 344.

! If symbols converge AT THE TOP, the stitches are crocheted off the hook together. If symbols converge AT THE BOTTOM, the stitches are worked INTO THE SAME INSERTION POINT.

Resources

Everything else to help with your crochet
project: answers to common questions,
an illustrated glossary, and tables with
useful information.

Stitch Keys, Tables, and Abbreviations

 Generally, the **POSITION OF THE CROCHET SYMBOL** in the crochet chart shows in which insertion point the stitch is to be worked. If it is not possible to spot with certainty, check the written out row-by-row instructions, description of the stitch pattern, or the crochet chart for further hints.

STITCH KEY FOR CROCHET CHARTS

Symbols used in crochet charts are internationally often similar, and in most cases also resemble the stitches they represent. However, there are no uniform standards. When other symbols are used in instructions, an appropriate stitch key is usually included. Following are the most common symbols; if more than one symbol is common for a stitch, multiple symbols are shown.

INDIVIDUAL STITCHES

⌒ • = 1 slip stitch

• ○ = 1 chain

❙ ✕ = 1 single crochet

❙ ┬ = 1 half double crochet

┼ ┬ = 1 double crochet

┼ ╫ = 1 treble crochet

‡ ‡ = 1 double treble crochet

SPECIAL INDIVIDUAL STITCHES

✕ = 1 center single crochet

✕ = 1 elongated single crochet

= 1 bullion stitch/ roll stitch

= 1 herringbone half double crochet

⊶ = 1 Solomon's knot

= 1 loop stitch of 4 loops

BEGINNING/STANDING STITCHES

Beginning stitches, or standing stitches, at the beginning of a row or round are depicted much bolder and stand out from all other stitches.

= 1 beginning/standing double crochet

= 1 beginning/standing treble crochet

= 1 beginning/standing double crochet, worked below

= 1 popcorn with beginning/ standing double crochet

SPIKE STITCHES

Spike stitches are prolonged at the bottom with a taper or hook-like attachment.

= 1 single crochet worked below

= 1 half double crochet worked below

= 1double crochet worked below

= 1 popcorn worked below

POST STITCHES

A crescent-shaped hook at the bottom end of a symbol indicates that a raised stitch is to be worked around the post. When it points to the right, a back post stitch is meant, when it points to the left, a front post stitch.

= 1 front post single crochet

= 1 front post double crochet

= 1 front post treble crochet

= 1 back post single crochet

= 1 back post double crochet

= 1 back post treble crochet

FOUNDATION STITCHES

A base loop is symbolized by an oval at the bottom of the stitch symbol.

= 1 foundation single crochet

= 1 foundation half double crochet

= 1 foundation double crochet

STITCHES WORKED THROUGH THE FRONT OR BACK LOOP OF THE STITCH ONLY

The insertion point is indicated by a dash or curved stroke at the bottom end of the stitch symbol. Ends curved downward mean "through the back loop," curved upward "through the front loop" of the stitch.

= 1 slip stitch through the back loop of the stitch only

= 1 single crochet through the back loop of the stitch only

= 1 elongated single crochet through the back loop of the stitch only

= 1 half double crochet through the back loop of the stitch only

= 1 double crochet through the back loop of the stitch only

= 2 double crochets into the same stitch through the back loop of the stitch only

= 1 single crochet through the front loop of the stitch only

= 1 half double crochet through the front loop of the stitch only

= 1 double crochet through the front loop of the stitch only

 In crochet charts, EVEN- AND ODD-NUM-BERED ROWS OR ROUNDS are often visualized in two different colors for better orientation. Sometimes SPECIAL STITCHES IN A STITCH PATTERN, such as post stitches, might be shown IN A DIFFERENT COLOR.

PICOTS

Picots are represented by their own symbol, with further explanations in the pattern instructions, or else all chains and other stitches are pictured in detail.

 = 1 picot (detailed explanation often to be found in pattern instructions)

 = 1 picot of 3 chains and 1 slip stitch back into the first chain

 = 1 picot of 4 chains and 1 single crochet back into the first chain

BOBBLES AND POPCORNS

The symbols for bobbles and popcorns resemble the symbols of the individual stitches of which they are composed.

 = 1 bobble of 5 or 7 chains

 = 1 bobble of (1 chain, 1 double crochet, 1 chain) into the same stitch

 = 1 bobble of 3, 4, or 5 half double crochets

 = 1 bobble of 3, 4, or 5 double crochets

 = 1 bobble of 3, 4, or 5 treble crochets

 = 1 popcorn of 4 or 5 double crochets

 = 1 popcorn of 4 or 5 double crochets. The first double crochet is being replaced by 3 chains.

 = 1 slanted popcorn of 5 double crochets around the post of 1 half double crochet

GROUPS OF STITCHES INTO THE SAME STITCH OR WORKED OFF TOGETHER

Generally, the following can be said: If symbols converge at the bottom, the stitches are worked into the same stitch. If symbols converge at the top, the stitches are worked off together.

 = 2 single crochets into the same stitch

 = (1 single crochet, 1 chain, 1 single crochet) into the same stitch

= (1 double crochet, 1 chain, 1 double crochet) into the same stitch

 = 3 single crochets into the same stitch

= (1 single crochet, 3 chains, 1 single crochet) into the same stitch

= (1 single crochet, 9 chains, 1 single crochet) into the same stitch

= 2 half double crochets, double crochets, or treble crochets into the same stitch

 = (1 single crochet and 1 half double crochet) into the same stitch

 = 5 double crochets into the same stitch

 = 2 half double crochets into the same stitch. The first stitch is being replaced by 2 chains.

 = 5 double crochets into the same stitch. The first stitch is being replaced by 3 chains.

 = 2 or 3 single crochets crocheted together

 = 2, 3, 4, or 5 double crochets crocheted together

 = 2, 3, or 5 double crochets crocheted together. The first stitch is being replaced by 3 chains.

CROSSED, X- AND Y-STITCHES

 = 2 crossed double crochets

 = 2 crossed double crochets with 1 chain in-between

 = 1 X-stitch in double crochet

 = 1 Y-stitch in double crochet

 = 1 inverted Y-double crochet stitch

MISCELLANEOUS

Chains can be depicted either showing all individual chains or simply as an arched line with a number for the stitch count.

 = 1 magic circle/adjustable magic ring

= 1 beginning picot of 4 chains and 1 single crochet back into the first chain

 = 1 chain/arc of chains

 = 1 crab stitch

 = 1 double crochet, in right-side rows worked behind the chain of the previous row, in wrong-side rows, in front of the chain of the previous row

 = decreases by short rows

 = arrows either indicate the direction of work or point to joining spots

4 = row or round numbers

| repeat | = repeat or pattern repeat

X Always also note the **ARROWS** indicating the **DIRECTION OF WORK.** Especially in **MULTI-COLORED PATTERNS,** there might be 2 right-side rows or 2 wrong-side rows one after another.

TUNISIAN CROCHET SYMBOLS

 = 1 Tunisian simple stitch

 = 1 Tunisian purl stitch

 = 1 Tunisian knit stitch

 = 1 yarn over

 = 1 Tunisian raised double crochet

 = 1 Tunisian cluster stitch

ABBREVIATIONS

This list contains the abbreviations used in this book as well as other common abbreviations you may encounter in crochet patterns. For individual patterns, an appropriate list is usually part of the pattern; in books or magazines, it can often be found in a central spot.

Abbreviation	Explanation	Abbreviation	Explanation
add'l	additional	M	marker
AMR	adjustable magic ring	MC	main color
approx.	approximately	ndl	needle
B	bobble	p	picot
bet	between	patt	pattern
blo	through the back loop of the stitch only	pc	popcorn
		PM	place marker
bpdc	back post double crochet	prev	previous
bpsc	back post single crochet	r(s)	row(s)
bs	bullion stitch	rem	remaining
CC	contrasting color	rep	repeat
ch	chain	RH	right hand
ch-sp	chain space	rnd	round
cl	cluster	RS	right side
cont	continue	rsc	reverse single crochet
dc	double crochet	sc	single crochet
dc2/3/4/5tog	2/3/4/5 double crochets crocheted together	sc2in1	2 single crochets in the same stitch
dec	decrease	sc2/3/4/5tog	2/3/4/5 single crochets crocheted together
dtr	double treble crochet		
fdc	foundation double crochet	scDec	single crochet decrease
flo	through the front loop of the stitch only	selv st	selvedge stitch
		sk	skip
foll	follow(ing)	sl-st(s)	slip stitch(es)
fpdc	front post double crochet	sp(s)	space(s)
fsc	foundation single crochet	st(s)	stitch(es)
hdc	half double crochet	tch	turning chain
hdcDec	half double crochet decrease	tog	together
hk	crochet hook	tr	treble crochet
inc	increase(s), increasing	trtr	triple treble crochet
JAYGO	join as you go	WS	wrong side
LH	left hand	yo	yarn over, yarn over hook
lp(s)	loop(s)		

GUIDE TO APPAREL/TEXTILE CARE SYMBOLS

Wash

Bleach

Dry

Iron

Dryclean

Machine Wash Cycles

 Normal

 Permanent Press

 Delicate/ Gentle

 Hand Wash

Water Temperatures

(Maximum)	(200F)	(160F)	(140F)	(120F)	(105F)	(65–85F)
Symbol(s)	95C	70C	60C	50C	40C	30C
	•••	•••	••	•••	••	•

 Any Bleach When Needed

 Only Non-Chlorine Bleach When Needed

Tumble Dry Cycles

 Normal

 Permanent Press

 Delicate/ Gentle

 Line Dry/ Hang to Dry

 Drip Dry

 Dry Flat

 In the Shade
(Added to Line Dry, Drip Dry, or Dry Flat)

Tumble Dry Settings

 Any Heat

High

Medium

Low

No Heat/Air

Iron—Dry or Steam, Maximum Temperatures

 200C (390F) High

150C (300F) Medium

110C (230F) Low

Dryclean, Normal Cycle

 (A) Any Solvent

(P) Any Solvent Except Trichloroethylene

(F) Petroleum Solvent Only

Dryclean, Additional Instructions

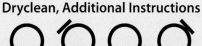 Short Cycle

Reduced Moisture

Low Heat

No Steam Finishing

Warning Symbols

 Do Not Wash

 Do Not Wring

 Do Not Bleach

 Do Not Dry *(Used With Do Not Wash)*

 Do Not Tumble Dry

 Do Not Iron

 No Steam *(Added to Iron)*

 Do Not Dryclean

HOOK SIZES

There are many different systems for indicating crochet hook sizes. The following table shows an overview, however, individual numbers for foreign manufacturers may vary. In any case, a gauge swatch will be indispensable.

metric hook size	US hook size			UK hook size (UK, Canada)		Japanese hook size
	steel	numerical	alphabetical	steel	regular crochet	
0.75 mm	14	–	–	–	–	–
0.85 mm	13	–	–	7	–	–
1.0 mm	12	–	–	6½	–	–
1.1 mm	11	–	–	6	–	–
1.25 mm		000	–	–	16	–
1.3 mm	10	–	–	5½	–	–
1.4 mm	9	–	–	5	–	–
1.5 mm	8	00	–	–	15	–
1.65 mm	7	–	–	4	–	–
1.75 mm	–	–	–	–	14	–
1.8 mm	6	–	–	3½	–	–
1.9 mm	5	–	–	3	–	–
2.0 mm	4	0	–	2½	–	–
2.1 mm	3	–	–	2	–	0
2.25 mm	2	1	B	1½	13	–
2.4 mm	–	–	–	–	–	1
2.5 mm	–	1½	–	–	12	–
2.7 mm	–	–	–	–	–	2
2.75 mm	1	2	C	1	–	–
3.0 mm	–	2½	–	–	11	3
3.25 mm	0	3	D	0	10	–
3.3 mm	–	–	–	–	–	4
3.5 mm	00	4	E	–	–	–
3.6 mm	–	–	–	–	–	5
3.75 mm	–	5	F	–	9	–
3.9 mm	–	–	–	–	–	6
4.0 mm	–	6	G	–	8	–
4.2 mm	–	–	–	–	–	7
4.25 mm	–	–	–	–	–	–
4.5 mm	–	7	–	–	7	8
4.8 mm	–	–	–	–	–	9
5.0 mm	–	8	H	–	6	–
5.1 mm	–	–	–	–	–	10
5.4 mm	–	–	–	–	–	11
5.5 mm	–	9	I	–	5	–
5.7 mm	–	–	–	–	–	12
6.0 mm	–	10	J	–	4	13
6.3 mm	–	–	–	–	–	14
6.5 mm	–	10½	K	–	3	–
6.6 mm	–	–	–	–	–	15
7.0 mm	–	–	–	–	2	7 mm
7.5 mm	–	–	–	–	1	–
8.0 mm	–	11	L	–	0	8 mm
9.0 mm	–	13	M/N	–	00	9 mm
10.0 mm	–	15	N/P	–	000	10 mm
15.0 mm	–	–	P/Q	–	–	–

Standard Yarn Weight System

Categories of yarn, gauge ranges, and recommended needle and hook sizes

Yarn Weight Symbol & Category Names	0 LACE	1 SUPER FINE	2 FINE	3 LIGHT	4 MEDIUM	5 BULKY	6 SUPER BULKY	7 JUMBO
Type of Yarns in Category	Fingering, 10-Count Crochet Thread	Sock, Fingering, Baby	Sport, Baby	DK, Light Worsted	Worsted, Afghan, Aran	Chunky, Craft, Rug	Bulky, Roving	Jumbo, Roving
Knit Gauge Range in Stockinette Stitch to 4 inches*	33–40 sts**	27–32 sts	23–26 sts	21–24 sts	16–20 sts	12–15 sts	7–11 sts	6 sts and fewer
Recommended Needle in Metric Size Range	1.5–2.25 mm	2.25–3.25 mm	3.25–3.75 mm	3.75–4.5 mm	4.5–5.5 mm	5.5–8 mm	8–12.75 mm	12.75 mm and larger
Recommended Needle in U.S. Size Range	000 to 1	1 to 3	3 to 5	5 to 7	7 to 9	9 to 11	11 to 17	17 and larger
Crochet Gauge Ranges in Single Crochet to 4 inches*	32–42 double crochets**	21–32 sts	16–20 sts	12–17 sts	11–14 sts	8–11 sts	7–9 sts	6 sts and fewer
Recommended Hook in Metric Size Range	Steel*** 1.6–1.4 mm Regular hook 2.25 mm	2.25–3.5 mm	3.5–4.5 mm	4.5–5.5 mm	5.5–6.5 mm	6.5–9 mm	9–15 mm	15 mm and larger
Recommended Hook in U.S. Size Range	Steel 6, 7, 8*** Regular hook B–1	B–1 to E–4	E–4 to 7	7 to I–9	I–9 to K–10½	K–10½ to M–13	M–13 to Q	Q and larger

   * GUIDELINES ONLY: The above reflect the most commonly used gauges and needle or hook sizes for specific yarn categories.

  ** Lace weight yarns are usually knitted or crocheted on larger needles and hooks to create lacy, openwork patterns. Accordingly, a gauge range is difficult to determine. Always follow the gauge stated in your pattern.

*** Steel crochet hooks are sized differently from regular hooks—the higher the number, the smaller the hook, which is the reverse of regular hook sizing.

*Source: Craft Yarn Council of America's **www.YarnStandards.com***

FAQs — 100 Most Frequently Asked Questions

YARNS, HOOKS, NOTIONS

1   I don't own any crochet hooks yet. Which ones should I buy? Many manufacturers offer sets containing multiple crochet hook sizes for the most common yarn weights. These hooks are all in the same design and often come in different colors for better differentiation, and a pretty matching case is often included as well. For this reason, a set like these is a good investment. These sets come in different materials and variations.

2   What does the number/letter for the size of the crochet hook mean? US sizes in numbers and letters are arbitrary sizes from smallest size to largest in ascending order. Sizes in millimeters are also typically given, which correspond to the diameter of the shaft. For tiny steel crochet hooks, the higher the number, the smaller the hook. The table on page 346 shows corresponding sizes.

3   Of what material should crochet hooks be made? This is a matter of personal preference and of the individual crochet technique. Very thin thread crochet hooks are, for reasons of strength, in most cases only available in steel; very thick crochet hooks due to their weight often only come in plastic. For all other hook sizes, everyone should try for themselves which material feels best in the hand and with which one can achieve the best crochet results.

4   There are many different crochet hook shapes, which do I need? Which crochet hook one needs depends on the respective technique. For traditional crochet, standard crochet hooks with a hook on one end and often a shaped handle or thumb rest are used. A few special techniques can be worked with these crochet hooks, too. For techniques such as hairpin lace and loop stitch crochet, in addition to a crochet hook,

other tools are needed. Knooking and Tunisian crochet require special crochet hooks.

5   How should I care for my crochet hooks? Crochet hooks should be stored in an orderly fashion and in a dry place, either in the original packaging or in a special storage system such as in fabric rolls. If hooks have become dirty or sticky, wooden or bamboo hooks should be wiped with a wet cloth and dried immediately. Plastic and metal hooks are easier to maintain and can be washed in warm water.

6   What other tools should beginners have on hand? In addition to crochet hooks in appropriate sizes, you will need a measuring tape, a few stitch markers, a medium-sized dull tapestry needle, and thread scissors.

7   I've found a yarn without a ball band. How can I find out what fiber it is made of? A burn test gives an indication of the fiber content. For this, the working yarn is carefully held to an open flame. If it burns with a bright flame, and the yarn turns to fine ash, it is probably made of cotton or viscose (rayon). Wool yarns burn with a smaller flame, the black ash smells of burned horn. Most synthetic fibers form a hard bead. A more precise classification and the testing of fiber blends are more difficult.

8   What information can I find on the ball band of the yarn? The yarn label indicates besides name and brand of the yarn also the fiber content, the yardage, the color number and the dye lot or batch number. Usually, information about the hook size and the optimal gauge are also included, however, these numbers apply in most cases to knitted fabric only. Additionally, the yarn label contains care instructions for the finished crocheted piece (> pages 345–347).

9   What are multicolor yarns good for? Multicolor yarns are self-patterning, creating a colorwork pattern in the crocheted piece without having to change colors during work. They should preferably be used for fabrics crocheted in basic stitches, since more complex textured patterns will be lost in the colors.

10   What does the dye lot number mean? When spun yarn is dyed, every batch can only accommodate a limited yarn amount: the dye lot. Individual batches always deviate slightly from each other despite using the exact same technology. For this reason, only yarns with the same dye lot number should be used together.

11   How do I store my yarn stash? When stocking up on wool yarns, it is especially important to ensure moth protection. The yarns should also be stored dry and without exposure to direct sunlight.

12   I have multiple projects planned and started. How can I keep track of them? Keep a project journal where you write down everything important about each project, such as hook size, yarn used, and pattern worked from.

13   Why should a special wool detergent be used? A wool detergent has a special ph-value, which allows for washing wool particularly gently.

14   Which yarn is suitable for beginners? For beginning crocheters, smooth, tightly plied cotton yarns in medium yarn weights are suitable.

CROCHET STITCHES AND TECHNIQUES

15   How do I hold the crochet hook? There are two basic positions for holding a crochet hook: from below like a pen or from above like a knife. The chosen method has no bearing on the resulting crocheted piece; it is just a personal preference.

16   Which are the basic stitches? The basic stitches in crochet are slip stitch, single crochet, half double crochet, and double crochet. These can be additionally varied in a variety of ways, such as by changing the way of inserting the hook.

17   Can I crochet cable patterns? Yes, with crochet one can create a look resembling that of knitted cable patterns. However, crocheted cables are not as prominently raised above the base fabric (> page 46).

18   How do I count the chains in a chain? Counting chains always begins at the stitch worked last, immediately below the crochet hook, counting back toward the beginning slipknot.

19   Does every crocheted piece have to begin with a foundation chain? No. When an especially stretchy beginning edge is desired, work foundation crochet stitches (> page 59). Pieces worked in the round can be started with other methods, too.

20   How many height-adjustment or turning chains must be worked? The number of required height-adjustment or turning chains depends on the height of the stitches that will be worked in the next row or round (> page 64).

21   How can I start a piece that's worked in the round? Depending on how large and adjustable the center opening is supposed to be later, circular pieces can be started with a magic circle or adjustable magic ring, a few chains, or one single chain (> page 67).

22   Does it make a difference whether I work in rows or in the round? Since when crocheting in turned rows fronts and backs of the stitches are alternatingly visible but when working in the round only the fronts of the stitches, it makes a significant difference for the stitch appearance whether crocheting in rows or rounds. Additionally, when crocheting in the round, under certain circumstances, fewer seams must be worked.

23   How do I close the rounds? Every round is usually closed with a slip stitch. You can also crochet without visible round transition in continuous spiral rounds (> page 71).

24   What do I do when I've reached the end of my skein? Depending on the type of yarn and type of crochet project, there are multiple ways to join a new skein to the existing piece to continue with a new skein. The ending tail of the old skein and the beginning tail of the new skein must be carefully woven in at the end.

25   How can I finish off a crochet part? At the end of a crocheted piece, secure the last working loop to prevent the crocheted piece from unraveling.

SHAPED TO PERFECTION

26   Crochet patterns often sound to me like a secret language. How can I better understand them? Crochet patterns are often written using standardized expressions, phrases, and abbreviations. The most important terms and phrases are explained on pages 340–343; the most common abbreviations are listed on page 344. With some practice, understanding crochet patterns will soon no longer be a problem.

27   How do I read a crochet stitch pattern chart? Every symbol in a crochet chart is usually assigned to a certain stitch type or group of stitches. In the legend or stitch key, these allocations are explained. The placement of symbols in relation to each other also shows the correct insertion points. When crocheting in rows, right-side rows are to be read and crocheted from right to left, wrong-side rows from left to right. For crocheting in the round, every round is read in the working direction in a counterclockwise direction.

28   What is the difference between a grid chart and a stitch pattern chart? Grid charts consist of rows of square-shaped boxes, and often show the allocation of colors in a colorwork pattern or of filled and empty boxes in filet crochet. The different stitches for Tunisian crochet are also sometimes visualized in the form of grid charts. Crochet stitch pattern charts, by contrast, show various symbols for different individual stitches and groups of stitches, and how they are arranged in relation to each other.

29   Do I have to make a gauge swatch? Even if one would like to begin right away with the actual crocheted piece, a gauge swatch is essential. This is the only way to ensure that the crocheted piece will turn out the correct size and intended drape.

30   Which factors affect the gauge? The gauge is affected by yarn weight, stitch pattern, hook size, fiber content, and the individual crochet technique.

31   What can I do if my gauge does not match the one stated in the pattern? Make a new gauge swatch with a different hook size and count the stitches in this new swatch. It is possible to reach the correct gauge this way; however, the crocheted fabric should not turn out too dense or too loose. If the gauge differs significantly, the whole project might need to be recalculated.

32   I want to substitute the yarn listed in the pattern with a different one. How do I go about this? This is most easily done by finding another yarn that is very similar to the original in gauge, weight, and texture. If a yarn with the same gauge cannot be found, the stitch counts for the project can often be easily recalculated. In any case, make a large enough gauge swatch!

33 The crochet pattern contains multiple sizes. How do I deal with that? When a crochet pattern has been graded for multiple sizes, all the numbers for different sizes are in most cases listed one after another divided by slashes, dashes, or brackets. If only one number is listed, it applies to all sizes. When you have determined the size to be made, highlight the relevant numbers for your size.

34 How can I find out which of the sizes to work? Every crochet pattern should contain information about the measurements on which the individual sizes are based. Often, these measurements can be gained from a schematic containing measurements. Take your body measurements for bust circumference, waist circumference, and hip circumference, and compare them with the numbers in the pattern. If they fall between two sizes, the larger size should be worked.

35 Which one is the right side of a crocheted piece? The "right side" is the public side of a crocheted piece, which faces the outside when the garment is being worn or a piece being displayed.

36 What is meant by "Right Front"? Usually, this denotes the "right half of the front when the garment is being worn," so it means on the right of the wearer of the garment.

37 How does a crocheted piece get a certain shape? Crocheting rows or rounds with the same stitch count throughout produces a straight piece. If a crocheted piece needs to be shaped, stitches must be purposefully increased or decreased, adding to or reducing the total stitch count. The placement and number of increases or decreases is determined by the desired shape.

38 On which side of a jacket do the buttonholes belong? For women, the buttonholes are worked on the Right Front, for men, on the Left Front.

39 Can I still add pockets to my crocheted garment afterward? Yes, patch pockets (> page 131) don't have to be taken into account from the outset in the planning process. They can be added as an afterthought.

40 What do I do if I can't find a zipper in a matching length? A zipper can simply be shortened to the required length. For this, sew multiple times over the chain, teeth, or coil with sturdy sewing thread, forming a stopper for the slider. Just cut off excess length.

FINISHING TOUCHES

41 How can I join two crocheted pieces with each other? Crocheted pieces can be either sewn or crocheted together in different ways.

42 What does "right sides facing each other" and "wrong sides facing each other" mean? For "right sides facing each other," the two pieces to be joined are placed onto each other with the better-looking sides of the pieces inward. After sewing or crocheting together, the piece needs to be turned inside out. "Wrong sides facing each other" means that the two better-looking sides of the pieces are facing the outside and the two wrong sides are facing each other. Here, the seam stays visible from the outside or right side of the fabric.

43 How do I set a sleeve cap into an armhole? A sleeve cap should first be pinned in the middle and at the sides and then gradually pinned further in small increments to evenly distribute the fabric. Then the sleeve cap is sewn in, since crocheting the seam would not produce a sufficiently even seam.

44 What is the best way to join multiple individual motifs such as granny squares? The easiest method for joining multiple individual motifs is to either sew them together or crochet them together with a flat seam. This allows for joining over a longer stretch at the same time, reducing the number of ends needing to be woven in.

45 Can I join motifs during crocheting? Using the "join-as-you-go" method lets you join every motif with already-completed motifs while crocheting its last round. This eliminates sewing altogether.

46 How can I secure the yarn tails? Yarn tails from adding a new skein or color within a row can be either immediately crocheted in or woven in later. Beginning and ending tail are woven in at the end. In any case, leave all yarn tails at least 4 inches (10 cm) long!

47 How can I attach crocheted lace edgings to woven fabric? The edge of the fabric must be specially prepared first. There are various methods (> *page 162*) to do this. After that, a border edging is crocheted directly onto the prepared edge of the fabric, or else an already-completed edging is joined with the fabric edge.

48 What are facings or bands needed for? Facings can cover up the unsightly tape of a zipper or reinforce an edge. Open edges look neat and professional with a crocheted-on edging. Choosing a different stitch pattern than the pattern used for the main piece and also creates very nice decorative effects.

49 Can I attach facings or bands only afterward or also crochet them at the same time with the main piece? Bands can be crocheted directly together with the main part of the piece if carefully planned in advance or crocheted on after crocheting the main piece.

50 Which stitch patterns are suitable for facings or bands? For sturdy bands, dense, compact stitch patterns are suitable. A stretchy cuff as a finishing edge can be produced in the knooking technique.

51 Which buttons are best for my crocheted piece? Retail stores offer a wide range of buttons in various colors, shapes, and sizes—most of which are suitable for crochet with a little planning for their use. Care should be taken that the size of the buttonholes matches the diameter of the buttons. You can also crochet a perfectly matching button over a button insert with the original yarn or a similar one. (> *page 185*).

52 What kind of needle do I use to embroider crocheted fabric? It is best to use a tapestry needle with a blunt tip that won't perforate the stitches in the crocheted fabric.

53 How can I make pom-poms quick and easy? Retail stores carry pom-pom makers, sets of special plastic disks that can be used to make pom-poms without having to cut cardboard rings every time.

54 How do I care for items crocheted in wool? Wool should always be laundered carefully, preferably by hand, in cold or lukewarm water, agitating it as little as possible. Always use a special wool detergent! Newer washing machines often also have good and gentle wool washing cycles.

55 How do I best store my crocheted pieces? Crocheted garments should be stored horizontally since they would permanently stretch out on a hanger due to their inherent weight. For crocheted pieces from wool and other animal fibers, don't forget moth proofing!

56 Why does the crocheted piece have to be blocked? Crocheted pieces obtain their final shape only after blocking, which smooths and relaxes the fibers. Only this way, stitch patterns constricted during crocheting can reach their full potential.

SOCKS, MITTENS, AND HATS

57 I don't want to crochet in the round. Can I still make socks? Yes! The seamed sock is completely crocheted in rows and only later sewn together (> *page 200*).

58 How can I crochet socks in different sizes? The different stitch counts and lengths for individual sizes are listed in a convenient table (> page 204).

59 Why are there special sock yarns? Sock yarns are often made of a blend of pure new wool and polyamide/nylon. The wool content is responsible for comfortable wearing characteristics, while the addition of polyamide makes the sock more durable.

60 Are crocheted socks stretchy enough? Yes. They are worked in elongated single crochet, which creates a very stretchy crocheted fabric.

61 How do I measure my mitten size? Measure your hand circumference above the thumb and the hand length from the tip of the middle finger to the wrist, and compare the numbers with the table on page 206.

62 Are hats very complicated to crochet? Not at all! Various basic shapes in the trendy chunky crochet look in half double crochet work up quickly and easily.

63 Should I crochet a hat from the top down or from the bottom up? It is recommended to start a hat at the crown and to work top down with increases. This makes it possible to try them on again and again during work, and to perfectly customize circumference and length.

CREATIVE CROCHET

64   How can I join working yarn in a new color? For a color change within a row, the last 2 loops of the last stitch before the color change are always finished with the new color. For a color change at the beginning of a new row, there are multiple ways—for instance, with standing beginning stitches or a beginning slipknot (> page 76).

65   What do I do with the colors not in use when working colorwork patterns? Unused colors can be either carried as floats or crocheted in.

66   Can I work stripes over an odd number of rows? Yes, stripes can be worked over an odd number of rows without having to break the yarn, if working in a certain order (> page 214).

67   How do I read colorwork pattern charts? Every box in a colorwork chart represents 1 stitch and shows in which color it is to be worked. Right-side rows are to be read from right to left, wrong-side rows from left to right.

68   Which stitch types are especially good for crocheted-in motifs? Geometric shapes can be worked well in double crochet. For more intricate motifs, single crochets in the round and knot stitch are suitable (> page 221), since these produce especially crisp outlines.

69   What's the difference between jacquard and intarsia crochet? For jacquard crochet, small motifs are worked multiple times one after another, often in the form of decorative bands. This method creates only short floats, which can be either carried or crocheted in. Intarsia creates large areas of color that would have too-long floats if left hanging. For this reason, every color section is worked from its own skein.

70   What is different about Tunisian crochet? For Tunisian crochet, during the forward pass, all stitches of a row are taken up one after another so that instead of one working loop, many loops sit on the hook. During the return pass, they are then crocheted off one after another. The result is especially dense and compact fabric.

71   Do I need special hooks for Tunisian crochet? Yes. For Tunisian crochet very long hooks without grip or thumb rest are needed so that all loops of all stitches have room and can slide well.

72   Can I also work Tunisian crochet with colors? Tunisian crochet is very well suited for playing with colors. You can create interesting stripe patterns, but also work in motifs very well since the stitches are nearly square-shaped.

73   What are crochet hooks with hooks at both ends good for? With these crochet hooks, you can work special stitches in Tunisian crochet in the round or in rows. Please note: Don't mistake them for regular crochet hooks with different hook sizes at both ends!

74   Where do I get inspiration for filet crochet? Besides special charts for filet crochet, embroidery patterns can also be used as templates, or you can design your own patterns and motifs on graph paper.

75   Can I also shape pieces worked in filet crochet? In the filet crochet technique, you can only increase or decrease in increments of whole filet boxes. It is also important whether the boxes are filled or empty.

76   What does "double-sided" mean? In double-sided crochet, two permanently joined layers are crocheted at the same time, but both can be designed independently from each other in color and stitch pattern. This creates a very dense crocheted fabric that works very well for potholders, among other things.

77   What are crochet hooks with a hole at one end intended for? These hooks are for the "knooking" technique. A cord for holding stitches is threaded through the hole to hold all stitches until they are worked.

78   Why does knooking appeal to crocheters? With this technique, a knitted fabric can be produced without having to knit. The cord for holding stitches, which is threaded through the hole in the hook's handle, replaces the second knitting needle; the hook end makes it easier to pull the working yarn through.

79   Can I crochet whole pieces in slip stitch crochet? With the traditional slip stitch alone, it's tedious to crochet larger pieces since this is a shallow stitch and using a regular hook size would produce a much too dense and compact fabric. The slip stitch crochet technique uses a number of modifications of the slip stitch, and everything is crocheted very loosely with a larger size hook, which creates impressive pattern effects.

80   What does "front loop only" and "back loop only" slip stitch mean? A few varieties of the slip stitch are not worked through both loops of the stitch but only crocheted through either the front or the back loop of the stitch.

81   Can pieces worked in slip stitch crochet also be shaped? Yes. In the slip stitch crochet technique, increases and decreases can be worked, too.

82   What is Irish crochet? In Irish crochet, filigree flowers and leaves are traditionally crocheted and combined into large all-over lace fabric or integrated into a mesh background. Irish crochet motifs can also be used individually very nicely as appliqués or eye-catchers.

83   What options exist for joining Irish motifs? The motifs can be directly crocheted together, crocheted into a crocheted mesh background, sewn onto the latter, or joined with wrapped connective bars.

84   What's the purpose of hairpin lace looms? Hairpin lace looms are used in conjunction with a regular crochet hook for hairpin lace crochet, also known as fork work. On these looms, strips of filigree loops are crocheted.

85   What can I make from hairpin crochet strips? Multiple strips can be joined into larger areas and designs for lacy garments. Individual strips of loops can also be crocheted into and used as decorative elements.

86   What's the difference between U-shaped and closed hairpin lace looms? The basic principle and result are the same for both types. They only need to be used slightly differently. Additionally, in closed hairpin lace looms, the spacing of the rods can often be changed, while U-shaped hairpin lace looms have fixed rods.

87   What does Bruges crochet have to do with the town of Bruges? Very fine and filigree laces traditionally originate from Bruges in Belgium. Bruges crochet imitates these through ribbons worked in double crochet and chain arcs.

88   What is the difference between hairpin lace crochet, fork work, and loop stitch crochet? In hairpin lace crochet, or fork work, individual narrow strips of loops, held together in the middle by a few stitches, are crocheted. Loop stitch crochet creates contiguous areas of any size, which consist of loops or into which loops are worked at intervals.

89   What kind of tool do I need for loop stitch crochet? Depending on the desired result, you need just a finger, a flexible or rigid flat stick, or a thick auxiliary needle ("broomstick").

90   What is special about lace? In the lace crochet technique, very thin yarns are worked with thick crochet hooks. This creates a fabric with a translucent, delicate lace structure.

91   How can I embellish my crocheted piece with beads or sequins? Beads and sequins can be added directly to the individual crochet stitches. They can also be sewn onto already-finished fabric afterward with sewing thread in a matching color.

92   What do I have to look out for when purchasing beads if I want to use them in crochet projects? The hole in the bead must be large enough to be able to pull at least a single or double strand (depending on the technique used) of the project yarn through. When working with a crochet hook or a sewing needle, the head of the crochet hook or the whole sewing needle, including doubled-up sewing thread, also must fit through. For garments decorated with beads, the beads must be washable.

93   I'm left-handed. Can I learn to crochet, too? Yes! Left-handed crocheters hold the crochet hook in the left hand and lead the working yarn over the fingers of the right hand. All working steps are executed mirror-inverted. *(> page 310).*

94   Which projects are suitable for crocheting and felting? Very well suited are bags, slippers, hats, and home decor items. For jackets and vests, the resulting felt is often too thick, and the fit after felting too unpredictable.

RESOURCES

95   In Blogs and Forums, I often read about UFOs. What does that mean? A UFO is an "unfinished object" (= project not yet fully completed). This is what crocheters call projects that were started a long time ago but are still not finished at present.

96   There are many crochet patterns in the Japanese language out on the Internet. How can I work from them? Japanese crochet patterns often contain very detailed crochet charts with crochet symbols similar to those used in European patterns, which makes them easy to work from if you can read charts. In any case, take note of the different hook size designations, and consider that the American, European, and Japanese clothing size systems are also different.

97   What is Ravelry? Ravelry (www.ravelry.com) is a community of knitters and crocheters as well as a marketplace for both crochet and knitting patterns. You can also log and keep track of your own projects there, similar to keeping a paper journal.

98   Can I sell what I have crocheted on the Internet? On the Internet, there are several platforms on which specifically handcrafted items, including crochet, can be offered for sale. Some designers prefer that you not sell what you make from their patterns, while others will state that it is fine to do so. Check the pattern notes and be mindful of designer's wishes.

99   Can I buy crochet yarns on the Internet? Crochet yarns are offered on the Internet by numerous suppliers, which often also carry rare brands and exclusive yarn lines. When purchasing yarn over the Internet, keep in mind that the colors of yarn on screens can vary significantly and are not reproduced true to the original. To be able to better judge the yarn weight and the drape of the finished fabric, it often helps to look at finished items in a particular yarn, for instance, via projects linked to the yarn page on Ravelry.

100   What is a CAL? The abbreviation CAL stands for "crochet-a-long." During a CAL, many crocheters work the same piece at the same time and communicate on the Internet about it. Particularly appealing are the many different variations and individual results you can see this way, and that experienced participants are often eager to help beginners.

A to Z – Glossary

adjustable magic ring Basis for crocheting in the round consisting of a circular-shaped loop around which stitches are crocheted, and which is then pulled small. This leaves a very small opening.

Amigurumi (Japanese for "knitted bundle") Crocheted or knitted small dolls, animals or items.

appliqué Sewn-on decoration, often of fabric, wool, or felt. Appliqués can also be crocheted.

* (asterisks) can be found in phrases such as "repeat from * to *" or "repeat from *." They indicate that the instructions listed between asterisks or after a single asterisk are to be repeated either continuously or as often as indicated.

at both ends of the row/at both ends/on both sides To work a symmetrical shape—at both ends of a crocheted piece the same actions are performed at the same height, for instance, increasing or decreasing a certain number of stitches.

back of work In most cases, the less presentable (wrong) side of a crocheted fabric, which later in the finished piece will be on either the inside or the back. This is also the side on which all ends should be woven in.

band Finishing strip of a crocheted piece, either crocheted onto the piece afterward or crocheted at the same time as the main part. Bands reinforce, but they also serve decorative purposes.

bead crocheting Crochet technique in which beads are worked into the crocheted fabric. The beads can be either threaded onto the working yarn before beginning of work, and then crocheted in, or placed onto the working loop with a thin crochet hook or a thread loop during crocheting.

beginning slipknot First loop with which a crocheted piece is started.

beginning with a wrong-side row If the more presentable side of a stitch pattern is on the actual back of work of the crocheted piece, the counting method changes. The first row after the foundation chain and all odd-numbered rows are wrong-side rows, all even-numbered rows are right-side rows.

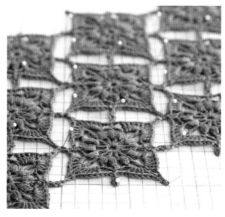

blocking After crocheting, finished crocheted pieces are pinned onto a suitable blocking mat with the help of tailor pins in the desired shape and to the measurements in the schematic, and steamed. This is especially important for lace patterns to give the stitch pattern its final shape.

bobble Multiple double crochets or treble crochets that are worked into the same stitch and crocheted together, and bulge outward three-dimensionally.

body/post of the stitch Denotes the complete stitch or the part of the stitch below the top loops.

border/edging Purely decorative ending of a crocheted piece, such as a lace trim, either crocheted directly onto the piece or worked separately and then attached to the main piece.

Boshi (Japanese for "hat") Trendy, sporty crocheted hat, often featuring contrasting color combinations, stripe patterns, and relatively thick yarn worked with hook size 6.0–10.0 mm (US J/10–N/15).

brackets Angular brackets [ ] indicate that all stitches listed within these brackets are to be read and worked as a group of stitches. Example: "[2 single crochets, 1 double crochet] 3 times" means that this sequence of stitches must be performed 3 times consecutively. Often, angular brackets are also used for consolidating groups of stitches that are to be worked into the same insertion point. **Parentheses ( )** often serve to explain something in more detail. Example: "1 double crochet into the next double crochet (the middle one of 5 double crochets of the previous round)" explains the specific insertion point—namely, the middle double crochet of a group of 5 of the previous round.

broomstick Auxiliary needle of a large diameter used for crocheting loop patterns such as broomstick lace or loop stitch.

Bruges crochet/Bruges lace Crochet technique modeled after bobbin lace.

bullion stitch Also called roll stitch. Before inserting the hook into a stitch of the previous row or round, the working yarn is wrapped multiple times (5 to 7 times) around the crochet hook. The stitch bulges out three-dimensionally to the front on the background fabric.

cables Created from raised stitches, which are crossed in regular intervals.

chain Basic stitch in a loop shape. Multiple individual chains crocheted one after another make a crocheted chain. Chains are in most cases used to begin a project or as chain arcs in lace patterns.

cluster (stitch) Multiple stitches worked into the same insertion point and crocheted together in half double crochets, double crochets, or treble crochets.

continuously Often found in conjunction with color sequences, stitch pattern sequences, or pattern repeats. It means that instructions are to be repeated or performed consecutively as often as possible until either the end of a row/round has been reached or there are no longer enough stitches left to work a full repeat.

contrasting color Color in a multi-colored stitch pattern that sets accents because it is very different from the main color.

crocheted edging Outer edges of a crocheted piece, composed of: bottom edge of the crocheted piece = beginning edge, top edge of the crocheted piece = the row worked last, side edges of the crocheted piece = edges at the right and left side of the piece.

crocheting off For each stitch, one or more yarn overs are placed onto the crochet hook, and the resulting loops crocheted off in multiple steps. For this, the working yarn is always pulled through one or more loops at the same time. "Crocheting off together" is the name for pulling the working yarn through individual loops or groups of loops, as well as the whole action of finishing a more complex stitch.

crocheting together Means to crochet stitches together: Every stitch is completed individually until one loop remains on the hook for each stitch, the working loop not included. Then a new yarn over is made onto the hook, and the working yarn is pulled through all loops on the hook at once. The stitch count decreases depending on how many stitches have been crocheted together.

crochet stitch pattern chart Drawing in which all stitches of a stitch pattern are represented through characters/symbols. It shows how a stitch pattern is constructed, whether it is crocheted in rows or rounds, and where the hook is inserted for individual stitches or where stitches are to be attached.

decreasing/decrease Reducing the number of stitches of a crocheted piece, either to shape the piece or to create a stitch pattern.

double-sided crochet Crochet technique in which two good sides with different colors and patterns are worked together and permanently joined during crocheting. Pieces worked in double-sided crochet are very thick and can be used as potholders, among other things

dye lot Number of the batch in which the yarn of a skein has been dyed. For a crochet project, make sure that all skeins used together are from the same dye lot.

edge stitch/selvedge stitch Name for the first and last stitch in a row of crochet.

ending tail/beginning tail Surplus remaining thread, either at the beginning or end of a crocheted piece or at the beginning or end of a skein. It will need to be woven in after having completed the crocheted piece or worked in while crocheting.

even- and odd-numbered rows The rows in a crochet pattern are numbered consecutively. The first and thus odd-numbered row is the row after the foundation/beginning chain row. If not otherwise stated, odd-numbered rows are right-side rows and form the public side of the crocheted piece, while even-numbered rows are wrong-side rows and later form the non-public side on the back of the finished fabric.

fiber Natural or synthetic raw material of which a yarn is made.

filet crochet Crochet technique in which a type of mesh or grid is worked using chains and double crochet, following a grid chart. Stitch patterns are created through the interaction of empty boxes and boxes filled in double crochet.

finishing Different procedures used for finishing a crocheted piece, such as sewing together, embroidering, crocheting on facings, or edgings.

foundation stitches These stitches do not need a base (such as typically chain stitches). The basis for the next stitch is worked directly from the previous stitch. Foundation crochet stitches are used for an elastic beginning row instead of chains or for increasing several stitches at the edge of a crocheted part.

from * /from * to * See Asterisks.

from the hook In the beginning chain, chains are not counted from the beginning tail to the crochet hook, but the other way around from the crochet hook back toward the beginning tail.

front of work The good (right) side of a crocheted piece, which will later be worn or displayed on the outside or the front of the piece.

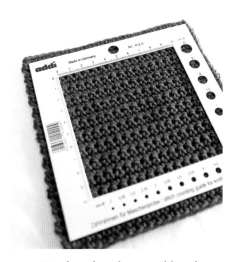

gauge Number of stitches in width and rows/rounds in height fitting in 4 inches (10 cm). Your own numbers should match those listed in the instructions in order to meet the measurements for the finished piece as shown in the pattern.

granny square A motif crocheted from the center out in the round, traditionally square-shaped but also sometimes used for numerous other shapes, in most cases crocheted in combinations of multiple colors.

grid chart Representation of a stitch pattern in form of filled-in and empty boxes for filet crochet and colored boxes for intarsia and jacquard. Each individual box corresponds to 1 stitch.

hairpin lace crochet Very old crochet technique, in the past also called hairpin crochet. Worked with a special fork or hairpin loom.

height-adjustment chains Name for the chains that are worked to reach the height of the first stitch of the row/round. The exact number of chains to be worked depends on the height of the following stitches.

hook size Denotes the thickness of the crochet hook at the shank. The International Standard Size (ISG) is indicated in millimeters, but in the USA and Great Britain as well as Japan, different systems are used, which can be converted with the help of conversion tables.

increasing/decreasing evenly distributed To avoid unsightly bulges, several stitches within a row/round are decreased not at once, but individually in evenly distributed spots.

increasing/increase The number of stitches of a crocheted piece is increased to shape the piece, or for creating a stitch pattern.

in front of work/in back of work This specification always refers to the side of work currently facing the crocheter, no matter whether this is the front or back of the crocheted fabric itself.

inserting the hook in rows below The insertion point for the new stitch is not located in the previous row or round, but one or several rows or rounds below. Either the crocheted piece is folded or the working yarn is pulled up to the height of the current row at the top edge. The insertion point at the top edge is not worked into.

insertion point Spot into which the hook is inserted for a new stitch before pulling the working yarn through the fabric. This can be at the top edge of the crocheted piece through both loops of the following stitch, or just the back or the front loop of the stitch. It can also happen that the hook is inserted into a stitch located one or several rows below, between two existing stitches, or in the chain space of a chain arc.

intarsia technique A method to work large areas of different colors, often for large motifs.

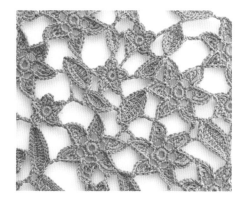

Irish crochet Crochet technique in which typical motifs such as flowers and leaves are crocheted individually and subsequently worked into a mesh background

jacquard technique Crocheting in multicolored, small-scale stitch patterns with two or more colors in one row or round. The unused colors are either carried on the wrong side of the fabric as floats or crocheted in during the current row or round

joining Attaching new working yarn within a crocheted piece. Also refers to crocheting or sewing two pieces of crochet together.

joining the round with a slip stitch When crocheting in the round, each round has to be joined/closed (i.e., the first and last stitch are joined with a slip stitch).

knooking Crochet technique in which a knitted fabric is created with a special crochet hook and corresponding cord.

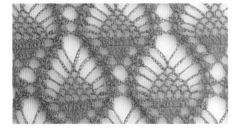

lace Openwork patterns made from very thin yarn with thick hook.

leaving stitches unworked/stitches not crocheted into To decrease multiple stitches at the end of a row, the last stitches are not crocheted into but just left unworked, and work is turned a number of stitches before the end of the row. The outside edge of the crocheted piece is therefore moved inward by the number of stitches to be decreased.

loop stitch crochet Crochet technique in which loosely suspended loops are worked in different ways into crocheted items, such as for fur pattern or as all-over stitch pattern.

main color/dominant color In a multi-colored stitch pattern, the color that stands out most because it is used more often than other colors.

main pattern The stitch pattern in which the main part or body of a piece is worked.

marking thread/piece of contrasting color yarn/ Piece of yarn in a stark contrast to the color of the project yarn. Serves for marking rows, rounds, or individual stitches.

mirror-inverted For symmetrically crocheted pieces, synonym for "mirrored." Example: If at the beginning of a row, the "second and third stitch" are crocheted together, then, at the end of the row, the "third-to-last stitch" must be crocheted together with the "next-to-last stitch."

motif crochet Crochet technique in which individual motifs are worked separately and often later joined into a larger item.

patchwork Assembling geometric crocheted motifs, such as squares, circles, hexagons, and so on, or flowers and leaves, into larger crocheted pieces.

pattern repeat Smallest self-contained unit of a stitch pattern, consisting of a specific number of stitches and repeated multiple times within a row or round. Crochet charts or written instructions for the stitch pattern often show or describe the pattern repeat only once with an indication how often it is to be worked.

picots Small decorative spikes or teeth of chains and slip stitches or single crochets that are either worked as edge finishing or used as small details in the pattern.

popcorn Multiple double crochets worked into the same stitch that are combined at the top edge during the last working step, resulting in a three-dimensional outward bulge.

post stitch/raised stitch Stitch such as single crochet or double crochet worked around the post of a stitch of the previous row or round, thus being raised above the background fabric.

previous row/previous round Denotes the row or round that has been worked immediately before the row or round currently in the process of being worked.

raised stitch patterns Stitch patterns with post stitches or stitches with a particular three-dimensional stitch appearance, such as bobbles, popcorns, cluster stitches, and so forth. Relief type stitch patterns with characteristic "high-low effect" are also created when double crochets or treble crochets are crocheted onto an area in single crochet, or when the hook is inserted through the back or the front loop of the stitch only.

repeat See Pattern Repeat.

right and left edge of the crocheted piece The indication of the position of the edge always refers to the position as viewed from the crocheter onto the crocheted piece when the front of work is facing up.

right and left side of the body For garments, the indication "right" or "left" for sleeves, fronts, shoulders, or pant legs always refers to the view from the wearer.

right-side row Row that is worked while the front of work is facing up, usually all odd-numbered rows.

right sides facing each other Two crocheted pieces are placed together with the fronts of work (= right sides) toward each other. Often, this is done before joining pieces by seaming. The piece is later turned outside out, so that in the finished object, the right sides of the fabric are located on the outside.

round transition Indicates closing a round with a stitch and beginning a new round, often with height-adjustment chains.

Russian Join Invisible join of two strands of wool yarn without knots.

schematic/garment pattern Representation of the individual parts of a piece, drawn in detail and with indicated measurements.

seam Spot where joined crocheted pieces meet.

shells/fans Stitch pattern in which multiple double crochets are worked into the same stitch, arranging the stitches in a fan or shell shape.

short rows Means that a row is not worked over all existing stitches of a row, but incrementally only over part of the stitches. Serves for shaping rounded edges or inserts.

single crochet Basic stitch with a compact body and no yarn overs prior to inserting the hook.

skipping/skip/leaving out/bridging Means that instead of crocheting into the following stitch, a certain number of stitches is not crocheted into, inserting the hook first in a stitch located further left. This is used for creating stitch patterns. Often, chain arcs are used to bridge skipped stitches.

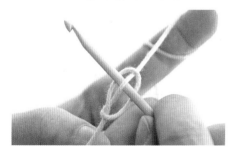

slipknot/adjustable loop/running slipknot Knot to form a beginning slipknot at the beginning of a crocheted piece.

slip stitch Very shallow basic stitch without post. Normally used for looping on working yarn, joining into the round, or for skipping stitches, but can also be worked as a technique on its own for whole pieces.

spiral rounds Rounds worked in a continuous spiral without joining into the round before a new round begins.

stitch appearance How the stitches appear in the crocheted fabric. An even stitch appearance is produced if the yarn is always worked at the same tension. If the tension of the working yarn varies within a crocheted piece, the stitch definition appears sometimes too loose, other times too dense. The stitch appearance can also be affected through the choice of hook size.

stitch marker/removable stitch marker/ open stitch marker Small safety-pin-type clasp made of metal or plastic that can be attached to individual stitches to mark specific stitches within the crocheted fabric.

surface crochet Stitches worked onto a crocheted base fabric, often slip stitches. It is used for creating colorwork patterns or decorative embellishments.

tawashi Japanese name for bath or cleaning sponge crocheted in sturdy cotton yarn and used for household cleaning or personal care.

top loops of a stitch V-shaped loops of the stitches positioned horizontally at the top edge of the crocheted piece. The part of the stitch that makes up the front leg is called "front loop of the stitch," the one that makes up the back leg "back loop of the stitch." When multiple stitches are crocheted together or worked off together, all of them together have one consolidated top loop of the stitch at the top edge of the crocheted piece.

top of the stitch Denotes the upper part of the stitch with the front and back loop of the stitch.

treble crochets and taller stitches Longer basic stitches for which the working yarn is placed onto the hook as yarn over multiple times before inserting the hook. The loops are crocheted off the hook in several steps. The more yarn overs have accumulated on the hook, the taller the stitch will turn out.

For a treble crochet, two yarn overs are placed on the hook prior to inserting the hook.

Tunisian crochet Crochet technique using a special long crochet hook. During the forward pass, all loops of the new stitches are placed onto the crochet hook, and during the following return pass, crocheted off the hook again. All rows are worked on the right side of the fabric.

turning At the end of a row, the crocheted piece is turned to the other side so that the beginning of the new row is again at the right and therefore located in the working direction. Front and back of the crocheted piece trade places.

turning chains Turning chains are crocheted to reach the height of the first stitch of the following row and also to prevent the crocheted fabric from constricting at the sides. Depending on the height of the following stitches, a certain number of chains is crocheted.

weaving in/sewing in ends/weave in Sewing/hiding and anchoring yarn tails on the wrong side of the fabric/inside of a crocheted piece.

welt Vertical or horizontal, round, narrow bulging fold.

with two strands of yarn held together Two strands of yarn, either from the same or from different skeins, are held together as one working yarn and crocheted with together.

working in rows When working in rows, at the end of every row, work must be turned, since every row is always worked from right to left (for left-handed crocheters, from left to right). After having turned, alternatingly either the front or the back of work is facing up.

working in the chain space/around the chains When working the stitches, the hook is not inserted into individual chains of a chain arc but into the space under and around the chain, and then the working yarn is pulled through underneath the chain.

working in the round Working without turning, always in the same working direction. As a rule, the front of work (= right side of the fabric) is always facing up or outward. A distinction is made between rounds that are closed with a slip stitch and continuous spiral rounds. In special cases, turned rounds can also be worked, working rows within a round.

working into the same insertion point Two or more stitches are crocheted into a single stitch of the previous row or round or into the same chain space. For this, after completion of the first stitch, for the next stitch the hook is again inserted into the same spot. Used to increase stitches, or to create stitch patterns.

working loop Single loop always remaining on the hook after having worked off all loops of all stitches.

working yarn The yarn leading from the working loop to the ball of yarn, used to crochet the piece.

wrong-side row Row that is worked while the back of work is facing up. All even-numbered rows are usually wrong-side rows.

wrong sides facing each other Two crocheted pieces are placed together so the backs of work (= wrong sides) are on the inside, and the right sides on the outside.

yardage How long a length of yarn is in relation to its weight, for instance, 219 yd/1.75 oz (200 m/50 g) means that 1.75 oz (50 g) of yarn have a length of 219 yd (200 m). The shorter the yardage for equal weight, the thicker the yarn.

yarn bobbin Small notched disc of cardboard, plastic, or wood onto which a supply of yarn is wrapped (often used for an area of color in the intarsia technique).

yarn label/yarn wrapper/ball band Paper strip wrapped around the skein of yarn. Contains all information about the respective yarn, such as fiber content, color, dye lot, yardage, hook size, gauge, care instructions, and manufacturer.

yarn over The working yarn is placed over the crochet hook one or more times from back to front. Made before inserting into a stitch or when crocheting off loops of stitch.

Index

ABOUT THE AUTHORS

BEATE HILBIG, after many years as a chemical laboratory assistant and in the business sector, turned her passion into a career in 1996, studying liberal arts in Nürtingen, followed by working as a freelance artist, designer, and author. She especially likes to combine her extensive knowledge of crafts, centered primarily around crochet, knitting, and embroidery, with artistic elements. In 2008, she changed her career path once more, and has been working as a specialist subject teacher since 2010.

BÉATRICE SIMON's path to designing crochet patterns began with translating craft books and her longstanding love for everything yarn and needles. Since 2007, she has been blogging in memory of her dear aunt Lilli, who taught her to crochet, under the screen name "lilli-croche." After many years of living abroad, she returned to her native Bretagne in 2009. Blog in French: lillicroche.wordpress.com, Blog in German: lillicroche2.wordpress.com

EVELINE HETTY-BURKART works as a freelance editor and author for magazine and book publishers. Her area of expertise includes a wide array of craft techniques, spanning from the initial design idea and creative implementation to pattern writing. Crochet is her favorite, as she loves trying new variations of traditional crochet stitches and experimenting with various materials. She lives with her husband and son near Hamburg, Germany.

SPECIAL THANKS

We would like to thank companies MEZ GmbH (Herbolzheim), www.mezcrafts.com, Prym Consumer GmbH (Stolberg), www.prym-consumer.com, Gustav Selter GmbH and Co. KG (Altena), www.addi-nadeln.de, Zweigart and Sawitzki GmbH and Co. KG (Sindelfingen), www.zweigart.de, RAYHER HOBBY GmbH (Laupheim), www.rayher-hobby.de and Pony NePremium Industries (India) Private Limited®, www.ponyneedles.com, for providing yarn and tool support for this book.

Expand your crochet library with these great books!

Bestselling Crochet Books

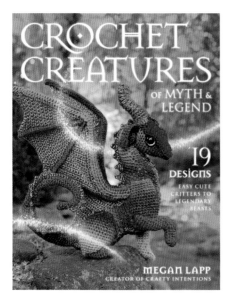

Megan Lapp
ISBN 9780811771481 * Paperback *
March 2023 * $28.95
Pages: 246 * Trim: 8 ½ x 11

Sascha Blase-Van Wagtendonk
ISBN 9780811738835 * Paperback * June
2020 * $22.95
Pages: 168 * Trim: 8 ½ x 11

Salena Baca, Danyel Pink, and Emily
Truman
ISBN 9780811737081 * Paperback * April
2019 * $24.95
Pages: 152 * Trim: 8 ½ x 11

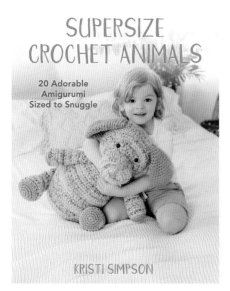

Kristi Simpson
ISBN 9780811771009 * Paperback *
November 2022 * $24.95
Pages: 144 * Trim: 8 ½ x 11

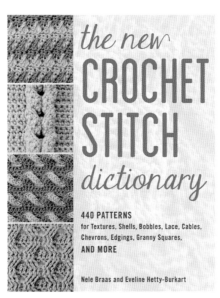

Nele Braas and Eveline Hetty-Burkart
ISBN 9780811738699 * Paperback * May
2021 * $27.95
Pages: 272 * Trim: 8 ½ x 11

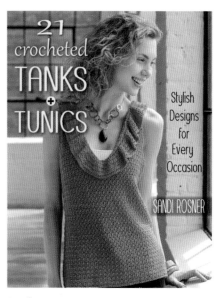

Sandi Rosner
ISBN 9780811714839 * Paperback * April
2022 * $24.95
Pages: 108 * Trim: 8 ½ x 11

Crochet Skills

Salena Baca
ISBN 978-0-8117-7074-3 * Paperback *
November 2022 * $24.95
Pages: 150 * Trim: 8 ½ x 11

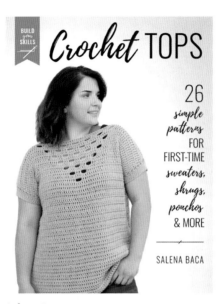

Salena Baca
ISBN 978-0-8117-3870-5 * Paperback *
March 2021 * $24.95
Pages: 120 * Trim: 8 ½ x 11

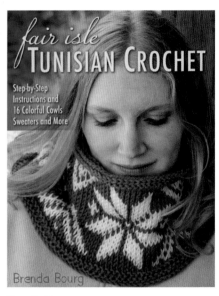

Brenda Bourg
ISBN 978-0-8117-1538-6 * Paperback *
January 2016 * $24.95
Pages: 112 * Trim: 8 x 11

Sharon Hernes Silverman, Photographs
by Alan Wycheck
ISBN 978-0-8117-7018-7 * Paperback *
October 2021 * $9.95
Pages: 32 * Trim: 8 ½ x 11

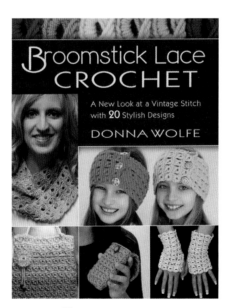

Donna Wolfe
ISBN 978-0-8117-1615-4 * Paperback *
November 2015 * $21.95
Pages: 128 * Trim: 8 ½ x 11

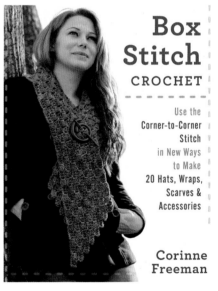

Corinne Freeman
ISBN 978-0-8117-1764-9 * Paperback *
September 2017 * $19.95
Pages: 96 * Trim: 8 x 10

Crochet Tops and Accessories

Salena Baca
ISBN 978-0-8117-3969-6 * Paperback *
February 2022 * $24.95
Pages: 144 * Trim: 8 ½ x 11

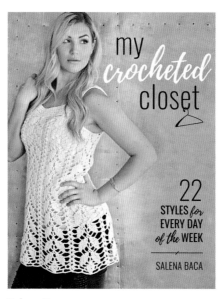

Salena Baca
ISBN 978-0-8117-1806-6 * Paperback *
October 2017 * $19.95
Pages: 112 * Trim: 8 x 10

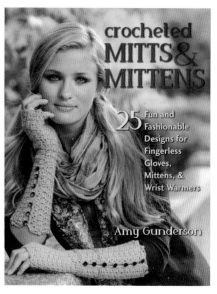

Amy Gunderson
ISBN 978-0-8117-1410-5 * Paperback *
May 2015 * $21.95
Pages: 160 * Trim: 8 ½ x 11

Salena Baca
ISBN 978-0-8117-3783-8 * Paperback *
August 2019 * $22.95
Pages: 120 * Trim: 8 ½ x 11

Julie King
ISBN 978-0-8117-1796-0 * Paperback *
September 2018 * $22.95
Pages: 128 * Trim: 8 ½ x 11

Sharon Hernes Silverman
ISBN 978-0-8117-1988-9 * Paperback *
December 2018 * $29.95
Pages: 176 * Trim: 8 ½ x 11

Crochet for Baby

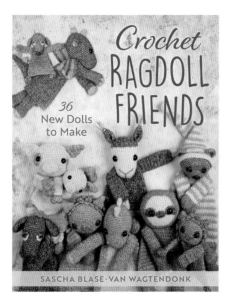

Sascha Blase-Van Wagtendonk
ISBN 978-0-8117-7170-2 * Paperback *
April 2023 * $24.95
Pages: 192 * Trim: 8 ½ x 11

Kristi Simpson
ISBN 978-0-8117-7000-2 * Paperback *
June 2022 * $24.95
Pages: 184 * Trim: 8 ½ x 11

Kristi Simpson
ISBN 9780811739474 * Paperback *
October 2020 * $9.95
Pages: 32 * Trim: 8 ½ x 11

Kristi Simpson
ISBN 978-0-8117-1258-3 * Paperback *
October 2013 * $19.95
Pages: 128 * Trim: 8 ½ x 11

Kristi Simpson
ISBN 9780811738385 * Paperback *
February 2020 * $22.95
Pages: 184 * Trim: 8 ½ x 11

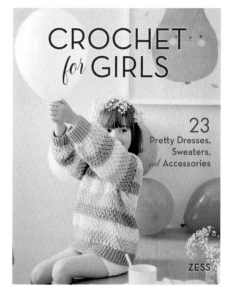

Zess
ISBN 9780811736510 * Paperback * May
2019 * $24.95
Pages: 128 * Trim: 8 x 10